Euro-
Politics

EURO-POLITICS

Institutions and Policymaking in the "New" European Community

Alberta M. Sbragia, Editor

The Brookings Institution
Washington, D.C.

Copyright © 1992 by
THE BROOKINGS INSTITUTION
1775 Massachusetts Avenue, N.W., Washington, D.C. 20036

Library of Congress Cataloging-in-publication data:

Euro-politics : institutions and policymaking in the new European
community / Alberta M. Sbragia, editor.

    p.   cm.

  Includes bibliographical references and index.

  ISBN 0-8157-7724-8 (cloth) — ISBN 0-8157-7723-X (pbk.)

  1. Europe 1992. 2. European Economic Community.

  3. European communities. I. Sbragia, Alberta M.

HC241.2.E77 1991

341.24'22—dc20   91-40355

                                      CIP

9 8 7 6 5 4 3 2 1

The paper used in this publication meets the minimum requirements
of the American National Standard for Information Sciences—Perma-
nence of paper for Printed Library Materials, ANSI Z39.48-1984

Foreword

Two views dominate the American view of the European Community. One sees the Community largely as an economic arena, an emerging common market populated by competing firms. The other, more attuned to politics, assumes that policymaking within the Community is roughly analogous to that found in the European nation-state. Yet the Community is far more than a common market. And its structures of governance differ profoundly both from those of the traditional European state and from those found in the United States. It is neither a "superstate" nor a potential "United States of Europe" in the way Americans would interpret the latter phrase.

In particular, national governments play a uniquely important—and yet uniquely constrained—role in collective decisionmaking. National governments are far more important in Community decisionmaking than state governments are in American national policymaking. European prime ministers are not about to become the equivalent of American governors. Yet their acceptance of the supremacy of EC law over national law, and their consequent acceptance of the rulings of the European Court of Justice, makes the Community very different from an international organization.

This volume explores the intricate relationships that exist between the Community's institutions and those of the member-state governments. It suggests that American policymakers and business people will need to maneuver within an extremely complex political system whose superficial similarities to the American experience may prove more misleading than helpful. The United States will face a Europe quite different from the image most Americans carry with them.

Alberta M. Sbragia, editor of this volume, is the director of the West European Studies program as well as an associate professor of political science at the University of Pittsburgh. The authors are David R. Cameron, professor of political science at Yale University; Peter Lange, professor of political science at Duke University and fellow at the Center for Advanced Study in the Behavioral Sciences at Stanford University; Gary Marks, associate professor of political science at the University of North Carolina, Chapel Hill, and fellow at the Center for Advanced Study in the Behavioral Sciences at Stanford University; B. Guy Peters, Maurice Falk Professor of American Government and chair of the Department of Political Science at the University of Pittsburgh; Martin Shapiro, the James W. and Isabel Coffroth Professor of Law at the University of California, Berkeley; and John T. Woolley, associate professor of political science at the University of California, Santa Barbara.

The editor wishes to thank those who commented on initial drafts of the chapters in this book: Peter Hall, Françoise de La Serre, Helen Wallace, Joseph Weiler, and Wolfgang Wessels. Helen Wallace, Joseph Weiler, and Michael Shackleton deserve special gratitude for their help with the entire project. Gertrude Gordon and Regina Takos of the West European Studies program provided invaluable secretarial assistance. At the Brookings Institution, Renuka Deonarain, Lisa Pace, Susan Thompson, and Antoinette Williams provided secretarial assistance; Sandy Riegler and Susan Stewart provided administrative assistance. Rozlyn Coleman, Caroline Lalire, and Venka Macintyre edited the manuscript; Todd L. Quinn verified its factual content; and Susan L. Woollen prepared it for typesetting. The index was compiled by Rhonda Holland.

The German Marshall Fund of the United States provided generous financial assistance for the project.

The views expressed here are those of the authors and should not be attributed to the people or organizations whose assistance is acknowledged or to the officers, trustees, or staff members of the Brookings Institution.

BRUCE K. MAC LAURY
President

December 1991
Washington, D.C.

Contents

1. Introduction   1
   Alberta M. Sbragia
   Scope of the Book   6
   The Community's Future   13

2. The 1992 Initiative: Causes and Consequences   23
   David R. Cameron
   Theoretical Perspectives   25
   History of the Internal Market Initiative   31
   Sources of the Internal Market Initiative   35
   Discussion   64

3. Bureaucratic Politics and the Institutions
   of the European Community   75
   B. Guy Peters
   The Institutions of European Government   77
   Fundamental Political Processes   92
   Institutional Analysis of the Community   105
   Conclusion   121

4. The European Court of Justice   123
   Martin Shapiro
   Foundations of the European Court of Justice   124
   Free Movement of Goods   128
   Deregulation and New Regulation   134
   Administrative Judicial Review   141
   Legal Basis   145
   Human Rights   148

The Future of Community Human Rights   152
Conclusion   154

5. Policy Credibility and European Monetary
    Institutions   157
    John T. Woolley
    The Problem of Policy Credibility   158
    The European Monetary System and Credibility   161
    Credibility of Economic and Monetary Union   172
    Conclusion   183
    Appendix: The Institutions of the European Monetary
        System   185

6. Structural Policy in the European Community   191
    Gary Marks
    The Growth of the Structural Funds   193
    Reform of the Structural Funds   206

7. The Politics of the Social Dimension   225
    Peter Lange
    The Social Dimension   229
    Interests, Rules, Governments, and the Social
        Dimension, 1985–90   235
    The Evolving Politics of the Social Dimension   244
    The Social Dimension and the Evolution of European
        Institutions   252

8. Thinking about the European Future: The Uses
    of Comparison   257
    Alberta M. Sbragia
    Federalism in Comparative Context   259
    Analytic Costs and Benefits of Comparison   264
    The Problem of National Governments   268
    Territory versus Electorate   277
    The Institutional Representation of Territorial
        Government   280
    The Question of Representation   287
    Conclusion   289

    Appendix: A Thumbnail Sketch of the Institutions of
        the European Community   293

    Index   295

Tables

2-1. Trade Dependence of the Member States of the European
Community, the United States, Canada, and Japan, 1960,
1972, 1985   37

2-2. Exports of the Member States of the European
Community to Other EC Members, 1960, 1972, 1985   38

2-3. Exports of the Member States of the European
Community to Other EC Members, 1960, 1972, 1985   39

2-4. Exports Minus Imports of Goods, Services, and Transfers
of the Member States of the European Community,
1973–86   40

2-5. Annual Rate of Economic Growth in the European
Community, 1973–86   41

2-6. Rate of Unemployment in the Member States
of the European Community, 1973–86   42

2-7. Realignments of Currencies in the European Monetary
System, 1979–90   46

2-8. Inflation Rates in Consumer Prices in the European
Community, 1980–88   48

2-9. Contributions to and Receipts from Budget of the
European Community, Average of 1982, 1983, and 1984   60

2-10. Exports of Member States of the European Community
to Other Member States, 1980, 1989   68

2-11. Balance of Trade (Exports minus Imports) of Member
States of the European Community with Other Members
of the EC, 1980–89   69

6-1. Hypothetical Payoffs Resulting from Economic
Liberalization and Structural Policy   195

6-2. Real GDP per Capita in EC Member States, 1960–88   200

6-3. Regional Growth in Real GDP, Population, and
Employment in the Twenty-five Strongest and Weakest
EC Regions, 1973–82   201

Figures

3-1. Directorates-General of the European Commission   87

6-1. Regions of the European Community Eligible under
Objective 1 of the Structural Funds   207

6-2. Regions of the European Community Eligible under
Objective 2 of the Structural Funds   208

Euro-
Politics

Chapter 1

Introduction

ALBERTA M. SBRAGIA

T HE TRANSFORMATION of the European continent has highlighted the importance of the European Community for that same continent. The Community's economic prosperity and political stability are a magnet for those nations that enjoy neither and therefore face an uncertain future. Yet, given its centrality to the political economy of Europe, the European Community is surprisingly little understood within the United States.

Two broad views dominate Americans' understanding of the Community. The first sees the Community largely as a free trade area in which markets and firms prevail. The political institutions of the Community and the institutional processes by which decisions are taken are given short shrift, for they are assumed to be marginal to economic forces. Thus, in this "economistic" view, the institutional dynamics of the Community are largely ignored or overlooked while the logic of interdependent economies is emphasized.

The "1992" program has often been analyzed through such a prism, especially in the United States. The drive to create an internal market for goods, services, capital, and labor by eliminating nontariff barriers seems to justify such an approach. By emphasizing the size of the Community's market and the opportunities and challenges it offers to American business, analysts have reinforced an essentially economistic definition of the Community. The important changes in the institutional dynamics of the Community that accompanied the decision to pursue an internal market, therefore, are frequently overlooked.

The second view, held by those more sensitive to the importance of political processes and institutions, assumes that the Community and its member states are governed in roughly the same way. It regards policymaking in the Community as similar to that in the European nation-state. Indeed, because of the increasing economic power to be derived from the creation of a single integrated market, as well as the historic integrative decisions taken at the Maastricht summit in December 1991, the European Community is sometimes thought of as an emerging "super-state," similar in its contours to a "United States of Europe." As such, in the view of many Americans, it would have centralized decisionmaking, a cohesive and uniform policy process, and, especially, institutional inde-pendence from the collective will of the member-state governments. Na-tional governments and bureaucracies would not be central to the analysis of politics and policymaking in the Community.

Readers will find little, if any, confirming evidence for either view in the chapters that follow. Interdependent economies certainly create their own logic, but political structures and institutions channel, shape, and influence the forms interdependence is allowed to take. The Single Euro-pean Act, the parent of the 1992 program, is significant because it both committed the Community's members to eliminate nontariff barriers *and* changed the decisionmaking procedures so as to facilitate the elimination of such barriers. The SEA changed the way the Community's institutions could operate and laid the groundwork for the institutional changes agreed to at Maastricht.

The changes introduced by the SEA and by the Maastricht summit do not fit with the notion of either a "superstate" or a "United States of Europe" in which the member states lose their sovereignty to a set of Community institutions independent from the member states themselves. The governments of the twelve members of the Community exert immea-surably more influence on Community policies than American state gov-ernments exert on federal policies within the United States. On the other hand, the Community is far more than a strong international organization. It is precisely the complexity of the meshing between national institutions and leaders, on the one hand, and Community institutions and leaders, on the other, which makes it difficult for those with only a cursory knowl-edge of the Community to understand how it functions.

The European Community is an extraordinarily complex political sys-tem, and its institutions and policymaking differ from those of the Euro-pean state as we have come to know it. Rather than use centralization, uniformity, coherence, and decisiveness to describe politics and policy-making, the authors in this volume tend to describe the Community in terms of leadership, coalitions, decentralization, diversity, bargaining, convergence, policy differentiation, and national government discretion. In fact, to the uninitiated, the sheer number and diversity of actors, institutions, policy communities, working groups, and governments can be overwhelming (for example, the very names of the Community's institutions—the European Council and the Council of Ministers in particular—are easily confused with the Council of Europe, an organization completely distinct from the European Community). The institutional consequences of the Single European Act and the decisions taken at Maastricht have moved the Community away from an international organization while not making it more similar to a traditional state.

To complicate matters, political and institutional arrangements differ widely among the Community's member states. Whereas the fifty American states are roughly similar in their institutional structures, the twelve members of the Community are not. The variation within the Community—whether measured in wealth, administrative capacity, cultural and linguistic heterogeneity, or political and institutional arrangements—is far greater than the variation within the United States. In fact, the EC's institutional structure is so complex in part because of the difficulty in managing the extraordinary diversity of its members.

Coexisting with this diversity are the very high levels of institutionalization within each member state. Even the "poor" members of the Community have more complex and well-institutionalized political and administrative systems than most other countries have. All EC states possess the administrative capacity to formulate and articulate their interests within the bargaining process characteristic of Community decisionmaking. Such institutional capacity translates into the effective representation of diverse national interests and needs at the Community level. All member governments make themselves heard—and in a variety of ways. Most prominently, their top political leaders meet collectively at least semiannually in the "summit meetings" officially known as the meetings of the European Council, and their ministers meet regularly in the Council of Ministers, but member states also communicate in many less-visible ways directly with the European Commission, the body that symbolizes the Community to much of the world.

The institutionalized representation of *governments* within the Community sharply distinguishes politics within the Community from politics within the U.S. federation. It has become customary to analyze "American politics" in terms of national politics only; state politics are put in a compartment separate from national politics. State legislatures and governors are not normally participants in *national* political conflict. Nor are there privileged institutional links between state government and national government. Governors play crucial policymaking roles only within their own states—the collectivity of governors does not challenge presidential or congressional policymaking prerogatives. Governors are not members of the U.S. Senate nor do they choose senators, and neither governors nor state legislatures choose the members of the president's cabinet. Associations of governors and state legislators do articulate and represent the views of state-elected officials, but such associations are viewed by national politicians as roughly analogous to interest groups; they do not have privileged constitutional status.

By contrast, one cannot discuss Community politics without incorporating the governments of the Community's member states. The EC is a political system in which the governments (and bureaucracies) of the member states play a crucial role. They are most prominently represented in the Council of Ministers and the institutionally distinct European Council. Yet the Community is not merely a collection of national governments bargaining with each other. The role of national governments is far more complex. The Commission and the European Court of Justice, linked to the national governments through appointment as well as other channels, are important institutions that bind the national governments into the Community. They are "European" while simultaneously linked to the national. National leaders, institutions, and political experiences influence both politics and policy within the Community, but they in turn are influenced by the dynamic of Community politics. Students of national governments cannot ignore the European Community, but neither can students of the Community easily disentangle the national governments from the Community.

The Community does not have a popularly elected president. Commissioners—who at least theoretically represent the Community's interests, provide a liaison with their national policymaking elites, initiate policy, and provide leadership—are appointed by national governments. Both the commissioners and the civil servants whom they oversee have extensive contacts with national representatives, whether the latter be civil servants or politicians. The judges on the European Court of Justice are also appointed by national governments. National government ministers, such as foreign, finance, agriculture, and environment ministers, personally make policy in the Council of Ministers. And national political leaders—

meeting in "summits" as the European Council—make the principal strategic decisions. The Maastricht summit was, in official terms, a meeting of the European Council. The European Parliament, which is directly elected by voters, is a relatively weak institution, though its powers were enhanced at Maastricht and will continue to be expanded during this decade. But even if future summits should extend its powers dramatically, national governments will still have a large say in Community policymaking.

Community politics and national politics are institutionally intertwined rather than insulated from each other. Although one can discuss American politics and policymaking without mentioning a single governor, it is impossible to exclude prime ministers and the French president (the French system has both a politically powerful president and a prime minister) from analyses of Community politics. This difference makes the Community particularly confusing to Americans. Because the single integrated market is a familiar notion, they expect to find a system of governance that is also familiar. Yet the privileged status enjoyed by member governments in the Community's political system has no analogue in the U.S. system. American state officials do not participate personally in national policymaking. For their part, American national politicians represent voters who happen to reside in states; they do not represent governors or state legislators. Thus, in the United States, the representation of the *institutional interests* of state governments in national policymaking is not constitutionally entrenched.

For Americans to begin to grasp the differences in institutional structure between the United States and the Community, they need to imagine a collective presidency composed of governors, who make the strategic decisions on the development of the constitutional and political system (the European Council); a cabinet (the Commission), which exercises a monopoly over policy initiation as well as considerable leadership, but which is chosen by the states' governors; a very strong Senate (the Council of Ministers), comprising top political leaders chosen by the governors and having the right to amend or veto all proposals made by the cabinet; and a weak House of Representatives (the European Parliament) elected by voters but having the right neither to initiate nor to veto most policy proposals. The Community, therefore, is constructing a single market quite similar to the U.S. market but a system of governance that differs profoundly from the U.S. federal system.

Scope of the Book

The chapters that follow highlight the intricate relationships between the Community's institutions and those of the member-state governments. In chapter 2 David Cameron describes and analyzes how and why the so-called 1992 program, the foundation stone for the decisions taken at Maastricht, came to be accepted. He argues against those who regard the Community as only the creature of the member states as well as against those who view the Community as largely independent from the member states. Incorporating both "neorealist" and "neofunctionalist" approaches, he gives an overview of the complex history of an initiative that is to take the Community from a modified customs union to a true common market.

Cameron's chapter makes the case for viewing the Community as responding to a complex, interdependent set of forces—including economic pressures internal and external to the EC, national leaders, convergent national experiences, and the EC institutions themselves, the Commission in particular. Both the Commission and national leaders, Cameron argues, played critical, and interdependent, roles in arriving at the Community's decision to use qualified majority voting rather than unanimity in the creation of a single integrated market by 1992. The 1992 project is about both economics and governance and thus its political history illuminates particularly well the main contours of the Community's policymaking process. Cameron's analysis gives the reader a sense of how complex the process of consensus building is within the Community when major institutional and policy innovation is at stake as well as how intertwined Community and national institutions are.

But how does such intertwining take place? How is the Community governed? Casual observers usually find the Community's governmental framework confusing, to say the least. Americans, as mentioned, do not find ready analogies in their own national experience for the process of EC decisionmaking, the interplay between national governments and Community institutions presenting particular difficulties.

In his overview of the Community's institutions in chapter 3, Guy Peters provides an introductory sketch of the Community's institutional and policymaking architecture which American readers unfamiliar with the Community will find particularly useful. Peters points out that governance in the Community can be only partly understood by referring to governing arrangements in either an international organization or a European parliamentary system. In sketching the singularities of the Community's decisionmaking institutions, he signals the importance of the dynamics of policymaking within the Commission and highlights the study of bureaucratic politics as providing a "very promising approach to understanding policymaking dynamics within the institutions of the European Community."

His chapter suggests that the policy process is significantly shaped by the fragmented nature of decisionmaking within the Commission, the role of national (and subnational) bureaucracies, and the increasing importance of regulative rulemaking. With regard to budgets and money, the governance of the Community differs from that of parliamentary systems in that spending is less important than regulating.

Peters explores the links between the Community and the national governments, but he also makes clear how important the Commission is for the Community's policymaking process. He sketches the possible evolution of the current system by suggesting that links between the Commission and non-national actors may, if developed over time, eventually permit the Commission to circumvent national governments as such. "Policy communities" are especially important in this respect, for they may either complement or offset "nationalist" pressures in policymaking. Although national governments acting through the Council of Ministers are important in the Community, Peters' analysis alerts us that other actors and networks also have a significant impact in the policymaking process.

While the Commission, the Council of Ministers, and the European Parliament are the Community's most visible institutions, careful observers of the Community point to the European Court of Justice as an institution of central importance both to the building of the Community as a system of governance and to the construction of the internal market. In fact, many consider the Court to have been the "motor of integration" during the 1960s and 1970s. Martin Shapiro, in a similar vein, argues in chapter 4 that the "the Court of Justice constituted the European Community."

Shapiro's chapter explicates the broad and overarching significance of the Court to the Community, firmly establishing the Court as a policymaker. Shapiro links the Court to both the institutional capacity of the Community and public policy. Its rulings, for instance, altered the way product standards were established and served as a catalyst for the internal market initiative. Shapiro also makes clear why the "technical" decisions of the Court are so important in shaping policy choice. He links the Court to the Community's policy dynamics by focusing on the Court's role in "deregulation and new regulation" and in administrative law. Both European and American readers will find his U.S.-EC comparisons insightful, and his discussion of the role of the Court in shaping the Community's regulatory framework expands on Peters' point that the Community is distinctive because regulation plays such a prominent role.

Although the Court has been pivotal in establishing the power of the Community over the member states in those areas agreed to by the Treaty of Rome (the Community's founding document), the member states nevertheless play an important, and to Americans surprising, role in the Community's judicial process. Given the Court's catalytic role, one might expect that the behavior of national institutions would be less important in the legal arena than elsewhere. Yet Shapiro argues that national courts, both high and low, have been critical to the success of the Court's exercise of judicial review. In brief, we find that the national judicial systems have advanced the cause of European integration in the legal arena.

Of the institution-building proposals accepted at the Maastricht summit, the construction of a central bank and the introduction of a common currency are among the most striking. They are also of paramount importance to U.S. policymakers. While the institutions discussed by Peters and Shapiro symbolize the institutional foundations and achievements of the past, a Community central bank and a common currency symbolize the future, expanding power of the Community. Neither a bank nor a currency, however, will emerge from a vacuum. Their institutional base, the European Monetary System, is now viewed as one of the Community's principal achievements in the last decade. The "EuroFed" (the central bank) and the European Monetary System are inextricably linked.

In chapter 5 John Woolley discusses both institutions through the prism of his general concern with policy credibility. He examines the relation between member states and the Community in the European Monetary System by focusing on the role of member governments in the construction of the EMS's policy credibility. In particular, he is concerned with how the European Monetary System acquired the credibility that then bolstered discussion about an EC central bank and a common currency. National governments were essential to the acquisition of such credibility, he argues, for their credibility in the area of monetary policy and that of the EMS developed *sequentially*. The EMS now carries weight, but in Woolley's analysis such power is not intrinsic to the EMS but has been given to it by governments.

Woolley forces readers to consider the linkages among the credibility of international institutions, the capacity and willingness of domestic actors to bear the costs associated with policies that increase credibility, and the benefits accruing to domestic actors from reinforcing the credibility of the international institution. Extrapolating his argument to economic and monetary union (EMU), he argues that "there will be more domestic political fights to be won before EMU can become a reality with high credibility pertaining to inflation policy."

Although the EuroFed (the federal structure of which resembles the Bundesbank more than the Federal Reserve System) will have all the characteristics of an independent central bank, such independence may not lead to low inflation, because of possible policy preferences for "easy money." Yet the combination of an independent bank and the opening of capital markets, Woolley points out, permits market forces to penalize any deviation from an anti-inflation stance. Finally, the EuroFed's structure is designed to allow it to serve as a scapegoat so that policymakers can pursue long-term goals which carry short-term costs.

In brief, Woolley's analysis compels readers to ask how much an institution really matters. Does the structure of an institution have implications for the substance of policy? Can EMU be separated from binding commitments in the areas of taxation and budget deficits? Can a Community institution be constructed so that it will be insulated from the policy preferences of the Community's member-state governments? Alternatively, can a Community institution succeed if national actors are not willing to fight domestic battles on its behalf?

While national governments are preeminent in debates over Community monetary policy, the Community, in other policy areas, is increasingly involved with national governments *along with* other bodies. Monetary policy, in fact, may represent an outlier case for illustrating the influence of national governments. That is, monetary policy may be one of a few policy sectors in which national governments and Community institutions do not need to include or respond to other actors. If monetary policy represents one end of a continuum, regional development policy (known as structural policy) may represent the other. Member governments, in ratifying the Single European Act, pledged to reduce the enormous gap in wealth among regions within the Community (similar pledges were made at Maastricht). And indeed the member governments have agreed to large increases in the amounts of Community money spent on a structural policy that in effect transfers funds from rich to poor countries. How can such a decision be explained?

In chapter 6 Gary Marks considers the argument that such a redistributive decision can be interpreted as simply a "bribe" or a "side payment" made by the rich countries to the poorer countries. Such a payment was necessary to obtain the assent of the poor countries to the creation of the single market because, the argument runs, the poor will be hurt by such a market. Marks, however, argues for a more complex explanation of why structural policy was given increased prominence under the rubric of 1992. Casting doubt on the proposition that the poor countries will inevitably be hurt by the single market, Marks suggests that the increases in funds might well be viewed as payments made to the poorer societies "because of their greater vulnerability to any given economic loss should it occur." Furthermore, conceptions of fairness and equity that have been used in national debates about national regional policy have entered the Community's political discourse.

In the policy area of the structural Funds, at least, Marks argues that the Commission has been able to increase its independence from the member states. It is also increasing its own "reach" and thereby penetrating member states. The Commission is now dealing directly with subnational bodies rather than restricting its contacts to national governments and bureaucracies. Marks focuses on the implications of the growing administrative autonomy the Commission is slowly constructing to handle structural policy. In effect, the Commission and subnational governments can each develop their respective autonomy by circumventing national governments.

In asking whether a "Europe of the Regions" is a likely outcome of the new policies put in place since 1988, Marks illuminates the complex set of relations that now exist among the Commission, national governments, and regional bodies. Although national governments are being challenged as the main gatekeeper to the Community, they will not be easily displaced from their preeminent role. They are mobilizing to protect their power just as subnational governments are battling to increase theirs. Not surprisingly, Marks argues against assuming that a "tidy polity" is being born.

The emphasis on governments—whether national or subnational—may surprise those familiar with the early scholarly work on the Community. Most analysts regarded Community-wide groups, such as functional interest groups and political parties, as critical to the future evolution of the Community, and many assumed that transnational groups would move

the Community toward further integration. Because of the strength of
interest representation in the member states, groups acting for the interests of business firms and of labor unions were expected to be very
powerful in shaping the eventual contours of the Community.

In chapter 7 Peter Lange examines the roles of business, labor, and
governments in the debate over the "social dimension." If transnational
partisan and interest group influence were to be preeminent in any policy
area, it would be natural to expect it here, for the social dimension refers
to a set of policy measures designed to improve the position of workers
within the new internal market. And if that were true, the politics of
the social dimension would largely replicate the politics of welfare state
development within the individual member states. Parties and interest
groups would thus play a central role.

Lange argues, however, that such is not likely to be the fate of the
social dimension. His analysis stresses that the future political dynamics
in this area are unlikely to be those of the past. The former British prime
minister Margaret Thatcher, in his view, allowed national governments to
engage in "cheap talk," since they knew that her opposition to developing
the social dimension protected them from actually having to implement
that for which they were arguing. Now that the Maastricht treaty has
exempted Britain from selected future Community decisions in the area
of social policy, the Thatcher-induced "symbolic politics" of the past may
give way to the politics of economic interest. But such politics will not be
centered around conflict between European confederations of unions and
employers, between European capital and labor. Rather, sector-specific
dynamics within each country may be most relevant, with some representation of sectoral interests being important at the European level as well.
In this scenario, there will be no serious ideological confrontation at the
Community level between those wanting an extensive European welfare
state and their opponents.

Lange finds, too, that national governments will continue to play a
critical role. Interest groups will continue to be important at the national
level, and when unions and firms disagree about specific EC proposals,
national governments will find that formulating a national position within
the Council of Ministers will be difficult. For their part, transnational
actors desiring to impose a Community-wide social dimension are not
likely to emerge. In fact, Lange argues, many unions may form alliances
with their firms to protect the firms' competitive position within the
internal market—and the union members' jobs. Further, Lange has not

found much enthusiasm within the Commission itself for the rapid development of a Community-wide welfare state, partly because of the Commission's concern that such a development would hurt the economic development of the poorer areas within the Community. In looking to the future, Lange provocatively concludes that "no general European social 'model' is likely to develop."

Although the authors in this volume came to the study of the politics and policymaking within the Community from very different conceptual backgrounds, they have each found that national governments are prominent actors in the Community, integral to its very identity. To discuss the Community as somehow detached from its member states is misleading. The notion of a United States of Europe, if based on the American model, is inappropriate for government, though perhaps useful for analyzing the creation of the internal market. Yet the Community is not a collection of cooperating sovereign states. National governments participate in a policymaking system that both includes and constrains them. If nothing else, the decisions taken at Maastricht have rendered the term *member state* more applicable to the Twelve than the term *nation-state*. Even if the decisions taken at the summit should be implemented more slowly than currently anticipated, the fact that they were taken at all is a watershed in the history of the European nation-state as we have known it.

The simultaneity of inclusion and constraint makes it difficult to analyze the Community by using frameworks developed in studying national politics and policymaking in advanced industrial democracies. The final chapter, therefore, considers how the role of national governments can be incorporated into a fuller understanding of policymaking within the Community.

How can the Community continue its attempts at integration while acknowledging and maintaining the importance of territorial representation at the Community level? Even if the powers of the European Parliament, elected by a European electorate, are vastly increased, the national governments are unlikely to yield their right to veto legislation approved by such a Parliament. The Council of Ministers would still retain considerable power under any foreseeable system of "co-decision." That being the case, are there any models one can use to help think about a system in which policymaking is controlled by the governments—rather than the electorate—of the constituent units?

In that spirit, the final chapter assumes, as do the others in this volume, that thinking about the Community comparatively will prove to be more fruitful analytically than simply describing the Community as "unique" and consequently analyzing it exclusively on its own terms. Theories, concepts, and knowledge drawn from the study of other polities can in fact be illuminating when applied to the study of the Community. Chapter 8 describes how several functioning federal systems—such as the Canadian, Australian, and American—have designed institutions in response to tension between the national public authority and the constituent units. It asks whether even thinking about a "center" is fruitful with regard to the Community, for a center implies, at least to Americans, the creation of institutions insulated from the constituent units. The American model of federalism, the analysis suggests, is not relevant, because governors in the United States do not participate in the making of national policy. Washington is a "center" in a way Brussels is not.

By contrast, German federalism presents a more useful (albeit imperfect) model for envisaging the future of the Community. The German system protects the collective power of state governments by giving them a crucial, participatory, role in much of the policymaking that goes on at the national level. State governments are indeed actors in national policymaking in a way that is unknown in the U.S. federal system. Their institutional interests are extremely well protected. In brief, the Federal Republic has already faced at least some of the same dilemmas confronting the Community. The German type of federalism, therefore, allows one to conceptualize a Community in which a "center" is created that is not completely independent from its constituent units. In the German model both electorates and constituent governments have significant influence, a balancing act that the Community may find of interest as it attempts to construct its own balance between voters and prime ministers.

The Community's Future

The European Community, as sketched in this book, is a partial polity that has developed institutionally in both asymmetrical and evolutionary ways. The European Court of Justice has worked to advance judicial review since the founding of the Community. The Regional Development Fund was established at the time of the first enlargement, grew more important after the second major enlargement, and will become even more important after Maastricht. The European Monetary System was established in 1979 by the original core of founding states, gradually attracted new members, and laid the groundwork for the acceptance at

Maastricht of a central bank and a common currency. The European Parliament was directly elected in 1979, the Single European Act, effective in 1987, increased the Parliament's power, and Maastricht increased it once again. The Luxembourg Compromise of 1966 retained the national veto, but the use of the veto was eroded by the SEA and again by Maastricht. Social policy, for its part, will also develop asymmetrically across the Community unless the British government changes the position it adopted at Maastricht (where it insisted that it be exempted from selected areas in which the other eleven members hope to legislate at the Community level).

This pattern of development has been shaped to some degree by the two main enlargements the Community has undergone—the United Kingdom, Ireland, and Denmark joined in 1973, and Spain and Portugal in 1986 (Greece was admitted in 1981). Each enlargement has created new problems and challenged institutional development. Future enlargements will certainly carry on that tradition. The pressure from Poland, Czechoslovakia, and Hungary (as well as the similar pressure likely to come from other post-Communist states) for eventual membership underscores the complexities of future enlargement. Admitting countries whose policy legacy is rooted in a command economy creates unique challenges as well as more generic ones, such as how to ensure that the wealthy countries will not be overwhelmed by those needing assistance, how to protect decisionmaking processes from paralysis, how to handle extraordinary cultural diversity, and whether to continue to require that member states accept all the Community's accumulated regulations (the *acquis communautaire*).

What are the implications of enlargement? It is tempting to use the past as a guide in answering that question, especially since the first enlargement in 1973 strongly affected the way policymaking, as well as political conflict, subsequently proceeded within the Community. Yet it may be best to be cautious here in one's use of history.

Members entering the Community before 1992 essentially joined, in economic terms, a customs union and an incomplete common market with a multiplicity of nontariff barriers. Agricultural policy was much more developed than industrial or financial policy. Countries entering the EC after 1992 will be joining an economic system with both a common agricultural policy and a largely completed common market in industrial goods and financial services, as well as a system committed to the creation of a central bank and common currency by the year 2000. They will therefore be joining an economic entity very different from that which Spain and Portugal joined as late as 1986. This will be true even if the single market is not fully constructed by 1992, if its implementation is delayed by slow economic growth, or if the Maastricht accords face difficulties.

As regards institutional arrangements, a small sample of what new members will face suggests what entering the Community in the 1990s will mean. Such countries will be joining a Community in which investigators from the Commission raid the files of private companies if they suspect price-fixing, in which countries with polluted beaches expect to be publicly identified and to suffer considerable economic damage, in which governments are restricted from subsidizing their industries, and in which national courts are expected to refer to the European Court of Justice. New members' businesses will need to conform to health, safety, and environmental standards now being formulated, monopolies will be open to serious challenge by the Commission (acting under article 90 of the Treaty of Rome as interpreted by the Court), and member states' national representatives can be outvoted in selected areas, including those pertaining to the creation of the internal market.

Furthermore, new members will participate in the making of a common foreign and security policy as well as cooperate in the areas of immigration policy and internal security. Although the implications of the Maastricht treaty will take time to become clear—if only because the Court of Justice will need to clarify some of its ambiguities—there is no doubt that the Community of the 1990s will be more cohesive than that of the 1980s. Thus, from the perspective of a new member, joining the European Community will be like joining a new European Community. It will be a qualitatively different step from that taken by Britain, Ireland, and Denmark in 1973 and will mean accepting more penetrating constraints than those accepted by Spain and Portugal in 1986.

Governments that decide to join an organization which has already become so integrated must accept a degree of constraint not found outside of a formally constituted federation. Joining the post-1992 Community will require a far greater commitment to political and economic integration than joining the pre-1992 Community did. That the waiting list is long— even before applicants know the final conditions they must accept—testifies to the Community's magnetic power. The expectations surrounding entry may therefore be different from those which earlier members had. Many basic decisions will already have been made about the Community's shape before the next member is accepted. Although current members may decide to change institutional features in light of impending enlargement (as the Ten did in accepting qualified majority voting vis-à-vis the single market before the entry of Spain and Portugal), new members will have to accept the status quo until a new round of negotiations emerges. Even so, much of the status quo will not be open to review.

The fact that the single market will have been largely constructed—and that a single currency has been agreed to—before new members have a place at the table has profound significance for the future politics of an enlarged Community. The logic of regulation and political conflict in a common market with a single currency is very different from that found in a customs union. Furthermore, the creation of that market makes the Community a much more attractive organization to belong to. Entry demands a relatively high price, but it will also grant relatively high benefits. Although entry is costly, so is remaining outside.

A ratio of costs and benefits, however, applies to both current members and new members. For current members, enlargement that brings in countries like Sweden and Austria has benefits, in that both are very rich (Sweden has already calculated that it will be a net contributor to the Community) industrial countries. The East European countries provide a far more complex set of calculations. Their economic and environmental problems are so serious, and yet their elites are so committed to "returning to Europe," that it is difficult to predict how much pain Poland, Czechoslovakia, and Hungary would bear to gain eventual membership. Joining only the customs union (as Andorra has done) might well expose their private sector to premature competition without their being able to qualify for help from the Community's structural Funds. Yet full membership, which would qualify them for such help, would also bring to the fore difficult questions about redistribution among current Community member states.

Concerns over enlargement focus on decisionmaking and on the future responsibilities of the Community. The more members, the more difficult it is to achieve consensus. Thus some fear (even after Maastricht) that widening the Community will hinder progress toward further integration, perhaps by encouraging intergovernmental cooperation rather than policymaking within the Community framework. The greater use of qualified majority voting (that is, its use in areas not linked to the creation of the internal market) is often proposed as a way to avoid decisional paralysis, and in fact was selectively agreed to at Maastricht. Such a response, however, could well backfire. Even now, the Twelve, though formally able to proceed by qualified majority voting on all decisions linked to the creation of the single internal market, prefer unanimity on major decisions having to do with the 1992 project. Such a preference may well reflect an accurate assessment of how difficult it is to integrate national systems that are as sophisticated, well developed, and complex as the Community's members. Forcing new members into a position of being outvoted even on issues of very high priority to them could lead to so much conflict that the policy process in the Community would be damaged far more than if it had relied on unanimity, with all its attendant problems.

An alternative response would be for the current members to decide to put into place all the main elements of a fully integrated Community before significant further enlargement takes place. An intergovernmental conference in 1996, called for in the Maastricht treaty, could agree to further steps toward integration, steps that new members would have to accept as a condition of entry. Acceptance by new members of such an integrative framework would narrow the range of important issues in which conflict would be expected and thus prevent consequent difficulties in decisionmaking from hurting the goal of integration.

It is up to the current members to decide how steep will be the "sunk costs" a new member will need to accept. The steeper such costs, the more committed a new entrant must be to accept them and the narrower the range of issues on which major conflict will be possible. To take an American analogy, when Kansas became a state, the issue of whether slavery should be permitted was extraordinarily divisive. Yet when Washington became a state, the issue of whether it should be "slave" or "free" was dead. The issue had been settled by the victor in the Civil War. Similarly, the greater the number of issues that become settled before further enlargement takes place, the fewer the issues that will need to be addressed by a larger Community. Just as the goal of eliminating nontariff barriers had to be accepted by Spain and Portugal, so other basic goals that are decided on by the current membership would have to be accepted by future candidates for membership.

However, the Twelve could decide to differentiate among new entrants. Such "variable geometry" would lead to a Community in which some new members would be asked to accept the entire Community framework already in place at the time of accession, while others would be held to a looser standard. All countries, therefore, would not be asked to pay the same price for entry. To many observers, this alternative seems a logical response to the transformation of the European continent. It would allow the Community to extend its influence, help stabilize democratization and the movement to free markets throughout the continent, and make "Europe" roughly synonymous with the Community in fact as well as in symbol.

The ostensible logic of variable geometry, however, tends to downgrade the role that values have played in shaping the Community's evolution. Yet it is precisely because of the importance of values that it will be difficult (though not impossible) for the Twelve to agree to create a tiered or segmented Community. The Community's six founding members (Belgium, the Netherlands, Luxembourg, the Federal Republic, Italy, and France) in particular have been deeply attached to a Community in which each member, upon admission, accepts equal responsibilities and obligations. Even for the creation of the EuroFed, where presumably a more economistic logic should reign, strong sentiment exists against institutionalizing distinctions among member states. Once states have joined the Community, they have subsequently been able to decide when to join institutions such as the EMS and even, in the case of Britain and social policy, have been exempted from decisions affecting the other Eleven. However, allowing new members to select among the *acquis communautaire* will be extremely difficult for at least several member states.

A Community already characterized by extraordinary diversity may not be able to incorporate variations in responsibility and commitment without altering its identity as well as the trajectory of institutional development. For many key elites in the founding member states, equality of commitment on the part of all members is an essential anchor for the Community. They see it as a necessary counterweight to the centrifugal forces that exist and that will continue to exist in the Community. Just as elites in the post-Communist states may be willing to pay a high price for entry, so elites in many of the Community's current member states may be willing to forgo the possible political and economic benefits of "variable geometry" in order to maintain the Community as a cohesive and, at least symbolically, an egalitarian unit.

If a tiered or segmented Community was accepted in principle, some countries, such as post-Communist states, might well choose political membership and defer the decision to join the internal market and the EuroFed. They might prefer participation in the foreign policy and security activities of the Community to full economic participation. Others, like Sweden and Austria, might choose membership in the civilian segment of the Community and forgo participating in defense-related activities. The dichotomy created by such choices highlights some critical questions facing the current Twelve. How should the Community deal with foreign, security, and defense policy? How much more closely should the Twelve member states cooperate? And what should the Commission's role be in formulating such cooperation?

The area of security policy is both pressing and particularly complicated for the Community. Even though the role of the North Atlantic Treaty Organization (NATO) will need to be reexamined in light of the Soviet Union's disintegration, it is far from clear what the ex-Soviet empire will look like in five years, and even less clear how much violence and conflict will accompany the shaping of that new look. What is clear is that many organizations, all established while the Soviet Union was a state, will be attempting to rethink their mission in a new context.

NATO, the Western European Union, and the Conference on Security and Cooperation in Europe as well as the Community will each have to redefine their roles. This redefinition will be affected by the debate over what role the United States should play in Europe, over whether the CSCE can overcome the problems inherent in collective security organizations, and over how important the WEU should be. But perhaps the central decision that will affect the shape of security on the European continent rests with the current Twelve. Will the Community actually be able to forge common foreign and security policies, and if so, how will defense policy be treated? The answer to that question will influence many decisions taken with regard to other security organizations. The fluidity of security, dramatized by the disintegration of the Soviet Union and the consequent uncertainty as well as by the fear of interethnic (and perhaps interstate) violence, puts the Community in a particularly strategic position to fashion the security landscape on the European continent.

How security will be organized raises another set of issues. Will the Community's security structure eventually become an integral part of the Community? Or will it retain the structure agreed to at Maastricht, in which foreign and security policy was not integrated into the Treaty of Rome, the European Court of Justice was explicitly excluded from exercising its jurisdiction, and the Commission was given a minimal role in the formulation of policy? Will the Commission be eventually involved in formulating such policy or will that remain primarily an intergovernmental effort? Such questions have to do with how power is organized inside the Community in the area of foreign and security policy, with the smaller countries generally afraid of being dominated by the larger ones and therefore wanting policy to be decided within the Community's institutions (with the Commission playing an important role) rather than in strictly intergovernmental settings. Furthermore, how will the Western European Union evolve? At Maastricht the WEU was identified as the Community's defense component but was also charged to work cooperatively with NATO. How the relationship between the member states (acting intergovernmentally), the WEU, and NATO will develop concretely is one of the major questions facing the Twelve during this decade.

Integration in foreign policy and security policy will probably be strengthened (regardless of the specifics decided at Maastricht and later) to the extent that the post-Communist states are viewed as sources of political instability for the entire region. Thus upheaval on the European continent, which threatens EC members with the specter of refugees, immigration, the flight of capital from Europe, and general instability, provides fertile ground for movement toward a Community foreign policy and security policy. In fact, the need to develop a broad Community approach to the explosive political issue of immigration may force the pace of integration in those areas. The desire to have "Europe" count as an international actor is one thing and may well not be strong enough to overcome long-standing notions of national sovereignty and historical legacies in foreign policy. By contrast, the political consequences of non-EC immigration could be so disruptive to the existing political order within member states that some integrative processes in the foreign and security policy area may well be accepted in the name of immigration policy, though they would be opposed if cast as traditional foreign policy issues.

The Yugoslav conflict, which began in mid-1991, was important, suggesting that violence in the East encourages integration in the West. The dynamics among the member states in responding to the crisis were significant in helping to build the foundations for the eventual common foreign policy called for at Maastricht. A common foreign policy will not be easy for the Community to achieve, but the efforts made to work together during the Yugoslav crisis, in spite of very different national views on the appropriate policy vis-à-vis Croatia, can be viewed as part of an evolutionary institution-building process in the arena of foreign policy.

Once the European Council decided to act in the Yugoslav crisis, the troika (consisting of the past, present, and future presidents of the Council of Ministers) immediately went into action. It was understood who would actually go to Yugoslavia to negotiate. That the actual membership of the troika changed so smoothly (the first group consisted of the Italian,

Luxembourg, and Dutch foreign ministers and the second of the Luxembourg, Dutch, and Portuguese foreign ministers) as the presidency shifted from Luxembourg to the Netherlands shows how much the Twelve have got used to working together. It also shows how institutionalized subgroups within the EC, such as the troika, have become. Finally, the institutional innovations (such as a force of observers and a peace conference) that the Community created on very short notice show that the member states can often agree when addressing conflicts fanned by nationalism and historical hatreds. Differences between the member states did not lead to hasty unilateral action by any member state, although they did prevent the Community from adopting specific measures such as economic sanctions, armed intervention, and the recognition of Croatia at the beginning of the crisis. Although the Federal Republic was criticized for insisting on the recognition of Croatia in the last days of 1991, it is significant, from the point of view of institution building, that the German government hewed to the Community position as long as it did, given the extraordinary strength of the multipartisan forces in the Bundestag demanding recognition of Croatia.

Nonetheless, that the Community became the central external power trying to resolve the conflict will make it even more important diplomatically and politically in the eyes of nonmembers seeking international assistance. The Community as an international player may be relatively effective in the post-Communist context because of its economic strength and is likely to benefit from the increasing entanglement of economic and diplomatic power. Threats of economic retribution and the denial of access to the Community's market may not be sufficient to prevent nationalism from taking a virulent and violent form, but they at least represent a firebreak.

Alternatively, the Community's hold on foreign policy may not develop uniformly across all sectors. Just as the Community became an international actor in external economic negotiations while maintaining member-state autonomy in other foreign policy areas, so it may strengthen its cohesion in some sectors while moving slowly in others. Thus it could move slowly in areas concerned with military power while becoming more integrated in, for example, the newly emerging area concerned with international environmental negotiations. In fact, a broad consensus seems to be forming across the Community in favor of far-reaching pro-environmental international measures. On that issue, the Community may well take the lead.

Such a result is especially likely if the Commission is given the same role in environmental negotiations that it has in external economic negotiations. It is now automatically the negotiator for all EC members in GATT negotiations, for example, but in environmental negotiations it must be asked to act as negotiator by the member states. Because the environment will be extremely visible on the international scene in 1992 and beyond, the Commission may be able to capitalize on increasingly strong proenvironmental sentiment among national governments to expand its own power in this area. If it succeeds, the United States may well find that the Community sets the agenda for international environmental negotiations.

Regardless of how integration in the foreign and security policy area proceeds, however, the ongoing integration of Europe, when viewed historically and comparatively, is a phenomenon that can only inspire amazement. It is not surprising that the process of integration is extraordinarily difficult, contentious, and asymmetrical. What is surprising, given the experience of past centuries and of other parts of the world, is that the process of integration exists at all. The fact that it has come so far and is continuing should alert Americans not to underestimate its long-term prospects.

The contributors to this volume have analyzed some (but by no means all) of the pieces making up a political structure that is recognizable as such yet differs from all existing models. Their chapters demonstrate why the Community is simultaneously intriguing and frustrating for both scholars and policymakers. We recognize it as a polity in the making, and thus it resembles processes and structures we understand because we have studied them (or variants thereof) elsewhere. At the same time, however, the Community diverges in many ways from established polities. It is that creative tension between the recognizable and the unique that informs this book.

Chapter 2

The 1992 Initiative:
Causes and Consequences

DAVID R. CAMERON

W HEN the European Council met in Milan in June 1985, the leaders
of the ten member states of the European Community (EC) had
two proposals before them. One, a White Paper, specified some three
hundred measures that would eliminate most of the barriers that still
impeded the free flow of goods, services, capital, and labor in the Community. The other, the Dooge Committee's report, specified several changes
that would improve the efficiency of decisionmaking in the Community,
render it less vulnerable to the veto of individual member states, and
expand the role of the European Parliament.[1]

The European Council provisionally approved both proposals and
recommended that the Council of Ministers convene an extraordinary
intergovernmental conference of the member states to consider the
proposals in detail, decide which elements of each should be adopted, and
then draft the necessary amendments to the treaties that govern the
Community.[2] The conference—essentially a series of meetings of the

For their comments and suggestions on various drafts of this chapter, the author wishes
to thank Jeffrey Anderson, Miriam Golden, Peter Hall, Ellis Krauss, Françoise de La Serre,
Peter Lange, Joseph LaPalombara, Steven Lewis, Helen Milner, Andrew Moravcsik, Simon
Reich, Helen Wallace, Joseph Weiler, Wolfgang Wessels, and Nicholas Ziegler.

1. For the text of the two proposals, see Commission of the European Communities,
Completing the Internal Market: White Paper from the Commission to the European Council
(Luxembourg, 1985); and Ad Hoc Committee for Institutional Affairs, *Report to the European
Council (Brussels, 29–30 March 1985)* (Luxembourg, 1985).

2. A decision to convene an intergovernmental conference requires a majority of the
member states (although any amendments to the Treaties of Paris and Rome adopted by
such a conference must be approved by all the member states and ratified by each national

Council of Ministers—took place in Luxembourg, which then held the rotating Council presidency, in the fall of 1985.[3] The ministers drafted the treaty amendments and incorporated them in the Single European Act (SEA). The amendments and the SEA were approved by the European Council at its December meeting and subsequently by the Council of Ministers.

During the first several months of 1986, the member states of the Community ratified the Single European Act. In so doing, they committed themselves to the progressive establishment, by the end of 1992, of an internal market, defined as "an area without internal frontiers in which the free movement of goods, persons, services and capital is ensured."[4] They also agreed to institute certain reforms in the internal legislative and executive procedures of the Community. Thus the nearly three hundred proposals that would create the internal market were to be implemented through a new cooperation procedure that gave the European Parliament a greater role in amending and approving the Commission's proposals. For most of the directives pertaining to the internal market, the act extended the principle of voting by qualified majority (that is, a weighted and larger-than-minimum majority), rather than by unanimity, in the Council of Ministers.[5]

On July 1, 1987, the Single European Act went into effect. As it did, the Community appeared to have heeded François Mitterrand's call, before the European Parliament in 1984, to "relaunch" itself. And with its renewed sense of purpose, Europe moved toward "1992" and beyond, along a road that, after Milan, passed through Hannover, Madrid, Rome, and then Maastricht on its way to economic, monetary, and political union.

---

legislature). At the Milan meeting, all the member states except Britain, Greece, and Denmark voted in favor of convening the conference. Those three did, however, agree to participate.

3. The presidency of the Council of Ministers, and therefore the chair of the various meetings of the Council, as well as those of the European Council, rotates in alphabetical order among the member states in six-month terms. See Colm O'Nuallain and Jean-Marc Hoscheit, eds., *The Presidency of the European Council of Ministers: Impacts and Implications for National Governments* (London: Croom Helm, 1985).

4. Article 13 of the SEA, which became articles 8a and 8b of the amended treaties.

5. The SEA retained the principle of unanimity in council voting for directives involving taxation, employment, and the movement of persons. For discussions of the institutional reforms, see Richard Corbett, "Testing the New Procedures: The European Parliament's First Experiences with Its New 'Single Act' Powers," *Journal of Common Market Studies*, vol. 27 (June 1989), pp. 359–72; and John Fitzmaurice, "An Analysis of the European Community's Co-operation Procedure," *Journal of Common Market Studies*, vol. 26 (June 1988), pp. 389–400.

What kind of supranational organization will the Community of the future be? Will it resemble the Community we now know? Or will its responsibilities and powers be markedly greater after 1992? In short, has the 1992 initiative launched Europe on a new trajectory, one that will take it ever closer to the goals—idealized by some and abhorred by others—of full economic integration and political federation? This chapter argues that the meaning and consequences of 1992—in particular, the extent to which it will change the developmental path of the Community—are revealed in its origins and in the process by which it came into being.

Theoretical Perspectives

There are two contrasting theoretical perspectives on the nature of politics and the process of change within the European Community. One derives from neofunctionalist theories of regional integration and the other from neorealist theories of international relations. From the former perspective, the 1992 initiative represents an integrationist impulse that is likely to strengthen the supranational institutions and responsibilities of the Community. From the latter, however, the Community remains, despite the 1992 initiative, the creation and instrument of national politics and national interests that will continue to constrain integrationist impulses within the Community.

Neofunctionalists treat regional integration as a process rather than an end-state. The process is said to consist of several phases. First, supranational institutions are assigned tasks that are *inherently expansive*. Then interest groups, political parties, and other national political elites begin to press for a strengthening and expansion of the functions of supranational institutions so that they can perform those tasks. As those new functions are carried out, support builds for the strengthened supranational institutions among both elites and the mass public.[6] Thus, to the extent that *inherently expansive* tasks are assigned to supranational institutions, the responsibilities and powers of, and support for, those supranational institutions will tend to increase in a spillover effect.

The 1992 initiative appears to offer some validation of the neofunctionalist theory of regional integration. The Single European Act and the commitment to achieve a single internal market by the end of 1992, followed

6. For the development of neofunctionalist theory in the European context, see Ernst B. Haas, *The Uniting of Europe: Political, Social, and Economic Forces, 1950–1957* (Stanford University Press, 1958); Haas, *Beyond the Nation-State: Functionalism and International*

by the commitment agreed upon at Maastricht in late 1991 to move to the third stage of economic and monetary union by January 1, 1999, at the latest, extended the responsibilities and powers of the supranational institutions of the Community and in so doing represent a return to the Community's early course of incremental, step-by-step institution building à la Monnet.[7] Soon after the ratification of the act, the Community began to pursue once more its long-standing objective of economic and monetary union (EMU).[8] The Commission of the European Commmunities formed a committee of experts to study the implications of an internal market, and in 1987 that committee, chaired by Tommaso Padoa-Schioppa, reported that free trade, capital mobility, fixed exchange rates, and national control over monetary policy constitute an inconsistent quartet

---

Organization (Stanford University Press, 1964); and Leon N. Lindberg, *The Political Dynamics of European Economic Integration* (Stanford University Press, 1963). See also, Lindberg and Stuart A. Scheingold, *Europe's Would-Be Polity: Patterns of Change in the European Community* (Prentice-Hall, 1970); and Reginald J. Harrison, *Europe in Question: Theories of Regional International Integration* (London: Allen and Unwin, 1974). For an insightful assessment of integration theory in the light of the 1992 initiative, see Robert O. Keohane and Stanley Hoffmann, "Conclusion: Community Politics and Institutional Change," in William Wallace, ed., *The Dynamics of European Integration* (London: Pinter Publishers, 1990), pp. 276–300.

7. Jean Monnet, a civil servant, businessman, and banker before World War II, served as high commissioner of the Plan for Modernization and Reequipment in France from 1946 to 1952. An essential concern of the office of the plan was the expansion of French steel production. Expansion could occur only if France obtained reliable access to large amounts of German coal and coke. By early 1949 the French government had concluded that only some form of association between the French and German coal and steel industries could ensure that access. In May 1950 the French foreign minister, Robert Schuman, announced a plan to put the German and French coal and steel industries under a joint High Authority. The plan, associated with Schuman's name but developed largely by Monnet and his colleagues in the plan, formed the basis of the European Coal and Steel Community (ECSC). The ECSC, created by the Treaty of Paris of April 1951, became the model for a parallel supranational organization designed to institute a common internal market among the then six ECSC members. That latter organization, the European Economic Community, was created by the Treaty of Rome in March 1957. Monnet served from 1952 until 1955 as the first president of the High Authority of the ECSC. See, among others, Alan S. Milward, *The Reconstruction of Western Europe 1945–51* (University of California Press, 1984), chaps. 4, 6.

8. EMU had first been identified as an objective by the six political leaders of the European Economic Community at their summit meeting in The Hague in 1969. At that meeting they formed a working group, chaired by Pierre Werner, the prime minister of Luxembourg, to examine the steps necessary for EMU. In October 1970 the Werner group issued its report: Commission of the European Communities, *Report to the Council and Commission on the Realization by Stages of Economic and Monetary Union in the Community* (Luxembourg, 1970). The objective was reaffirmed at the summit meeting of the six member states in Paris in 1972 and again at the summit meeting of the nine members in 1974.

that could only be resolved by the creation of a single, Community-wide monetary policy.[9]

At its June 1988 meeting in Hannover, the European Council decided to devote its 1989 meeting in Madrid to discussing the means of achieving economic and monetary union. It appointed a committee, chaired by Jacques Delors, the president of the Commission, to study and propose the necessary steps to EMU. The committee's report, issued in April 1989, concluded that economic and monetary union implied "irrevocably fixed exchange rates between national currencies and . . . a single currency. This, in turn, would imply a common monetary policy and require a high degree of compatibility of economic policies and consistency in a number of other policy areas, particularly in the fiscal field." As a result, the Community would need new institutions to implement monetary policy— most notably, a "European System of Central Banks"—and a *transfer of decision-making power* from Member-States to the Community as a whole . . . in the fields of monetary policy and macroeconomic management."[10]

In short, after adopting the proposal for an internal market, the Community moved quickly, and in a manner consistent with neofunctionalist theory, to consider an economic and monetary union featuring a single central bank and a single currency. And, indeed, at its December 1991 meeting at Maastricht, the European Council agreed to create both a European central bank and a single currency—the essential elements of the third stage of EMU—by 1999. An image of the European Community of the future then began to take shape—an image of a supranational organization endowed with new and strengthened institutions and responsibilities and even, perhaps, a federal form of government.

Those of the neorealist frame of mind, however, are not convinced that the Community is now moving, or is likely to move, inexorably toward greater economic integration and political federation, at least as the latter is typically defined. (See chapter 8 for a discussion of alternative models of federation.) This perspective has its roots in the modern realist theory of international relations elaborated by Hans Morgenthau, among others.

9. See Tommaso Padoa-Schioppa, *Efficiency, Stability, and Equity: A Strategy for the Evolution of the Economic System of the European Community: A Report* (Oxford University Press, 1987), pp. 23–24.

10. European Economic Community, Committee for the Study of Economic and Monetary Union, *Report on Economic and Monetary Union in the European Community* (Luxembourg, 1989), paragraphs 16, 19; italics in the original (also known as the Delors Report).

According to realist theory, states are the essential and most important actors in international politics, behave rationally (that is, in a self-interested manner), and are motivated by their desire to maintain and enhance their power relative to that of other states. Neorealism, as expounded by Kenneth Waltz, assumes that states are self-regarding (although it relaxes the assumption that power is the only, or even primary, objective of state behavior). In addition, neorealism asserts that states interact in a *structured* system—that is, the system of states is governed by certain principles (most notably, decentralization and anarchy), and the states within it are differentiated by and vary with regard to their capabilities, which depend on their size, wealth, power, form, and so on.[11]

From the neorealist perspective, the essential components of the Community are said to be the member states, and the Community itself is seen as a gathering of sovereign *states*—that is, an *international* rather than a *supranational* organization. It follows (by definition) that the authority for essential economic, monetary, political, and security matters will always be vested in the member states. Thus, whatever the extent of the new and expanded powers of the Community's institutions, the ultimate authority for all policy will continue to reside, as it has in the past, in the member states. From this perspective, the accumulation of power by existing or newly created supranational institutions in the Community only reflects the desire of the member states to cede or delegate authority to those institutions. If the states wish, they can recall or revoke that authority. Thus, if the Community appears to be evolving toward a more integrated and more institutionally elaborate supranational organization, it is only because the member states have decided that such an organization best serves their national objectives and interests.

In the neorealist image, the Community of the future is an essentially unintegrated—or at best loosely integrated—confederation of sovereign states, rather than a tightly integrated protofederation of states that have agreed to pool and otherwise limit their sovereignty. This image derives in part from the theory's state-centric notion of sovereignty. But it also

11. For the classic statements of modern realism and neorealism, see, respectively, Hans Joachim Morgenthau, *Politics among Nations* (Knopf, 1948); and Kenneth N. Waltz, *Theory of International Politics* (Addison-Wesley, 1979). For a comprehensive discussion of the attributes, strengths, and weaknesses of neorealist theory, see Robert O. Keohane, ed., *Neorealism and Its Critics* (Columbia University Press, 1986), especially chap. 4 (by Waltz), chap. 6 (by John Gerard Ruggie), and chap. 7 (by Keohane).

reflects the legacy of certain political leaders—most notably, Charles de Gaulle and Margaret Thatcher, both of whom lost no opportunity to assert the primacy of the nation-state in supranational Europe. If de Gaulle's legacy was to delay British membership by a decade and retain the national veto, via the Luxembourg Compromise, Thatcher's eleven years in office gave the Community the air of a forum in which member states pursued their particular national interests by bargaining, negotiating, and forming coalitions and alliances with other member states.[12] As a result, politics and policymaking in the Community in the Thatcher era appeared to revolve around the recurring conflicts, negotiations, and bargains worked out in the intergovernmental fora of the Community—that is, in the Council of Ministers and, above all, the European Council.[13]

If the neorealist image of the Community as a confederation of sovereign states depended only on Thatcher's presence, her resignation in November 1990, and the circumstances that provoked it, might lead one to doubt its validity as a predictive guide to the future. However, the historic changes in the Soviet Union and Eastern Europe since Gorbachev's accession to power have given new life to the neorealist perspective. The collapse of the Communist regimes in Eastern Europe and the former Soviet Union, the unification of Germany, and the obsolescence of the European security alliances have raised the possibility of a further enlargement and "widening" of the Community. In the wake of that "widening"— exemplified by the applications for membership by Austria and Sweden, pending applications from most of the other members of the European

12. At Luxembourg in January 1966 the member states ended France's six-month withdrawal from the Council of Ministers—the period of the "empty chair"—by agreeing that a state's "very important" interests would be protected against an adverse majority vote in the Council by a shared commitment to continue negotiations. As part of the compromise, France (but not the others) expressed the view that negotiations would continue until unanimity prevailed, implying that without unanimity decisions on such matters could not be taken. The six agreed to disagree about how to proceed if no agreement ensued. See W. Nicoll, "The Luxembourg Compromise," *Journal of Common Market Studies*, vol. 23 (September 1984), pp. 35–43. For a discussion of de Gaulle and the Community, see, among many, Stanley Hoffmann, *Decline or Renewal? France since the 1930s* (Viking, 1974), chaps. 10, 12.

13. For discussions of intergovernmentalism in the Community, see, among others, Paul Taylor, *The Limits of European Integration* (London: Croom Helm, 1983), chap. 2; Helen Wallace, William Wallace, and Carole Webb, eds., *Policy-Making in the European Community*, 2d ed. (Wiley, 1983), chaps. 2, 13; and Andrew Moravcsik, "Negotiating the Single European Act: National Interests and Conventional Statecraft in the European Community," *International Organization*, vol. 45 (Winter 1991), pp. 19–56.

30   DAVID R. CAMERON

Free Trade Association, and association agreements with several of the Eastern European nations—the Community faces the prospect of an increasingly complex array of intergovernmental relations, tensions, conflicts, and negotiations among a larger number of participating member states. As Thatcher well understood when she pressed for early enlargement to the nations of EFTA and Eastern Europe, "widening" may well inhibit a further "deepening" of the integrative process by increasing the frequency and intensity of conflicts and tensions among the member states.

Which of the two contrasting images of the future Community is accurate? Do the recent initiatives that fall under the 1992 label represent a significant relaunching of European integration, and will the Community's supranational institutions find their authority increasing in the 1990s and that of the member states beginning to decline? Or will the Community remain, as it has always been, a vehicle for expressing state interests and an international confederation of sovereign states rather than a supranational organization moving toward full economic integration and political federation?

This chapter deals with these questions by examining the history of the 1992 initiative; the most important economic, institutional, and political factors affecting the development of the initiative; and the interaction of the contrasting impulses of integration and intergovernmentalism in the Community.

When all the factors are reviewed, *neither* neofunctionalism nor neorealism seems to fully explain the process by which 1992 came into being. And, taken alone, neither serves as a reliable guide to the Community of the future. Rather, the 1992 initiative was the product of a complex interaction between forces and actors that, self-consciously or otherwise, moved the Community toward greater economic and political integration, on the one hand, and, on the other, forces and actors that reflected the diverse national interests of the member states of the Community and the intergovernmental politics among those states. In other words, the discussion suggests that *both* neofunctionalism and neorealism—taken together rather than as alternative approaches—are useful for, and indeed necessary to, an understanding of the 1992 initiative.

The chapter concludes by considering some of the implications and possible consequences of a process of politics in the Community that is characterized, simultaneously, by accelerating economic integration and supranational institution building and by institutionalized intergovernmentalism among its member states.

History of the Internal Market Initiative

The decisions to create an internal market and to take the first steps toward economic and monetary union are often viewed as the result of a new commitment to Europe spearheaded in 1984 and 1985 by François Mitterrand, Jacques Delors (the newly named president of the European Commission), and other proponents of a stronger, more integrated, and more federal European Community. In fact, those decisions represent the culmination of a long process of policy development within the Community, which spanned two decades and had produced a commitment to a single internal market long before Delors assumed the presidency.

The Paris summit conference of December 1974 laid at least some of the initiative's foundation. The summit reaffirmed the commitment, first made in The Hague in 1969 and reiterated in Paris in 1972, to economic and monetary union by the end of 1980 and invited Prime Minister Leo Tindemans of Belgium to provide a comprehensive review of the prospects for such a union.

Taking as a model the Werner Report issued in response to the request of the leaders' meeting at The Hague, Tindemans reviewed the place of economic and monetary union in a Community that had recently experienced enlargement, the oil price shock of the Yom Kippur War, the acceleration of inflation, and recessions. In discussing the need for greater harmonization of fiscal, monetary, and exchange rate policy, Tindemans put a major component of the internal market initiative on the table for the first time when he recommended that the member states gradually abolish national obstacles to the free movement of capital.

In July 1980 the European Council appointed Gaston Thorn, the former prime minister of Luxembourg, as president of the Commission for a four-year term beginning in January 1981. Responsibility for the internal market and customs union was assigned to Karl-Heinz Narjes, a Christian Democratic deputy in the German Bundestag.[14] The new Commission took office in January 1981. Soon thereafter the European Council voiced, for the first time, its concerns about the state of the internal market in the Community and, in so doing, initiated the policymaking process that was to culminate several years later in the 1992 initiative.

14. Commission portfolios are assigned to the individuals nominated by the member states to be commissioners. In the 1960s Narjes had served as the *chef de cabinet* of Walter Hallstein when the latter was president of the Commission. He subsequently headed the Directorate-General for press and information before returning, in 1972, to German politics.

At its meeting in Luxembourg in June 1981, the European Council expressed alarm about the state of the internal market. Trade, it argued, was increasingly being threatened by unintentional as well as intentional barriers, subsidies, and other market-distorting policies. To remedy the situation, the council endorsed a "concerted effort . . . to strengthen and develop the free internal market."[15] At its next meeting, in London in November 1981, the European Council asked both the Commission and the Council of Ministers to report to it on the state of the internal market in the Community and, more generally, on the state of economic and monetary union some six years after the Tindemans report.[16]

The Commission prepared an extensive study of the state of the internal market, and Thorn reported its main conclusions to the European Council at its Copenhagen meeting in December 1982. The Commission recommended that the council take steps to remove nontariff barriers in the Community, simplify frontier formalities, increase competition in the public procurement of telecommunications services, equalize the legal rights and simplify the tax codes for companies based in one member state and doing business in another, and open up trade in services, especially in the financial field. This set of proposals contained the first elaboration of the core of the internal market initiative.[17]

At Copenhagen the European Council not only endorsed the concept of strengthening the internal market by eliminating restrictive trade practices, but also created a special council within the framework of the Council

15. "19th and 20th Sessions of the European Council," *Keesing's Contemporary Archives*, vol. 27 (November 13, 1981), p. 31199.

16. Moravcsik, "Negotiating the Single European Act," p. 33 and n. 33, argues that no internal market initiative was considered seriously by the major member states before 1981 and that no consensus for reform existed before 1984, when the French assumed the council presidency. In fact, however, by 1984 the heads of state had been publicly committed to EMU for more than a decade (since the Paris summit of 1969). And at least since the Tindemans Report of 1976—if not that of Werner five years earlier—they understood that EMU involved in part the creation of an internal market for goods, services, and capital. Likewise, to argue that no consensus in favor of reform existed until 1984 ignores the historical record—specifically, that a consensus existed as of the Luxembourg meeting of the European Council in mid-1981 (at the latest) and that that position was reiterated by the council every time it met during the next four years.

17. It is perhaps worth highlighting the fact that this core of the internal market initiative was produced by the Thorn Commission, which almost invariably has been perceived by academic commentators as ineffective and largely irrelevant to the development of the initiative.

of Ministers to identify priority measures for creating an internal market. [18] At the next meeting of the heads of government in Brussels in March 1983, the council reviewed the progress made by the new Internal Market Council, which had gone through about two dozen proposals (some pending as far back as 1977) that were designed to open up internal frontiers and remove barriers to trade and financial services, such as insurance, within the Community. The council also asked the Internal Market Council to speed up its consideration of such issues as the mutual recognition of diplomas, the right to provide services in the Community, and the removal of frontier barriers and various documentary inconveniences that had confronted the transportation sector.

Three months later, in June 1983, the European Council (meeting in Stuttgart) went over the progress made in strengthening the internal market in such areas as the development of technical standards and company law. And in what must surely have been taken as a measure of their dissatisfaction with the pace of work by the Internal Market Council, the heads of government noted with regret that progress on some key aspects of the internal market was not yet forthcoming and called on the Council of Ministers, at its meeting later in that same month, to "make every effort to settle as many of the outstanding internal market matters as possible." The European Council concluded its postsummit declaration by recalling that the "completion of the internal market must remain a priority aim . . . [and that] work must therefore continue . . . on the removal of the various forms of distortion of competition that still exist, including trade barriers in the form of differences between national standards, as well as in the services sector."[19]

Much of 1984 was consumed with the ongoing negotiations and disputes between Britain and the other EC members over rebates for its budget contributions. But at the June 1984 meeting of the European Council at Fontainebleau, the leaders returned to the issue of the internal market

18. As Bieber and others note, this institutional innovation, by which the Council of Ministers was, for the first time, defined by a particular task, rather than by the conventional grouping of common portfolios of government, played an important role in promoting a coherent and coordinated response to the European Council's initiative among the member governments of the Community. See Roland Bieber and others, eds., *1992: One European Market?: A Critical Analysis of the Commission's Internal Market Strategy* (Baden-Baden: Nomos, 1988), p. 319.

19. "26th European Council Meeting in Stuttgart," *Keesing's Contemporary Archives*, vol. 29 (September 1983), p. 32406.

and formally pledged themselves to "the creation of a genuine economic union."[20] Their first priority would be to strengthen the internal market. The Commission had already presented a report on this task calling for the "decisive simplification" of formalities in trade and a modernization of customs; the harmonization of European standards and products; an opening up to European competition of public procurement contracting; a liberalization of trade in services such as transportation, banking, and insurance; and the elimination of many of the national legal and tax regulations faced by multinationals operating in the Community.

The European Council asked the Council of Ministers to examine the Commission's proposals with a view to acting on those in line with the stated objectives of the economic union and a strengthened internal market. The Commission was invited to report on its progress in this field in time for the European Council's June 1985 meeting.[21]

Shortly after the Fontainebleau meeting the European Council announced that Jacques Delors would succeed Thorn as president of the Commission. Delors and the other newly appointed members of the Commission took office in January 1985. By that time, the internal market initiative was well under way. Indeed, it had been brewing for more than three years—largely under the direction of the European Council, which had long been committed to economic and monetary union and which viewed the creation of a single internal market as an important component of EMU. Since the early 1980s the council had been encouraging the Commission and the Council of Ministers to develop, approve, and implement proposals for a single market, and literally hundreds of proposals covering a wide range of economic activity had been drafted by the time Delors took office. But they had not yet been put together in a package that would be politically attractive to the leaders of the Community.

At its Brussels meeting in March 1985 the European Council again called for "action to achieve a single large market by 1992, thereby creating a more favourable environment for stimulating enterprise, competition, and trade." In addition to assigning, for the first time, a target date for the completion of the internal market, it called on the Commission to draw up

20. "29th European Meeting at Fontainebleau," *Keesing's Contemporary Archives*, vol. 30 (October 1984), p. 33165.

21. At the Fontainebleau meeting the council also created the Ad Hoc Committee on Institutional Affairs to examine and suggest improvements in the operations of the European institutions. Ireland assumed the presidency of the council for the last six months of 1984 and Prime Minister FitzGerald appointed Senator Jim Dooge of Ireland to head the committee, which was instructed to report to the council at its March 1985 meeting.

a "detailed programme with a specific timetable before its next meeting."[22] That meeting, scheduled for Milan in June, was only three months away— which may explain why the White Paper prepared by Lord Cockfield, the new commissioner in charge of the internal market, had a slapped-together quality, consisting as it did of three hundred proposals covering a wide range of trade and commercial issues, most of which had already been developed by the Commission and were taken "off the shelf."[23]

In instructing the Commission to submit its proposals swiftly for the consideration of the intergovernmental conference, the European Council suggested that the following measures be given high priority: the removal of physical barriers to the free movement of goods; the removal of technical barriers to the free movement of goods (through the adoption of common or compatible standards for new technologies that would, in turn, open up public procurement to greater competition); the creation of a free market in the financial services and transport sectors; the granting of full freedom to professionals to practice throughout the Community; and the liberalization of capital markets. These actions were to be guided by three basic principles: the equivalence of each member state's legislative objectives; the institution of minimum standards when harmonization was required; and a reliance on the concept of mutual recognition to avoid, whenever possible, the complications involved in formulating and harmonizing Community-wide standards.

Sources of the Internal Market Initiative

The critical factors that contributed to the development of the 1992 initiative can be grouped into three categories: economic, institutional, and political.

22. "31st European Council Meeting in Brussels," *Keesing's Contemporary Archives*, vol. 31 (May 1985), p. 33597.

23. Colchester and Buchan state that Cockfield, drawing on his considerable experience, wrote the section on taxation—in particular, the harmonization of indirect taxation—himself. For the rest of the White Paper, however, Cockfield's job "was more one of trawling and sieving than of inventing. An immense amount—perhaps half—of the required European rule-making was already in draft form after years of effort by the Commission." Nicholas Colchester and David Buchan, *Europower: The Essential Guide to Europe's Economic Transformation in 1992* (Economist Books, 1990), pp. 30–31. Cockfield was, of course, one of Margaret Thatcher's two nominees to the Commission. Earlier he had served as minister of state for the Treasury (from May 1979 to April 1982), secretary of state for trade (from April 1982 to June 1983), and chancellor of the Duchy of Lancaster (from June 1983 until his nomination to the Commission in September 1984). While he was secretary of state for trade, he served as Britain's representative on the Internal Market Council.

Economic Factors

The policy choices of European leaders—including those that resulted in the internal market initiative—do not occur in a vacuum. They are greatly influenced by the international economic context in which their countries functioned. The brief survey in the previous section of the development of the internal market initiative suggests that its origins lie in the early 1980s. That being the case, it is necessary to consider in some detail the economic context of that period. Here I consider four aspects of that context: the growing dependence, in the period before the development of the initiative, of the member states on trade with other member states; conditions in the international economy and within the economies of the member states in the late 1970s and early 1980s; the creation of the European Monetary System and its evolution into a quasi-fixed exchange rate regime in the early 1980s; and the interests, desires, and economic objectives of certain segments of European business in that period.

INCREASING DEPENDENCE ON INTRA-COMMUNITY TRADE. The member states of the European Community are all open economies.[24] They depend to a considerable degree on external markets for the consumption of their goods and services and on external producers for a considerable portion of the goods and services they consume. Table 2-1 presents a measure of this openness, or trade dependence. The measure is simply the ratio of exports to gross domestic product.

According to the table, the member states depend, to a high degree, on external markets. They are considerably more open, and dependent, than the United States and Japan. Furthermore, this dependence has been steadily increasing. To cite a typical example, Germany's exports rose from 19 percent of GDP in 1960 to 32 percent in 1985 and thus outpaced the German economy as a whole.

The increase in openness was by no means a Community-specific phenomenon. The period 1960–85 saw similar increases in Spain and Portugal—which were not yet members of the Community in 1985—and in the

24. For discussions of openness see, among others, David R. Cameron, "The Expansion of the Public Economy: A Comparative Analysis," *American Political Science Review*, vol. 72 (December 1978), pp. 1243–61; and Peter J. Katzenstein, *Small States in World Markets: Industrial Policy in Europe* (Cornell University Press, 1985), chap. 3. For analyses of the economics of openness, see, among others, Rudiger Dornbusch, *Open Economy Macroeconomics* (Basic Books, 1980); and John Williamson, *The Open Economy and the World Economy: A Textbook in International Economics* (Basic Books, 1983).

Table 2-1. *Trade Dependence of the Member States of the European Community, the United States, Canada, and Japan, 1960, 1972, 1985*
Exports as a percent of GDP

Country	1960	1972	1985
West Germany	19.0	20.9	32.4
France	14.5	16.7	23.9
Italy	13.0	17.7	22.8
Netherlands	47.6	45.0	63.5
Belgium	38.4	51.1	76.9
Luxembourg	86.5	82.6	108.4
United Kingdom	20.9	21.8	29.1
Ireland	31.6	34.5	60.8
Denmark	32.2	27.1	36.7
Greece	9.1	11.8	21.2
Spain	10.2	14.6	23.4
Portugal	17.3	27.2	37.3
United States	5.2	5.8	7.1
Canada	17.2	22.0	28.4
Japan	10.7	10.6	14.6

Source: Organization for Economic Cooperation and Development, *OECD National Accounts*, vol. 1: *Main Aggregates, 1960–88* (Paris, 1990), tables 13, 17, pp. 126–29.

United States, Canada, and Japan. However, the ratio of exports to total economic product increased much more rapidly in the member states than in Japan and the United States, and thus made the Community highly dependent on trade.

As the member states became more dependent on trade in general in the decades before the development of the 1992 initiative, they also became more dependent on trade with other members of the Community. Table 2-2 presents a measure of the concentration of trade within the Community. The measure is simply the ratio of each nation's exports to other Community members relative to its total exports. These data demonstrate that the concentration of trade within the Community has increased markedly. Germany, France, and Italy, for example, sold less than 30 percent of their exports within the Community in 1960, but by 1985 that figure had risen to almost 50 percent. In contrast to trade dependence, however, the degree of trade concentration appears to have increased at different times in different countries. The largest increases occurred in the 1960s in the six original members of the Community, whereas in Denmark, Ireland, and Britain the largest increases occurred between 1972 and 1985—that is, in the period spanning their entry. (Note,

Table 2-2. *Exports of the Member States of the European Community to Other EC Members, 1960, 1972, 1985*
Percent of all exports

Country	1960[a]	1972[a]	1985[b]
West Germany	29.5	39.9	47.4
France	29.8	48.8	47.6
Italy	29.6	45.0	46.1
Netherlands	45.9	64.8	72.5
Belgium-Luxembourg	50.3	68.3	69.1
United Kingdom	15.2	22.5	46.1
Ireland	6.5	15.6	67.8
Denmark	27.5	22.1	43.4
Greece	32.9	48.7	53.1
Spain	38.5	35.4	49.9
Portugal	21.5	20.2	58.4

Sources: International Monetary Fund, *Direction of Trade Statistics: Yearbook, 1990* (Washington, 1990), and *Yearbook, 1979*; and International Monetary Fund, *Direction of Trade: Annual 1960–64* (Washington, 1965).

a. Trade with the Six: Belgium, Netherlands, Luxembourg, Germany, France, and Italy.

b. Trade with the Ten: Belgium, Netherlands, Luxembourg, Germany, France, Italy, Ireland, the United Kingdom, Denmark, and Greece.

too, the extent to which Spain and Portugal had already become integrated into the Community as trading partners by the time of their entry in 1986.)

Increasing dependence on trade in general, and increasing concentration of trade within the Community, has increased the dependence of the member states on intra-Community trade (see table 2-3). Over the past three decades exports from France, Italy, and Germany rose from 4 to 6 percent of GDP to between 10 and 15 percent; and exports from Belgium-Luxembourg and the Netherlands increased from about 20 percent of GDP to approximately 50 percent. Note that even for the largest, and least trade-dependent, member states, exports to other members are equivalent to 10 to 15 percent of GDP.

Although this growing economic dependence on intra-Community trade did not dictate the development of the 1992 initiative, it undoubtedly increased the awareness of national political and economic elites of the Community as an export market—and of the innumerable ways in which easy access and equality in competition were impaired for exporters within the Community.[25]

25. A small anecdote that illustrates the growing sensitivity to protectionism within the Community involves two businessmen, Basil de Ferranti of Britain and Karl von Wogau of Germany. They began swapping stories soon after their election to the European Parliament

Table 2-3. *Exports of the Member States of the European Community to Other EC Members, 1960, 1972, 1985*
Percent of GDP

Country	1960	1972	1985
West Germany	5.6	8.3	15.4
France	4.3	8.1	11.4
Italy	3.8	8.0	10.5
Netherlands	21.9	29.2	46.0
Belgium-Luxembourg	20.4	38.0	54.0
United Kingdom	3.2	4.9	13.4
Ireland	2.1	5.4	41.2
Denmark	8.9	6.0	15.9
Greece	3.0	5.7	11.3
Spain	3.9	5.2	11.7
Portugal	3.8	5.5	21.8

Sources: See tables 2-1 and 2-2.

INTERNATIONAL AND NATIONAL ECONOMIC CONDITIONS. In the early 1980s, for the second time in less than a decade, the member states of the European Community experienced the complex economic phenomenon popularly known as stagflation.[26] The rate of change in prices accelerated, imports rose, the balance of trade deteriorated, growth slowed, and unemployment increased.

As table 2-4 reveals, the Community as a whole and several of its larger members experienced a sharp decline in their current account balances in 1979 and 1980. The trade deficit continued into 1981 and 1982, undoubtedly as a result of the higher cost of energy imports in the wake of the Iranian Revolution and second OPEC price shock and the loss of export markets due to rising domestic prices and recessions in several trading partners (notably Britain and the United States).

Tables 2-5 and 2-6 demonstrate the domestic consequences of a deterioration in trade in economies that are highly dependent on trade. As already

---

in 1979 about the innumerable impediments to trade within the Community. Out of those conversations that occurred over dinners at the Kangaroo restaurant in Strasbourg, the Kangaroo Group emerged within the Parliament to press for the elimination of nontariff barriers to trade. See Colchester and Buchan, *Europower*, pp. 26–27.

26. Among the many studies of inflation and economic stagnation in the 1970s and early 1980s, see Michael Bruno and Jeffrey D. Sachs, *Economics of Worldwide Stagflation* (Harvard University Press, 1985); Peter Gourevitch, *Politics in Hard Times: Comparative Responses to International Economic Crises* (Cornell University Press, 1986), chap. 5; and Leon N. Lindberg and Charles S. Maier, eds., *The Politics of Inflation and Economic Stagnation: Theoretical Approaches and International Case Studies* (Brookings, 1985).

Table 2-4. *Exports Minus Imports of Goods, Services, and Transfers of the Member States of the European Community, 1973–86*
Percent of GDP

Country	1973	1974	1975	1976	1977	1978	1979	1980	1981	1982	1983	1984	1985	1986
West Germany	1.5	2.8	1.0	0.8	0.8	1.4	-0.7	-1.7	-0.5	0.8	0.8	1.6	2.6	4.4
France	0.6	-1.4	0.8	-1.0	-0.1	1.4	0.9	-0.6	-0.8	-2.2	-0.9	-0.2	-0.1	0.3
Italy	-1.5	-4.3	-0.3	-1.3	1.0	2.1	1.6	-2.2	-2.2	-1.5	0.4	-0.6	-0.9	0.4
Britain	-1.3	-3.8	-1.4	-0.8	-0.1	0.6	-0.3	1.4	2.7	1.7	1.3	0.6	0.9	0.0
Belgium-Luxembourg	2.9	1.4	0.3	0.6	-0.7	-0.9	-2.7	-4.1	-4.3	-2.8	-0.5	-0.1	0.8	2.7
Netherlands	3.8	3.1	2.4	2.8	0.6	-1.2	-1.4	-1.6	2.0	2.9	3.0	4.1	4.1	2.6
Denmark	-1.7	-3.0	-1.5	-4.8	-3.7	-2.5	-4.5	-3.7	-3.2	-4.0	-2.1	-3.0	-4.6	-5.5
Ireland	-3.5	-9.6	-1.5	-5.2	-5.4	-6.7	-13.5	-11.5	-14.7	-10.6	-6.8	-6.4	-4.1	-3.1
Greece	-7.3	-6.1	-4.5	-4.1	-4.1	-3.0	-4.9	-5.5	-6.5	-4.9	-5.4	-6.3	-9.8	-4.3
Portugal	3.0	-6.2	-5.2	-8.4	-5.8	-2.5	-0.2	-4.2	-10.4	-13.4	-4.0	-2.5	-1.9	3.8
Spain	0.8	-3.7	-3.3	-4.0	-1.6	1.1	0.6	-2.4	-2.6	-2.4	-1.6	1.3	1.7	1.7
Entire EC	0.4	-1.0	0.0	-0.6	0.0	0.9	-0.2	-1.3	-0.7	-0.6	0.2	0.5	0.7	1.4

Sources: Organization for Economic Cooperation and Development *OECD Economic Outlook* 46 (December 1989), table R20, p. 185; and *OECD Economic Outlook* 45 (June 1989), table R20.

Table 2-5. *Annual Rate of Economic Growth in the European Community, 1973–86*
Percent change in real GNP or GDP

Country	1973	1974	1975	1976	1977	1978	1979	1980	1981	1982	1983	1984	1985	1986
West Germany	4.7	0.2	-1.4	5.6	2.7	3.3	4.0	1.5	0.0	-1.0	1.9	3.3	1.9	2.3
France	5.4	3.1	-0.3	4.2	3.2	3.4	3.2	1.6	1.2	2.5	0.7	1.3	1.9	2.3
Italy	7.1	5.4	-2.7	6.6	3.4	3.7	6.0	4.2	1.0	0.3	1.1	3.0	2.6	2.5
Britain	7.3	-1.9	-0.9	2.8	2.3	3.7	2.8	-2.3	-1.2	1.7	3.6	2.2	3.7	3.4
Belgium	6.0	4.2	-1.4	5.7	0.6	2.9	2.2	4.1	-0.9	1.5	0.4	2.1	0.9	1.8
Luxembourg	8.6	4.2	-6.2	2.4	1.9	3.9	2.7	1.2	-0.2	1.5	2.9	6.2	3.7	4.7
Netherlands	5.0	7.6	-0.5	4.9	2.7	2.4	2.1	1.1	-0.7	-1.5	1.5	3.2	2.6	2.0
Denmark	3.6	-0.9	-0.7	6.5	1.6	1.5	3.5	-0.4	-0.9	3.0	2.5	4.4	4.3	3.1
Ireland	4.0	4.3	2.1	0.5	7.0	5.5	2.7	2.7	2.6	-0.7	-1.6	2.3	0.8	-1.1
Greece	7.3	-3.6	6.1	6.4	3.4	6.7	3.7	1.8	0.1	0.4	0.4	2.8	3.1	0.8
Portugal	11.2	1.1	-4.3	6.9	5.6	3.4	6.1	4.8	1.3	2.4	-0.3	-1.6	3.3	4.3
Spain	7.7	5.3	0.5	3.3	3.0	1.4	-0.1	1.2	-0.2	1.2	1.8	1.8	2.3	3.3
Entire EC	6.0	2.2	-1.1	4.9	2.8	3.3	3.6	1.4	0.1	0.8	1.7	2.5	2.4	2.6

Source: *OECD Economic Outlook* 46, table R1, p. 166.

Table 2-6. *Rate of Unemployment in the Member States of the European Community, 1973–86*[a]

Percent

Country	1973	1974	1975	1976	1977	1978	1979	1980	1981	1982	1983	1984	1985	1986
West Germany	1.0	2.1	4.0	4.0	3.9	3.7	3.3	3.3	4.6	6.7	8.2	8.2	8.3	7.9
France	2.7	2.9	4.2	4.5	5.0	5.3	6.0	6.3	7.5	8.2	8.4	9.8	10.2	10.4
Italy	6.4	5.4	5.9	6.7	7.2	7.3	7.8	7.7	8.5	9.2	10.0	10.1	10.2	11.2
Britain	2.1	2.2	3.6	4.8	5.2	4.9	4.5	6.1	9.1	10.4	11.2	11.4	11.6	11.8
Belgium	2.3	2.4	4.4	5.8	6.6	7.1	7.3	7.7	10.0	11.7	12.9	13.0	12.0	11.3
Luxembourg	0.0	0.1	0.2	0.3	0.5	0.8	0.7	0.7	1.0	1.3	1.6	1.7	1.6	1.4
Netherlands	3.1	3.7	5.3	5.6	5.5	5.5	5.6	6.3	9.2	12.4	15.0	15.4	14.2	13.2
Denmark	1.0	2.3	5.3	5.3	6.4	7.3	6.2	7.0	9.2	9.8	10.4	10.1	9.0	7.8
Ireland	5.7	5.3	7.3	9.0	8.8	8.2	7.1	7.3	9.9	11.4	14.0	15.5	17.4	17.4
Greece	2.0	2.1	2.3	1.9	1.7	1.8	1.9	2.8	4.0	5.8	7.8	8.1	7.8	7.4
Portugal	2.2	n.a.	3.5	5.8	7.1	7.9	8.2	8.0	7.7	7.5	7.9	8.6	8.7	8.6
Spain	1.9	2.7	4.3	4.8	5.2	7.0	8.6	11.5	14.3	16.4	18.2	20.1	21.5	21.0
Entire EC	2.7	2.9	4.3	5.0	5.3	5.5	5.7	6.4	8.2	9.5	10.6	11.2	11.3	11.4

Source: *OECD Economic Outlook* 46, table R18, p. 183.

n.a. Not available.

a. Definitions are those most commonly used in each nation. In most cases, the rates are close to those produced by a standardized measure; however, because they are not standardized across the nations, the measures are not exactly comparable. But they maximize cross-temporal comparability.

mentioned, the current account deteriorated in 1979 and 1980. Roughly a year later, the rate of economic growth deteriorated, and after another year or so, unemployment began to climb, rising from 6.4 percent in 1980 to 10.6 percent in 1983, and more than doubling in some nations (most notably, Germany and the Netherlands).

The Community and the national governments of the member states began searching for an economic antidote. According to conventional macroeconomic theory, they needed to expand fiscal and monetary policy to remedy the economic stagnation and rising unemployment. But an expansionary policy at a time when the rate of inflation was already unusually high and the governments were already incurring large budget deficits would only exacerbate the economic ills besetting Europe. And as the French experience of 1981–82 demonstrated only too well, reflation could not be counted on to improve the balance on current accounts. Such a policy would only add to the region's economic woes and have an adverse effect on growth and employment.[27] Instead, the situation called for a policy of noninflationary growth, one that would simultaneously improve the rate of economic growth (and thus the rate of employment) and the balance on current accounts.

A nation's current accounts can be improved through a variety of defensive and offensive measures. On the defensive side, domestic producers can be protected by limiting imports through the application of quotas, tariffs, voluntary export restraints, and other similar devices. The member states of the Community entered the 1980s with a considerable array of such defensive devices already in effect and were not averse to supplementing then with new ones to halt the deterioration in their external accounts. Thus a variety of barriers were erected against imports from Japan: France, Britain, Italy, and Spain applied import restrictions or export guidelines to automobiles and color televisions, France instituted its much-publicized customs inspection of video recorders, voluntary export restraints were negotiated for cathode ray tubes and recorders, and more than two hundred antidumping investigations were initiated by the

27. On the French experience, see, among many, Philippe Bauchard, *La Guerre des Deux Roses: Du Rêve à la Réalité, 1981–1985* (Paris: Grasset, 1986); Alain Fonteneau and Pierre-Alain Muet, *La Gauche Face à la Crise* (Paris: Fondation Nationale des Sciences Politiques, 1985); George Ross, Stanley Hoffmann, and Sylvia Malzacher, eds., *The Mitterrand Experiment* (Oxford University Press, 1987); and David R. Cameron, "The Colors of a Rose: On the Ambiguous Record of French Socialism," Harvard University, Center for European Studies Working Paper, 1988.

Commission in the half-dozen years after 1983.[28] Protectionism also gained appeal as a means of maintaining the export and domestic markets of producers located within the Community. Thus by 1982 the Commission was called on to investigate more than 750 instances of intra-EC protectionism.[29]

But such defensive measures carried a price. If pursued further, they would have undoubtedly incurred the wrath of Europe's trading partners, who might then be tempted to reciprocate against European exports. Given Europe's considerable reliance on exports, such action could adversely affect growth and employment. Most important, insofar as such protectionist measures would merely deny Europe's trading partners the rewards of their competitive advantage rather than lessen Europe's relative disadvantage, they would subsidize and perpetuate global inefficiency and impede long-term growth in Europe.

In view of the inherent long-term disadvantages of an exclusively defensive trade policy, it was perhaps inevitable that Europe would search for an alternative approach in the early 1980s, one that would rectify the trade deficit by expanding exports rather than by constricting imports. One possible offensive strategy for the Europeans was to undervalue exchange rates in relation to those of their external trading partners, either through unusually large unilateral devaluation or through systematic undervaluation over the long term.[30] However, undervaluation was not actually pursued because it might exacerbate inflation rates that were already high, because external trading partners might reciprocate with their own policy of undervaluation, and because certain member states (most notably, Germany, the Netherlands, and Britain) were committed at the time to a strong national currency.

To avoid the potential inflationary and provocative consequences of undervaluation, the Europeans instead sought a strategy that would lower the domestic costs of goods and services. One answer was to create the potential for economies of scale in the production of goods and services

28. See Kenneth Flamm, "Semiconductors," in Gary Clyde Hufbauer, ed., *Europe 1992: An American Perspective* (Brookings, 1990), pp. 277–78.

29. Colchester and Buchan, *Europower*, p. 26.

30. An example of the former occurred in Sweden in late 1982, when the newly elected Social Democratic government devalued the krona by 16 percent. The non-Socialist government had devalued the crown by 10 percent in the previous year. The double devaluation caused the predictable outcry among Sweden's trading partners. On the policy of aggressive devaluation, see, among others, Peter Swenson, *Fair Shares: Unions, Pay, and Politics in Sweden and West Germany* (Cornell University Press, 1989), chap. 5.

by expanding the size of the potential market available to producers while lowering or removing the political, economic, and legal barriers to trade. This, of course, was precisely the objective of the internal market initiative.

It is difficult, a decade after the fact, to ascertain the degree to which such factors motivated the political elites who advocated the internal market initiative within the EC Commission and the European Council in the early 1980s. But since the presumed benefits of economies of scale figure prominently in official Community assessments of the initiative, such motives may well have influenced its development.[31] Perhaps it was therefore no coincidence that the initiative began to take shape in a period in which the Community experienced, in the aggregate, a deficit in the balance on current accounts.

THE EUROPEAN MONETARY SYSTEM. One of the most consequential developments in the past three decades of the Community's existence was the creation of the European Monetary System (EMS).[32] When President Valéry Giscard d'Estaing of France and Chancellor Helmut Schmidt of

31. Cecchini and Emerson and others estimated that the gains from scale economies, restructuring, and increased competition in the single market would be equivalent to between 4.3 and 6.4 percent of aggregate GDP. See Paolo Cecchini, *The European Challenge, 1992: The Benefits of a Single Market* (Aldershot: Wildwood House, 1988); and Michael Emerson and others, *The Economics of 1992: The E.C.'s Commission's Assessment of the Economic Effects of Completing the Internal Market* (Oxford University Press, 1988). For a more modest estimate of the gains from these microeconomic effects, see Merton J. Peck, "Industrial Organization and the Gains from Europe 1992," in "Symposium on Europe 1992," *Brookings Papers on Economic Activity*, 2:1989, pp. 277–99.

32. The literature on the EMS is voluminous. See, among many, Marcello De Cecco, *International Economic Adjustment: Small Countries and the European Monetary System* (Oxford: Basil Blackwell, 1983); De Cecco and Alberto Giovannini, eds., *A European Central Bank? Perspectives on Monetary Unification after Ten Years of the EMS* (Cambridge University Press, 1989); Francesco Giavazzi, Stefano Micossi, and Marcus Miller, eds., *The European Monetary System* (Cambridge University Press, 1988); Giavazzi and Giovannini, *Limiting Exchange Rate Flexibility: The European Monetary System* (MIT Press, 1989); Giavazzi and Marco Pagano, "The Advantage of Tying One's Hand: EMS Discipline and Central Bank Credibility," *European Economic Review*, vol. 32 (June 1988), pp.1055–75; Paolo Guerrieri and Pier Carlo Padoan, eds., *The Political Economy of European Integration: States, Markets, and Institutions* (Harvester Wheatsheaf, 1989); Peter Ludlow, *The Making of the European Monetary System: A Case Study of the Politics of the European Community* (London: Butterworth Scientific, 1982); Frank McDonald and George Zis, "The European Monetary System: Towards 1992 and Beyond," *Journal of Common Market Studies*, vol. 27 (March 1989), pp. 183–202; Horst Ungerer, "The European Monetary System and the International Monetary System," *Journal of Common Market Studies*, vol. 27 (March 1989), pp. 231–48; and Jacques van Ypersele with Jean-Claude Koeune, *The European Monetary System: Origins, Operation, and Outlook* (Brussels: Commission of the European Communities, 1984). See also John Woolley's chapter in this volume.

Table 2-7. *Realignments of Currencies in the European Monetary System, 1979–90*

Date and currency	Percent change	Date and currency	Percent change
September 1979		*March 1983 (Cont.)*	
Deutsche mark (DM)	+2.0	F franc	$-2\frac{1}{2}$
Krone	-2.9	Lira	$-2\frac{1}{2}$
November 1979		Punt	$-3\frac{1}{2}$
Krone	-4.8	*July 1985*	
March 1981		All except lira	+2
Lira	-6	Lira	-6
October 1981		*April 1986*	
DM	$+5\frac{1}{2}$	DM	+3
Guilder	$+5\frac{1}{2}$	Guilder	+3
F franc	-3	Krone	+1
Lira	-3	B franc	+1
February 1982		F franc	-3
B franc	$-8\frac{1}{2}$	*August 1986*	
Krone	-3	Punt	-8
June 1982		*January 1987*	
DM	$+4\frac{1}{4}$	DM	+3
Guilder	$+4\frac{1}{4}$	Guilder	+3
Lira	$-2\frac{3}{4}$	B franc	+2
F franc	$-5\frac{3}{4}$	*June 1989*	
March 1983		Peseta entered (±6)	
DM	$+5\frac{1}{2}$	*January 1990*	
Guilder	$+3\frac{1}{2}$	Lira	-3.7[a]
Krone	$+2\frac{1}{2}$	*October 1990*	
B franc	$+1\frac{1}{2}$	Pound sterling entered (±6)	

Source: Horst Ungerer and others, "The European Monetary System: Developments and Perspectives," International Monetary Fund Occasional Paper 73 (Washington, November 1990), table 3, p. 95.
a. Range reduced to $\pm 2\frac{1}{4}$

Germany proposed the EMS in 1978, they did not anticipate that it would evolve into a system of relatively stable exchange rates resembling a fixed exchange rate regime. They simply sought a "zone of monetary stability." By the mid-1980s, however, the EMS had become a quasi-fixed exchange rate regime, thereby greatly facilitating trade and commerce among the member states.

Table 2-7 presents information on all the currency realignments in the EMS since its founding in March 1979. Note in particular the gradual reduction in the frequency of multicurrency realignments. Whereas seven realignments occurred in its first four years, of which five represented multicurrency realignments, in the past eight years there have been only five realignments, and only three of those involved more than one currency. This change suggests that exchange rate fluctuations have been stabilized over the past dozen years, with the result that the EMS has taken on some of the qualities of a fixed exchange rate regime. In the process, the dominant currency within the EMS, the deutsche mark, has come to resemble a reserve or anchor currency.

Although these realignments have been somewhat arbitrarily divided into two periods at March 1983, this date is nevertheless a meaningful point of demarcation. The 1983 realignment—precipitated by continued downward pressure on the French franc in response to continued trade deficits, budget deficits, and high inflation rates—demonstrated that countries could not reflate against the tide of German price stability. If they did, they would eventually find themselves in the position of the French Socialists in 1983. That is, they would have to either sacrifice demand stimulation for austerity and price stability or leave the EMS.[33]

One of the most important consequences of the creation of the EMS can be seen in consumer prices in the member states of the Community—both those that participated in the exchange rate mechanism of the EMS and those that did not (table 2-8). All the member states, but especially those in the EMS, experienced lower rates of inflation as the 1980s progressed. Furthermore, and again especially in the EMS, the differential between the rate of inflation in Germany and that in the other member states decreased over the period. In other words, the EMS may have promoted greater price stability throughout the Community by providing an institutional device through which Germany's long-standing aversion to inflation and preference for price stability could be generalized to the Community.

In instituting a monetary regime that stabilized exchange rates and prices, the Community created the monetary foundation for a single internal market. By stabilizing exchange rates and prices, in an era after the collapse of the Bretton Woods system of fixed exchange rates when currencies were fluctuating and floating, the EMS facilitated trade and commerce among the member states of the Community. In a sense, the creation of the EMS, or something like it, represented a necessary precondition for

33. For an elaboration of this argument, see Cameron, "Colors of a Rose"; and David R. Cameron, "French Socialism and the Creation of the European Monetary Regime," Yale University, 1991.

Table 2-8. *Inflation Rates in Consumer Prices in the European Community, 1980–88*
Percent change

Country	1980	1981	1982	1983	1984	1985	1986	1987	1988
Currency in the EMS									
West Germany	5.5	6.3	5.3	3.3	2.4	2.2	−0.2	0.2	1.2
France	13.6	13.4	11.8	9.6	7.4	5.8	2.7	3.1	2.7
Italy	21.2	17.8	16.6	14.6	10.8	9.2	5.9	4.7	5.0
Netherlands	6.5	6.7	5.9	2.8	3.3	2.2	0.1	−0.7	0.7
Belgium	6.6	7.6	8.2	7.7	6.3	4.9	1.3	1.6	1.2
Luxembourg	6.3	8.1	9.4	8.7	5.6	4.1	0.3	−0.1	1.4
Denmark	12.3	11.7	10.1	6.9	6.3	4.7	3.6	4.0	4.6
Ireland	18.2	20.4	17.1	10.5	8.6	5.4	3.8	3.2	2.1
Currency not in EMS									
Spain[a]	15.6	14.5	14.4	12.2	11.3	8.8	8.8	5.2	4.8
Britain[b]	18.0	11.9	8.6	4.6	5.0	6.1	3.4	4.2	4.9
Greece	24.9	24.5	21.0	20.2	18.4	19.3	23.0	16.4	13.5
Portugal	16.6	20.0	22.4	25.5	28.8	19.6	11.8	9.4	9.7

Source: *OECD Economic Outlook* 46 (December 1989), table R11, p. 176.
a. Joined in June 1989.
b. Joined in October 1990.

the free flow of goods, services, and capital within the Community.[34] Thus it is understandable that the European Council would not consider an internal market until the EMS had been formed but that, once formed, attention would immediately turn to creating an internal market.

THE INTERESTS OF EUROPEAN BUSINESS. There can be no doubt that one of the main beneficiaries of the internal market initiative will be European business. The initiative offers European producers of goods and services the prospect of competing in a market consisting of more than 300 million people. Moreover, they will have a privileged position in relation to non-European producers.[35] The reduction or elimination of national barriers to trade and commerce—whether in the form of frontier formalities,

34. That an internal market requires, at some point in its creation, the institution of a system of stable exchange rates among the member states that constitute the market is suggested by an earlier European experience. In 1818 Prussia established a uniform tariff. Over the next fifteen years most of the other independent German states either joined the Prussian Customs Union or formed other comparable unions. In 1834 most of the states joined in the Prussian-dominated German Customs Union (*Zollverein*). Four years later, the union fixed the ratios among the coinage systems of the states, thereby creating a partial fixed exchange rate regime. And in 1847 the union formulated a code governing bills of exchange, thereby extending the regime to all currency in circulation.

35. For a discussion of the Community's external trade policy after 1992, see Gary Clyde Hufbauer, "An Overview," in Hufbauer, ed., *Europe 1992*, pp. 1–64.

technical standards in public procurement, or company law—offers European firms an opportunity to reduce transaction costs, achieve economies of scale, and thereby improve profitability. The liberalizing and deregulatory thrust of the 1992 initiative encourages firms to obtain those scale economies rapidly, through cross-national alliances and joint ventures.[36]

In light of the obvious benefits that the internal market will bestow on some segments of European business, it is not surprising that some firms operating throughout the Community, or with the potential to do so, were strong advocates of the internal market initiative and played an important role in its development. Individually and collectively, businesses promoted the idea. The Confederation of European Industries of the European Community, the most important European business association, actively supported the single market initiative. And in 1983 the leaders of European multinational enterprises such as Philips Petroleum, Fiat, Volvo, and Siemens created the Roundtable of European Industrialists, which made the creation of a single market within the Community one of its most important objectives.

Nonetheless, the actual effect of that advocacy is uncertain, in part because most of those who supported the initiative did not become vocal until well after it had already been conceived. A significant number of other European business leaders were indifferent or opposed to it.[37] Moreover, of course, advocacy—to the extent it occurred—did not necessarily constitute influence and cannot be taken as evidence of influence.

Business leaders may have played a more influential role in the development of the initiative through their private consultations with national and Community leaders. Particularly important in this respect were the consultations that Etienne Davignon organized in the early 1980s among the leading telecommunications and electronic firms. Davignon, who had served as the commissioner in charge of the internal market in 1977–81, became vice president of the Commission with special responsibility for

36. For a discussion of European multinational business in the Community, see John H. Dunning and Peter Robson, eds., "Special Issue: Multinational Corporations and European Integration," *Journal of Common Market Studies*, vol. 26 (December 1987). For a discussion of the surge in cross-national alliances and joint ventures in the 1980s, see Douglas E. Rosenthal, "Competition Policy," in Hufbauer, ed., *Europe 1992*, pp. 293–343.

37. See Moravcsik, "Negotiating the Single European Act," pp. 45–46, who argues that transnationally organized business interest groups were *not* a critical moving force in the development of the 1992 initiative. Wayne Sandholtz and John Zysman take the opposite view in "1992: Recasting the European Bargain," *World Politics*, vol. 42 (October 1989), pp. 95–128.

industry, energy, and research in 1981, whereupon he created a commission to bring together the twelve major European firms involved in microelectronics and advanced information technologies to discuss technical standards and emerging technologies. That initial experience in cross-national collaboration led to the development of the billion-dollar Mega-project in 1983, a scheme to induce Siemens and Philips to collaborate in the design and production of memory chips.

These first efforts to encourage European firms to collaborate in the design and development of advanced technologies were followed in 1984 by the European Strategic Program for Information Technology (ESPRIT). Funded in part by the Community and launched under the supervision of Davignon, ESPRIT engaged firms and research institutes in some 450 cooperative projects whose purpose was to develop new microelectronic technologies. Of particular relevance to the single market initiative, ES-PRIT was designed to improve the integration of technological research in the Community by encouraging pan-European alliances among firms.[38]

The Davignon initiatives were not the only means by which European business leaders could communicate with Community policymakers and, if they were so inclined, influence the development of the internal market in the early 1980s. But they suggest the complex way in which that influence may have worked. By sponsoring a series of collaborative ventures among the most technologically advanced firms in Europe, the Community incorporated the views of the leaders of those firms into its deliberative process. As those leaders participated in Community ventures that were deliberately pan-European in scope, they may have come to support—if they did not already—the principle of a single European market and may have been impelled not only to advocate that principle in public, as some did, but, more important, to advocate it in private communications with members of their national government. At a more abstract level, those initiatives may have laid the groundwork for an internal market by encouraging European firms in one important sector of the economy to pool their research efforts and take advantage of economies of scale in research, development, and production.

Institutional Factors

The 1992 initiative—when it occurred, how it occurred, and the form it took when it did occur—was influenced not only by economic context but by institutional actors within the European Community. Among the

38. Flamm, "Semiconductors," p. 282.

most important were the Commission, the Court of Justice, and the European Parliament.

THE COMMISSION AS POLICY ENTREPRENEUR. Of all the actors that contributed to the development of the internal market, it is probably the Commission that is most frequently credited with bringing the idea to fruition, particularly under the guidance of Jacques Delors. But Delors and the Commission that took office in January 1985 came on the scene well after the initiative had already taken shape. By early 1985, when Delors was searching for a cause to champion and settled on the internal market, the European Council and the Commission had in fact been working on the creation of such a market for almost four years. Indeed, by then the Community was in the concluding stages of putting the initiative together.

It is nevertheless true that Delors and his Commission did play a major role in the successful completion of the initiative. By setting a specific date in the not-so-distant future (1992) for the creation of the internal market and by including in the Commission's 1985 White Paper some three hundred proposals concerning every conceivable aspect of market enlargement, Delors and Lord Cockfield scored a public relations coup. They gave to a complex, technical, and business-oriented process of market enlargement that was likely to drag on for years the image of a simple and finite adventure in "building Europe." Furthermore, in proposing to the European Council at its Milan meeting in June 1985 that an intergovernmental conference be convened to consider both the White Paper on the internal market and the Dooge Committee's report on institutional reform, Delors may have increased the initiative's chances of being adopted. By broadening the range of issues to be discussed at the conference, Delors created the possibility for bargains, trade-offs, and alliances to be struck *across* the issues of market reform and institutional reform. Moreover, in proposing an intergovernmental conference on the two subjects of reform, Delors and his Commission succeeded in giving the internal market initiative the aura of progressive, democratizing reform. The conflation of market enlargement and institutional reform may have further promoted the internal market initiative by attracting to it some segments of the political elite and the public who would otherwise have been opposed to it or, at best, indifferent.

The preceding Commission, headed by Gaston Thorn, played an especially decisive role in the development of the initiative. It was Thorn's report to the European Council in Copenhagen in 1982 that outlined the largest obstacles to the free movement of goods, services, and capital in the European market; elaborated, for the first time, the core of what would subsequently become the internal market initiative; and stressed the need to simplify frontier formalities, increase competition in public procurement, equalize the legal rights of firms throughout Europe, simplify tax codes for business, and increase European trade in financial services. Subsequent reports by the Commission to the Internal Market Council and the European Council in 1983 and 1984 provided a continuous stream of proposals for eliminating national barriers to trade and commerce within Europe. Indeed, it was during Thorn's tenure as president of the Commission (1981–85) that most of the proposals eventually included in the 1985 White Paper were discussed and drafted in DG III, the Directorate-General in charge of the internal market.

The Thorn Commission also encouraged businesses to pursue Europeanwide economies of scale. Especially through the initiatives of Davignon, it promoted cross-national alliances among firms specializing in telecommunications, electronics, and computers to pool and share their technological expertise, thereby creating in one sector of the economy a prototype of the industrial structure that might exist in a single market. In addition, it undoubtedly created—in the firms that participated in such initiatives as the Information Technologies Commission, Megaproject, and ESPRIT—strategically important proponents of the market-enlarging initiative.

THE COURT OF JUSTICE AND CASSIS DE DIJON. The Court of Justice played as important a role as the Commission in the development of the internal market initiative—primarily through a decision handed down in 1979. The court had earlier issued several important rulings—most notably, in *Van Gend en Loos (1963)*, when it held that EC law has a "direct effect" and is binding not only on member states and Community institutions but also on citizens and companies, and in *Costa* v. *ENEL (1964)*, when it held that, in conflicts between the two, EC law dominates national law.[39] But it was the Court's decision in 1979 in *Cassis de Dijon* that, in establishing a new legal standard for the resolution of trade disputes among the member states, made it plausible for Community elites to envision the creation of a single internal market. As Colchester and Buchan point out,

39. See Colchester and Buchan, *Europower*, p. 133–34.

Crème de Cassis, the blackcurrant elixir which transforms white wine into kir, also transformed the nature of Europe's common market. It is largely due to a famous European Court case involving this liqueur that the 1992 single-market initiative has been able to do so much to restore progress to the European Community.[40]

The *Cassis de Dijon* case was brought by a German importer, Rewe Zentral AG, which wished to import the French liqueur into the Federal Republic. Since under German laws the liqueur has too little alcohol to qualify as a liqueur and too much to qualify as a wine, Rewe was not allowed to import it. After the German courts upheld the ruling, Rewe took the case to the European Court of Justice in 1978. It ruled in favor of Rewe, arguing that if the cassis met French standards for a liqueur, then it could be sold as a liqueur in Germany. In so ruling, the Court established the principle of mutual recognition and thereby created a simple standard for resolving trade disputes that would have far-reaching consequences in the years ahead.

The new doctrine uttered in *Cassis de Dijon* greatly facilitated the resolution of trade disputes within the Community. Whereas before the laws of separate states had to be harmonized and made identical in their effects and consequences, the new ruling simply required each state to accept as legitimate the laws of other states as long as certain health and safety concerns were satisfied. As a result, Europe for the first time had available to it a means of bypassing what would otherwise have been a nearly impossible task in the creation of a single internal market—that of harmonizing the countless European national laws pertaining to goods, services, capital, and labor. Instead, via mutual recognition, Europe could simply move to the lowest common denominator among the national laws. In fact, the process of creating a single market was greatly accelerated once the Commission could simply codify the lowest common denominators in one domain after another.[41]

THE EUROPEAN PARLIAMENT AND THE IMPULSE FOR INSTITUTIONAL REFORM. One of the issues on the agenda of the European Community since at least

40. Colchester and Buchan, *Europower*, p. 79.
41. The doctrine of mutual recognition established in the *Cassis de Dijon* case had, it should be noted, other important and far-reaching implications—for example, for the role of national laws and national jurisprudence and for the Court itself. Not only did it create a

1974 has been institutional reform, particularly with regard to expanding the role of the European Parliament in Community decisionmaking and extending majority voting within the Council.[42] Through a series of coincidental developments in the early and mid-1980s, both became closely associated with the internal market initiative, which was taking shape at the time.

In mid-1980 Altiero Spinelli and a group of European parliamentarians launched an initiative to greatly expand the powers of the Parliament. And early in 1981 Hans-Dietrich Genscher, the foreign minister of West Germany, launched an initiative calling for the improved coordination of security policy and expansion of the role of the staff of the European Council. Genscher also called for a stronger role for the Parliament in Community policymaking and greater reliance on majority voting in the Council of Ministers, which meant reserving the national veto only for exceptional circumstances.

The Genscher initiative, modified slightly in the course of discussions in the German cabinet and with Italian Foreign Minister Emilio Colombo (whose name thus became frequently attached to the initiative), was presented to the European Council at its London meeting in November 1981. The European Council then asked the Council of Ministers to examine it. At about the same time, the proposal also received support from a number of members of the European Parliament—most significantly, perhaps, Leo Tindemans, who became the foreign minister of Belgium in December 1981 and the chair of the Council of Foreign Ministers in the first six months of 1982.

The foreign ministers reported their views on the Genscher-Colombo initiative to the European Council at its meeting in Stuttgart in June 1983. At Stuttgart, the heads of government issued a declaration on European union calling for greater cooperation in foreign and security policy and an increased role for the Parliament in Community decisionmaking. They also suggested that the Council of Ministers should facilitate decisionmaking by

means of bypassing the complex problem of the harmonization of distinctive national laws, but it also created the precedent that a supranational institution—the Court—would serve as the arbiter of disputes pertaining to mutual recognition. See chapter 4 in this volume.

42. At their Paris meeting in 1974, all of the leaders except those of Denmark and Britain agreed on the direct election of members of the European Parliament (subsequently implemented in all member states in 1979). And all nine agreed to renounce the practice of making decisions within the Council of Ministers conditional on the attainment of unanimous agreement. The latter agreement represented an effort to overcome the lingering effects of the Luxembourg Compromise.

encouraging the use of abstention instead of the veto—thereby endorsing greater use of majority voting.[43]

The Stuttgart declaration was followed by several proposals for reform. In February 1984 the Parliament approved Spinelli's proposal for a European Union by a vote of 237 to 31. The Spinelli plan recommended not only increasing the powers for the Commission and Parliament in Community policymaking but also abolishing the national veto. In May François Mitterrand, in an address to the Parliament, indicated that the European Council would study the Spinelli plan carefully and proposed that the national veto be restricted to "specific" (but undefined) cases rather than be abolished. And at its meeting in Fontainebleau in June, the European Council created the Ad Hoc Committee on Institutional Affairs to consider these proposals and the larger issue of institutional reform in the Community.

The ad hoc committee, chaired by Senator James Dooge of Ireland, issued a report in March 1985 calling (over the resistance of Denmark, Britain, and Greece) on the European Council to convene an intergovernmental conference to draft the amendments to the Treaty of Rome that were necessary to implement European union. In particular, it proposed a much wider use by the Council of Ministers of qualified majority voting and an enlarged role for the Parliament in debating and amending Commission proposals. In view of the disagreements within the committee (which, of course, reflected the disagreements among the member states), the council simply took note of the report at its March meeting in Brussels and carried it over to its next meeting, scheduled for Milan in June. Thus it was that the European Council had two proposals to consider at Milan— one pertaining to the completion of the internal market and the other pertaining to institutional reform.

At Milan, the council decided to convene an intergovernmental conference to consider the ad hoc committee's report as well as related proposals from the Italian council presidency. It was this conference that drafted the treaty amendments, through which the Community increased the role of the Parliament (via the cooperation procedure) and extended the range

43. The precedent for the use of abstention had been established the previous year. In May 1982 the Council of Agricultural Ministers had considered increasing some farm prices. Britain stated that it would oppose the increases until it had received satisfaction on its request for a budget rebate. Claiming the issue affected its national interests, Britain therefore invoked its right to veto the increases. The other members disputed the claim and insisted on a vote by qualified majority. The increases were approved, with Britain, Denmark, and Greece abstaining from the vote.

of issues that would be subject to a qualified majority vote in the Council of Ministers.

Of the European Council's decisions pertaining to insitutional reform, the extension of majority voting may be the most important. As Sbragia argues, the broader application of majority voting has changed the political calculus of Council of Minister members, who must now search for allies in majoritarian coalitions.[44] Moreover, in its broader application majority voting implies that national preferences are more likely to be overridden and, as a result, that national sovereignty might be eroded.

It should also be noted that the linkage of institutional reform with the internal market initiative had important consequences for the development of the initiative. Among other things, this linkage transformed what had begun as a commercial and legal program designed to benefit certain sectors of the business community into one that expanded the responsibilities and authority of the supranational institutions of the Community. And in so doing, the linkage with institutional reform may have brought to the rather mundane and commerce-oriented task of creating the internal market the support of those who favored the Genscher-Colombo initiative, the Stuttgart declaration, and the Spinelli proposal—that is, all those whose ambition was to relaunch the Community and move it toward the integrated and federal ideal envisioned by its founders.

Political Factors

The origins of the initiative can also be found in certain aspects of the politics within and among the member states, especially the ideological preferences of their national governments, the bargaining that occurred between the member states, and the role of the European Council as the political executive of the Community.

THE POLITICAL-IDEOLOGICAL PREFERENCES OF NATIONAL GOVERNMENTS. One of the most important political developments within the Community in the early 1980s was a series of changes in the partisan composition of the national governments. The magnitude of the changes varied. Some involved dramatic changes in the ideological center of gravity of government as one party replaced another in office. In other cases one party in a coalition government was replaced by another, and there was even

44. See Alberta M. Sbragia, "Asymmetrical Integration in the European Community: The Single European Act and Institutional Development," in Dale L. Smith and James Lee Ray, eds., *The 1992 Project and the Future of Integration in Europe* (Shape, forthcoming).

one important ideological and programmatic switch in a government that remained in office. The changes shared one feature in common: they all represented a shift toward a more conservative position.

The most marked change occurred in Britain, in 1979. With the election of a Conservative majority and Margaret Thatcher as prime minister, the British government embarked on a radical program of tax reduction, disinflation, privatization, and deregulation, which, in sanctifying the principle of the market, sought to reduce or eliminate various government-imposed barriers to commercial activity. Throughout the 1980s the Thatcher government was a strong proponent of pro-market positions within the Community, including the elimination of national barriers to trade and commerce.[45]

In 1981 and 1982 three of the member states experienced changes in the composition of their coalition governments. Although less dramatic than the change in Britain, all three resulted in a rightward ideological shift. The first of these occurred in Belgium after the parliamentary election of November 1981, when Wilfried Martens formed a center-right government composed of the two Christian Social parties—the CVP in the Dutch-speaking region and the PSC in the French-speaking region of the country—and the two Liberal parties—the PVV (Dutch) and the PRL (French). That government was renewed after the 1985 elections.

The Netherlands experienced a similar realignment of government in May 1982 when a center-left coalition of the Christian Democrats, the Labor party, and a smaller center-left party was succeeded by a center-right government, headed by Ruud Lubbers and formed by the Christian Democrats and the right-wing People's Party for Freedom and Democracy. Like the center-right government in Belgium, that government was renewed in office in the subsequent election in the mid-1980s.

When the Social Democratic minority government in Denmark resigned in 1982, it was succeeded by a four-party non-Socialist government, formed by the Conservative party, the Liberal party (as in the Low Countries, a conservative party despite its name), the Center Democrats, and the Christian People's party. Although a minority government, this coalition, headed by Poul Schlüter, remained in office throughout the 1980s.

45. For useful summaries of the early program of the Thatcher government, see Peter A. Hall, *Governing the Economy: The Politics of State Intervention in Britain and France* (Oxford University Press, 1986), chap. 5; Kenneth Hoover and Raymond Plant, *Conservative Capitalism in Britain and the United States: A Critical Appraisal* (London: Routledge, 1989), chaps. 7-9; Joel Krieger, *Reagan, Thatcher, and the Politics of Decline* (Oxford University Press, 1986), chaps. 3-4; and Ralph Miliband, Leo Panitch, and John Saville, eds., *The Socialist Register, 1987* (London: Merlin Press, 1987).

At about the same time, the coalition of Social Democrats (SPD) and Free Democrats (FDP), which had been in power in West Germany since 1969, began to break up. In part because of disagreements over economic strategy, public expenditure, and the size of the budget deficit, the FDP decided in June 1982 to ally itself with the opposition Christian Democrats (CDU) in the state of Hesse. In September the FDP ministers in the federal government, headed since 1974 by Helmut Schmidt, resigned and their party began negotiations with the CDU and its Bavarian sister party, the CSU, to form a new government. In October 1982, after a "constructive" vote of no confidence in the Schmidt government, a three-party coalition, formed by the CDU, the CSU, and the FDP and headed by Helmut Kohl, took office.[46]

In each of these five cases, a Labor, Socialist, or Social Democratic party was replaced with one or more non-Socialist parties. France, however, shifted toward the right not because one party replaced another in government but because the Socialist government elected in 1981 changed its program. The story of that shift, which occurred in 1982 and 1983, has been told in great detail elsewhere and need not be repeated here.[47] Suffice it to say that in the wake of three devaluations of the franc between October 1981 and March 1983 the Socialist-controlled government shifted from its initial policy of reflation to one of fiscal and monetary restraint. By 1983–84 restraint had evolved into full-fledged austerity in spending, consumption, and incomes, and active support for profit-making, investment, and corporate restructuring and reorganization.

As different as these six changes in government were, all represented, in varying degrees, a rightward shift in the ideological center of gravity. Taken together, they may have greatly facilitated the development of an

46. It should be noted that unlike the Belgian and Dutch liberal parties, the German FDP is a centrist party. And unlike the situation in the Low Countries, the Christian parties in Germany (and especially the CSU) are located in the conservative area of the ideological spectrum. For a comparative assessment of the ideological position of these and other European parties, see Francis G. Castles and Peter Mair, "Left-Right Political Scales: Some 'Expert' Judgments," *European Journal of Political Research*, vol. 12 (March 1984), pp. 73–88.

47. See, among many, Bauchard, *Guerre des Deux Roses*; Fonteneau and Muet, *Gauche Face à la Crise*; Ross and others, *Mitterand Experiment*, chaps. 2 and 3; Cameron, "Colors of a Rose"; Hall, *Governing the Economy*, chap. 8; and Organization for Economic Cooperation and Development, *Why Economic Policies Change Course: Eleven Case Studies* (Paris, 1988), chap. 5.

initiative that, above all, sought to create a market free of the intrusions and obstacles erected by interventionist governments.

BARGAINING AMONG THE MEMBER STATES. France and Germany, with the Benelux countries, constitute the core of the European Community, as they have since the formation of the European Coal and Steel Community in 1950–51. For that reason, the history of the Community consists, to a considerable extent, of the bargains and agreements negotiated among those member states. Especially after Charles de Gaulle and Konrad Adenauer signed the Treaty of Friendship in 1963 and French and German heads of state began to exchange visits on a regular basis, the privileged partnership became an important source of policy initiatives within the Community.[48]

Although the Franco-German relationship constitutes the pivotal bilateral relationship within the Community, its role in the development of the 1992 initiative was nevertheless muted. The French preoccupation, during the first years of the Mitterrand presidency, with domestic politics and economic policy, coupled with the fact that the policy challenged the orthodox views held by certain other members—most notably, the Germans—caused the Schmidt-Mitterrand relationship, and, after October 1982, the Kohl-Mitterrand relationship, to be more formal and distant than that between de Gaulle and Adenauer or Giscard and Schmidt.

The Franco-German relationship, however, reasserted itself in late 1983 and 1984, at a time when Mitterrand had called for a relaunching of Europe and for institutional reform in the Community. In a complex bargain struck at the European Council meeting at Fontainebleau in June 1984, which resolved the long-standing dispute between Britain and the Community over its net contribution and claim for a budget rebate, Germany concocted a compromise that essentially provided Britain the amounts Thatcher had demanded.[49] Besides obtaining some financial benefits in return, Germany, which had always supported the principle of

48. See Haig Simonian, *The Privileged Partnership: Franco-German Relations in the European Community, 1969–1984* (Oxford University Press, 1985).
49. The previous council meeting in Brussels had ended in a series of disagreements about the budget issue and agricultural prices and quotas. Britain had claimed it made a net contribution to the Community of almost 2 billion European currency units (ECU) a year. After Britain had subsequently accepted the criteria and methodology of calculating the net contribution used by the other member states, it was agreed that Britain had a net payment of ECU 1.6 billion in 1983, for which it had received, via earlier negotiations, a rebate of

Table 2-9. *Contributions to and Receipts from Budget of the European Community, Average of 1982, 1983, and 1984*
Millions of ECUs

Item	West Germany	France	Italy	Netherlands	Belgium-Luxembourg	Britain	Ireland	Denmark	Greece
Contributions									
Value added tax	−3,585	−2,934	−1,778	−652	−479	−2,656	−109	−253	−198
Customs duties	−1,957	−1,005	−643	−608	−408	−1,794	−97	−155	−98
Agricultural duties	−408	−356	−362	−206	−292	−435	−17	−39	−53
Total	−5,950	−4,295	−2,783	−1,466	−1,179	−4,885	−223	−447	−349
Percent of GDP	0.9	0.8	0.8	1.1	1.3	1.0	1.2	0.8	0.9
Receipts									
FEOGA[a]	2,602	3,133	2,869	1,581	574	1,573	616	655	821
Structural Funds	216	473	694	50	53	703	284	67	241
Specific measures	140	0	102	0	0	1,271	43	0	66
Costs of collection	243	139	102	83	71	229	12	20	16
Total	3,201	3,745	3,767	1,714	698	3,776	955	742	1,144
Net contribution (−) or receipt	−2,749	−550	984	248	−481	−1,109	732	295	795
Percent of GDP	0.4	0.1	0.3	0.2	0.5	0.2	3.8	0.5	2.1
Net incidence of budget[b]	−2,938	849	−964	1,276	−552	−2,631	1,456	1,176	392

Source: Brian Ardy, "The National Incidence of the European Community Budget," *Journal of Common Market Studies*, vol. 26 (June 1988), pp. 410, 413, 420.
a. European Agricultural Guidance and Guarantee Fund.
b. Includes estimated incidence of Common Agricultural Policy and customs duties.

institutional reform, was able, with the support of France, a recent convert to the principle, to persuade the other states to create the Ad Hoc Committee on Institutional Affairs.

The recent history of the Community consists not only of the bargains struck among its core members but also of the long series of disputes and negotiations between Britain and the Community—over membership in the 1960s, the terms of entry and their renegotiation in the 1970s, budget contributions and rebates in the 1980s, and entry into EMS and EMU in the 1990s.[50] It is therefore something of a paradox that the single most important initiative developed by the Community in recent years involves a program that is entirely consistent with the former British prime minister's ideological commitments and domestic programs. Is the apparent convergence between much of Thatcher's domestic program during her eleven years in office and the effort to strengthen the internal market, liberalize trade in financial and transport services, and eliminate legal and tax obstacles to firms operating in Europe coincidental? Or does it reflect, instead, Britain's ability to influence Community policy in spite of its isolation and its rather obdurate stance on many issues?

Several features of the relationship between Britain and the Community had an effect on the development of the internal market initiative. First, the period in which the initiative was developed—that is to say, the first half of the 1980s—was marked by severe conflict between Britain and the Community. Second, that conflict, which involved the size of Britain's net contribution to the budget of the Community, reflected a legitimate grievance by Britain about the terms of its membership.

An analysis of the contributions, receipts, and net incidence of the Community budget for 1982–84 indicates that during the early 1980s, and in spite of specific ameliorative measures adopted in 1980, Britain was a net contributor to the Community budget, rather than a net beneficiary (see table 2-9). Largely because of its small farming sector and the unusually small amount of agricultural payments it receives from the Community

---

ECU 750 million. Thatcher asked for a rebate of ECU 1 billion in 1984, 1.1 billion in 1985, 1.25 billion in 1986, and a settlement for future years based on the 1986 rebate. The nine refused to go beyond ECU 1 billion per year for five years, after which a permanent system would be instituted to deal with the issue. At Fontainebleau, the Community agreed to provide Britain ECU 1 billion in 1984 and, from 1985 onward, an annual correction of two-thirds of the gap between its payments and expenditures.

50. For discussions of Britain's relationship with Europe, see, among many, William Wallace, *Britain's Bilateral Links within Western Europe* (London: Routledge and Kegan Paul, 1984); and Wallace, ed., *Britain in Europe* (London: Heinemann Educational, 1980).

(FEOGA in the table), British contributions to the Community exceeded its receipts by more than 1 billion ECUs—an amount equivalent to roughly 0.2 percent of its GDP.[51]

Britain is not, of course, the only net contributor to the Community. Nor is it, for that matter, the net contributor that pays the largest share of its GDP (that honor is shared by Germany and Belgium-Luxembourg). Nevertheless, Britain does pay into the Community significantly more than it receives. After one also takes into account the likely nonbudgetary effects of the Community's customs duties and agricultural program, Britain appears to have lost more than any other member, with the possible exception of Germany. Thus, in terms of the net incidence of Community membership (which combines these probable nonbudgetary consequences with the net budget contribution), Britain lost between 2 and 3 billion ECUs (European currency units) to the other member states in the 1982–84 period (see table 2-9). When calculated as a share of GDP, that net incidence is larger for Britain (0.5 percent) than for the wealthier Federal Republic (0.4 percent) and is second only to that for Belgium-Luxembourg (0.5 percent).

A third conclusion derives from the other two. The existence of a serious conflict between Britain and the Community over the size of its budget contribution and the fact that Britain appeared to have a legitimate grievance in that regard may have had an effect on its bargaining power in the Community. Although the long-standing dispute might have been expected to isolate the country within the Community, possibly Britain's belligerence instead *enhanced* its bargaining position. By taking a somewhat intransigent stance on one issue, such as budget rebates, Britain may have been able to obtain a better agreement on another issue in exchange for some accommodation on the first.

The British rebate issue arose at roughly the same time the internal market initiative was being prepared. And, as noted earlier, the issue was settled by the European Council at Fontainebleau at precisely the moment

51. For recent discussions of the agricultural programs of the Community, which consume much of its budget, see Dimitrios G. Demekas and others, "The Effects of the Common Agricultural Policy of the European Community: A Survey of the Literature," *Journal of Common Market Studies*, vol. 27 (December 1988), pp. 113–45; and Alan Swinbank, "The Common Agricultural Policy and the Politics of European Decision Making," *Journal of Common Market Studies*, vol. 27 (June 1989), pp. 303–22.

it formally and publicly committed itself to the creation of a single market.[52] Moreover, immediately after the Fontainebleau meeting, in the negotiations among the national governments about the allocation of portfolios in the new Commission that would assume office the following January, one of Thatcher's trusted cabinet members received the portfolio for the internal market.

THE EUROPEAN COUNCIL AS POLITICAL EXECUTIVE. The European Council, the recurring summit meeting of the leaders of the member states of the Community, is not, strictly speaking, a Community institution, since it was not created by the treaties. Nor can it be regarded as a *supranational* institution like the Commission, the Court of Justice, and Parliament. Instead, it must be regarded as an extra-treaty manifestation of *institutionalized intergovernmentalism*. That does not, however, lessen the importance of the council in the development of an initiative that had obvious integrationist consequences. Virtually every decision that affected the development of the internal market since the early 1980s was taken by the heads of state or government in their periodic meetings as the European Council. Therefore, the history of the internal market initiative is to a significant degree the history of those meetings—Luxembourg and London in 1981, Copenhagen in 1982, Brussels and Stuttgart in 1983, Fontainebleau in 1984, Brussels and Milan in 1985.

This is not to say that the European Council acted alone. Obviously, many institutions and actors—the Commission, business executives and organizations, agencies within the national governments, and the like— influenced the decisions taken with regard to the single market. But the European Council—that is, the leaders of the national governments of the member states, acting collectively through the institution their predecessors had created in 1974—was the decisive actor, the final arbiter, in the development of the internal market.

The European Council did not simply ratify the choices already made by subordinates or by Community officials. More than any other actor or institution, the council consistently provided the policy leadership in the early 1980s necessary for the development of the internal market, by expressing its alarm over the present state of the market, by continually

52. For a useful discussion of the Fontainebleau meeting and Britain's bargaining power in relation to France and Germany, see Moravcsik, "Negotiating the Single European Act," pp. 37–38.

requesting reports from the Commission, and by occasionally prodding the Commission and the Council of Ministers to work more expeditiously in preparing proposals that would contribute to the creation of a single market. And at the end of the process, of course, it was the European Council that convened and presided over the intergovernmental conference that, in drafting and approving the Single European Act, gave the internal market initiative the imprimatur of the national governments and prepared it for ratification by the parliaments of the member states.

Discussion

What is the meaning and significance of the 1992 initiative? Does it represent, as many assume, a significant relaunching of Europe and a major step forward on the road to economic integration and political federation? My examination suggests that the initiative was the product of complex economic, institutional, and political forces. Several of those forces—most notably, those involving changes in the European and international economy and the role of the supranational institutions of the Community—were, indeed, fundamentally integrationist in their impact. Hence the growing dependence on intra-Community trade in the 1960s and 1970s, the deterioration in the world economy and the economies of the member states in the late 1970s and early 1980s, the development of the European monetary system as a quasi-fixed exchange rate regime, and the desire of European business leaders to develop advanced technologies and to lower costs through economies of scale—all of which promoted a more integrated European economy—gave a powerful impetus to the idea of a single internal market. In addition, the supranational institutions of the Community played a significant role in the development of 1992—the Commission through its agenda-setting and entrepreneurial activities, the Court of Justice through the transformative effects of its decision in the *Cassis de Dijon* case, and the European Parliament through its continued promotion of a larger role for itself and, more generally, institutional reform within the Community.

But these were not the only forces that worked in favor of 1992. Political forces were also influential—the shifts in the partisan and ideological centers of gravity of several governments of the member states, the bargaining between member states (for example, during Britain's pursuit of budget rebates), and the role of the European Council as the collective executive of the Community. These forces were not inherently integration-ist but reflected, instead, the continued presence, and indeed growing importance, of *national* and *intergovernmental* politics within the Commu-nity—that is, the conflicts, coalitions, alliances, and antagonisms within and between the member states.

In view of the role of both integrationist and intergovernmental forces in the development of the 1992 initiative, one must conclude that the initiative did not represent simply a process of supranational institution building and integration. It also reflected the national politics of the member states and the intergovernmental conflicts and bargaining among those states. For that reason, the initiative should not be considered merely an expansion of supranational authority that will erode the author-ity, power, and sovereignty of the member states.

As the neofunctionalist perspective described earlier would suggest, there were powerful integrationist pressures and impulses at work within the Community that generated the 1992 initiative and that were, in turn, stimulated by the initiative. But as the neorealist perspective might con-tend, those pressures and impulses were given voice and mediated through national politics and the institutionalization of intergovernmental-ism within the Community, and the member states were able to act collectively not only to accelerate but also to control economic integration and supranational institution building. In short, then, the 1992 initiative was the product of a complex interaction among several economic, institu-tional, and political factors, some of which were integrationist and others intergovernmental.

Implications for Policymaking in the Community

Recognizing that the internal market initiative was influenced by both intrinsically integrationist and intergovernmental forces is essential in order to understand Community politics in the 1990s, particularly with respect to the policymaking process. For example, by introducing the domestic politics of the member states into the policymaking of a suprana-tional organization such as the Community, institutionalized intergovern-mentalism erodes the conventional distinction between foreign policy and domestic policy.

Few scholars would defend a simplistic dichotomy of foreign and domes-tic policy, for it is by now a truism that policies developed in one domain have consequences in the other. Put in the context of the European Community, for example, policies developed in negotiations among heads of state—which by definition involve foreign policy—often are about, and have consequences for, domestic policy, just as policies enacted by the national governments of the member states influence negotiations and bargaining among those states.[53]

However, institutionalized intergovernmentalism in a supranational organization produces a more consequential effect than this simple spilling over from one domain to the other. Foreign and domestic policies become increasingly *intertwined* because national political leaders, in negotiating among themselves in the Community, are *simultaneously* making foreign policy and domestic policy. Thus, when they meet in the European Council to deliberate on a piece of legislation proposed by the Commission, they are obviously involved in international relations and in the making of foreign policy. But they are also involved, as they consider that legislation, in internal politics (both their own and those of their partners) and in domestic policymaking (not only in their own country but also within the other member states). In other words, to use Robert Putnam's metaphor, they are engaged in "two-level games," playing simultaneously at the "domestic" and the "international" table.[54]

One result of executive policymaking in an intergovernmental body of a supranational organization, then, is that the national political leaders find themselves acting both as representatives of their nations in negotiation

53. On this, see Peter Gourevitch, "The Second Image Reversed: The International Sources of Domestic Politics," *International Organization*, vol. 32 (Autumn 1978), pp. 881–912; David R. Cameron, "Distributional Coalitions and Other Sources of Economic Stagnation: On Olson's *Rise and Decline of Nations*," *International Organization*, vol. 42 (Autumn 1988), pp. 561–603; and Gabriel A. Almond, "Review Article: The International-National Connection," *British Journal of Political Science*, vol. 19 (April 1989), pp. 237–59.

54. See Robert D. Putnam, "Diplomacy and Domestic Politics: The Logic of Two-Level Games," *International Organization*, vol. 42 (Summer 1988), pp. 427–60. For applications to international summits, see Putnam and Nicholas Bayne, *Hanging Together: The Seven-Power Summits* (Harvard University Press, 1984); and Putnam and C. Randall Henning, "The Bonn Summit of 1978: A Case Study in Coordination," in Richard N. Cooper and others, eds., *Can Nations Agree? Issues in International Economic Cooperation* (Brookings, 1989). For similar analyses of "nested" or "overlapping" games—that is, games in which one actor is playing in multiple and distinctive arenas—see George Tsebelis, *Nested Games: Rational Choice in Comparative Politics* (Berkeley: University of California Press, 1990); and James E. Alt and Barry Eichengreen, "Parallel and Overlapping Games: Theory and an Application to the European Gas Trade," *Economics and Politics*, vol. 1 (July 1989), pp. 119–44. For an application to the negotiations among the heads of government in the European Council, see Simon Bulmer, "The European Council's First Decade: Between Interdependence and Domestic Politics," *Journal of Common Market Studies*, vol. 24 (December 1985), pp. 89–104.

with representatives of the other nations over matters of national interest and as national leaders with domestic interests, constituencies, and ambitions. And like policy, politics has two concerns: one involves internal issues within each state; the other involves international issues between the states. In conducting politics at one level in a Community marked by institutionalized intergovernmentalism, the heads of government are inevitably and simultaneously conducting politics at the other level. And thus, in the Community of the 1990s, the old and easy distinction between foreign and domestic policies and politics will become less significant as the two domains become increasingly entwined and entangled.

The New Germany in the Community of the 1990s

As foreign policy and domestic policy become conflated, Community policymaking in the 1990s is likely to reflect and respond to the domestic politics of the member states. And as that happens, policymaking and its outcomes in the Community in the 1990s are likely to reflect the interests, objectives, and internal conflicts of the most important member states. That being the case, it is likely that policymaking will be shaped, influenced, constrained, and occasionally determined, above all, by *German* perceptions of national interest.[55] The new, unified Germany is indisputably the most important economic actor in the Community. Indeed, it had become the most important actor long before the Berlin Wall came down and the Communist regime collapsed in 1989–90. Thus, as the exchange rate mechanism of the European Monetary System gradually evolved into a quasi-fixed regime, the deutsche mark assumed the role of anchor currency in the Community. As Nicholas Colchester and David Buchan point out, "The Bundesbank in Frankfurt has become Europe's de facto central bank. Other EMS participants have to ape a German monetary policy in which they have no formal say."[56]

55. On the role of Germany in the Community, see Simon Bulmer, *The Domestic Structure of European Community Policy-Making in West Germany* (Garland, 1986); Bulmer and William Paterson, *The Federal Republic of Germany and the European Community* (London: Allen and Unwin, 1987); and Bulmer and Paterson, "West Germany's Role in Europe: 'Man-Mountain' or 'Semi-Gulliver'?" *Journal of Common Market Studies*, vol. 28 (December 1989), pp. 95–117. For more general overviews, see Wolfram F. Hanrieder, *Germany, America, Europe: Forty Years of German Foreign Policy* (Yale University Press, 1989).

56. Colchester and Buchan, *Europower*, pp. 160–61. Or as Mitterrand bitterly put it after the third French devaluation in March 1983, "We are not masters of our own policy.

Table 2-10. *Exports of Member States of the European Community to Other Member States, 1980, 1989*
Percent of total intra-EC exports

Country	1980	1989	Percent change
West Germany	26.1	27.6	+1.5
France	15.9	15.5	−0.4
Italy	10.4	11.7	+1.3
Netherlands	14.9	11.9	−3.0
Belgium-Luxembourg	13.0	10.8	−2.2
United Kingdom	11.4	11.3	−0.1
Ireland	1.8	2.3	+0.5
Denmark	2.4	2.6	+0.2
Greece	0.7	0.7	0.0
Spain	2.9	4.4	+1.5
Portugal	0.7	1.3	+0.6
Total	100.0	100.0	...

Sources: IMF, *Direction of Trade Statistics: Yearbook, 1990,* and *Yearbook, 1987.*

Tables 2-10 and 2-11 present two measures of the relative position of Germany in the Community. Table 2-10 presents each country's exports to the other member states as a proportion of total exports within the Community. From this simple measure of national market shares, it is clear that Germany accounts for far more of the Community's exports than any other nation. By 1989, it was exporting more than twice as much as Britain and Italy, 10 percentage points more than France, and considerably more than the Benelux countries taken together. And over the course of the 1980s Germany, though already the largest exporter, experienced the largest increase in its share of exports.

Table 2-11 illustrates the extent to which, in the wake of the EMS-induced stabilization of exchange rates, Germany dominated and benefited from intra-Community trade. From the annual and cumulative balance of trade among Community members during 1980–89 in the table, one can see that Germany had a cumulative surplus of more than $200 billion over this period! The Netherlands (which deliberately tied its exchange rate and hence its monetary and fiscal policy to Germany's) was the only other

By remaining in this system [the EMS], we are in fact condemned to the policy of a dog that kills itself swimming against the current. Only for the profit of Germany." Quoted in Serge July, *Les Années Mitterrand: Histoire Baroque d'une Normalisation Inachevée* (Paris: Grasset, 1986), p. 96 (translated from the French).

Table 2-11. Balance of Trade (Exports minus Imports) of Member States of the European Community with Other Members of the EC, 1980–89

Billions of dollars

Country	1980	1981	1982	1983	1984	1985	1986	1987	1988	1989	Cumulative total 1980–89
West Germany	7.5	6.4	11.7	7.4	9.2	10.9	23.9	34.8	46.3	50.3	208.4
France	-5.0	-5.4	-10.1	-8.4	-7.0	-7.7	-7.8	-9.6	-7.1	-8.4	-76.5
Italy	-5.7	-4.1	-1.9	-0.4	-3.2	-4.8	-3.1	-5.5	-6.2	-7.3	42.2
Netherlands	10.8	13.5	13.0	13.1	13.8	12.6	12.0	10.9	13.2	15.1	128.0
Belgium–Luxembourg	1.2	0.9	0.5	-0.2	-1.4	-1.5	0.7	1.5	1.0	3.2	5.9
United Kingdom	0.8	-1.0	-3.7	-5.6	-5.9	-4.3	-14.0	-16.6	-26.6	-26.9	-103.8
Ireland	-1.6	-2.1	-1.1	-0.2	0.3	0.5	1.3	2.8	3.6	4.0	7.5
Denmark	-0.9	-0.8	-0.7	-0.2	-0.8	-1.4	-2.0	-0.9	0.1	0.9	-6.7
Greece	-1.8	-2.6	-2.7	-2.4	-2.0	-2.4	-3.0	-3.6	-4.2	-5.4	-30.1
Spain	0.2	-0.1	0.0	0.3	2.3	1.6	-1.2	-5.0	-7.9	-11.1	-20.9
Portugal	-1.5	-2.1	-1.9	-0.8	-0.2	0.1	-0.7	-2.6	-3.7	-3.7	-17.1

Source: See table 2-10.

country to accumulate a significant trade surplus from the Community over this period. Almost every other nation registered a sizable trade deficit. Intra-Community trade by Britain, for example, produced a cumulative deficit of more than $100 billion—vastly more than the sum of all the annual net budget contributions that became such a contentious issue for Thatcher in the mid-1980s. France suffered a cumulative deficit of more than $75 billion over the decade, which was hardly rectified by the government's austerity policy of 1982–83. Italy suffered a deficit in excess of $40 billion. And Spain appeared in the late 1980s to be on the road to equally large deficits.

These data do not prove that Germany has become, or is becoming, a "regional hegemon." But they do show that it is not only the dominant economy within the Community but also the main economic beneficiary of intra-Community trade.[57] Thus it is not surprising that Germany has consistently supported the creation of the single internal market and has often been willing to assume a disproportionate share of the costs of maintaining a well-functioning Community. And for the same reason, it should not be surprising if Germany remains deeply committed to the Community during the 1990s, despite the distractions created by unification, and actively supports and promotes the initiatives to create an economic, monetary, and political union.[58]

To assert that the Community of the 1990s will, more than ever, be influenced by German political and economic interests does not mean, of course, that those interests will always be articulated in a coherent and consistent manner. In fact, as the domestic debate over German economic and monetary union demonstrated in the first part of 1990, the presence in the government for the foreseeable future of three parties (the CDU, CSU, and FDP), the independence of the Bundesbank, and the existence of large and powerful state governments almost guarantee that the "national interest" will be defined differently by different German actors. But it does mean that German interests, however confusing and contradictory in their definition and articulation, will pervade the Community of the 1990s. Indeed, to the extent that foreign policy and domestic policy in the

57. For discussions of the concept of hegemony in the international economy, see, among many, Charles P. Kindleberger, *The World in Depression, 1929–1939* (Berkeley: University of California Press, 1973); and Robert O. Keohane, *After Hegemony: Cooperation and Discord in the World Political Economy* (Princeton University Press, 1984).

58. For a discussion of the possible impact of German unification on the Community, see Directorate-General for Research, European Parliament, *The Impact of German Unification on the European Community* (Luxembourg, 1990).

Community become increasingly entangled, German concerns will also intrude into the domestic politics of the other member states. This would have been the case even if the East German regime had not collapsed. But the fact that it did and that the new unified Germany now forms a single state of almost eighty million will only accentuate the tendency. This will be true whether unification proves to be a blessing, a curse, or a mixture of both for the German economy, the Bundesbank, the deutsche mark, and the political leaders of the new Germany.

Beyond 1992

The passage of the Single European Act appeared to put the European Community back on a welcome trajectory after two decades of bickering about Britain's role, contributions, and rebates, and other issues such as the common agricultural policy and enlargement—a trajectory that is likely to take the EC significantly closer to the economic integration and political federation envisioned by some of its founders and early adherents. Thus, at its Madrid meeting in June 1989, the European Council agreed that the Delors Committee's report defined a process that might lead to economic and monetary union and agreed to begin the first stage of the committee's three-stage process by July 1, 1990.[59] The council also agreed to convene an intergovernmental conference, once stage one had begun, to consider the amendments to the Treaty of Rome necessary for the implementation of the subsequent stages in the transition to this union.[60] It subsequently decided to begin the conference in December 1990, and, in fact, did so at the conclusion of its meeting in Rome that month.

As the Community moved toward economic and monetary union, the ambitions for union were extended to the political sphere as well. In April 1990 François Mitterrand and Helmut Kohl, meeting in a "friendship

59. The first stage of EMU, according to the committee, entailed completion of the removal of barriers to the internal market; reform of the structural funds for regional development and a doubling of their resources; strengthened coordination of economic and fiscal policy among the member states in the Council of Ministers; creation of a single financial area marked by the unimpeded flow of monetary and financial instruments and the uniform treatment of banking, securities, and insurance services; expansion of the research, consultative, and advisory activities of the Committee of Central Bank Governors; and inclusion of all currencies in the exchange rate mechanism of the European Monetary System. Delors Report, paragraphs 50–54 (see note 10).

60. In stage two of its proposed transition, the Delors Committee called for an increase in the powers of the Commission to establish and monitor the observance of nonbinding rules regarding national budget deficits and their financing. And it proposed the creation of a European system of central banks that would begin developing the capacity to formulate and

summit," called on the heads of government to commit themselves to political union. They proposed that the council invite the foreign ministers to prepare the ground for an intergovernmental conference on political union that would occur simultaneously with the conference on economic and monetary union. The purpose of this second conference, according to Kohl and Mitterrand, would be to accelerate the political construction of Europe and transform the relations among the members into a European union. The proposed conference was expected to amend the treaties in order to reinforce the democratic legitimacy of Europe; improve the operational efficiency and coherence of the institutions of the Community in economic, monetary, and political matters; and define and put into effect a common foreign and security policy.

At its Dublin meeting in April 1990, the European Council adopted a deadline of December 31, 1992 (the target date for the approval of all directives pertaining to the internal market), for the ratification and implementation of the treaty changes necessary for economic and monetary union. And it called on the foreign ministers to develop detailed proposals for the strengthening of Community institutions and instructed them to advise the council at its regular meeting in Dublin in late June regarding a parallel conference pertaining to political union. At its June meeting, the council decided to convene the second conference in Rome in mid-December 1990, the time and site of the conference on economic and monetary union, and the conference on political union held its first session at that time.[61] And at its historic meeting in Maastricht in December 1991, the council agreed to the treaty amendments drafted in the two conferences—amendments that would ensure the creation of a European central bank, a single currency, and a single Community-wide monetary policy and that would also extend the competence of Community institutions in foreign, security, and possibly defense policy.

In moving quickly from the internal market initiative to the larger issues of economic, monetary, and political union and in speaking explicitly, as the Delors Committee did, of a transfer of power from the national

---

implement a common monetary policy. Stage three would involve the establishment of binding rules and procedures for budgetary policy (for example, upper limits on budget deficits, restrictions of access to central bank credit, limits on borrowing in non-Community currencies) and the irrevocable locking of exchange rates, the pooling of official reserves, the transition to a single monetary policy, and the creation of a single currency. Delors Report, paragraphs 50–60.

61. As a further development on the integrationist trajectory, one should note the agreement between Germany, France, Belgium, Luxembourg, and the Netherlands signed

governments to the existing Community institutions and such new ones as an autonomous and federal European system of central banks, the Commission and the council appear to have reinforced and extended the integrationist impulse of the Single European Act. Taken together, the content and timing of the proposals for union convey an impression of the likely character of the European Community of the 1990s: a supranational entity endowed with new and strengthened institutions and powers, able to influence and constrain, if not determine, the domestic economic policies of its members; led by a highly visible, respected, and activist Commission president; poised to cross the threshold to full economic integration; and increasingly taking on some of the forms and functions of a political federation.

In this emerging image of the Community of the 1990s, the member states appear in a secondary role, to some extent the supporting actors in a drama of historic proportions about the inexorable economic and political integration of the European continent. Certainly, the states will retain control over the Community through the Council of Ministers. And their leaders may often rail against, and occasionally succeed in stalling, the movement toward an integrated Europe. But over the longer term, the institutions and powers of the Community will continue to expand into new spheres of action, and certain policymaking powers, heretofore vested in the member states, will be delegated or transferred to, or pooled and shared with, Community institutions. As a result, the sovereignty of the member states will increasingly and inevitably be eroded.[62]

To what extent does this impression capture the reality we are likely to witness in the 1990s? As the discussion of the sources of the internal market initiative has suggested, powerful economic and institutional forces have impelled the Community toward greater integration over the past decade. Indeed, the continuing movement toward economic and monetary union and further institutional reform symbolized by Maastricht suggests

---

in Schengen (a village in Luxembourg) on June, 19, 1990. The agreement created a free travel zone within which passports and border controls for travel among the five nations are to be eliminated.

62. The issue of sovereignty, of course, invokes the legal realm, the concepts and distinguishing traits of confederal and federal systems, the role of the European Court of Justice, and the Community case law that has accumulated since *Cassis de Dijon*. For useful discussions of some of these issues, see the contributions by Stanley Hoffmann, Joseph Weiler, and William Wallace in Loukas Tsoukalis, ed., "Special Issue: The European Community: Past, Present, and Future," *Journal of Common Market Studies*, vol. 21 (September–December 1982), as well as chapter 4 in this volume.

that the Community has already embarked on the next phase in supranational institution building—one that will ultimately bring it ever closer to its founders' ideal of an integrated and federal Europe.

At the same time, however, the impulses and pressures moving the Community toward supranational integration are mediated, to a large extent, through intergovernmental politics and institutional arrangements. As a result, politics in the Community—even when concerned with integration and supranational institution building—remains grounded in the politics within and among the member states. Thus, however inexorable the integrationist impulses in the Community, in the final analysis it will be the states, acting through the European Council, rather than the supranational organizations of the Community, that will by and large define, shape, and control policy, at least in the realm of economic, monetary, and political union. This is likely to be true notwithstanding the real supranational institution building that is occurring, the evident expansionism of an activist and well-led Commission, the apparent erosion of the sovereignty of the member states by decisions of the Court of Justice, and the creation in the late 1990s of a European central bank.

Community politics in the 1990s will inevitably involve a complex interaction of integrationist impulses, pressures, and institutional actors *and* national and intergovernmental politics—that is, political conflicts, coalitions, antagonisms, and alliances—among and within the member states. For however powerful the economic and institutional forces favoring integration may appear, and however consequential the spillover effects of the 1992 initiative, the Community has been, is now, and will remain a community of states.

Chapter 3

Bureaucratic Politics and the Institutions of the European Community

B. GUY PETERS

T HE MOVE toward a single internal market among the twelve countries of the European Community by 1992, as well as the goals agreed to at the Maastricht summit of December 1991, presents many interrelated challenges to individuals and organizations in Western Europe. Some are economic and managerial and have been forced upon firms that want to do business within the new market. Other challenges are to member governments, which will need to adjust their own policies and modes of governing to fit the reality of a stronger Community. The most difficult challenge, however, will probably confront the institutions of the EC: to become the governing bodies for an immense and complex economic unit composed of many political units with varying degrees of commitment to the new political center. These European institutions are to be both the governing bodies for an enhanced, if not exactly new, autonomous political entity and the locus of international diplomacy, negotiation, and even confrontation over the nature of that emerging entity. Because of the rapid changes in Western Europe in the late 1980s and early 1990s, the institutions of the European Community have sometimes seemed to be racing desperately to stay abreast of events and in coordination with one another. The institutions have different amounts of sail and anchor for

The author is grateful to Helen Wallace and Wolfgang Wessels for their helpful comments on an earlier version of the chapter. The author is also grateful to Anthony Zito for research assistance.

integration, so that coordination among them can be difficult. Yet they must find a way to supply that scarce commodity "governance" to the Community.

The purpose of this chapter is to introduce those unfamiliar with European politics or the Community to selected aspects of the Community's policymaking process. In other words, it tries to provide a way for those just becoming interested in the EC to understand how governance is supplied within the Community. I therefore at times simplify an extremely complex and unusual policymaking system in the interests of comprehensibility and general, rather than detailed, understanding. Although Americans often think of the Community as either a proto-parliamentary system or an international organization, neither conventional models of governing in an international organization nor those of governing in a European parliamentary democracy are adequate for understanding the institutions designed to govern the European Community. Instead, governing occurs on two levels. One is the level of very visible *haute politique*, in which the leaders of the member nations meet as the European Council to negotiate among themselves over the future shape of Europe. At these discussions the Community itself, usually represented by the president of the Commission of the European Communities, Jacques Delors, has played an increasingly important role. The momentous decisions bringing Europe from "Eurosclerosis" to "Europhoria" have been announced from these meetings, which take place at least semiannually. At times the European Council's decisions have seemed counter to the interests of the participants, since their own powers may be reduced, but the decisions have been made nonetheless.

The second level of policymaking is the bureaucracy functioning within the Commission. This activity is less visible to the average observer but has been important for moving forward enhanced policy integration within the Community. With that enhanced policy integration has come a greater need for political integration. This level of policymaking, and therefore of politics, is characterized by a gradual accretion of common policies and standards through the European bureaucracy (and its masters within the Commission) and through its contacts with national bureaucracies and with national and transnational interest groups.

Policymaking at the bureaucratic level seems fragmented into fairly narrow, specialized fields of competence. I argue here that the apparent fragmentation of policymaking within the Commission and the increased linkages of the components of the Commission to components of national bureaucracies is the crucial aspect of decisionmaking within the EC. Indeed, the main argument of this chapter is that the politics of the European Community is best understood as bureaucratic politics.[1] Further, the tendency of bureaucratic decisionmaking to occur within policy communities (especially those of a technical nature) has been able to depoliticize what could have been highly divisive issues, and thereby the less overt politics of the EC has been able to force, or perhaps cajole, integration along.

The chapter has three main divisions. The first part briefly describes the principal institutions (except for the European Court of Justice) of the European Community. The second part considers some of the fundamental political processes in which these institutions are involved, such as budgeting and rulemaking. Again, the discussion will concentrate on the role of the European bureaucracy within the system of policymaking and the complex linkages it has to national governments and to interest groups. Further, it will point to the importance of regulation and lawmaking, as opposed to large taxing and spending programs, in the progress of the Community. A regulative style of intervention can be less divisive than taxing and spending, and winners and losers in policy can be less clearly identified. The final section discusses in greater detail analytical models for understanding institutional decisionmaking within the Community that may be more appropriate than either the international organization or parliamentary government models. This section emphasizes the bureaucratic politics model and the importance of understanding policymaking fragmentation within the Community in order to understand policy outcomes.

The Institutions of European Government

The European Community is at once an international organization and the proto-government for some future political entity, the contours of which are not yet fully understood. As such, the institutions within the EC share some of the qualities of other international organizations, but have always had a greater governmental role than most. As the institutions

1. See Jerel A. Rosati, "Developing a Systematic Decision-Making Framework: Bureaucratic Politics in Perspective," *World Politics*, vol. 33 (January 1981), pp. 234–52.

have evolved, they have come to look more like those of a national government, even though the analogues with legislatures and executives are not exact. Understanding these European institutions, therefore, requires understanding that they perform several kinds of tasks and that both the legislative and executive functions are divided between two organizations. It also requires understanding the evolutionary path on which the institutions are embarked. Finally, it requires understanding the importance of the executive, and especially the fragmented nature of the executive, in segmenting conflict and allowing decisionmaking in what might otherwise be difficult political circumstances.

Council of Ministers

The Council of Ministers is the institution most similar to one that might be found in a conventional international organization.[2] It very clearly represents the nation-states that constitute the European Community, and its interactions depend to a great extent on diplomacy and bargaining among representatives of national interests rather than on the more collegial interactions that might be expected within an organization pushing toward full economic integration in a relatively short time. The Council often operates as the brake on movement toward a Single Europe. However, the movement toward fuller economic integration could not have occurred unless the Council had made the decision to move. It is at this level, and in the European Council, composed of the Heads of State (for France) and Government of the member states, that the most visible decisions about integration are processed. Further, there have been individual members of the Council of Ministers who have been instrumental in encouraging integration, so that individuals as well as institutions have mattered at this level.

As its name implies, the Council of Ministers is composed of ministers appointed (one each) by member governments. In addition, the Commission appoints one member to the Council to propose and defend policies and to represent the interests of the Community as a whole. Members of the Council of Ministers are elected from the member countries and rotate according to the issue being debated. If agriculture is on the agenda, ministers of agriculture will occupy the seat for each country. When particularly important matters are being debated, the foreign minister of

2. A. LeRoy Bennett, *International Organizations: Principles and Issues*, 3d ed. (Prentice-Hall, 1984); and Ernst B. Haas, *When Knowledge Is Power: Three Models of Change in International Organizations* (University of California Press, 1990).

each country attends council meetings. The presidency of the Council of Ministers rotates among the member countries every six months, and toward the end of each presidency of the Community there is a meeting of the European Council, comprising the prime ministers (the president in the case of France), the foreign ministers of each of the twelve member states, and the Commission president and one other commissioner.[3] These meetings have been a prime source of movement toward greater economic and, especially, political integration. For example, the Maastricht meeting in 1991 moved the Community somewhat closer to a federal solution for its political structure.

Because the ministers who sit in the Council of Ministers are leading political figures in their own countries, considerations of national politics motivate their behavior. They must be concerned about the impact of any decisions made in Brussels on the people back home and about the impact of those decisions on any upcoming elections (there is almost always an election of some sort looming somewhere in the twelve countries). As the populations of the member countries become increasingly aware of the importance of the EC for their economic and political futures, it has become more difficult for politicians to escape repercussions for decisions they may make within the European framework.[4] At this level at least, politics in the European Community resembles Putnam's idea of a two-level game, although for most policymaking within the Community that idea is much too simplistic.[5] Besides playing national and supranational games, actors (especially ministers of functional departments) are also involved in games over particular policy interests.

COMPONENT COUNCILS AND COREPER. The Council of Ministers functions through a number of component councils. In the early days of the Community there was so little business that the work of the councils could be processed by the general Council of Ministers, usually composed of foreign ministers of the member countries. As the work became more extensive

3. Colm O'Nuallain, with Jean-Marc Hoscheit, eds., *The Presidency of the European Council of Ministers: Impacts and Implications for National Governments* (London: Croom Helm, 1985).

4. For example, the poor showings of the Conservative party in Britain in both local elections and the European elections in 1989 were attributed at least in part to the anti-European attitudes of Margaret Thatcher and her willingness to broadcast those views in official venues.

5. Robert D. Putnam, "Diplomacy and Domestic Politics: The Logic of Two-Level Games," *International Organization*, vol. 42 (Summer 1988), pp. 427–60.

and had more policy concerns, more specialized councils became necessary. The most important is the General Affairs Council, comprising the foreign ministers or their deputies. Of several other long-standing and important councils, one of the most important is ECOFIN, the Council of Economics and Finance Ministers, which is responsible for coordinating and harmonizing monetary and fiscal policy among the member countries. It also monitors the European Monetary System and the place of the European currency unit (ECU) in international financial markets.[6] The Agriculture Council, also long-standing, is composed of the agricultural ministers of the members. The very large proportion of the EC budget going to agricultural programs, the importance of agricultural constituencies, and the central place of the agricultural program in EC politics has made this an extremely important locus of policymaking.[7]

The councils functioning under the umbrella of the Council of Ministers include councils dealing with fisheries, budgets, the nonfinancial aspects of the internal market, foreign aid, social affairs, environment, science and technology, and transportation, among others. Each involves the relevant ministers from the member countries and establishes, if nothing else, a basis for ongoing personal cooperation and negotiation among executives working in the policy area. Given that 1992 involves greater coordination of all these activities, the councils' work will inevitably increase. In addition to these councils there is the Committee of Permanent Representatives (COREPER) beneath the Council of Ministers, composed of senior civil servants from the member countries, to assist in preparing and managing the work of the Council.

The functional differentiation of the councils is an important element of EC governance. Differentiation at once contributes to the complexity of governance and tends to mask potentially divisive issues beneath a proliferation of professional and expert language. Further, the councils are linked directly to experts at the national level, and both national and European levels are lobbied by interest groups. The specialization and differentiation make EC policymaking look somewhat more like policymaking in the U.S. federal government than that in most parliamentary governments. The many policy communities or networks appear to exert

6. Jacques van Ypersele, with Jean-Claude Koeune, *The European Monetary System: Origins, Operation and Outlook* (Cambridge: Woodhead-Faulkner, 1985).

7. See Joan Pearce, "The Common Agricultural Policy: The Accumulation of Special Interests," in Helen Wallace, William Wallace, and Carole Webb, eds., *Policy-Making in the European Community*, 2d ed. (Chichester: Wiley, 1983), pp. 143–75.

great influence, if not control, over public policy, more than in most national governments in Europe.[8] Just as differentiation minimizes conflict within the United States, in the EC it reduces redistributive conflicts between different interests and therefore between member countries. The councils are also linked to the "comitology" of the Community, the numerous committees linking the Council of Ministers and the Commission, with further links to national bureaucracies. These committees defuse institutional and national tensions and are places to work out the details of policy in a more private setting.

COREPER analyzes draft legislation coming to the Council from the Commission and to some degree monitors the decisions taken in the Commission in the name of the EC. The Commission is the principal source of the large volume of rules and regulations required to implement the Treaty of Rome and the other agreements having the force of law for the EC. COREPER also assists the Council in overseeing the actions of the Commission. It is, in essence, an institution of executive officials exercising oversight over an executive body, although the Council is really more like a legislative body. The Council is organized for the analysis of draft decisions and oversight through a large number of working groups. These groups comprise members of the permanent missions of the member states as well as national civil servants who fly back and forth to Brussels. As with the full Council of Ministers, its component councils, and COREPER, the Commission has a representative on each working group to defend its position, to present draft texts, and perhaps thereby to advance the cause of increased integration. Although national positions are voiced in opposition to specific Commission proposals, Commission representatives do have an opportunity to defend the proposal. The links between the two institutions mean they can minimize conflict over policy, resolve most potential conflicts in committee, and act more as a unified set of policymakers.

The Council of Ministers remains the locus of what to Americans seems parochialism in the European Community, and indeed was conceived as an institution that would permit member nations to express national views about policy. There are, however, supranational checks on that nationalism. First, at every level of the Council's operations a member of the Commission represents the "European" perspective and prevents any

8. Hugh Heclo, "Issue Networks and the Executive Establishment," in Anthony King, ed., *The New American Political System* (Washington: American Enterprise Institute for Public Policy Research, 1978), pp. 87–124.

nationalism from going unanswered in debates. Here the style may be more that of discussion within a partnership than of one between adversaries, but there will be debate. Second, with at least two levels of officials functioning beneath the more manifestly political level of activity, much of the work of the Council can be performed with less regard to domestic political considerations. At least national considerations may be slightly blurred. Likewise, involving professional civil servants from the member nations may mean that decisions at the official level are made in conformity with the technical standards prevailing in the policy area rather than along national lines. Again, a bureaucratic or "policy community" perspective can be more appropriate for understanding policy in the EC than more political or nationalist perspectives.

It is especially important that the agenda and draft decisions are prepared for the Council of Ministers by COREPER and by the Secretariat of the Council and other permanent officials. If some issues can be kept off the agenda and others defused by the time they reach the agenda, parochial conflict can be minimized. This is one indication of the importance of bureaucratic processes for understanding politics in the European Community, an importance that will be even more evident when I look at the role of the Commission in fostering integration and at the role of national bureaucracies in implementing European policy. The cause of movement toward a single market and toward greater political unification is perhaps better served by nonpolitical processes (political here meaning partisan and national). Progress toward supranationalism seems possible when manifestly political institutions are confined to the mere enregisterment of decisions made elsewhere,[9] a point raised earlier in much of the functionalist and neofunctionalist literature on integration.[10] The institutions of the European Community have not achieved that bureaucratized state perfectly, but they do permit substantial policymaking activity by bureaucracies before political officials ever see the prospective decisions.

QUALIFIED MAJORITY VOTING. Changes in the decisionmaking rules in the Council have begun to alter its role and to some extent to change the

9. Alfred Grosser, "The Evolution of European Parliaments," cited in Mattei Dogan, "The Political Power of the Western Mandarins: Introduction," in Dogan, ed., *The Mandarins of Western Europe: The Political Roles of Top Civil Servants* (Beverly Hills: Sage Publications, 1975), p. 7.

10. Ernst B. Haas, *Beyond the Nation State: Functionalism and International Organization* (Stanford University Press, 1964).

entire Community. Since the Council was designed as a venue where national representatives could defend their national interests, the voting rules before acceptance of the Single European Act required unanimity on most issues. The rules have now been changed, so that for a larger number of matters qualified majority voting is sufficient to enact policies. The basic rules governing the use of qualified majority voting extend it to issues linked to the completion of the single market. Of the eighty-five issues under active consideration by the Council in October 1989, only eleven (for example, tax harmonization) were deemed to require unanimity, although the issues requiring unanimity are often the most fundamental for the Community and its members.[11] The voting rules for qualified majorities are designed so that the four largest nations (France, Germany, Italy, and the United Kingdom) cannot make decisions on their own, but they can make decisions with the addition of at a minimum three smaller countries to a coalition.[12] Likewise, the smaller countries cannot together force a decision on the larger countries, but with the addition of two larger countries they can produce Community action. Size, of course, is not the only basis of coalition, and several of the larger countries (the United Kingdom and, earlier, France) have been at odds more often with the other larger countries than have the Netherlands and other smaller countries.

Qualified majority voting has moved policymaking in the Community away from what might be expected in an international organization and toward what might be expected in policymaking and coalition formation in a parliamentary democracy. Although certainly more powerful, the large countries cannot dictate policy to the smaller members. The large countries are also protected against having the smaller countries impose policies they might not favor or that may require more from their larger economic contributions to the Community budget. Decisionmaking within the Community therefore relies more on coalition building than on national vetoes for protection. Countries need not be the only players in the coalition game, so that the Directorates-General within the Community bureaucracy (see below) can attempt to form their own policy coalitions.[13]

11. "State of Play," *Advance 1992*, newletter, June 1989, pp. 2–15.

12. France, Italy, the United Kingdom, and Germany have ten votes each; Spain has eight; Belgium, Greece, the Netherlands, and Portugal have five; Denmark and Ireland have three; and Luxembourg has two. Fifty-four votes constitute a qualified majority, and twenty-three a blocking coalition.

13. See Neill Nugent, *The Government and Politics of the European Community* (Duke University Press, 1989), pp. 249–51.

More subtle procedural changes have also influenced the way in which the Council of Ministers functions. After the "Luxembourg Compromise" in 1966, although the Treaty of Rome called for moving toward qualified majority voting at that earlier date, the tendency had been to negotiate until a clear consensus could be reached without a vote; this pattern accommodated among others the French and their (then) skepticism about the EC.[14] Package deals (analogous to logrolling in American legislatures) that gave all parties some benefits were a usual means to generate consensus, although sometimes an expensive one. In 1985 in the Milan summit meeting of the European Council, Prime Minister Bettino Craxi (then holding the presidency of the council) began to call for votes, and from these votes it became clear that the then chief skeptical voices (Margaret Thatcher and Britain, along with Greece and Denmark) were clearly in the minority and could be outvoted under the rules of the treaty.[15] Although the change in procedures under the Single European Act has been far from successful in silencing British opposition (or that from others such as Greece), the pattern of decisionmaking within the European Council has been changed to permit decisions to be made, and there is a sense that isolation is perceived as a real danger.[16] For example, British opposition to movement toward monetary union in the EC in the autumn of 1990 was perceived as a serious threat to Britain's role in the EC and was a precursor to Thatcher's leaving office.[17]

Greater use of qualified majority voting in the Council of Ministers also may alter the dynamics of policymaking. If countries risk becoming isolated by bargaining too hard on an issue, they may be more compromising and become more willing to accept some short-term losses to perceived national interests so as to avoid losing a vote publicly. Further, if one country was to lose frequently, it would risk becoming a pariah within the Community and losing even more power and influence with

14. That position has changed significantly, so that France is now one of the chief proponents of increased European activity. See, for example, Roger Morgan and Caroline Bray, eds., *Partners and Rivals: Britain, France, and Germany* (Aldershot: Gower, 1986).

15. Emile Noël, "Reflections on the Community in the Aftermath of the Meeting of the European Council in Milan," *Government and Opposition*, vol. 20 (Autumn 1985), pp. 444–52.

16. Wayne Sandholtz and John Zysman, "1992: Recasting the European Bargain," *World Politics*, vol. 42 (October 1989), pp. 95–128; and Andrew Moravcsik, "Negotiating the Single European Act: National Interests and Conventional Statecraft in the European Community," *International Organization*, vol. 45 (Winter 1991), pp. 19–56.

17. David Buchan and John Wyles, "Thatcher Left Trailing as Summit Fixes Emu Date," *Financial Times*, October 29, 1990, p. 1.

other countries; it might simply not be trusted as a reliable coalition partner.[18] Isolation would be a much greater danger for smaller countries, but the pattern of politics in which playing the game is as important as winning all the time is more familiar in those countries.[19] The Low Countries in particular have managed a pattern of inclusion and accommodation that has helped preserve the democratic stability and effective decisionmaking crucial for the success of the EC once the euphoria over 1992 wanes.

Commission of the European Communities

The Commission is the executive of the European Community and has been the source of much of the movement toward greater unification. Although the Commission originates almost all policy proposals, it is dependent on the member states' bureaucracies for executing the decisions made by the Council of Ministers. The Commission per se comprises seventeen members, appointed to four-year terms by member governments. (France, Italy, Spain, the United Kingdom, and Germany have two commissioners each; the other countries have one each. But the Maastricht treaty calls for the Commission's membership to be reviewed.) Once appointed, commissioners take an oath of loyalty to the European Community and pledge to accept no national instructions on policy. Although they are somewhat difficult to characterize, they are often people who have been politically active but who have decided, for personal or ideological reasons, to leave the fray of national politics and work on the European stage. Perhaps less generously, the Commission has become a place where national governments can "exile" politicians too difficult to have at home or who need to be retired with an honorable (and remunerative) position. The impolitic Nicholas Ridley once referred to the Commission as "failed politicians." This pattern is changing somewhat, with younger and more technocratic commissioners being appointed.[20] What

18. Linda Cornett and James Caporaso, "And Still It Moves!: State Interests and Social Forces in the European Community," paper presented at the 1990 meeting of the American Political Science Association.

19. Martin O. Heisler, with Robert B. Kvavik, "Patterns of European Politics: The 'European Polity' Model," in Heisler, ed., *Politics in Europe: Structures and Processes in Some Postindustrial Democracies* (David McKay, 1973), pp. 27–89.

20. Richard O'Toole, "The Decision-making Process within the Commission of the European Communities in Light of the Single European Act," *Irish Studies in International Affairs*, vol. 2 (1986), pp. 65–76.

is most interesting is that politicians who have been deeply involved in national affairs (Roy Jenkins and Jacques Delors among others) honor their oaths of office and become rather quickly active in and committed to broader European issues. Some commissioners have, on the other hand, been criticized for being extremely anxious to receive portfolios from which they could benefit their home countries and for remaining too much national representatives.

The European Council chooses the president of the Commission for a two-year, renewable term. The Maastricht treaty calls for the appointment of the president to be made "after consulting the European Parliament." (Furthermore, once the entire Commission has been selected, it will be subject to a vote of confidence from the Parliament.) The understanding has been that the presidency will alternate between larger and smaller member countries. To date, there have been two presidents from France, one each from the other founding nations, and one from the United Kingdom. The member countries tend to nominate their commissioners to reflect in large part national political pressures and issues.[21] The United Kingdom, for example, in the past decade has had one commissioner from the government party and a second from the opposition Labour party. Clearly then, although the Commission is a European and supranational institution, it also has direct and important links to national politics and interests.

Besides applying to the college of politically appointed commissioners, the term "commission" is also applied to all the permanent staff of the Community—the "Eurocrats."[22] At present the Commission employs approximately 2,500 senior civil servants and more than 10,000 additional staff. Some are on secondment from their national governments, but the large majority are direct employees of the European Community. Though certainly smaller than the bureaucracies of any of the member nations, this is still a sizable staff with impressive (if unevenly distributed) professional capabilities for rulemaking and enforcement.

As noted earlier, the Commission has been the locus of much of the movement toward greater economic and political integration. A great deal

21. Klaus van Miert, "The Appointment of the President and the Members of the European Commission," *Common Market Law Review*, vol. 10 (1973), pp. 257–73.
22. The term comes from Altiero Spinelli, a principal advocate of European federalism; see also Joseph Jamar and Wolfgang Wessels, eds., *The Community Bureaucracy at the Crossroads* (Bruges: Collège d'Europe, 1985).

of this movement has resulted from gradual bureaucratic pressure rather than from more dramatic political decisions. The political decisions of the European Council may receive greater media attention, as the passage of the Single European Act and the Maastricht accords certainly did, but day by day, drafting regulation after regulation, the Commission and its Eurocrats have been constructing a public policy foundation for the integration envisaged by those political acts. Likewise, their seemingly incremental and bureaucratic activities interpret and ramify the meanings of political actions and may at times push integration even further than intended (or would be possible) by the more politicized council. For example, the Treaty of Rome provides the Community with no competence in public health policy, but it has acquired one through creative bureaucratic use of other powers.[23]

The EC bureaucracy is divided into twenty-three Directorates-General, usually referred to by number (table 3-1). These have been assigned specific functional tasks, but the evolving character of their work has meant that it is easier to use simple numerical designations. New tasks can be added to one or another Directorate, although not without debate, and the work of the Commission can continue. The organizational location of important new functions may be the subject of intense bureaucratic infighting among the Directorates, but that can be managed without having to alter titles and the organization chart.[24] The internal structure of the Directorates varies; the general model is to have a member of the Commission (the analogue of a minister in a parliamentary system) shadowed by a European civil servant (the director general) at the top and served by a small cabinet, and then a typical hierarchical proliferation of Directorates and sections underneath the top leadership structure. Some Directorates have more than one commissioner responsible for part of their work—DG XV (Financial Institutions and Company Law) at present has three. Given the sensitivity of the Commission's work and the possibility of trampling on national sensibilities, component sections of the Directorates tend to work on a somewhat shorter leash from their political leaders than might be true in many national bureaucracies.

23. Michel Ronnier, "How the European Community Went into Public Health," Center for International Affairs, Harvard University, n.d..

24. Helen Wallace, "Negotiation, Conflict and Compromise: The Elusive Pursuit of Common Policies," in Wallace, Wallace, and Webb, eds., *Policy-Making in the European Community*, pp. 43–80.

Figure 3-1. *Directorates-General of the European Commission*

DG I	External Relations
DG II	Economic and Financial Affairs
DG III	Internal Market and Industrial Affairs
DG IV	Competition
DG V	Employment, Social Affairs and Education
DG VI	Agriculture
DG VII	Transport
DG VIII	Development
DG IX	Personnel and Administration
DG X	Information, Communication and Culture
DG XI	Environment, Consumer Protection and Nuclear Safety
DG XII	Science, Research and Development
DG XIII	Telecommunications, Information Industry and Innovation
DG XIV	Fisheries
DG XV	Financial Institutions and Company Law
DG XVI	Regional Policy
DG XVII	Energy
DG XVIII	Credit and Investments
DG XIX	Budgets
DG XX	Financial Control
DG XXI	Customs Union and Indirect Taxation
DG XXII	Coordination of Structural Instruments
DG XXIII	Enterprise

The work of the Commission is analogous to that of a public bureaucracy in a nation-state except for one important factor: the European bureaucracy is concerned less with direct implementation of laws. It must, in most instances, depend on national bureaucracies (including national police forces) to implement Community law.[25] The principal task of the Commission is thus to generate rules, in particular, most European rules. Much as a national bureaucracy would make secondary legislation—in American terms "regulations"—to codify primary legislation made by the

25. Heinrich Siedentopf and Jacques Ziller, *Making European Policies Work: The Implementation of Community Legislation in the Member States* (London: Sage Publications, 1988).

legislature, the Commission generates rules and regulations in pursuit of the Treaty of Rome, the Single European Act, and other primary agreements governing the Community. These rules are monitored by working groups within the Council of Ministers as well as by committees in national governments, and most must be approved by the Council of Ministers. The initiative, however, is in the hands of the Commission, which gives it tremendous influence over the final shape of policy within the Community.

The Commission also has the exclusive right to introduce legislation to the Council of Ministers. The Council may or may not accept a proposal, but it cannot act without initiation by the Commission. Few items ever come to the Council without previous widespread discussion in its working groups in COREPER and thus to some extent with national governments, but the Commission sets the agenda. This right gives it the ability to speed the pace of integration or at least to attempt to do so. At times it may be able to accelerate the pace simply by its volume of activity. With hundreds of employees and with highly specialized personnel in the Directorates, it can overwhelm the more political bodies of the Community by sheer volume and speed of action. Again, this may be analogous to the position that permanent bureaucracies have achieved in most national political systems. Further, the Commission has met with reactions analogous to those in national systems: the Secretariat serving the Council and the Permanent Representations of the members has been expanded to ensure that the more political arms of government can make their voices heard.

The position of the Commission is something of a dilemma for it and for its leadership. On the one hand, it is recognized as the conscience of the Community and as the greatest force for a more integrated Europe. On the other hand, it and its members have a large "democratic deficit": their appointive and bureaucratic nature makes them appear remote and intrusive to many national governments, if not to the average citizen in Europe. Thus the Commission must at once be active in advocating its own agenda and be cognizant of the needs of the individual member countries and their political leaders. This dual responsibility results in its using bureaucratic politics to preserve its position. That is, the Commission is conscious of the need to build coalitions with national politicians and bureaucrats whose interests may be affected by a proposal. This is not democracy in the usual sense but does constitute a means of responding to functional and national demands.

The European Parliament

The third main political institution of the European Community is the European Parliament. Examining the evolution of the Parliament tells a great deal about the development of the European Community.[26] The Parliament began as an institution in which national governments were in reality the dominant players; the members were appointed by their national parliaments and behaved somewhat like ambassadors from the national governments. But the Parliament has evolved to the point that it can compensate for some of the democratic deficit of the Community. Citizens now have a direct electoral relationship with their Euro MPs. The Parliament is also attempting to emulate the role of a legislature in a conventional parliamentary democracy. There is still a good bit to be done before that degree of power can be achieved, but progress has been steady and substantial and sustained by the expansion of power agreed to at Maastricht. And the need of the Community for greater legitimation, as it feels the strains that will inevitably accompany 1992, will enable the Parliament to further assert its powers. The EC Commission and the Council of Ministers may continue to have greater decisionmaking authority, but the Parliament will be needed to make their actions appear legitimate to populations accustomed to being governed through legislative bodies and cabinet governments.

Among the most important features of the European Parliament is that it now has a partisan rather than a national basis. Euro MPs belong to political parties organized on a Europewide basis or ones that at least campaign in several countries.[27] And Euro MPs sit in Strasbourg by party rather than by nation, with nine party groups now represented. There may be national caucuses of members from the same party, but the basic organization is partisan and supranational. This does not mean that the issues on which candidates are elected are necessarily pan-European; many campaigns are concerned with the relationship of the nation-state to Europe, as the electoral difficulties experienced by British Tories in

26. Michael Palmer, "The Development of the European Parliament's Institutional Role within the European Community, 1974–83," *Journal of European Integration*, vol. 2 (1983), pp. 183–202.

27. Geoffrey Pridham and Pippa Pridham, *Towards Transnational Parties in the European Community* (London: Policy Studies Institute, 1979); and R. Bourguignon-Wittke and others, "Five Years of the Directly Elected European Parliament: Performance and Prospects," *Journal of Common Market Studies*, vol. 24 (September 1985), pp. 39–59.

the summer of 1989 indicated. Still, there are Europewide issues (not the least of which is how the Community should evolve) that are also a component of electoral campaigns.

One feature enhancing the decisionmaking powers of the European Parliament is its well-articulated committee structure. Unlike many national parliaments, the Parliament has developed an elaborate structure of eighteen permanent committees specialized by policy area. Members are assigned to a committee at the beginning of a five-year term of office (roughly according to partisan composition in the Parliament) and can serve long enough to develop substantial policy expertise. Further, unlike the full body, the committees meet in Brussels and can thus oversee the work of the Commission and Council of Ministers more closely. The committees review most legislation drafted by the Commission and Council and informally, if not always formally, may have a significant impact on the shape of the final rules.

The committee structure also helps Commission bureaucrats in the equally differentiated Directorate structure work with the Parliament. Policy segmentation is the predictable outcome, much as in the United States. The evidence is as yet limited, but the committees will probably develop some form of symbiotic working relationship with the Directorates whose work they oversee, a relationship heightened by the connections of both with European and national interest groups. Policy communities are already forming around each of the main issue areas within which the Community has competence.[28]

The Single European Act substantially increased the powers of the European Parliament (and the decisions taken at the Maastricht summit confirmed the trend). The act requires that the Parliament approve all accession and association agreements with other states before the agreements are considered by the Council.[29] The act also requires two parliamentary readings of some Community legislation. Before the act's passage, the Parliament would render an opinion on legislation proposed

28. See, for example, Peter M. Haas, "Do Regimes Matter? Epistemic Communities and Mediterranean Pollution Control," *International Organization*, vol. 43 (Summer 1989), pp. 377–403. The concept of epistemic communities is similar to policy communities but depends more on the existence of a common professional or scientific basis for the formation of the community.

29. Richard Corbett, "Testing the New Procedures: The European Parliament's First Experiences with Its New 'Single Act' Powers," *Journal of Common Market Studies*, vol. 27 (June 1989), pp. 359–72.

by the Commission before the Council took final action, but the opinion had little influence. Now Council decisions are not final, and the Parliament reviews the Council's "common position." The Parliament has three options: the position can be approved or simply not disapproved within three months; the position can be rejected, in which case the legislation fails unless the Council acts unanimously (with approval of the Commission) within three months; or the Parliament may propose amendments that, if supported by the Commission, require unanimity on the Council to overturn (a qualified majority accepts the amendments). Amendments rejected by the Commission require unanimity on the Council. Rejection or amendment of Council positions requires a simple majority of the Parliament. These new powers appear to provide the Parliament the basis for becoming a real force in decisionmaking within the Community, an indication of which is its assertion of the power to control automobile exhaust emissions.[30] Once the Maastricht treaty goes into effect, the Parliament will be able to propose amendments to some bills directly to the Council of Ministers as well as exercise a veto, again on selected bills.

The European Parliament is involved in two political games simultaneously. In one, it influences the policies of the European Community— although the Treaty of Rome and its addenda tightly circumscribed the Parliament's political powers, the Single European Act and the Maastricht summit expanded its policymaking influence. The limitations on its powers led the Parliament to take part in a second game of attempting to assert its own powers and prerogatives vis-à-vis the other institutions in the Community. These two games are very much interdependent. If the Parliament was able to become an effective decisionmaking body in the first game, it would more likely be granted enhanced power and authority—or would at least be involved more frequently, even if not required constitutionally—and therefore would be more successful in the second game. But if the Parliament bogs down in bickering, delay, and obstruction, it will not do well in either game. For advocates of increased parliamentary powers, the Parliament's record since the passage of the Single European Act has been responsible, which has made some governments more willing to envisage enhanced powers for it.[31]

30. Francis Jacobs and Richard Corbett, with Michael Shackleton, *The European Parliament* (Boulder, Colo.: Westview Press, 1990).

31. David Buchan, "MEPs Seek to Lay Down Law on Legislative Powers," *Financial Times*, August 13, 1991, p. 2.

Fundamental Political Processes

Policymaking in the European Community must allow for dichotomies between national and supranational interests and for dynamic interactions among people and institutions representing those interests. It must also allow for the importance of bureaucratic decisionmaking within the Community. Although the Community is not dominated by permanent bureaucrats in the Commission, it is heavily influenced by them and by their interactions with the bureaucracies of member states. Finally, the Community as yet lacks a strong democratic relationship with its citizens, and although the European Parliament is forging those links, Europe is some distance from being a parliamentary democracy.

Comparing the institutions of the Community with the parliamentary democracies of Western Europe should not be extended too far, however. For example, although revenues and expenditures are important for the Community, such matters are not as central as they are for national governments. Rather, the Community's impact on its constituent nations is increasingly through law and regulation. This choice of policy instruments may be wise because regulative instruments tend to mask the effects of policies and to make winners and losers less visible than expenditure programs do. Regulatory policy may thus minimize (although not eliminate) national, regional, and even class conflicts over Community policy. The choice also enhances the relative powers of the Commission and the bureaucracy.

The Budget Process

The budgetary process is crucial in any political system, even one with an emphasis on legal and regulatory policy. The question of "who gets what" is always important and "who pays what" is of equal importance, especially when that question has implications for individuals as well as nations.[32] For example, several countries with efficient agricultural sectors have expressed reservations about subsidizing less efficient agricultural operations. One needs therefore to understand where the money to run the European Community comes from, where it goes, and who makes the

32. Brian Ardy, "The National Incidence of the European Community Budget," *Journal of Common Market Studies*, vol. 26 (June 1988), pp. 401–29; and Helen Wallace, "Distributional Politics: Dividing Up the Community Cake," in Wallace, Wallace and Webb, eds., *Policy-Making in the European Community*, pp. 81–113.

decisions. The adequacy of the funding arrangements for any movement toward greater integration, especially greater political integration, will also determine the likelihood of greater integration.

REVENUE. Compared with most international organizations, the European Community can raise money easily from four designated revenue sources, three of which it can claim as its own. It does not have to beg member countries for funds—although countries have used funds collected on its behalf as a lever to gain concessions on policy.[33] Thus, compared with the United Nations, or even the central government in the United States under the Articles of Confederation, the Community is reasonably sure of receiving its rightful revenues. Still, its revenues are often thought of in national terms—who is "contributing" how much. Arguments about fairness concern national considerations more often than socioeconomic class, progressivity, or even the horizontal neutrality of the revenue structure. The Community does not receive revenues directly from its citizens; it depends on indirect taxes collected by national governments. Therefore national governments continue to play an obvious and significant role in the revenue process.[34]

The four sources of EC revenues are as follows.[35] The first is a common levy on industrial imports from outside the EC, similar to national governments' tariffs on imports, except that the customs agents remain national but hand the money over to the Community. The second source is a levy applied to all relevant agricultural products imported from outside the Community, collected in much the same way as the common industrial tariff. For the third source, the Community is entitled to 1.4 percent (1 percent before 1984) of the base used by member nations for collecting the value-added tax.[36] The base on which the VAT will bc extracted has been harmonized, but members are largely free to establish the rates at

33. Paul Taylor, "New Dynamics of European Integration," in Juliet Lodge, ed., *The European Community and the Challenge of the Future* (London: Pinter, 1989), pp. 4–7.

34. Citizens are not totally unaware that some portion of their taxes goes to fund the European Community, but the process remains less visible than direct EC taxation.

35. Michael Shackleton, "The Budget of the European Community," in Lodge, ed., *European Community.*

36. This base is to be calculated on a harmonized principle, and bargaining over tax harmonization is one of the most difficult issues in moving toward a single market. See Lucy Kellaway, "Commission to Study Tax 'Threat' to Single Market," *Financial Times*, February 23, 1990.

which they will extract the tax.[37] Thus the EC's revenue is not 1.4 percent of national VAT but 1.4 percent of the base used to calculate the national VAT obligations of businesses.

The fourth revenue source for the EC is a recent addition, and remains controversial. This revenue source grew out of the Community's financial crises during the mid-1980s and came into being in the Brussels agreements of 1988.[38] These agreements established a negotiated level of resource availability based on a percentage of the combined gross national products of the member countries.[39] If Community revenues from the other three sources, which tended to be stable or even declining in real value, were insufficient to meet the budgetary requirements within this GNP ceiling, an additional levy could be made on the member countries. In 1989, for example, a difference of ECU 3.9 billion was met by a levy of approximately 0.1 percent of the GNP of each country. This "fourth resource" at once strengthened the financial basis of the Community and raised doubts about its financial future. It allowed Community resources to keep up with expenditure demands, acknowledged that the Community had to have sufficient money to implement its programs and that expenditure commitments would to some extent determine the size of the final EC budget, and was flexible and could be used without regard to the volume of international trade or other uncontrollable economic aggregates. But the new source of revenue also represented a step back from the fiscal independence implied by the EC's having its own source revenues and put it more at the mercy of the member countries.[40] This potentially greater dependence occurred just as the Community was striving toward a more independent role through the Single European Act.

Even more than revenue processes within countries, EC revenue processes seem to be virtually automatic.[41] Two of the four sources depend

37. Donald J. Puchala, *Fiscal Harmonization in the European Communities: National Politics and International Cooperation* (London: Pinter, 1984).

38. Michael Shackleton, *Financing the European Community* (London: Pinter, 1990).

39. The percentage of GNP available to the Community was to increase gradually from 1.15 percent in 1988 to 1.2 percent in 1992. The original Commission target had been 1.4 percent.

40. However, when the member countries (more precisely Britain in 1983) have withheld the revenue collected for the Community, the European Court has ruled (case 93/85) that they were, in essence, *ultra vires* and required them to pay interest.

41. See for example, David A. Good, *The Politics of Anticipation: Making Canadian Federal Tax Policy* (Ottawa: Carleton University, School of Public Administration, 1980).

more on trade and implementation by national governments than on decisions made in Brussels. The third, the percentage of the VAT base, is also beyond the control of Community policymakers because it depends on the member countries' tax systems. The Community must decide (through summit meetings such as Fontainebleau or through the Council of Ministers) what the EC percentage of the national tax base will be, but once the decision is made, the process becomes automatic and dependent on economic activity. Likewise, after the initial agreement on the fourth source the process appears largely statistical; the national governments decide whether they will use these financial obligations to influence EC policy. The automatic nature of the collection process may be only apparent, however, and revenue issues remain as crucial to EC politics as they are for national politics.

EXPENDITURES. The EC budgetary process is now largely driven by expenditure commitments. The budgetary agreements of the 1980s established a ceiling, linked to the total GNP of EC members, above which expenditures should not go. But below that ceiling, expenditure commitments determine how much money will pass through the Community budget.[42] The Community now spends money for a wide variety of purposes. Unlike other international organizations, it pays for policies that have a direct effect on citizens of the member countries, the most familiar being agricultural policy, which currently accounts for about 60 percent of total EC expenditures. Other important purposes of Community spending are to help compensate member countries for economic adjustments resulting from integration (structural funds), to promote economies of scale (such as research), and to handle external affairs (including an increasing amount of foreign aid).

Like that of national governments, much EC spending is largely uncontrollable. Because agricultural expenditures are mandatory under the treaty and the agreements arising out of it, any Community budget will have forecasts of expenditures in this area rather than ceilings on the amount that can be spent legally, as it would for most budgetary items. In 1984 the Council of Ministers decreed that the rate of increase of agricultural spending should not exceed the rate of increase in its own source revenues. Though an admirable guideline, in practice it is useful primarily for determining how much excess spending has occurred. Subsequent changes in agricultural policies, such as introducing declining levels

42. Shackleton, "Budget of the European Community."

of support for cereals after 160 million tons of production, have brought some real control to agricultural expenditures in the Community.[43] And Commission decisions have also tended to reduce agricultural expenditures.[44] Agriculture is forecast to be a declining component of EC expenditure, dropping to 55 percent by 1992, and it is hoped that even greater budgetary control may be obtainable.

Despite the uncontrollable element of expenditure determined by the treaty, the process for determining EC expenditures is more that of a national government than is the process for determining EC revenue. The European Parliament has a greater role in expenditure than in revenue and can, as it did in 1979 and again in 1984, reject the budget presented by the Commission. Further, the Parliament can affect the amount and purpose of expenditures not resulting directly from treaty provisions ("noncompulsory expenditures"). Perhaps most important is that total expenditures have not kept pace with the ceilings established in the Brussels agreements; unlike most legislatures in contemporary democracies, the European Parliament has some slack with which to finance policy initiatives. That financing will not, however, occur without politics. As the poorer member nations press for full use of the GNP ceilings to fund development programs for themselves, the more affluent countries press for greater financial restraint and for the expansion of high-tech research and development projects likely to benefit their citizens. The need to finance development in Eastern Europe is also placing heavy additional strains on the Community budget.

ASSESSMENT. The budget has often been one means through which central governments in newly formed federations have expanded their influence and power over their constituent units. The evidence to date about the success of European institutions in using the budget in that way is mixed. On the one hand, the European budget remains a small component—about 3 percent—of total public expenditures made in the twelve member nations. Even with GNP ceilings to provide greater latitude for European spending, the Community operates under a greater budget constraint than does any member nation. If for no other reason, the EC

43. Michael Shackleton, "The EC's Budget under a Single Market," paper presented at the 1989 Meeting of the American Political Science Association, Atlanta, Ga., August 29–September 2.

44. Shackleton, "The EC's Budget under a Single Market."

is forbidden by the Treaty of Rome (article 199) from running a deficit.[45] And, as mentioned, most European spending has been on a single program—agriculture—that has become controversial in many member countries as well as for many individual Europeans. Thus, the EC has gained somewhat less public support (except among agricultural interests) through public expenditure than its advocates might hope.

On the other hand, the budgetary base of the European Community has expanded. The GNP ceiling has given decisionmakers considerable latitude to make new initiatives using expanded revenues. And the Parliament is taking a greater role in setting expenditure priorities and advocating nonmandatory expenditure programs, such as research and development, the structural funds, and aid to Eastern Europe. The Community will find it difficult to withdraw from these activities once they have begun, so public expenditure may be "ratcheted up" as in national governments.[46] Further, some of the most effective instruments for integration are regulatory and may not require great financial resources to implement. Because the Community institutions now have a stronger financial base and a stronger budgetary process than earlier, their supranational policymaking activity should grow.

Executive Accountability

The European Community has an executive and a parliament. What it lacks as yet is a clear, democratic means of linking the two. The members of the Council of Ministers will remain accountable to their national governments; therefore, if any executive is held accountable to the European Parliament, it will almost certainly be the EC Commission. As now constituted, the Commission is a responsible body but not an accountable or responsive body in the usual sense. The commissioners are responsible (primarily to their own consciences) to act in a European manner and to defend the treaty. But because the Community is not yet a conventional democratic government, few means are available for directly enforcing responsibility or accountability on the members of the Commission, or perhaps even on the bureaucrats employed by the Commission. The only real check available to the European Parliament is to dismiss the entire

45. There are, however, a variety of borrowing arrangements financed by the Community, although these activities are "off budget" and do not figure as part of the official Community Budget.

46. Alan T. Peacock and Jack Wiseman, *The Growth of Public Expenditure in the United Kingdom*, 2d ed. (London: Allen and Unwin, 1967).

Commission. Such a dramatic action, which would produce great disruption and might serve little purpose, is unlikely until Community institutions are better entrenched and legitimated. But even if such dismissals occurred, nothing would prevent national governments from simply reappointing the same commissioners and thereby provoking an even greater political crisis within the Community. For the foreseeable future, the accountability of the commissioners must remain to their own consciences and to one another. Some governments have expressed hopes for an enhanced role for the European Parliament in executive accountability, but these are as yet only hopes.[47]

This system of responsible government has worked. Many commissioners have been deeply committed to the Community and its goals, and most have acted responsibly. Indeed, most members and especially the presidents of the Commission have pushed supranational values and integration forward and have been driving forces in increasing Community powers over policy. Still, if the EC is to become a genuine political entity, better mechanisms of popular and political accountability need to be articulated for the Commission. As it is, the Parliament has almost no control over the appointment of commissioners and must depend on the goodwill and competence of national governments to send the correct people to Brussels.

Some changes have made EC institutions more closely resemble the governments of European nations. Budgetary accountability to the Parliament has been institutionalized, and the Parliament has twice rejected budgets submitted by the Commission. The power of the purse has historically been the central lever for legislative acquisition of power, and the development of legislative-executive relationships in the EC will apparently be little different. In addition, a "question hour" has been institutionalized in the Parliament, with members of the Commission required to attend when issues under their control (within their Directorates) are discussed.[48] Likewise, members of the Commission are increasingly expected to attend meetings of committees of the Parliament and may have to respond to questions advanced there.

47. This assumes, of course, that an accountable executive in the usual sense is indeed a goal of institutional development within the EC. It may be that the mixture of emerging federal regime and supranational organization will require alternative definitions of accountability.

48. Juliet Lodge, "The European Parliament after Direct Elections: Talking Shop or Putative Legislature," *Journal of European Integration*, vol. 5 (1982), pp. 259–84.

What is missing is a clear conception of cabinet government and ministerial responsibility. If the president of the Commission is to become the analogue of a prime minister, he or she should be able to select the other members of the "cabinet"—at present all commissioners are appointed. The Dooge Committee (1985) on the functioning of Community institutions suggested that the president be able to select the other EC commissioners, subject to review by the national governments, but this suggestion has not been accepted.[49] The president has the power to assign portfolios and can try to bury a less competent or cooperative commissioner in a minor position, but that person remains a commissioner until removed by the national government. Also, a mechanism for the Parliament to dismiss individual commissioners, rather than have to dismiss the entire Commission, would be required. Given the delicate balance that exists between national interest and the role of the Commission, this reform would be hard for many governments to accept. But such a change in organization would be almost inevitable if governance as understood in European democracies were to be institutionalized within the EC. And permitting the dismissal of individual members of the Commission could lead to the idea that the Parliament should also appoint the Commission, as the analogue of its cabinet.

Policymaking

Rather than be called policymaking, this section might better have a more formal appelation, such as law making. The focus is on how institutions of the European Community decide what proposals to accept as authoritative, and therefore which proposed laws they should try to implement. A decision at the Community level, more than at a national level, involves strategic questions as well as the usual questions about the desirability and feasibility of a policy. Leaders of Community institutions must decide not only what they want to do substantively but also how fast and how far they can push member governments and citizens of member countries. Although some dedicated Europeanists are willing to push very hard and very far, they risk creating manifest opposition to 1992 and to the EC more generally. If the European Community and its integration is a "bicycle" that remains upright so long as it is going forward, then to create manifest

49. Ad Hoc Committee for Institutional Affairs, *Report to the European Council (Brussels, 29–30 March 1985)* (Luxembourg, 1985).

(and needless) opposition is dangerous.[50] The feasibility of a proposal is used too easily to constrain policymaking at the national level, but it becomes a crucial consideration at this level.[51] The regulatory issues central to the Community generate considerable controversy but not usually as much as fiscal issues in which the winners and losers are more visible.

In the initial formulation of decisionmaking in the Treaty of Rome, the Commission prepared draft legislation, and the Council of Ministers made the principal decisions. For a few matters, the Commission could issue laws and engage in quasi-legislative activities, a process analogous to secondary legislation by national bureaucracies. In this arrangement the European Parliament was largely excluded. It might debate the merits of legislation but had little effect on final decisions. The Single European Act changed the relative powers of institutions. It introduced a "cooperation procedure"—the second reading described above—that gives the Parliament limited powers of co-decision with the Council over a range of important policy issues. Besides the formal changes brought about through this procedure, there is now much more consultation and indirect contact between the Parliament and the other institutions.[52]

As a result of the Single European Act, the European Parliament became a significant legislative body for the first time, a change important for reasons other than simply relative institutional power. Because of its increased powers, the Parliament, like the Commission, seems to have a more European perspective than the Council of Ministers, a perspective demonstrated in the workings of unofficial components of the Parliament such as the "Crocodile Club" and in the official support of the Parliament for federalist solutions to European political relations such as the draft European Union Treaty.[53] If the Parliament continues to be granted a larger role in European legislation, the rider on the bicycle may have to pedal very fast to keep up with the changes in the political system.

50. Michael Emerson, "1992 and After: The Bicycle Theory Rides Again," *Political Quarterly*, vol. 59 (July–September 1988), pp. 289–99.

51. Giandomenico Majone, "The Feasibility of Social Policies," *Policy Sciences*, vol. 6 (March 1975), pp. 49–69.

52. John Fitzmaurice, "An Analysis of the European Community's Co-operation Procedure," *Journal of Common Market Studies*, vol. 26 (June 1988), pp. 389–400.

53. Rita Cardozo and Richard Corbett, "The Crocodile Initiative," in Juliet Lodge, ed., *European Union: The European Community in Search of a Future* (Basingstoke: Macmillan, 1986), pp. 15–46; and Panayiotis Ifestos, *European Political Cooperation: Towards a Framework of Supranational Diplomacy?* (Aldershot: Avebury, 1987).

In fairness, it would be easy to make too much of the "cooperation" procedure for decisionmaking. The ultimate powers of decisionmaking remain in the Council of Ministers so long as it can achieve unanimity. The Parliament has to date rejected outright several "common positions" from the Council. For one on occupational health, there was no chance of unanimity and a compromise emerged. On others, the Council achieved unanimity.[54] This pattern of rulemaking makes the relations between these institutions somewhat like the separation of powers in the United States, except that a quasi-executive body (the Council of Ministers) has the right to overturn the veto and therefore to make the final decision, rather than vice versa. Moreover, the unanimity rule is a much tougher standard—even if the Council has worked with such a rule when not technically required—than is the two-thirds requirement for Congress to overturn a presidential veto.

As important as the Council and parliamentary levels of decisionmaking are for the Community, the impetus for most European rulemaking comes from a lower level, usually the Commission and its component units. Other than broad legislative statements, rulemaking in the Community comes in three forms. The simplest—and most compelling—must be put into effect automatically by national governments simply by virtue of their being issued.[55] These rules (called *regulations*) are directly binding on national governments and other actors (corporations, individuals, and so forth) and pass into national law without additional action. Regulations may be made by a simplified written procedure rather than by the more complex oral procedure required for most rulemaking.

The second level of rules are called *directives*. While the goals expressed in a directive are binding, the actual content remains open to some variation and interpretation by the member nations. Unlike the handling of a regulation, national governments can decide how they put a directive into effect. That gives them the opportunity for delay, for bargaining with the Commission, and for bargaining with interests within their own borders. To become effective, such rules must be incorporated into national law in some manner, and this method of rulemaking may provide substantial latitude to national governments to impose their own priorities.[56] The third levels of EC rules are called *decisions*. They are

54. Corbett, "Testing the New Procedures," p. 364.
55. Siedentopf and Ziller, *Making European Policies Work.*
56. Heinrich Siedentopf and Cristoph Hauschild, "L'Application des Directives Communautaires par les Administrations Nationales (Etude Comparative)," *Revue Française d'Ad-*

very specific and apply only to the individuals or governments to which they are directed, but they are binding on the target of the action.

Although the Council has preponderant authority in making Community decisions, the Commission has some direct and indirect powers of its own. For administrative matters, it can make binding declarations and issues several thousand rules of its own each year. As the experience with secondary legislation at the national level shows, "administrative" can include many different issues and can have important policy consequences. At least twice, for example, the Commission has had to decide on the amount of price supports in the Common Agricultural Program because the Council was deadlocked.[57] The Commission also decides what cases should be submitted to the European Court of Justice, so it can essentially (if successful) use the Court to make rules on its behalf. Finally, at times simply by announcing its opinion on an issue, the Commission (and especially its president) seems able to gain compliance without formal rule-making. Some of that power may be a function of the personal influence of Delors himself rather than a function of his office, but in the short run the Commission does have such influence.

THE ROLE OF IMPLEMENTATION. Although the discussion above was phrased legalistically, in reality national bureaucracies have great power over the implementation of EC rules. What does it mean, for example, that a government must "automatically" enforce the regulations made by the Commission and Council? Any number of studies of national policy-making show that a legalistic conception of how administrative systems perform in implementation is at best self-delusory on the part of politicians.[58] In fact, a great deal of interpretation and even redefinition of policy occurs during implementation. Unless they understand that influence of administration on policy intentions, analysts risk making errors in assigning responsibility for policy failures, or even policy successes.[59]

ministration Publique, vol. 48 (October–December 1988), pp. 547–55; and Giuseppe Ciavarini Azzi, ed., L'Application du Droit Communautaire par les Etats Membres (Maastricht: European Institute of Public Administration, 1985).

57. Alan Swinbank, "The Common Agricultural Policy and the Politics of European Decision Making," Journal of Common Market Studies, vol. 27 (June 1989), pp. 303–22.

58. The classic study is Jeffrey L. Pressman and Aaron Wildavsky, Implementation (University of California Press, 1973).

59. Morris P. Fiorina, Bureaucratic Failures: Causes and Cures (Washington University Press, 1981); Nelson W. Polsby, Political Innovation in America: The Politics of Policy Innovation (Yale University Press, 1984); and John E. Schwarz, America's Hidden Success: A Reassessment of Public Policy from Kennedy to Reagan (Norton, 1988).

Implementation in the European Community is no less subject to the implementing agents. The EC process is analogous to the implementation of policies in a federal regime, such as the Federal Republic of Germany, in which policies are made centrally and implemented by subnational governments. Thus, even if policy now comes out of Brussels, the national governments are by no means impotent.[60] They can bargain over policy and its meaning with their counterparts in Brussels and can then try to interpret policy in their own terms. As the existing evidence shows, national actions can affect the implementation of EC directives and regulations and indeed alter the meaning of regulations in practice.[61] These findings further reinforce the multilevel "interlocking" or *engrenage* interpretations of the Community, with winning and losing the game being defined differently at different levels and at different stages of the process.[62] Losing at the policymaking stage may not be so important if there is a second round at the implementation stage when the national government, through its bureaucracy, has an opportunity to determine what will actually happen in the policy area in that country.

THE SPECIAL CASE OF FOREIGN POLICY. Up to now I have been primarily discussing "domestic" issues in Europe—or issues that would be classified as domestic within a single nation-state. Foreign policy has been considered the preserve of national governments, and for Europe to create a common foreign policy presents more difficulties than even the thorniest economic issues (such as a common currency or a common central bank). But the EC needs a common foreign policy in order to be a meaningful international actor. The decision taken at Maastricht to act collectively in the foreign and security policy arena was a major step forward even if actually formulating common policy may prove difficult. Furthermore, the decision to eventually "frame a common defense policy" moves Europe forward a good deal toward its goal of "asserting its identity on the international scene."

A framework for establishing a common foreign policy had been created, and to some extent incorporated into the EC institutional framework during

60. Werner J. Feld and John K. Wildgen, "National Administrative Elites and European Integration: Saboteurs at Work?" *Journal of Common Market Studies,* vol. 13 (March 1975), pp. 244–65; and Brigid Laffan, "The Challenge of 1992 for the Irish Administrative State," *Seirbhis Phoibli,* vol. 9 (November 1988), pp. 37–41.

61. Siedentopf and Ziller, *Making European Policies Work.*

62. Wolfgang Wessels, "The Dynamics of Administrative Interactions: Towards a European System of Co-operative States," paper presented at the Workshop on the Dynamics of European Integration, Florence, September 1989.

the 1970s. The movement toward European political cooperation (EPC) began in 1969 (leaving aside earlier unsuccessful attempts such as the Defense Community), and has proceeded through a Council (initially Conference) of Foreign Ministers, a Political Committee for administrative purposes, and a Group of Correspondents in member countries monitoring the activities of EPC.[63] Linkage between the Community and the EPC organization was deepened in 1983 with the Solemn Declaration on European Union, and the Commission began to be represented in EPC meetings. The relationship between the EC and this more foreign policy and security conscious European organization became more formalized through the Single European Act, with its requirements for consultation and policy consistency between the two organizations. Finally, the Maastricht summit moved the Community significantly closer to a truly integrated foreign, security, and defense policy. Although the member states will cooperate within an intergovernmental rather than a Community framework, thereby minimizing the role of the Commission, many member states hope that foreign and security policymaking will eventually move into the Community's policy processes and become incorporated into the Treaty of Rome.

The movement toward a single market in 1992 can only exacerbate pressure for greater political and foreign policy cooperation among members of the EC.[64] Europe will increasingly function as a single entity in international economics, a condition that necessarily implies greater political cooperation and agreement among members. The need for unitary action will be true if the economic powers involved in the negotiations are nation-states (Japan and the United States) or other regional blocs (the ANDEAN Pact). Coping with the admission of new members, or some form of associative relationships with European countries not now members, may also have important political implications besides the economic ones over which the EC already has competence.[65]

Institutional Analysis of the Community

The analysis in this section, which focuses on approaches to understanding the European Community and the movement toward the single market envisioned for 1992, will be done from the perspective of the institutions

63. Juliet Lodge, "European Political Cooperation: Towards the 1990s," in Lodge, ed., *European Community*, pp. 223–40.
64. Lodge, "European Political Cooperation."
65. "The Nordic Countries in a Changing Europe," Insert, *Financial Times*, February 21, 1990, pp. 35–40.

discussed in the other sections. Although much of the day-to-day movement toward a single market might be explained through functionalist logic, the major transformations of the EC remain political acts.[66] Some of these have been individual acts of leadership, such as those taken by Roy Jenkins in relation to monetary and fiscal policy, and Jacques Delors in advocating the Single European Act and the target date of 1992. Individual actions, however, must be translated into an institutional framework if they are to persist and produce the policy outcomes intended. I therefore examine alternative approaches to change that are already on the intellectual table and assess them as aids to understanding. In conclusion I suggest an approach that draws on the "new institutionalism" in political science as well as on the old bureaucratic politics of the real world.[67] None of these approaches should be seen as the ultimate answer to the complex, analytic problems. Rather, each is useful in dealing with some aspect of the problems.

An institutional analysis of the European Community must recognize the several different but interconnected "games" being played simultaneously within the Community. The idea of a two-level game is too simplistic to capture the complexity of motives and interactions.[68] There are at least three large games being played. One is the national game, in which individual nations attempt to extract as much as possible from the EC, while relinquishing as little (financially or in terms of sovereignty) as possible; phrased differently, this is a game of coping with interdependence. The second game is among the institutions themselves, each seeking to gain more power relative to the others. This game may be played for the right reasons—for example, the Commission believes it is the protector of the treaty, while the Council of Ministers considers itself the protector of national interests—but it is a complex, multifaceted game nonetheless. This second game is, of course, intimately linked with the first.

66. Paul Taylor, "The New Dynamics of EC Integration in the 1980s," in Lodge, ed., *European Community*, pp. 3–25; and Richard Corbett, "The 1985 Intergovernmental Conference and the Single European Act," in Roy Pryce, ed., *The Dynamics of European Union* (London: Croom Helm, 1987), pp. 238–72.

67. James G. March and Johan P. Olsen, *Rediscovering Institutions: The Organizational Basis of Politics* (Free Press, 1989).

68. George Tsebelis, *Nested Games: Rational Choice in Comparative Politics* (University of California Press, 1990).

The third is a bureaucratic game that is apparently becoming an important subtext for everything else happening within the EC. The twenty-three Directorates-General appear to be developing their own organizational cultures and approaches to policy. As in most governmental structures the boundary lines among policy competences are not entirely clear, and the Directorates may compete for policy space: where, for example, is the boundary between research and development and the telecommunications industry or science policy? Even within a single Directorate there may be conflicts over policy definitions: is vocational education an education or a labor market policy concern? The components of the European bureaucracy also seem to be developing their own working relationships with national governments, or at least with relevant elements of national governments. Likewise, individuals and organizations in the national bureaucracies are promoting their own relationships, and their own policy goals, with organizations in Brussels. At times, policies with little support within a nation (the environment in Britain?) may have a great deal of support in Brussels. Although these developments in the Community may lead to the diminution of national dominance over policy, they also raise a potential concern: the European government may have to fight the "government against subgovernment" battle familiar at the national level. [69] It is important to remember that all three games are occurring simultaneously and that strategies adopted in one may have real consequences for outcomes in another. [70]

The National Basis

It would be incorrect to undertake an analysis of the changes occurring in Europe solely from the perspective of the European Community and its institutions. Obviously the member states have played, and will continue to play, an important role in those changes. And because policy choices made by the member states are to some extent conditioned by

69. Richard Rose, "Governments against Subgovernments: A European Perspective on Washington," in Rose and Ezra N. Suleiman, eds., *Presidents and Prime Ministers* (Washington: American Enterprise Institute for Policy Research, 1980), pp. 284–347.

70. There may also be still other games being played simultaneously. The nation-states themselves are not homogeneous actors, and components—public or private—may be using the EC as an arena to advance their own purposes. Firms, for example, may believe they would find a less restrictive regulatory environment if the Community had greater control of environmental policy. Also, interest groups that have been unsuccessful at home may find the European arena more congenial.

events in their own international economic and political environments, it would also be incorrect to think about change without considering what has been happening outside Western Europe. The European Community is becoming a prime actor on the international stage, although it has yet to fully supplant the nation-states that are affiliated with it, or to become capable of steering the international political economy.[71]

A notable development for the European Community has been the tendency of many member states to minimize their central governments' role in the delivery of services and even in policymaking. At the least extreme, this has meant turning over many policymaking and implementation activities to subnational governments, even in states (France, Spain) that have historically been centralized.[72] At a more extreme level, a number of governments have undertaken to supply public services through para-governmental or "third party" organizations.[73] At the most extreme, most European governments have privatized many public corporations and public services.[74] Again, privatization has occurred in governments with traditions of *étatiste* management of their economies and societies as well as in those with histories of laissez-faire policies.

The principal question has become whether the nation-state is important any more. Many governments, and a particularly large number of politicians, have chosen a governing style that permits the private sector to make an increasing number of decisions that once would have been made by government. If government is not the best way to make policy decisions—especially about the economy—then perhaps it does not matter so much who constitutes the government. Although that is an overstatement—some politicians (Thatcher is a prime example) most dismissive of government in general have been the most opposed to rapid movement into a single European political unit—the devaluing of government may

71. John Fitzmaurice, "European Community Decision-Making: The National Dimension," in Juliet Lodge, ed., *Institutions and Policies of the European Community* (London: Pinter, 1983), pp. 1–8. Some argue that the nation-states have been strengthened through the integration process. See Stanley Hoffmann, "Reflections on the Nation-State in Western Europe Today," *Journal of Common Market Studies*, vol. 21 (September–December 1982), pp. 21–37.

72. Michael Keating, "Does Regional Government Work? The Experience of Italy, France and Spain," *Governance*, vol. 1 (April 1988), pp. 184–204.

73. Christopher Hood and Gunnar Folke Schuppert, *Delivering Public Services in Western Europe* (London: Sage Publications, 1988).

74. Charles de Croisset, Boudouin Prot, and Michel de Rosen, *Dénationalisations* (Paris: Economica, 1986); and Cento Veljanovski, *Selling the State: Privatisation in Britain* (London: Weidenfeld and Nicolson, 1987).

make the creation of a more powerful "European government" more palatable to politicians and citizens alike.

Governing in the early 1990s may not be so much undesirable as impossible, or at least very difficult. Interdependence has become a buzz word to describe changes in the international political economy and, like most clichés, contains some element of truth.[75] National governments, or even large blocs like the EC, are increasingly incapable of determining their own economic futures. As a consequence, to be forced to take responsibility as a national government is often to be handed a poisoned chalice; to take credit for the good times in the 1950s, 1960s, and 1970s makes it difficult not to take the "credit" for the economic slowness of the 1980s. Adopting a more cooperative attitude toward Europe and permitting more economic decisions to be made in Brussels (or perhaps in Frankfurt) is a way to avoid blame for anything that goes wrong, and perhaps to make a few things go right. Indeed, politics in this era has been described as "blame avoidance" rather than credit claiming.[76]

Federalism

This institutional option most clearly addresses the issue of the national game. To many people, especially long-standing advocates of federalism, the political situation of the EC appears ripe for a federal solution. A number of independent and equal (at least in international law) political entities are seeking some form of closer linkage; in effect, they want mutual governance of at least part of their common economic and social interests. The institutions devised remain somewhat more like those of an international organization than those of a national government, although it is felt a closer political linkage will be necessary if this enterprise is to succeed. In addition, activists concerned with forming and perpetuating this linkage have envisioned a closer political union, to keep the peace and to create a common European identity that transcends nationalism.[77] Some kind of a federal arrangement seems to be a natural way to accommodate the existing nation-states while still providing a superordinate government for the aggregation.

75. Richard N. Cooper, "Economic Interdependence and Foreign Policy in the Seventies," *World Politics*, vol. 24 (January 1972), pp. 159–81.
76. R. Kent Weaver, "The Politics of Blame Avoidance," *Journal of Public Policy*, vol. 6 (October–December 1986), pp. 371–98.
77. Most famous among these was Altiero Spinelli. See Michael Burgess, *Federalism and European Union: Political Ideas, Influences, and Strategies in the European Community, 1972–1987* (London: Routledge, 1989).

But if indeed there is to be a federal solution to the European political question, what type of federalism is meant? For Anglo-Saxons, the contractual and constitutional model of federalism is the most logical answer to that question. In this approach, component governments, acting as independent and autonomous units, initially agree to establish a new level of government and to grant certain specified powers to a new, superordinate entity. The granting of those powers is never clear enough to prevent a need for future elaboration and interpretation, but some attempt is made to allocate powers and to form a binding and enduring contract. In other such federal arrangements, power has tended to gravitate toward the highest level of government, in part because of the availability of financial resources and in part because of spillover effects.[78] Those outcomes are analogous to the effects deemed to be important by functionalist and neofunctionalist theorists of supranational integration.[79] That is, in most federal systems it quickly becomes apparent that only the higher level of government is capable of regulating the many interactions and externalities that result from the independent actions of individuals and subnational governments.

For many Continental Europeans, federalism may have a very different connotation, stemming from the concept of "subsidiarity" in Catholic social thought.[80] Jacques Delors, for example, has been committed to this version of federalism for the European Community. If Europe becomes federal, this is the most likely approach. It was written into the proposals for amendment of the Treaty of Rome to create political union,[81] and in fact the Maastricht treaty includes language defining the principle of subsidiarity. By the term *subsidiarity* Delors implies that all actions in social and political life should be performed by the smallest possible unit. This view suggests a more organic view of society and political life than does the more mechanistic and legalistic approach of Anglo-Saxon federalism. In the context of

78. See Michael Emerson, "The Finances of the European Community: A Case Study in Embryonic Fiscal Federalism," in Wallace E. Oates, ed., *The Political Economy of Fiscal Federalism* (Lexington, Mass.: Lexington Books, 1985), pp. 129–69.

79. Robert E. Riggs and I. Jostein Mykletun, *Beyond Functionalism: Attitudes toward International Organization in Norway and the United States* (University of Minnesota Press, 1979).

80. Rolf G. Heinze, ed., *Neue Subsidarität: Leitidee für eine zukünftige Sozialpolitik?* (Opladen: Westdeutscher Verlag, 1986); and Hans von der Groeben, *Legitimationsprobleme der Europäischen Gemeinschaft* (Baden-Baden: Nomos, 1987).

81. Commission of the European Communities, "Commission Opinion of 21 October 1990 on the Proposal for Amendment of the Treaty Establishing the European Economic Community with a View to Political Union," COM(90)600 (Brussels, October 23, 1990).

the European Community, this approach would mean that the EC "government" would do as little as possible, leaving most functions to the national and, perhaps especially, subnational governments. It may even mean that as many things as possible would be done by private and voluntary organizations rather than by any form of government. This approach would seem to give the subnational governments an important place in European government, even though the European Court has ruled that it is the responsibility of national governments to make subnational governments conform to European policy (a European "Dillon's rule"?).[82] The approach also leaves much room for interpretation, most obviously in determining the "lowest possible" unit to perform a function.

From the perspective of the national "game" being played in Europe, these alternative visions of federalism would have rather different implications. The Anglo-Saxon version would make the nation-state central in bargaining over the shape of a future political entity in Europe. In essence, the nation-states would be bargaining over how much of their "sovereignty" to grant to the European Community in exchange for benefits derived from the coordination of policies, reduced trade barriers, and perhaps direct subsidies for some sectors, such as agriculture and less developed regions. In the Continental conception of federalism, the nation-states are important but are only one among many sets of institutions that have a right to participate in the bargaining. The "subsidiarity" approach, therefore, may permit the EC to deal directly with subnational governments, interest groups, and citizens without concerning itself much with the rights of nation-states (a European repudiation of the doctrine of "interposition"?).[83] Of course, the Community is already involved in relationships that circumvent national governments, so the acceptance of subsidiarity as the concept of federalism might only institutionalize and legitimate what is already being done.[84]

82. Dillon's rule is taken from a statement in an Iowa Supreme Court case ruling that local governments were "creatures" of the state government and that the state governments could establish the guidelines for the management of local policy. See John G. Grumm and Russell D. Murphy, "Dillon's Rule Reconsidered," *Annals of the American Academy of Political and Social Science*, vol. 416 (November 1974), pp. 120–32.

83. "Interposition" is a state's-rights doctrine arguing that state governments could interpose themselves between their citizens and the actions of the federal government. The term is especially associated with John C. Calhoun of South Carolina.

84. Jacques Biancarelli, "La Communauté et les Collectivés Locales," *Revue Française d'Administration Publique*, vol. 48 (October–December 1988); and Jill Preston and Chris Hogg, "European Community Integrated Operations and the Power Dependence Model," *Public Policy and Administration*, vol. 3 (1988), pp. 29–40.

Although federalism and other ideas about intergovernmental relations are usually discussed in terms of the political relationships among the political units, one should also note that these alternatives may have consequences for the other "games" being played within the Community. In particular, accepting the Continental version of federalism might make it more likely that "picket-fence federalism" and intergovernmental relations similar to those in the United States will develop.[85] If a nation-state, as the analogue of the state in the United States, has no special claims to bargaining on behalf of its constituent units, a government in Brussels can seek out smaller units where policy can be made and implemented. Those units may be political (local governments), or functional (interest groups, businesses). In any case, policymaking is likely to develop along functional lines, with the important linkages being forged between Brussels and the smaller units. That will, in turn, increase the powers of the Directorates-General within the Commission, or of any other bureaucratic structures managing these interactions with the entities actually delivering services.

If the pattern of intergovernmental relations within the Community assumes this functional style, in which the intermediate political institutions (in this case those of the nations) might be bypassed, most vertical, constitutional models of federalism would appear to be inapplicable. In their place, something more like the "policy community" approach would seem to make greater sense for understanding those relationships.[86] In particular, any top-down conception of intergovernmental relations dominated by the center and involving virtually diplomatic relations between the levels of government would not be applicable. Rather, problems would "bubble up" more than trickle down for consideration, and multilateral negotiations (including all or several nation-states) would be the more appropriate way to solve problems. Further, because the general approach used for much of European policymaking has changed from harmonization to mutual recognition, close coordination and control from the center is less necessary. So long as the constituent units act as they are expected (the analogue of "full faith and credit" in the United States is clear), there is less need to impose Community rules and standards from the center.

85. See Deil S. Wright, *Understanding Intergovernmental Relations*, 3d ed. (Pacific Grove, Calif.: Brooks-Cole, 1988). "Picket-fence federalism" refers to the tendency of interactions to develop among experts and administrators along functional lines, such as health and education, rather than between political actors, such as presidents and state governors.

86. See R. A. W. Rhodes, *Beyond Westminster and Whitehall: The Sub-Central Governments of Britain* (London: Unwin Hyman, 1988).

The European Polity

In a European Community requiring unanimity among the members on almost all issues, all countries could expect to be heard and to have a great influence over policies. They could therefore also afford to bargain hard for their national interests, with only the loss of goodwill and the intangible commodity "political influence" as possible costs. Much of this political period within the Community occurred during a period of affluence, so that countries could extract substantial "side payments" if they conceded on a point that other members of the Community (and perhaps most or all of the Commission itself) wanted to have approved.[87] The changes in the voting rules of the Community toward qualified majorities has apparently ushered in a different political dynamic and may help lessen some of the problems of the "joint-decision trap" identified by Fritz Scharpf.[88] This dynamic could well be one like those of smaller European democracies attempting to accommodate multifarious interests within potentially fragile political systems; Heisler and Kvavik referred to this pattern as "the European Polity."[89]

The fundamental dynamic of the European Polity is that the members must adopt more constrained strategies to remain active and effective participants in the political process. In this kind of political system, continuing to play the game is as important as winning or losing any single decision. Although nation-states within the Community would almost certainly never be excluded from participation as interest groups might be in a single nation, they could be isolated and barred from the informal stages of policymaking. Participation in bargaining and coalition formation have become crucial now that unanimity is no longer required, and a number of possible winning coalitions exist on any policy. Nations may become willing to accommodate to others to ensure that they will continue to have access to the early and often determinative stages of negotiations and that they will be consulted throughout the policymaking process. Bargaining too implacably for national interest under majority rule may ultimately produce formal inclusion for a nation, but exclusion when it counts the

87. The pattern of decisionmaking, the so-called package deals, was similar to the pattern of logrolling noted in many legislative bodies. While useful in assembling coalitions, it is an expensive way to make public policy.

88. Fritz W. Scharpf, "The Joint-Decision Trap: Lessons from German Federalism and European Integration," *Public Administration*, vol. 66 (Autumn 1988), pp. 239–78.

89. Heisler, with Kvavik, "Patterns of European Politics."

most. In some instances unanimity is still required, especially in responding to the European Parliament, but the changes in the rules are sufficient to produce some rethinking of the policymaking dynamics within Europe.

It could be argued that the events surrounding the Milan summit constituted a first step toward instituting this type of political system within the Community. At that summit it became clear that Britain was taking somewhat different positions from the other member countries and was running the risk of becoming isolated within the EC, particularly in view of the continuing cooperation of France and Germany in Community affairs.[90] Although by no means becoming a committed European unionist overnight, Margaret Thatcher did begin to modify her more extreme stances and to play a more positive and conciliatory role. Some evidence shows that Greece, recognizing the risk of isolation, has also modified some of its more extreme positions toward the single market.

If this model of politics is appropriate for the Community, it will feed back into at least one of the institutional decisionmaking processes discussed earlier. That is, it will make coalition formation within the Community seem much more like coalition politics in a nation-state. Further, as Heisler and Kvavik argue, the European Polity model is "co-optive"; a central component of the dynamic is that the actors have more to gain by being co-opted into the encompassing system than they have to gain by going it alone.[91] As Wessels has argued, participation in the EC can be analyzed in terms of the costs and benefits of national involvement, with an increasing number of decisionmaking situations within the Community becoming positive-sum games.[92] Likewise, some of the pressures for 1992 have come from widely publicized reports of projected large-scale economic benefits arising from full integration.[93] The one country that has appeared to question this positive balance most often is Britain, but the events previously mentioned, and the elections of 1989, tend to make that questioning less vigorous. Moreover, once involved, actors must bear some responsibility for the actions taken by the political unit—participation is traded for complicity in decisions. This complicity means that

90. Haig Simonian, *The Privileged Partnership: Franco-German Relations in the European Community, 1969–1984* (Oxford: Clarendon Press, 1985).

91. Heisler, with Kvavik, "Patterns of European Politics."

92. Wessels, "Dynamics of Administrative Interactions."

93. Paolo Cecchini, with Michael Catinat and Alexis Jacquemin, *The European Challenge, 1992: The Benefits of a Single Market* (Aldershot: Gower, 1988).

national governments, to be credible, will have few options of returning home and blaming Brussels—they are now a part of Brussels even more than in the past.

The European Polity model diverges in part from the bureaucratic politics model described next. It depends more on the individual nation-states' deciding that participation in the system is a benefit for them, or at least a greater benefit than the costs of membership. They therefore need to make overt choices about continued involvement in, and acceptance of, the policy decisions made within the EC. Whereas the bureaucratic politics style of governing, and the regulatory policies associated with it, seeks to disguise decisions and obfuscate the values inherent in choices, the European Polity model is more political, stressing understanding and making decisions about participation and acquiescence. It may be that policymaking in the EC oscillates between large-scale politics and small-scale addition of regulation, and that no single model is able to capture all the motives and processes required to build Europe.

Bureaucratic Politics

A third, and very promising, approach to understanding policymaking dynamics within the institutions of the European Community is bureaucratic politics. This approach is closely linked with many ideas such as the picket-fence federalism mentioned earlier, but it considers the linkages existing within a policy area from the perspective of the bureaucratic organizations rather than from that of the national or subnational governments. In this approach, made popular by Graham Allison, among others, for international politics, and Anthony Downs, among others, for domestic politics, the component units of a government administrative apparatus are assumed to be quasi-autonomous actors with their own goals, which they pursue through the policymaking process.[94] Many or most of those goals may be held in common with other organizations in government, though some are confined to a particular organization. All, or almost all, the organizations will assume they are indeed serving the public interest by pursuing their more individualized goals. Some organization goals are *purposive*, being concerned with achieving policy goals (including in this case achieving greater integration within the EC), while other goals may

94. Graham T. Allison, *The Essence of Decision: Explaining the Cuban Missile Crisis* (Little, Brown, 1971); and Anthony Downs, *Inside Bureaucracy* (Little, Brown, 1967).

be *reflexive*, having to do primarily with enhancing the power and prestige (or at a minimum the survival) of the organization itself.[95] With reflexive goals it may be difficult to distinguish the individual goals of key members from the collective goals of their organizations.

For the European Community, bureaucratic politics may be occurring on two levels. The first is that of the principal institutions—the Council of Ministers, the European Commission, and the European Parliament— taken as a whole. The goals pursued by some institutions may be attainable only if certain changes occur in the structure of the Community. If the Parliament is to achieve greater power, for example, it may be successful only if the EC itself obtains greater power vis-à-vis national governments, and there is consequently an even greater need to fill the democratic deficit of the Community. Similarly, the Commission may perceive the Council members as its natural rival for power and authority within the Community, sensing that they are playing a "zero-sum" bureaucratic game, with movements toward or away from greater European unification as their intermediate goal. In short, if the bureaucratic politics model is to be applied to interorganizational interactions and change, the analyst must be clear when purposive and reflexive goals are being pursued (if the two types can be separated), and what the main actors are attempting to gain through their interactions with other institutions.

In this process the president of the Commission has become central to European policymaking, especially during the presidency of Jacques Delors.[96] From the perspective of bureaucratic politics, the question arises whether the institutional goals of the presidency are compatible with specific policy goals. By trying to focus attention on himself, the power of the Commission, and very broad goals of supranationalism, the president may be able to minimize the potential national opposition to specific policy initiatives within the Council. Also, focusing on the presidency may help reduce fragmentation within the Commission itself; Delors seems to have accepted a central role at times to the exclusion of other members of the Commission.[97] For example, he has issued some Commission papers almost without prior consultation with other commissioners and has made some

95. Lawrence B. Mohr, "The Concept of Organizational Goal," *American Political Science Review*, vol. 67 (June 1973), pp. 470–81.

96. Previous presidents also helped to define the nature and speed of progress toward European solutions to policy problems. Guy de Bassompierre, *Changing the Guard in Brussels: An Insider's View of the EC Presidency* (New York: Praeger, 1988).

97. See Lucy Kellaway, "Delors Shines amid a Bunch of Managers Rather Than Thinkers," *Financial Times*, January 3, 1991, p. 3.

important economic policy issues his concern rather than the concern of the commissioner nominally in charge of economic affairs. Such focus on the president can minimize the balkanization of the European bureaucracy brought about by its apparent concentration on functional policies.[98] But as with any application of the bureaucratic politics model, these assumptions impute motives to leaders that may not exist, and assume greater rationality in the pursuit of those motives than may be present. Still, many would argue that EC presidents must take leading roles as institutional actors and must pursue both institutional goals of unity and coherence and more specific policy goals.

The president of the Commission is not the only (or perhaps even the main) actor in the game of bureaucratic politics; coalition formation over issues and agendas is an important aspect of that game. Here the second level of bureaucratic politics in the EC begins to emerge, the politics of functional policy areas. In organizational terms each of these policy areas is populated with its allotment of organizations—Directorates and their commissioners, European Parliament committees—and with representatives of the affected interests. As was discussed earlier, forming coalitions is crucial for determining the final shape of European policies. Given the decentralized structure of policymaking in Europe, with multiple actors at the European level and even more at the national level, it should not be surprising if policies were the product of loosely organized and flexible policy communities. Moreover, once a coalition can be formed within the policy area, another must be constructed across the institutions of the Community as well as with the relevant portions of the national government.

There are several very important features of the fragmentation of policymaking and politics in Community affairs. First, coalition formation and bargaining occur at several points throughout the policy process: between interest groups and the functional ministry in the nation-state, and between those groups, Europewide interest groups, and the relevant Directorate(s)-General in Brussels.[99] Extensive discussions must also take place

98. This is not the only way, however. "Comitologie," or the development of numerous advisory and oversight committees in the Council, is another way to ensure some control over the powers of the Commission. The basic framework for this oversight is provided in *Official Journal of the European Communities*, L 197, vol. 30 (July 18, 1987), pp. 33–35.

99. Wessels, "Dynamics of Administrative Interactions"; and Philip A. Butt, "Pressure Groups in the European Community and Informal Institutional Arrangements," in Rita Beuter and Panos Taskaloyannis, eds., *Experiences in Regional Cooperation: Prepared in the Framework of EC-ASEAN Cooperation* (Maastricht: European Institute of Public Administration, 1987).

within the Commission itself, since first a policy must be allocated among commissioners and Directorates and then coordination among policies must be achieved. Consultations are often required with the advisory committees organized by the Commission for various policy areas.[100] Then, at both the national and supranational levels, there must be negotiations between functional government organizations and the rest of the government (cabinet and Commission, respectively). Discussions can then begin between the national government and the EC, at the functional or general political level, or both. Policymaking will be iterative, and preliminary decisions, the bargaining over policy ideas, and so forth, will flow throughout this system time and again. Such a fragmented arrangement for policymaking provides multiple points of access and may make coherent policymaking difficult. Whether or not the bureaucracy, either European or national, is the dominant player (and it often is), the policymaking process has the characteristics of decentralization and local control typical of the bureaucratic form of policymaking.[101] Institutionally, the actors will strive to preserve their own powers, perhaps even if it means reducing the capacity of the resulting arrangements to make "good" policy for the Community as a whole.

Policymaking may be further fragmented by the increased powers of the European Parliament.[102] First, adding second-reading and "cooperation" provisions (as discussed earlier) makes the Parliament a player to be reckoned with in almost all policy decisions, and its role will be enhanced once the Maastricht treaty goes into effect. If nothing else, the majority of the Parliament may be able to form blocking coalitions with other parties (for example, with a single nation-state, where unanimity is required to override parliamentary wishes). This at once makes decisionmaking more difficult and provides additional incentives for anyone seeking quick results to pursue action through bureaucratic channels (perhaps at home) rather than through the more overtly politicized channels. Of course, that option is not available for all issues, but it may be for many, and a seemingly slower accretion of decisions may in the long run be faster than accretion through dramatic political action.

100. Economic and Social Committee of the European Communities, *Community Advisory Committees for the Representation of Socio-Economic Interests: The Machinery for the Consultation and Participation of Socio-Economic Interests in Community Decision-Making* (Farnborough: Saxon House, 1980).

101. Scharpf, "Joint-Decision Trap."

102. Fitzmaurice, "An Analysis," pp. 389–400.

The Council of Ministers retains (now after consultation with the Parliament) the final powers of decision within the Community, but the Commission has an increasing number of weapons and apparently a growing influence. This is in part due to the sheer volume of decisions that must now be processed—especially in preparation for 1992. Although the Council is a well-articulated structure and with its working groups can monitor the activities of the Commission, it still cannot compete with the expertise at the disposal of the Commission and its Directorates. Also, the Commission sets the agenda for decision, albeit after extensive discussion with the relevant national and European actors. The linkages that the Directorates have with national governments tend to be functionally specific, so that professional and technical criteria often guide decisions more than the national concerns which may arise in the Council. This tendency may become more the norm as standards for integration shift from harmonization to mutual recognition. Finally, the Commission can claim the moral high ground of being the defenders of Europe and of being above national concerns.

The shift toward bureaucratic politics and policymaking in the Community also has important implications for the kind of policies that will be made for Europe. As I have argued, decisionmaking in the Commission is a crucial element of policymaking in the EC, and the Commission's apparent increasing power makes the transition toward a single market easier. In essence, attention has shifted from large-scale budgetary issues (from the beginning of the British claims for renegotiation of contributions in 1979 through the mid-1980s) toward regulatory issues and indirect interventions.[103] Commission regulations over competition policy and Court cases on different topics have supplanted the budget as the most visible concern in Brussels, although that could change again. Such an emphasis on regulatory policymaking has the advantage of obscuring who wins and who loses in the policies; the outcomes are uncertain and vary widely within individual countries.[104] Issues of revenue collection and spending, in contrast, make redistributive issues readily apparent to national participants. Relying on bureaucratic decisionmaking and regulative

103. Geoffrey Denton, "Re-structuring the EC Budget: Implications of the Fontainebleau Agreement," *Journal of Common Market Studies*, vol. 23 (December 1984), pp. 117–40; and William Nicoll, "From Rejection to Repudiation: EC Budgetary Affairs in 1985," *Journal of Common Market Studies*, vol. 25 (September 1986), pp. 31–49.

104. This is a familiar argument of Theodore J. Lowi, "Four Systems of Policy, Politics, and Choice," *Public Administration Review*, vol. 32 (July–August 1972), pp. 298–310.

rulemaking should, all else being equal, make the transition to 1992 less divisive.

Although less divisive, rulemaking through the bureaucracy may not necessarily produce the "best" objective policy decisions for Europe or Europeans. If the EC is indeed engaging at all in the fragmented policymaking described above, its policymaking is beginning to resemble that of American government. The traditional "iron triangles" in American politics may have been replaced by "big sloppy hexagons," with a wider range of interests represented in policy decisions, but the tendency to subdivide policies remains.[105] In the European context such fragmentation is heightened by the shift from harmonization to mutual recognition of policies and standards as the criterion for having attained integration. No longer will a common European standard necessarily prevail if each member country can agree to accept the laws and standards of the others. Furthermore, with decisionmaking through qualified majorities there will be less need to package decisions to produce agreement, so that another cross-check on policy may be undermined. Since policymaking is fragmented among the policy communities within the EC itself, and further fragmented among national policymaking systems, policymaking may now be somewhat easier, but be less effective in producing coherence and uniformity. The political question this raises is, what are the appropriate trade-offs between the values of simply making decisions that are "European" versus the value of making the best possible decisions in the name of Europe?

Scharpf's characterization of the "joint-decision trap" in European policymaking also points to the problem of coherence in decisionmaking.[106] Scharpf argues that because of the need to obtain agreement between at least two levels of government, European policymaking, like that of Germany and other federal systems, tends to produce suboptimal decisions. This problem is exacerbated when unanimity is required among the constituent units before a decision can be reached. According to Scharpf, this pattern of joint decisionmaking enables those units to extract resources from the center, with a resulting high level of cost relative to output in the system as a whole and incoherent policies adopted to satisfy particular constituencies. The powers of the Commission and its component units to structure the agenda for decisionmaking may be understated in this

105. Charles O. Jones, *The United States Congress: People, Place, and Policy* (Homewood, Ill.: Dorsey Press, 1982).
106. Scharpf, "Joint-Decision Trap."

analysis, and the move to qualified majority voting may also help alleviate some of the worst problems. This analytic perspective does raise, however, interesting and important questions about the institutional dynamics of European policymaking.

Finally, to return to the "games" metaphor used earlier, one can see a number of games nested within the decisionmaking process.[107] At the largest level, nation-states play games to gain as much as possible in financial and policy terms, while the European institutions try to press their common agendas against those of the nation-states. Within each of the European institutions, functional differentiation results in contests over the allocation of money and policymaking attention. Fragmentation may further result in policy patterns that are not well coordinated unless the president or the Commission as a whole can intervene. After decisions are made at the European level, the interactions between EC institutions and the member states (and interest groups) begin again, because strategies for implementation must be developed. In short, policymaking within Europe is highly differentiated and functionally specific. Although the great decisions about Europe may be made at the level of prime ministers, much of what happens depends on less glamorous bureaucratic interaction and bargaining.

Conclusion

Two observations summarize the argument of this chapter. First, institutions do matter. The formal institutions established by the Treaty of Rome and other basic agreements, and the rules governing the relationships of those institutions, have established the range of action for the European Community. The complexity built into the institutional relationships has been increased by the structural elaboration needed to handle increased workloads, the increased pace of movement toward a single market, and the far-reaching decisions taken at Maastricht. These institutions may also help define the possibility of movement toward a closer political bond such as federalism. As much as or more than theoretical devices like functionalism, the institutional relationships within the EC have defined the pace of integration and the nature of the emerging European political and economic system. The institutions are not static

107. Tsebelis, *Nested Games.*

structures processing demands from the outside; they themselves provide a dynamic of change within the Community.

Second, institutions do not matter too much. They may only establish the bounds within which individuals and groups function. Such changes in the institutional rules of the game as going from unanimity to qualified majorities for most decisions will matter insofar as the actors permit them to matter. If the preexisting patterns of decisionmaking persist (as with the Luxembourg Compromise in 1966), such changes will not make much difference. In particular, there is no institutional way to predict the influence of individual leaders in moving the process of integration forward, or retarding it. Apparently the use of qualified majority voting has had the desired effect, and perhaps an even greater effect than anticipated. But the complex patterns of consultation and bureaucratic involvement in policymaking that have been created could not have been predicted adequately from the formal institutional patterns. Institutions do matter, but so do individual policymakers and informal understandings among the staff of the institutions.

Chapter 4

The European Court of Justice

MARTIN SHAPIRO

THE EUROPEAN Court of Justice has played a crucial role in shaping the European Community. During long years in which the political development of the Community seemed to have ground to a halt, it was the Court that kept alive the vision of the Community as something more than a trade alliance. In a sense, the Court created the present-day Community; it declared the Treaty of Rome to be not just a treaty but a constitutional instrument that obliged individual citizens and national government officials to abide by those provisions that were enforceable through their normal judicial processes. A treaty among individual sovereign states was transformed through international law into constitutional and legal obligations directly binding on citizens. Moreover, these obligations took priority over conflicting legal obligations derived from the laws of the members. Although the word was not used, authority to make laws binding directly on all individuals and superior to all other laws is usually said to be *sovereign*. Thus, not simply in the fancy language of modern political theory, but in a very real and concrete sense, the Court of Justice constituted the European Community.

Other organs of the Community have now taken over from the Court much of its constitution-building role. Many of the Court's important future decisions will seem somewhat more routine elaborations of constitutional law or even "smaller" applications of administrative and regulatory law. As the administrative and regulatory powers of Europe move increasingly from member states to the Community, it would be foolish for students of the Community to repeat the earlier mistake of Americanists and ignore a court because it appears to make small, technical decisions embedded in the mysterious administrative and regulatory "lawyers' " law. Much policymaking power is vested in a court empowered to review the legality of agency actions and regulations. To understand policymaking, one must hunt where the ducks are—even if they are in the deep thickets of the law.

Foundations of the European Court of Justice

The several treaties establishing the European Community provide for a Court of Justice and for the judicial review of Community acts and those of member states. The Court consists of one judge from each of the twelve member states plus one additional judge and five advocates general who advise the sitting judges on how they should decide cases but do not themselves participate directly in the decisionmaking. The member states must agree unanimously on the membership of the court. Once appointed, however, the judges do not serve as representatives of their states. The Court is divided into a number of chambers for hearing cases of lesser importance. Major cases are decided by the full Court; dissents and votes are not reported. The opinions, together with the addresses of the advocates general to the Court, build up a large and influential body of case law.[1]

The European Commission, the Council of Ministers, and the European Parliament may challenge the legality of one another's acts without the need to show any particular injury. Each organ of the Community may also judicially challenge a failure by another to act when required to do so by the treaties.[2] Member states, too, may challenge acts of the Community organs by bringing a variety of actions before the Court.[3] The actions need not meet any requirements of particularized injury or involvement and so may challenge either in the abstract or in the context of particular disputes.

1. For a leading case in which the Court invalidated an act of a Community organ, on the ground that it was in conflict with the treaties, see *Jean Reyners* v. *Belgian State*, Case 2/74 (1974) ECR 631. Precisely because of the absence of dissenting opinions and recorded votes, it is extremely difficult to track the influence of individual judges' policy preferences and political philosophies on the institutional output of the Court. For this reason, I tend to write in terms of the Court, not the judges, but I do not mean to imply that judging in the Community, any more than elsewhere, is impersonal or entirely objective.

2. Koenraad Lenaerts, *Le Juge et la Constitution aux Etats-Unis d'Amérique et dans l'Ordre Juridique Européen* (Brussels: Bruylant, 1988), p. 296.

3. Lenaerts, *Le Juge et la Constitution*, p. 302.

Individuals are more limited in their capacity to invoke review. They may not seek such review in the abstract, but only where they can show some particularized, individual detriment flowing from a Community act. Such concrete review may arise directly by an individual challenge to the application of a Community act or indirectly where the validity of a Community act becomes an issue in a suit in a national court between individual parties or between a government and an individual. In all instances in which an individual claim is involved, a Court of Justice decision against the legality of a Community act only has the effect of invalidating the application of that act, or the rules or other legal consequences flowing from it, to the challenging individual. Where the individual challenge to a Community act has arisen in litigation in a national court, the Court of Justice will provide review only in the form of a binding rule to the national court as to the proper interpretation of the treaties; the Court does not make an explicit decision about the case. One of the most important functions of the Court's review is to establish uniform interpretations of Community legislation. [4]

Articles 169 and 170 of the Treaty of Rome provide that the Commission or a member state may bring an action in the Court of Justice against another member state for violating its obligations under the treaty. Article 171 provides that a member state that has been found by the Court to have failed to meet its treaty obligations must comply with the Court's judgment. In actual practice the Court has ranged from very general judgments of noncompliance to very detailed specifications of what the member state would have to do to comply. The Court may not, however, actually invalidate a member-state statute or administrative act as the U.S. Supreme Court can do under the supremacy clause. It is up to the member state to amend its own statutes or administrative regulations and practices. There are notable instances in which states have not done so.

Actions under articles 169 and 170 are typically like American cases, for the Commission or member state will usually be challenging not the offending member state's statute or administrative regulation in the abstract but the statute's application to a particular class of business transactions or tax payments. The Commission or claimant member state does not have to meet the kinds of "standing" requirements that would be

4. See Jürgen Schwarze, *The Role of the European Court of Justice (ECJ) in the Interpretation of Uniform Law among the Member States of the European Community* (Baden-Baden: Nomos, 1988).

imposed on an individual, such as showing particular injury or exhausting administrative remedies.

The *Marbury* v. *Madison* of the European Court is not the establishment of review, but the movement of the review of member-state acts from the sphere of international law to that of constitutional law. The Court has declared that through their treaties the member states have surrendered some of their sovereignty to the Community. The treaties, therefore, are not simply agreements under international law but create a constitutional regime, and the treaties themselves, as well as the Community acts done under their authority, take precedence over the domestic law of the members and have "direct effect," that is, pass directly into the domestic law of the member states without the need of any independent, intervening action on their part.[5] Given the constitutional status of Community law, it is that law which must prevail in such a conflict.

It is not the conversion of the treaties into a constitution or the direct-effect doctrine that alone creates the Court of Justice's powers of judicial review; rather, it is the existence of those Court-announced doctrines in conjunction with article 177 of the Treaty of Rome. Article 177 provides that should a question of Community law arise in the course of an ordinary lawsuit in a national court, that national court can apply to the Court of Justice for a preliminary ruling. Highest national courts have an obligation to do so; lower national courts may do so. In such a preliminary ruling, the Court of Justice may advise the national court of the proper interpretation of Community law. In theory, such a ruling is never an actual invalidation of any national law, regulation, or administrative action, but only an "interpretation" of the treaties to guide a national court in the decision of a particular case. In practice, however, the Court of Justice may render, in the form of a preliminary ruling, a judgment of "unconstitutionality" of a national statute, regulation, or administrative decision (or, as already mentioned, of any act of the Community itself). Only the national court, not the litigating parties, may seek a ruling based on article 177, and, if it does, it is bound by the resultant interpretation. Still, rulings under the article do not decide cases; only national courts can do that.

In the European Parliament's draft of what became the Single European Act (SEA), provision was made for individuals to seek Court of Justice review of national courts' refusals to invoke article 177 and their failures

5. The major cases are 26/62, *Van Gend en Loos* v. *Nederlandse Administratie der Belastingen* (1963) ECR 1, and *Costa* v. *ENEL* (1964) ECR 585. Community *directives* have direct effect on member-state governments, but because they are written in general language,

to properly follow such rulings when those courts had applied. Significantly, that provision was dropped before the SEA was accepted.[6] Community members still are not prepared to convey direct judicial supremacy over their own courts to the Court of Justice.

The direct-effect doctrine combined with article 177 also extends the Court's powers to purely private—that is, nongovernmental—actions that violate the treaties. The Court has ruled that the treaty provisions directly bind private citizens and enterprises of member states. Thus, in the course of regular lawsuits in national courts, individuals may claim that their legal rights under those treaty provisions that provide for direct effect and under the Community regulations (but not directives) that enforce those provisions have been violated by other individuals. Article 177 offers a channel for referring such claims to the European Court. The success of federalism, or vertical review, has therefore depended heavily on the behavior of national courts and particularly of "lower" national courts. Under the direct-effect doctrine, national trial and intermediate appellate courts, not just the highest national courts, may invoke article 177. It has come as something of a surprise that lower-court judges have so frequently invoked the article, thus enhancing the power of the Court of Justice and detracting from that of their own national high courts, given that such judges must attend to their career prospects within hierarchically organized national judicial systems.

During the 1960s and 1970s the Court was clearly the most energetically forward-thrusting element of the Community. In this period the Commission and the Court often seemed to form a working alliance, and the Commission sought to accentuate the positive by highlighting the role of the Court. The Court itself spoke the brave language of teleological interpretation. And in some areas, such as member-state tax measures, which really were disguised tariffs or subsidies to internal industries, the Court made great progress toward integration.[7] Nevertheless, much of the actual legal doctrine created by the Court in these decades was relatively modest and set few limits, either substantive or procedural, on the organs

---

they only have direct effect on individuals through their implementation in member-state regulations. Community *regulations*, which are detailed, have direct effect on individuals within member states.

6. Anthony Arnull, "European Communities: 2. Institutional and Jurisdictional Questions: The Single European Act," *Current Survey of the European Communities* (Spring 1989), p. 359.

7. Jules Lonbay, "The Single European Act," *Boston College International and Comparative Law Review*, vol. 11 (1988), p. 47.

of national and Community government. Bold establishment but modest application of the tenets of constitutional judicial review seems to be the pattern of the Court.

Free Movement of Goods

Clauses governing the free movement of goods are the very heart of the Community. Much of the pessimism about the Community in the 1960s and 1970s stemmed from the facility with which many member states replaced tariffs with other barriers to Community-wide trade. From both the wording of the treaties and the Community's own case law, at the behest of either the Commission or private litigants, the Court was able to declare unlawful many national tax and subsidy arrangements that it equated with tariff protections. The member states were, however, adept at employing national health, safety, and consumer-protection regulations, as well as other "technical standards," to protect national markets. Even if the French found it increasingly difficult to levy a tax on imported German refrigerators, or indirectly subsidize French refrigerator makers, they could still write national standards for wiring or shelf arrangement that German refrigerators did not meet. Such regulations become the principal barriers to the free movement of goods.

The most obvious response to these national ploys was to exercise the harmonization provisions of the treaties, which provided a mechanism through which conflicts among the various national product regulations and standards could be eliminated. A second response involved the even more communitarian mode of writing single Europeanwide standards. Both options required vigorous action and mutual cooperation by the Commission and Council of Ministers. Implementation, however, did not go well for several reasons. First, just as the U.S. Occupational Safety and Health Administration and Environmental Protection Agency discovered, the Commission found that setting standards for products in a modern, capitalist, industrial economy is extremely difficult and time consuming. Even in a single nation there are many producing, consuming, and employee groups with differing interests. It is often difficult or impossible to obtain the data for determining what products exist and how safe or how durable they are. Moreover, the products themselves and the production technology often change so rapidly that standards obsolesce in the process of producing them. Where ten or more nations are involved, these problems multiply. Second, the Council had established specialized working committees with which the Commission had to cooperate in standard setting. This second technical bureaucracy, responsible to a Council whose members were each responsible to their individual national governments, aggravated the process. Finally the Council, which ultimately had to approve harmonization measures and enact Community-wide standards, was operating under a rule of unanimity. In the end, little "harmonization" was achieved and few Community-wide standards were even drafted, let alone enacted.

In its turn, the Court weighed in on the product standards issue. In surely the best known of the Court's decisions, aside from those that declared its judicial review powers, *Cassis de Dijon*,[8] the Court held that receiving nations must accept the standards of the producing nation. A product lawfully produced and marketed in one member state must have access to the others. Refusal to do so violates the clause providing for the free movement of goods. Thus the Court cut through the whole harmonization and standard-setting tangle by establishing this principle of "mutual recognition."[9] Of course, the Court could not declare an absolute prohibition. Peculiar local conditions and needs might sometimes provide a legitimate justification for enforcing a national standard, even when its effect was to disadvantage or preclude imported goods. *Cassis* provides for such exceptions when national governments can make a case for them.

Another area of doctrine impinges on and supplements the *Cassis* decision. To American constitutional scholars it is familiar as the "negative" or "dormant" commerce clause. The European treaties provide that the organs of the Community shall legislate to achieve free movement of goods. If the Community has so legislated, conflicting national legislation is condemned. Article 36 of the Treaty of Rome provides, however, that the free movement of goods "shall not preclude prohibitions or restrictions on imports . . . justified on grounds of public morality, public policy or public security; the protection of health and life of humans, animals or plants; the protection of national treasures. . .; or the protection of industrial and commercial property. Such . . . restrictions shall not, however, constitute a means of arbitrary discrimination or a disguised restriction on

8. *Rowe-Zentral AG* v. *Bundesmonopolverwaltung für Branntwein*, Case 120/78 (1979) ECR 649.
9. Renaud Dehousse, "The Institutional Dimension of the Internal Market Programme" (Florence: European University Institute, 1989), pp. 5–18.

trade between Member States." The Court itself added in its case law that national restrictions on imports might be justified if they were based on "imperative requirements."[10]

If the Community has not legislated on free movement, to what extent may the member states pass laws or regulations that, in the pursuit of health, safety, and welfare goals, impinge upon it? If the Community has legislated on a particular trade area, but in a fragmentary rather than a comprehensive way, may member-state regulations coexist with Community-wide regulations? And even if the Community has legislated comprehensively, when can the member state invoke article 36? To use the American language, in a series of cases, the Court granted the member states wide concurrent powers to regulate so long as their regulations did not "discriminate." It allowed nondiscriminatory state regulation to coexist with Community regulation whenever the Court did not perceive a Community intent to "preempt" the field in its regulations, that is, to totally exclude state regulation. And it rarely found that the Community had preempted.[11]

Again to use American language, the Court's operating test of both "discrimination" and "preemption" was composed in part of judicial attempts to discern the actual intent of the enactors and in part of a "balancing" standard. Where it was clear from the historical context that the member state was regulating to disadvantage foreign goods, then there was discrimination. Where the historical context did not give an answer, the Court imputed discrimination to the member state when the burden on free movement outweighed whatever interest in local health, safety, morals, or welfare the member state purported to be pursuing by its regulation.

As American constitutional scholars know, whenever a court moves toward such a balancing standard, a supplementary standard almost inevitably arises, which may be called the "least," or "minimum-means," test. Where a state regulation impedes interstate commerce but also achieves legitimate local goals, such as health protection, then American courts will ask: is the local goal achieved by those means that are least destructive to

10. The "imperative requirements" doctrine may or may not have been narrowed or eliminated by the SEA. See C.D. Ehlerman, "The Internal Market following the Single European Act," *Common Market Law Review*, vol. 24 (September 1987), p. 393; and Lonbay, "Single European Act," pp. 66–67. The SEA clearly adds protection of the environment and the working environment to the list of values justifying national limitations in imports.

11. Lonbay, "Single European Act," pp. 44–45.

free commerce? If the court can conceive of less damaging means, then the court will find that the state government has discriminated. Borrowing a well-known concept from the general body of continental law, Europeans call this balancing, least-means approach the test of "proportionality."[12] A member state may not adopt a means of pursuing its legitimate interests that disproportionally hampers the free movement of goods, even when that state has not overtly discriminated against other member states or has not enacted rules that conflict with Community rules or entered areas preempted by Community regulation.

This full body of jurisprudence gives enormous discretion to judges. Whether or not a member state really was discriminating and whether or not the Community really was preempting are often judgment calls. No state is going to say openly it is discriminating, and Community legislation often does not say explicitly whether it has or has not preempted. Under the doctrine of proportionality, just how much benefit to the health and welfare of a locality outweighs just how much "incidental" impedance to the free movement of goods? There is no simple, objective way of weighing the two pounds of reduced cancer risk to Frenchmen against the eight pounds of salami that Italy is blocked from selling to France. Proportionality is by its very nature in the eye of the beholder.

Thus *Cassis* comes very close to saying that each importing state must defer to the product standards of the producing state unless it can give the European Court a convincing reason for enforcing its own standards on the goods seeking entry. (The Court also employs the same doctrines to enforce other parts of the treaties, such as article 59 on the free movement of services and the right of "establishment.")[13] It is the *Cassis* approach to product standards that became the center of the initiative called the 1992 process. Central to the Single European Act are articles 13 and 14, which became articles 8a and 8b of the Treaty of Rome and provide that "the Community shall adopt measures with the aim of progressively establishing the internal market [by] 31 December 1992. . . . The internal market shall comprise an area without internal frontiers in which the free movement of goods, persons, services and capital is ensured in accordance with the provisions of this Treaty."

In order to achieve "the internal market," articles 18 and 19 of the SEA create articles 100a and 100b of the Treaty of Rome and specify a detailed

12. Joseph H. H. Weiler, "Eurocracy and Distrust," *Washington Law Review*, vol. 61 (April 1986), pp. 1131–32.
13. Lonbay, "Single European Act," p. 50.

process for dismantling obstructive national product standards and other devices. These articles instruct the Commission to draw up an inventory of national regulations impinging on the internal market. In the meantime, the Commission is to have sought to draft measures for the "approximation" or harmonization of national regulations impinging on the internal market. Such harmonization measures are now to be enacted by the Council of Ministers, not under a unanimity rule but by qualified majority. By 1992, where unharmonized national regulations still appear on the Commission's inventory, the Council, by qualified majority vote, may decree that "the provisions in force in a Member State must be recognized as being equivalent to those applied by another Member State." In other words, where the Commission and Council do not succeed by the end of 1992 in writing Community-wide product and other standards, then the Council, by qualified majority vote, may decree what *Cassis* already holds, that a receiving state must accept goods manufactured and marketed under the laws of the sending state.

Like *Cassis*, articles 100a and 100b also provide for exceptions. First of all, the qualified majority rule does not apply to harmonization measures for fiscal matters, free movement of persons, or "rights and interests of employed persons." Harmonization in these areas still requires Council unanimity. In other words, "internal market" largely means the free movement of goods and services. Second, a member state that wishes to persist in applying its national standards, and has good, "proportional" reasons of the kind required in *Cassis*, must notify the Commission of its continued national standards. Moreover, article 100a specifically provides that harmonization measures may include clauses specifically authorizing such exceptional national regulations. But the Commission must determine whether national regulations are legitimate or discriminatory.

Clearly what the Single European Act does is create a risk, and manipulate that risk in order to achieve greater economic integration. The risk is familiar in all federal states as the "race to the bottom." If each state must admit the product of every other, whatever state has the lowest standards for a particular product ought to become the situs for most Community production of that product. In a price-competitive market, the least-regulated product should become the cheapest and thus the most purchased. Faced with this prospect, member states desiring higher standards will be motivated to accept harmonization and Community-wide standards. They now need only a qualified majority rather than unanimity to achieve that goal. Again judging from American experience, members wishing to speed up this process may prefer enactment of private standard settings, and the Single European Act contemplates this strategy.[14] Often a private standard-setting group, like Underwriters Laboratories or a trade association, can arrive at a draft standard more quickly than a government bureaucracy. And rather than settle for the lowest standard, the Commission and the Council may endorse the official adoption of such drafts establishing basic, "essential" European health and safety standards.[15]

Where harmonization does not occur, however, the race to the bottom may heat up the business of the Court. Given the inertia of regulatory regimes everywhere, it is unlikely that more "advanced" nations will quickly lower their product standards. Disadvantaged national producers may press governments both to lower their domestic standards in the long run and to enforce existing standards, or enact new ones, in the short run, claiming that such enforcements qualify under the exceptions specified in the Court's case law and in the treaties as supplemented by the Single European Act. If national standards are enforced so as to limit imports, litigation will almost certainly result—litigation in which the Court wields considerable discretion under its discrimination approach and proportionality doctrine.

Indeed, the Single European Act explicitly invites such judicial supervision. The act specifically authorizes the Commission to challenge in the Court national regulations that do not meet articles 30–36's free-movement criteria or qualify for their exceptions favoring national regulation for legitimate health, safety, environmental, and welfare purposes. The provisions of the SEA that authorize member states to enact temporary measures derogating from the harmonization "for one or more of the noneconomic reasons referred to in article 36" explicitly empower the Commission and member states to directly challenge such derogations before the Court. Such challenges will, of course, be decided under the Court's broad proportionality discretion.[16]

As in the American cases involving the negative commerce clause, the European Court's decisions regarding free movement of goods are not easily characterized substantively, except to say that the Court has granted itself broad discretion and issued opinions that go in all directions. After establishing its free-trade principles, and most particularly the doctrine of mutual recognition in *Cassis*, the Court has tended to allow the member

14. Dehousse, "Institutional Dimension," pp. 29–31.
15. Lonbay, "Single European Act," p. 46.
16. Dehousse, "Institutional Dimension," p. 18.

states broad leeway and the benefit of the doubt on proportionality. Given current levels of concern over health, safety, and the environment, states frequently make persuasive cases for all but overt discrimination. Yet, precisely because of the new emphasis and the legitimacy assigned to the *Cassis* approach by the 1992 measures, the Court cannot help but feel vindicated and supported. If 1992 means anything, it must be that everyone must now take the free movement of goods seriously. Against this background and with the legitimacy of the Court's *Cassis* approach singularly confirmed by the political process, member states probably should look forward to relatively low batting averages in defending nondeference to producing states' product standards. Indeed, even with the retreat from unanimous voting, the committee system promises slow going for harmonization and, therefore, at least in the short run, increased Court attempts to enforce the new *Cassis*-like regime and to enforce it more vigorously than when it was merely case-law doctrine.[17]

Deregulation and New Regulation

Much of the impetus for 1992 came from political and business elites. From their point of view, the crux of the integration process is deregulation, and it is hard to imagine 1992 having been initiated except for the swing away from socialism and toward free markets that occurred in the 1980s. Mutual recognition, as established in *Cassis* and adopted by the SEA, is massive deregulation, in the sense that producers will now face only one set of regulations, those of their home nation, rather than a dozen sets, one for each member state. Harmonization is deregulation in the same sense. Perhaps more important, when harmonization is driven by the threat of mutual recognition should harmonization attempts fail, then even achieved harmonizations will tend toward the low end of the potential regulatory spectrum. This tendency occurs because mutual recognition itself contains a strong potential for a rush to the bottom in which production will shift to the least-regulated nation. In the face of this threat, those participants in harmonization who desire the highest level of regulation should choose to moderate their demands in order to achieve harmonization and avoid mutual recognition. Qualified majority voting also reduces the ability of the most highly regulated states to use the threat of veto to push harmonization up to their standards. Thus, both

17. Dehousse, "Institutional Dimension," pp. 39–43.

harmonization and mutual recognition should lead to fewer sets of regulations and less severe regulation than previously imposed by the members with the highest regulatory standards. This tendency will, however, be countered by the increased environmental, health, and safety concerns felt worldwide. It remains to be seen to what extent the members with the lowest levels of current regulation will yield their potential advantages in economic development in order to achieve higher quality-of-life standards.

Yet the deregulatory thrust of 1992 is not nearly as strong as its initiators desired. Early drafts proposed that after 1992 all unharmonized national regulations impinging on the internal market would automatically shift to the mutual recognition, equivalent-effect regime. The final Single European Act provides that only by qualified majority vote may the Council order mutual recognition where harmonization has not occurred. And although article 100b(3) implies that the Council ought to finish its harmonization by the end of 1992, there does not appear to be any basis for bringing a legal action before the Court to compel it to do so.

American readers will hardly be unfamiliar with the argument that the 1980s were not simply a period of deregulation but one in which some regulatory regimes were eroding and others flourishing. Old-style market regulation in which regulatory statutes granted certain interest groups legally guaranteed quasi-monopolist positions from which they drew rents (unearned income) was denounced. Trucking and airline regulation are the best-known examples. On the other hand, new-style regulation, designed to foster health, safety, and the environment, which was justified both deontologically and in the economic language of externalities, flourished. And it flourished particularly because it shifted the costs of public benefits to the private sector at a time when support for bigger government budgets and taxes had eroded. In short, old-style "economic" regulation was unmasked as a set of benefits to private interests at public expense, and new-style regulation was perceived by the naive as a set of public benefits at no one's expense and by the less naive as public benefits at the expense of private interests. The least naive might see the situation as one of public benefits at the expense of the consumer but benefits that the public wanted and was prepared to pay for as consumers, if not as taxpayers. Health, safety, and environmental regulation thus became the American equivalent of the European value-added tax.

American readers who are familiar with the "new" regulatory statutes will also be familiar with another phenomenon. Those statutes typically

contain highly aspirational language that appears to demand the achieve-
ment of an absolutely healthy, safe, and beautiful working and living
environment with no consideration of costs. More deeply buried in the
same statutes are vague language, exceptions, and hedges of myriad sorts
that allow some balancing of benefits and costs and some amelioration of
effects. If left unameliorated, the rapid implementation of many of the
regulatory goals would have rendered their putative beneficiaries jobless
and homeless. Much of this cautionary language is the product of regulated
groups that were not strong enough to block the legislation but were
strong enough to get some possible escape hatches. In the struggle
between the aspirational and the regulated, the frequent result was
compromise: vague statutory language. These complex, unclear, and
partly conflicting legislative pronouncements thus became treasuries of
potential statutory interpretation in which administrative and judicial
interpreters had wide leeway in deciding what the law really was. This
interpretative potential was enormously amplified because the statutes
frequently delegated vast rulemaking powers to administrative agencies.
Each rule had to be tested by reviewing courts as to its obedience to the
governing congressional statute, and each such test required a judicial
interpretation of the statute.

The internal market and other provisions of the SEA have exactly this
mix of "down with the old, up with the new" regulation and of aspiration
with exception. For example, there is a grand aspirational statement in
article 13 of the SEA (8a of the Treaty of Rome) establishing the internal
market; then comes a long series of fudge factors. Article 13 itself says that
the internal market is to be achieved "without prejudice to the other
provisions of this Treaty." Article 14 of the SEA (8b of the Treaty of Rome)
requires "balanced progress in all the sectors concerned." Then, article 15
(8c of the treaty) is one long hedge, allowing "derogations . . . of a
temporary nature and [with] . . . the least possible disturbance to the
functioning of the common market" to reduce the initial impact of the
internal market on the least economically advanced member states. Article
16 of the SEA amending article 57(2) of the Treaty of Rome provides a
special treatment for access to professions. Article 16(4) of the SEA com-
mands the Council of Ministers to achieve "the highest possible degree of
liberalization" of capital movements and requires unanimity rather than
qualified majority voting on capital-movement directives that constitute a
"step back" in such liberalization.

Article 18 and article 19 of the SEA establishing the new articles 100a and 100b of the Treaty of Rome first prescribe the new, easier, qualified-majority method of eliminating conflicting member-state regulations. No sooner is the new method stated than "fiscal" matters, "free movement of persons," and "rights and interests of employed persons" are excepted from the method. New article 100a(4) of the treaty then preserves the exceptions clause of old article 36, which allows states, even after harmonization, to continue a national regulation in order to further "public morality, public policy or public security [and] the protection of health and life of humans." Moreover, 100a(4) knocks down the old article 36 jurisprudence of the courts, which held that once harmonization had occurred the members could not write new national regulations under the exceptions clauses. Now members may write new exceptions even after harmonization occurs. If they invoke such an exception, however, the state must notify the Commission, and the Commission must determine whether the state act is discriminatory or a disguised restriction on trade. Either the Commission or a member state may then go directly to the Court of Justice to challenge the state action. Also, according to article 100a(5), such exceptions may be written directly into harmonization provisions as temporary measures. Article 100b(1) repeats the preservation of article 36 exceptions for mutual-recognition decrees. These provisions will undoubtedly be read by the Court as incorporating its own previous article 36 jurisprudence of nondiscrimination and proportionality.

Some, but by no means all, of this statutory stretching is a result of seeking to accommodate acceleration of the new regulation with deceleration of the old. Although the Community had already been active in environmental matters using some of the general provisions of the treaties, the Single European Act contains a whole new title (title VII) consisting of three articles (130r, s, and t) specifically mandating highly aspirational environmental policies for the Community and specifically permitting member states to go further than the Community. Article 100a(3) provides that in "health, safety, environmental protection and consumer protection," the Commission "will take as a base a high level of protection." Article 100a(4) adds to article 36 of the Treaty of Rome another basis on which a member state may apply national regulations contrary to harmonized standards, "protection of the environment or the working environment." And article 100a(5), echoing well-established Community law, refers to the article 36 exceptions as "non-economic reasons." In short, member states may not derogate from the internal market by persisting in old "economic" regulation that grants semimonopolies and rents to selfish interests, but may derogate when they want to achieve higher levels of the good new regulation protecting "non-economic" public interests in health, safety, and the environment.

Of course, the new regulations are really just as "economic" as the old. Much old bad monopoly granting can be easily disguised as new wonderful greening, and, unsurprisingly, uncertainties in the new language are enormous. How high is "the highest possible degree" or "a high level"? What is "balanced progress"? What measures on capital movements are "step[s] back" rather than steps forward? Are measures about "the working environment" also measures about "interests of employed persons"?

It is possible that the new qualified majority voting provisions and other factors will lead to a heyday of Commission–Council–member state cooperation on both harmonization and mutual-recognition decrees that contain few exceptions and are joyously followed by all the member states. The Commission White Paper that is the partner to the SEA contains 300 proposed harmonization measures—most of which fall under the qualified majority procedure. By mid-1989 the Council had enacted nearly half of these.[18] So the start is promising, but it is still unclear how many claims for national exception there will be. And the SEA specifically invites quick judicial review of such claims in the future. Moreover, in the past a major segment of the Court's caseload has involved allegations of faulty compliance by member states with Community directives quite apart from formal claims to exceptions.

Indeed, the problem of compliance has been serious enough that the SEA specifically addresses it. In the past, harmonization was by directive, that is, by a generally worded Community enactment that required detailed regulations written by each member state for its implementation. Considerable disparity might develop between a directive and member-state regulations. The new article 100a speaks of "measures for the approximation" of member-state law, thus allowing the Council to enact not only harmonization directives but detailed regulations too. Yet in most instances the Council will probably stick to directives, although the tendency toward more detail may accelerate. (In the declarations accompanying the final adoption of the Single European Act, it was provided that the Commission "shall give precedence" to the use of directives rather

18. "Survey: Europe's Internal Market," *The Economist*, July 8, 1989, p. 12.

than that of regulations in the harmonization of member-state statutes.) Even detailed directives do not, according to article 189 of the Treaty of Rome, have direct applicability to individuals in the member state in the absence of state implementing regulations. Community regulations do have such direct application. If the Council moves toward regulation, the Court may encounter more requests for article 177 preliminary rulings in cases in the member states involving private parties who wish to use Community regulations to shelter themselves from national regulations. To the extent that the Council adopts more detailed measures, whether directives or regulations, the Court will encounter more pressing preemption claims. The more detailed a statute, the more likely it is to appear to have occupied the field.

It is not unreasonable to expect that the Court will see a substantial number of disputes about a member state's cooperation in the SEA program. Probably the Court's earlier "free movement of goods" jurisprudence, now transposed into "internal market" jurisprudence, and broadened and burdened with much new statutory language, will become an extremely active part of its domain. Increasingly, that part of its domain will be marked not only by clashes between national and sectoral economic interests in the narrow sense but between production-oriented and environmentally oriented interests. In its previous article 36 jurisprudence, the Court has tended to talk a bold game but in fact to defer to national interests when they could plausibly invoke a health, safety, morals, or welfare, as opposed to an economic, claim.[19] The temptation to invoke good new regulatory reasons to camouflage old rent-granting motives, and the political realities that often lead national legislatures and administrations to closely brigade the old and the new, is likely to seriously challenge the Court. It may respond by a posture of judicial self-restraint, deferring to member states. The SEA provides specifically for Commission and Council surveillance of such behavior, and the Court may leave it entirely up to them. For instance, under Directive 83/189 (of January 1, 1985) member states must now inform the Commission when they are preparing to introduce new technical standards and must explain the need for them. If the Commission or member states object, the implementation of the standard must be delayed. This arrangement seems to be working.[20] In

19. Dehousse, "Institutional Dimension," pp. 29–31. See, for instance, *Commission* v. *French Republic*, Case 188/84 (Jan. 28, 1986) ECR 419; and *Commission* v. *Italian Republic*, Case 35/84 (Feb. 18, 1986) ECR 545.

20. Lonbay, "Single European Act," p. 46.

spite of some success with such systems, however, the Court may become an active supervisor. If it does, it will become a major policymaker not only in the trade-offs between Community development and national autonomy but in the trade-offs between regulation and deregulation and between productivity and the environment.

The Court's previous article 36 cases have nearly all involved attempts by member states to preserve "higher" national standards against "lower" harmonized standards. The Court sometimes has been sympathetic to such pleas. Now it may also hear cases in which members seek to preserve their higher standards against the lowest standards of some other state to which the Council has ordered them to give mutual recognition. The Court will have great discretion in deciding whether to grant many such exceptions. It may grant exceptions liberally in order to minimize the race to the bottom. Or it may push mutual recognition hard, either because it appears to be an effective tool of integration itself or because pushing it will build pressure for more harmonization, harmonization that article 100b(3) requires take place at a high level of protection for health, safety, and other public concerns.

More speculatively, one might anticipate a new Court jurisprudence dealing with the race to the bottom. In the past, the Court dealt largely with complaints that higher national standards served as a kind of tariff barrier keeping other members' goods out. Where a member state preserves or establishes very low internal standards in areas where harmonization has not been achieved and mutual recognition is required, can the Court reject such state policies through some kind of analogy to "dumping" or unfair competition? The dumping analogy is far from exact because the producing state presumably would be protecting its own citizens as little as it protects those of the member states to which it exports. But what if hardly any of the product is consumed in the producing country with low standards? Unfair competition comes closer, particularly where a markedly lower standard in one producing state results in a product that can be sold at a much lower price than can comparable items from other producing states. There must be something "discriminatory" about such member-state practices. Given qualified majority voting, the political process may push harmonization as an appropriate response in such situations. It seems probable, however, that the fertile minds of Community lawyers will find some way of tempting the Court into a response as well.

It would be foolish to believe that the Court's positions on either activism versus self-restraint or regulation versus deregulation will be determined solely by the words of the SEA. It would be just as foolish to believe that those positions will be determined solely by the general political forces at play in the Community and its member states. To a significant degree, the Court's positions on these matters will be determined by the judicial, economic, and social philosophies of the Court's current and future members. Here, there enters a kind of chicken-and-egg problem: if the Court is more active, the member states will be more conscious of and more strategically motivated in their appointments. So, to a degree, what the judges do determines who they will be as well as what they do. The outcome of these circular politics is far from clear.

Administrative Judicial Review

The new regime of deference to the lowest product standard among the member states (mutual recognition), plus limited harmonization by qualified majority voting in the Council, plus secondary, technical, Community-wide standard setting by private organizations, all raise new opportunities for the administrative-law jurisdiction of the court.

I have already shown that the Court of Justice exercises "constitutional" judicial review over all the organs of the Community, and that it decides whether the actions of those organs accord with the provisions of the Treaty of Rome (as amended), which is the Community's constitution. In addition, the Court exercises "administrative" judicial review over organs of the Community, most typically over the Commission when the Commission enacts secondary rules designed to implement Community legislation enacted by the Council. Such administrative review asks not, "Is the legislation or rule in accord with the treaty?" but rather, "Is the rule made by the Commission in accord with the law enacted by the Council?"

Moreover, the Court exercises administrative judicial review over many actions of the member governments. The Council issues two kinds of statutes. The first is called a directive, which is relatively general in character. Directives must be implemented through more detailed regulations enacted by the member-state governments, but in certain situations individuals may claim that directives have direct effect. The member-state governments, in some sense, are exercising Community-delegated lawmaking power when they enact implementing regulations. The second kind of Council statute, a regulation, is more detailed and is directly applicable to individuals and enterprises without the need for further implementing regulation by member states. Thus the entities of the Community most analogous to agencies exercising delegated legislative powers (that is, the writing of implementing regulations) are the governments of the member states themselves. Many provisions of the treaties grant the Commission oversight powers over this work of the national governments. As already mentioned, for instance, when a member state invokes the exemption clauses of article 100a(4), the Commission must verify that the member state is not engaged in "arbitrary discrimination" or "a disguised restriction on trade." More generally, article 169 of the Treaty of Rome requires the Commission first to deliver "a reasoned opinion" declaring that a member state has "failed to fulfill an obligation under this Treaty" and then to challenge the member state in the Court of Justice. Often the Court will then exercise its judicial powers over implementing regulations of the member states or over their failure to implement in the form of a constitutional "federalism" review. For most, such review will be in the context of a dispute among an organ of the Community, the Commission, and a member-state government. Although the form is constitutional, however, much of the doctrine will be drawn from administrative-law jurisprudence very similar to that of each of the member states and, for that matter, to that of the United States.

For instance, in two recent cases the Court has invoked familiar administrative-law doctrines to uphold member states against Commission actions. In *Commission* v. *French Republic* it held that the Commission had not prepared an adequate showing on the record that German product standards for woodworking tools ensured as much safety as French standards and so were entitled to mutual recognition by the French.[21] In *Commission* v. *Italian Republic* the Court upheld an Italian refusal to allow the importation of curd cheese from another member state on the grounds that the Commission's and Italy's scientific evidence were in conflict and potentially serious health risks were involved.[22] This kind of "frontiers of science" or "scientific uncertainty" rationale is familiar in American administrative law, where its normal function is to excuse an agency from having to make a convincing case on the record for its proposed regulation. In the American context, doctrines such as an adequate rulemaking record and frontiers of science are typically used by courts to referee disputes between federal agencies and regulated private enter-

21. Case 188/84.
22. Case 35/84.

prises. In the Community context, they serve the same purposes but are also available to referee disputes between Community regulators and member-state regulators, thus simultaneously serving as administrative-law and constitutional-law (federalism) doctrines.

In addition, the Court will invoke administrative-law jurisprudence to deal with disputes between individuals, or more frequently between private enterprises and member-state regulatory agencies, brought to it by the article 177 preliminary ruling route. Many of these disputes present classic administrative-law problems, with the enterprise asserting that the member state's regulations do not comply with the Community directives that they purport to implement or do not qualify for exemption from those directives.

The Commission itself exercises some delegated authority to write regulations, largely those governing the operations of the administration of the Community itself. The Court of Justice, of course, exercises administrative review over such regulations and other administrative acts and decisions of the Commission, most notably in personnel management. Thus, in one of those meldings of administrative and constitutional review that occur in federal and quasi-federal systems, the Court is often in a position to demand that organs of the member states and the Community follow proper procedures and give good reasons for their policies. For instance, article 36 authorizes member states to enact health and safety regulations that may interfere with free movement. But the Single European Act even more specifically authorizes and limits such derogations from free movement and from harmonized Community standards protecting free movement. In those instances in which the Court treats member states as exercising concurrent free-movement jurisdiction, member states enacting health and safety product legislation may be seen by the Court as exercising the delegated powers of the Community to control movement. In all such instances, then, the member states may be subject to the Court's supervision on administrative-law questions.

The SEA provides that the product standard of the producing state must be accepted by the importing state whenever the Council so decides. It may well be argued that the Community has occupied the field and preempted further member-state activity in any area of standard setting where the Council has ordered mutual recognition. In such instances, the Council might be seen as having enacted a "complete" regime of product standards, namely, the product standards of all the producing states, each of which, like other Community enactments, has direct effect within all the member states. In this view, member states setting new product standards are now wielding authority delegated to them by the SEA because a producing state's standards only became directly effective throughout the Community by virtue of the SEA's provision of mutual recognition. Moreover, when importing states do attempt to enact product standards binding on imported goods, those standards dominate the standards of the producing member state only when they are authorized by the exceptions clause of the SEA. Thus the enactment of those standards, too, can be seen as the exercise by member states of delegated Community power. In short, it may be argued that through the SEA all product standards have become Community standards, and that the member state's making and enforcing them is the wielding of delegated Community authority. Old and, particularly, new member-state regulations that do not grant full respect to the standards of the producing state may certainly be seen in this light. And private standard setting in support of new harmonized or Community-wide general product standards will necessarily be seen so.

In the past, the Court has typically granted the member states a wide "margin of appreciation" in determining when they will enact health and safety standards infringing on free movement of goods. It will be recalled, however, that as a matter of constitutional review—that is, of review for compliance with the treaties—the Court's proportionality doctrine and its whole antidiscrimination and balancing approach effectively demand that member states give good reasons for their infringements. Under the Single European Act, special member-state regulations over and above what is required by the producing state are rendered more suspect and appear to be exceptional exercises of free-movement powers delegated by the Community. Because health and safety are involved, and because such regulations are often highly technical, the Court of Justice may still be loath to handle such derogations frontally. It could, however, increasingly find that the member state had not given good enough reasons for what it had done.

American courts have used the good reasons approach to move to vigorous administrative-judicial review of federal regulations. The approach has the advantage of not telling the agency that its regulations are wrong and cannot be maintained. Instead, it says that we, the judges, cannot uphold your, the agency's, regulations at this time because you, the state, have not given us good enough reasons for them. If you can come back to us with sufficient reasons, perhaps you can have your regulations. In the hands of the Community judges this approach is even more gentle because the Court of Justice cannot directly invalidate regulations of the member states.

Thus one can envision a scenario in which the Court of Justice, relying on the well-developed administrative-law doctrine of giving reasons, would turn the proportionality doctrine and the derogation provisions of the SEA into a powerful suspensive judicial veto. In this way, at least at the first attempt, the Court could strike down member-state resistances to the free-movement goals of 1992 that are camouflaged as health and safety product standards. Striking them down by asking for better reasons would itself call Community-wide attention to them and push them into a more salient position in the Community's political process. That process might then bring them to heel during the time period in which the member state was mustering its new reasons.

Legal Basis

Closely connected with the jurisprudence of the internal market under the SEA is the jurisprudence of the "legal basis" of Community actions. As in American constitutional theory, the new central government created by the "constitutional" text, in this instance the treaties, is seen as enjoying only those powers assigned to it by the text; the rest of the governing power remains with the member states. Thus every act of the Community must be authorized by a specific clause of the treaties. The Court has been somewhat cautious about notions of "implied" and "inherent" powers, preferring to read particular clauses relatively broadly rather than saying that some Community competencies flow from the structure or the general nature of the treaties.

Article 235 of the Treaty of Rome provides that "acting unanimously on a proposal from the Commission and after consulting the European Parliament," the Council may "take the appropriate measures . . . to attain . . . one of the objectives of the Community" when "this Treaty has not provided the necessary powers." The Court has interpreted article 235 relatively narrowly as providing only for the creation of particular instruments or devices that were not specifically provided for in the treaties. Basically it treated the article as a "necessary and proper" clause that allowed the Community to adopt whatever measures were appropriate to carrying out its mandates as enumerated in other clauses.[23] Community action is rarely justified by the Council or Commission by reference to article 235 alone but usually by reference to a goal enunciated by some explicit treaty provision, and a means to that goal justified by reference to article 235. Article 100 of the Treaty of Rome provides that, acting unanimously on a proposal from the Commission, the Council may "issue directives for the approximation of" member-state legal acts that "directly affect the establishment or functioning of the common market." In every one of its legislative initiatives proposed to the Council, the Commission specifies the clause or clauses of the treaties authorizing the proposal. Before the passage of the Single European Act, many of these "legal basis" issues interested only the handful of Community-law specialists, for many of the Commission's proposals clearly would fly under a number of different clauses and the "correct" choice made no immediate difference. Only where there was no correct choice, that is, where someone argued that no treaty provision, including article 235, could be read as authorizing Community action, were there major stakes.

The SEA changes all this because it authorizes qualified majority voting by the Council for legislative acts under some clauses of the treaties and the SEA itself, but does not alter the unanimous voting convention for others. By choosing one legal basis or another for its proposals, the Commission now chooses the voting rule under which the Council considers its proposals.

The SEA amendments of article 100 now move to qualified majority voting on harmonization measures and to "internal market," which may or may not be a more encompassing term than "common market." It also provides, however, that the old article 100 (unanimous voting and common market) still applies to fiscal provisions, free movement of persons, and rights and interests of employed persons. Thus article 100a may have become a broader general clause than article 100 is, and obviously disputes will arise as to whether a given harmonization measure should fall under the unanimity requirement of the former or the qualified majority requirement of the latter.

Similarly, article 99 requires unanimous decisions in harmonization of tax laws. As just shown, article 100a specifies qualified majorities in harmonization to complete the internal market, but excepts fiscal provisions. Given the complexity of modern regulatory statutes, it will be difficult

23. Joseph Weiler, "Pride and Prejudice—Parliament v. Council" (Florence: European University Institute, 1989).

to tell whether many member-state regulations are sufficiently related to taxation or fiscal policy to escape article 100a majority-vote harmonization.

In many situations, it will be natural for litigants to allege that the Commission has shoehorned some of its proposals into the majority-vote clauses that correctly belong under unanimity-triggering clauses. Then the stakes will become higher. Indeed, the Commission has changed direction on article 235. It used to be quite fond of the article as a way of avoiding squabbles about legal basis because nearly anything could go under the article. Although article 235 required unanimity, so did most other articles. Now the Commission frequently challenges Council invocation of article 235 as a basis for its acts. The Commission is anxious to shift the legal basis of Council actions away from the article and toward others that specify qualified majority voting, particularly toward article 100a with its broad "internal market" language that can be made to serve as the legal basis for nearly anything the Council does. Without repudiating its older line of cases interpreting article 235 rather broadly, the Court more recently seems to be interpreting the article more narrowly, particularly in cases where a member state challenges an action taken by a qualified majority of the Council on the grounds that the legal basis of the action should have been article 235 requiring a unanimous vote.[24] So the Court now has two lines of precedent to call upon. Moreover, the SEA contains a number of relatively complex rules and exceptions to its majority-voting designations that will facilitate such litigational claims. A large body of law exists about what kinds of Council acts go with which clauses—a case law that was not made with a judicial eye to majority versus unanimity voting because it was developed before the SEA was enacted. This jurisprudence will provide a rich mine for litigants.

Without in any way being able to predict whether the future legal-basis jurisprudence of the Court will enhance or inhibit Council majority voting, one can assume that the number of "legal-basis" cases will pick up and that the Commission will often face the Hobson's choice between putting forward a legal basis that will surely withstand Court review but requires a unanimous Council vote or proposing one that requires only a qualified majority vote but risks invalidation by the Court.[25]

Majority voting also raises, again, fundamental questions of federalism. Under a unanimity rule each member state could police what it regarded as

24. Weiler, "Pride and Prejudice," p. 4.
25. Such cases have already begun to occur. See *Commission* v. *Council*, Case 45/86, Common Market Reporter CCH 14,421, March 26, 1987.

the proper boundary between its own and the Community's competencies. With unanimity replaced by majority voting in key areas, calls are already being made for the Court of Justice to police Community competencies more vigorously. Given that new Community harmonization legislation undoubtedly will adversely affect many economic interests embedded within particular member states, the Court can expect to receive more claims that the Community has exceeded its competence.[26]

Human Rights

The Court of Justice has discovered "fundamental rights" in the treaties.[27] Once the Court had proclaimed that the member states had surrendered part of their sovereignty, it could easily go on to argue that the members surely would not have made such a surrender to a governing entity authorized to run roughshod over individual rights. And if the acts of that entity had direct effect, it could hardly be argued that the Community could employ that direct effect to reach down into the member states and destroy the individual rights of their citizens. If the Community is a constitutional regime, then it could hardly be that the Western European nations which had created that regime intended that the Community's own organs might violate fundamental individual rights. Thus fundamental human rights comes to the Community not as a constitutional bill of rights constraining the actions of the member-state governments but as an implied constraint on the organs of the Community itself.

Once having recognized that the organs of the Community were bound by "fundamental rights" constraints, the Court of Justice had the difficult problem of discovering what those fundamental rights were, given the absence of rights provision in the treaties. The Court has bridged the lacuna by inventing a formula: "fundamental human rights . . . inspired by the constitutional traditions common to the Member States . . . are enshrined in the general principles of Community law and protected by the Court."[28] The Court also said "international treaties for the protection of human rights on which the Member States collaborated or of which

26. See Jean Paul Jacqué and Joseph Weiler, "On the Road to European Union—A New Judicial Architecture" (Florence: European University Institute, 1990).

27. Weiler, "Eurocracy and Distrust."

28. Combining language in *Stauder* v. *City of Ulm*, Case 29/69 (1969) ECR 419 at 425, with language in *Internationale Handelsgesellschaft mbH* v. *Einfuhr- und Vorratstelle für Getreide und Futtermittel*, Case 11/70 (1970) ECR 1125 at 1135.

they are signatories, can supply guidelines."[29] It is these rights that the organs of the Community may not violate. Obviously the formula is shaped so that the Court can make reference to the text of the European Convention on Human Rights and the decisions of the Court of Human Rights without being formally bound by them or making formal interpretations of them. It also carefully avoids committing the Court of Justice either to the lowest common denominator among the member states of any particular right or to the highest national level of such a right announced by any member state.[30] Instead, the Court gives itself a free-roving role as practitioner of European comparative constitutional law. Interestingly, though, for all the academic attention to the Court's bold invention of fundamental rights,[31] the Court so far has rendered few fundamental rights decisions.

The Court of Justice does find that one of the fundamental rights of the Community is that, as specified in article 173 of the Treaty of Rome, Community organs meet "essential procedural requirement[s]" in their decisions affecting individuals. The Court is creating the law of "essential procedural requirements" case by case. In the United States, such procedural law straddles the boundary between what lawyers call "administrative law" and "constitutional law," and American experience indicates that assertions of freedom of speech, privacy, and other rights are often packaged as procedural claims. Judicially enforced norms about how administrative agencies must behave are part of administrative law. Continental countries typically have a statutory code of administrative law establishing such norms and a special administrative court system. Procedural law, thus, is grounded not in a constitutional provision but in a statute; procedural law questions are handled not by the constitutional courts but by the administrative ones. Paradoxically, the Community

29. *Nold, Kohlen- und Baustoffgrosshandlung* v. *Commission*, Case 4/73 (1974) ECR 491 at 507.

30. See Cases 46/87 and 227/88, *Hoechst A.G.* v. *Commission*, Advocate General's opinion of 21 Feb. 1989, para. 103 (unpublished).

31. See Andrew Clapham, "Human Rights and the European Community: An Assessment of the Acquis Communautaire" (Florence: European University Institute, 1989); Meinhard Hilf, Gritta Ciesla, and Eckhard Pache, "Rights vis-à-vis the Administration" (Florence: European University Institute, 1989); Jurgen Schwarze, "The Administrative Law of the European Community and the Protection of Human Rights," *Common Market Law Review*, vol. 23 (March 1986), pp. 401–17; and Joseph Weiler, "The European Court at a Crossroads: Community Human Rights and Member State Action," in F. Capotorti and others, eds., *Du Droit International au Droit de l'Intégration: Liber Amicorum Pierre Pescatore* (Baden-Baden: Nomos, 1987), pp. 821–42.

situation more closely approximates the American scenario precisely because the Community "constitution," the treaties, says nothing about procedural norms. Thus the Court has had to introduce norms of administrative procedure and to decide issues of procedural law case by case. As a result, Community procedural law has been "constitutionalized." Nevertheless, European lawyers think about all such law as administrative law, and the court itself is in the process of reinventing roughly the same norms that exist in the administrative law of the member states. European lawyers see clearly this intimate connection between what they have always seen as administrative law and the human-rights law of the Community. Moreover, as already noted, where a member state implements a Community program, it may be conceived of as acting as a Community delegate falling under proportionality review of the Court of Justice, and proportionality review may be argued to require a review for human-rights violations. The Community's human-rights concerns may be conceived as a segment of the Community norms that member states are obligated to respect in the implementation of Community programs.[32]

One must look a little more closely at the background of the current European enthusiasm for rights. The new national constitutions enacted after World War II were written under American influence, in the midst of partisan struggles between Socialist and non-Socialist parties, and in response to earlier fascist regimes. There was great interest in rights of personal autonomy, negative rights against state interference with individual freedom. The French Declaration of the Rights of Man and the American Bill of Rights were models of the enunciation of such rights. Socialists and communists, however, denounced such an approach as hopelessly bourgeois. They argued for the creation of social charters of positive rights—such as the right to a job, the right to education, and the right to housing. In most of the new European constitutions, a compromise was struck in which negative rights were specifically enumerated and "juridicized" while social rights were broadly stated in aspirational language. By juridicized, I mean that the negative rights were stated in such a way and surrounded with such institutions that individuals could vindicate them by litigation leading to specific judicially ordered remedies.

In Europe, there have been occasional judicial forays into enforcement of aspirational, positive rights. Most notable, perhaps, is the German

32. See the articles cited in note 31.

constitutional courts' invalidation of limitations on enrollment in the professional schools of the universities, thus creating a positive claim to government educational services out of what appeared to be the basic laws' purely negative right to freely choose one's profession.

The treaties reflected the concerns of the political Left with welfare rights. They contain economic and social provisions to balance the free-trade, laissez-faire orientation of the Community. At the time of this writing, there is a draft Community Charter of Fundamental Social Rights being considered by the European Parliament.[33]

If one puts all these phenomena together, a possible future for the fundamental, or human, rights jurisdiction proclaimed by the Court of Justice emerges that may appear more than a little imaginative. The building blocks in the imaginary edifice stand as follows. The Court has the power to order organs of the Community itself to obey the Community's "constitution." That constitution now includes the substantive rights of the European Convention on Human Rights or something very close to them. It also includes whatever rights the court says are fundamental, based on its interpretation of the European national rights traditions—traditions that include the positive social rights declarations built into the postwar constitutions by the Socialists. That those constitutions build in substantive rights without providing much by way of procedures for judicial enforcement of them may not be important to the Court of Justice. It can pick up the substantive rights and add them to the procedures that the treaties and the Court's interpretation of them have created for the vindication of individual rights.

Moreover, the judges of the Court can complete the wonderful circular pass. A national constitution may create a right with no national, individually triggered judicial remedy. Suppose, however, that the individual *can* raise an issue of Community law in a lawsuit in a national court and persuade the national court to seek a preliminary ruling from the Court of Justice. Then the Court can proclaim that the national constitutional right is actually a fundamental Community right and so has direct effect. Then it can "advise" the national court that, as a matter of Community law, it ought to vindicate the right against any national action infringing upon it. In this way, the Court of Justice can create a capacity in the citizens of a European nation to acquire enforcement by a national court

33. Clapham, "Human Rights and the European Community," pp. 29–31.

of a national constitutional right that is stated in aspirational terms only and that the national courts have hitherto refused to enforce. Thus, not only can the Court enforce in the Community organs whatever "fundamental rights" it discovers in its independent interpretations of the rights traditions of the member states and in the international obligations upon which they have entered, but it can enforce those same rights in the governments and private entities of the member states, at least when they are implementing Community law.

Furthermore, where a member state chooses to enact a regulation that impedes free movement and wraps it in the language of health, safety, or welfare, the Court may sustain such regulations if they are proportional. Fundamental-rights language is a wonderful lever on proportionality. National-sectoral interests hit either by the true comparative advantage of other countries or by the rush to the bottom of mutual recognition can wrap protective measures in positive social-charter-style language. Greens can wrap more vigorous national environmental and safety regulation in rights language. In many instances, then, what the national government will assert as a sufficiently weighty counterbalance to its infringement on free movement, under article 36 or article 100ab, will be not a mere national interest but the vindication of a fundamental right.

Thus institutional alliances may collide. On one side might be the Commission, supporting pro–free movement and deregulation, and the Council, dominated in its newly installed qualified majority voting by those members inclined to deregulation. On the other could be those nations or national sectors that become post-1992 losers and the Court that would extend them generous article 36 or article 100ab protections under the banner of fundamental, positive social rights. Free-market deregulators versus regulators, with the Court on the side of the regulators, is, of course, a far cry from protectionist national governments versus free-movement enthusiasts with the Court on their side, which has been the standard pre-1992 picture and a fundamental precursor to 1992 itself. Fundamental rights as a banner for national regulation is, nonetheless, a possible starter even if a long shot.

The Future of Community Human Rights

The Council and Commission, perhaps under goading from the Parliament, may begin legislation in the human rights area. Such directives do not have "direct effect." Treaty provisions, however, do have direct effect. If it wishes, the Court can always use Community directives on human rights as best evidence of the fundamental rights prevalent in the member states, just as it can use the Convention on Human Rights as such evidence. Thus Community human-rights directives can be seen as best evidence of what human rights are in the treaties, and whatever rights are in the treaties do have a direct effect. In this way, Community human-rights directives could have a direct effect. Thus a coalition of Commission, Council, and Court could turn the Community into a full-scale constitutional human-rights regime.

It is possible, then, that the current rudimentary fundamental-rights jurisprudence of the Court of Justice could greatly expand. The most natural way to think about such expansion, particularly for those of standard liberal persuasions who think of "progress" in civil rights and liberties, is toward a more elaborate litany of individual guarantees against abuses both by the organs of the Community itself as those organs grow in power and by member-state organs implementing Community policies. This picture of "reverse incorporation" is standard in most writing on Community human rights. Because the treaties themselves lack a bill of rights binding on the organs of the Community, the Court will incorporate one into the treaties, binding its central organs to the human-rights practices of the member states. Such a development would be the mirror image of what the U.S. Supreme Court has done in incorporating the Bill of Rights of the Constitution into the Fourteenth Amendment, making central rights practices binding on the member states. And having incorporated human rights into the treaties limiting Community organs, the Court can then also enforce those human rights in member-state governments as well, at least when the member states are implementing or making exceptions from Community law.

For those of less sanguine disposition, it seems quite possible to tell a different story for the future. Various national-sectoral sufferings and regulatory versus deregulatory clashes will occur after 1992. There will be a growing tendency to express various environmental, health, and safety concerns in rights language. European lawyers are daily becoming more skilled at American-style political-legal maneuvering and at litigating in transnational courts. The Court may be pressed to acknowledge and vindicate "rights" that are in fact devices for defending national regulatory measures that are more enlightened, in the minds of some, than are those of some other producing nation. It may also be pressed, in the name of rights, to grant priorities to the interests of some groups over others or to shelter some persons from the ill effects of post-1992's freer competition. In other words, the Community law of fundamental rights is now a potential weapon in the armory of those who would resist the strategy of free movement through deregulation, which is one of the strands of 1992. One does not know how much the weapon will be used or how the Court will respond to it.

Conclusion

T. Koopmans has suggested that after an initial phase of institution building, including building its own powers of review, the Court entered a stage of vigorously pushing forward substantive policies of European integration and then, some time ago, entered a less active stage. That stage he describes as policing minimums, such as nondiscrimination, in areas of established policy but leaving new policy initiatives to the political branches. Basically, he favors this approach, as apparently does Hjalte Rasmussen.[34] Koopmans concludes, however, by hedging his bets and calling for some continued level of judicial activism.

It is possible that this assessment somewhat underplays several aspects of the Court's activities in relation both to the initiation of the Single European Act and to policymaking under it. As already noted, the degree to which the Court built the *Cassis* doctrine of mutual recognition became the catalyst of a key feature of the SEA. In the tax area, the Court practically rewrote by interpretation a Community value-added tax directive, and its approach was then incorporated in the SEA.[35] Koopmans cites a Court decision of May 1985 in which it denounced the state of Community transport policy but left policy improvement to future legislative action as an example of the newer minimalist stage of Court action.[36] Yet that decision was followed by commitments by the Council of Ministers in November 1985 and June 1986 to end all quantitative restrictions on truck licenses by 1992. It may be true that the Court will less often try to go it entirely on its own, making the treaties themselves do what is better done

34. T. Koopmans, "The Role of Law in the Next Stage of European Integration," *International and Comparative Law Quarterly*, vol. 35 (October 1986), pp. 925–31; and Hjalte Rasmussen, *On Law and Policy in the European Court of Justice: A Comparative Study in Judicial Policymaking* (Dordrecht: Martinus Nijhoff, 1986).

35. Lonbay, "Single European Act," p. 49.

36. *Parliament v. Council*, Case 13183.

in tandem by the treaties and Community legislation. Given the new Council voting mechanisms and the somewhat increased vitality of Parliament, it may be that the Court will often feel that it can afford to wait for legislative help. More of its policy initiatives may come in the realm of statutory interpretation and administrative review and less in the sphere of the constitutional law of the treaties.[37] Even this prediction must, however, be qualified by the reminder that the Court has a whole new treaty, the SEA, to work with, and numerous interests that will be pressing it to clarify and elaborate this new "constitution."

The Community may indeed be entering a period in which the Court is not going it alone, but that does not necessarily mean a period in which the Court ceases to participate actively in policymaking. The period of the Court's most obvious activism was when it was acting on its own because the Council, under a unanimity agreement, was often such a drag on the Commission that the Community's legislative capacities were attenuated. Whatever got done had to get done judicially. The SEA invites a higher level of legislative activity. Heightened legislative activity, however, does not necessarily compel judicial surrender of policymaking. Instead it may presage a period of increased interaction between legislative and judicial institutions in policymaking in which, à la *Cassis*, value-added tax, and transport policy, the Commission, Council, and Parliament react to Court initiatives or cries for help, and the Court responds to legislative action. Americans have learned that judicial activism can occur not only when the courts wave the big, dramatic stick of constitutional judicial review but also when they work small in the realms of statutory interpretation and administrative review.

So if the Court of Justice remains as integrationist as it appears to have been in its activist period, it will have little difficulty in pursuing integrationist activism, though now in an arena in which there are more active players. What may be new after the SEA is that in the struggles between regulation and deregulation, high productivity and the environment, and advanced and nonadvanced regional and sectoral economies, just who the good guys are and who the bad guys are may not be as clear to the judges as when the fight was simply between integration and national sovereignty. "Smaller" judicial decisions may well jawbone more and

37. The Community is currently considering a draft directive creating the possibility of Community-wide corporations. If it is enacted there will be a whole new field of Community corporation law for the Court.

command less. More lines of equal but opposite precedents may arise. More whittling and less monument building may occur. Those things, however, are not necessarily signs of a retreat to judicial passivity. Instead, they may well be symptoms of a Court more deeply embedded in a complex policymaking process filled with many actors and interests.

Chapter 5

Policy Credibility and European Monetary Institutions

JOHN T. WOOLLEY

I N LIGHT OF the commitments of European Community member states to the European Monetary System, creating a single market in financial services had important implications for monetary policy. The Delors Committee studied those implications and, in 1989, proposed a plan of action. The Delors Report included a plan for economic and monetary union, a common currency, and a European central bank. Member states in effect adopted the Delors plan at the 1991 Maastricht summit.[1]

Almost from the outset, the Delors Report emphasized that monetary policy must pursue the goal of price stability. The report stressed one of the great successes of the European Monetary System: the imposition of an "exchange rate constraint" that helped countries with high inflation to "gear their policies, notably monetary policy, to the objective of price stability" (paragraph 5). The importance of improving institutions for policy coordination, the need to adopt "binding procedures" to constrain national policy authorities, and the need to reinforce commitments to price stability were themes of the report.

The Delors Committee also discussed the possibility of establishing a

I have benefited especially from comments and advice from Benjamin J. Cohen, John Goodman, Peter Hall, Wolfram Hanrieder, Robert Keohane, Leon Lindberg, Jean-Jacques Rey, and Wolfgang Wessels, and from the able research assistance of Martin Jarvis.

1. European Economic Community, Committee for the Study of Economic and Monetary Union (Delors Committee), *Report on Economic and Monetary Union in the European Community* (Luxembourg, 1989) (Hereafter Delors Report). There are different versions of the Delors Report with different pagination, but the paragraph numbers are the same throughout. See the appendix to this chapter for an explanation of the institutions of the EMS.

European reserve fund "to be the symbol of the political will of the European countries and thus reinforce the credibility of the process towards economic and monetary union" (paragraph 53). The committee foresaw a European system of central banks "committed to the objective of price stability" and "independent of instructions from national governments and Community authorities" (paragraph 32). In macroeconomic policy, "countries would have to accept that sharing a common market and a single currency area imposed policy constraints" (paragraph 30).

This theme of constraints and commitments is of interest not only because it is central to the 1992 program but also because concern for the conditions that create political commitments and the dangers of unconstrained policy discretion have become prominent in academic political economy theory. Here I address this question from both sides—academic theory and substantive program. The two are, without question, intertwined in the thinking of key participants. The central issue concerns the structure of political institutions and how that creates substantive policy commitments. The way commitments in one policy area relate to commitments in other policy areas is a related issue.

Overall, I argue that the contribution of institutions to policy credibility must be understood as an unfolding historical process. Critical to this process is the creation of domestic political coalitions in support of substantive policy objectives. Political coalitions create credibility by bearing the costs associated with their commitments. International institutions acquire credibility initially because of domestic political commitments. However, if successful, these institutions create new benefits for domestic political actors. In turn, these new benefits raise the costs of breaking commitments. Economic and monetary union would be difficult to reverse, and in that sense, a highly credible commitment. But to credibly commit the central bank in such a union to an anti-inflation policy may be more difficult.

The Problem of Policy Credibility

Separate literatures in political economy pose the problem of whether and how policymakers can make credible commitments about their future conduct. The structure of institutions and elections may make any promises about future behavior unbelievable. Similarly, the structure of the economy (and the working of politics) may present policymakers with difficult trade-offs between short-run policy benefits and long-run policy costs. The implications of these literatures are profoundly interesting for any exercise in institution building.

Some literature, focusing on the mechanisms of effective electoral control of incumbents, raises questions about the conditions in which elected officials might be expected to adhere to their campaign promises rather than merely serve their narrow self-interest or pursue private ideological goals. That literature concludes that continuing electoral competition (that is, an infinite iterated game) can be effective in binding politicians to their pledges.[2] The more politicians care about the future (that is, the less they discount the future), the more likely they are to abide by their promises.[3] If voters can agree on general standards for evaluating incumbent behavior (rather than on the particularistic benefits delivered to their group), they can effectively punish incumbents who fail to keep promises.[4]

Other literature examines how the structure of the economy may induce policymakers to seek short-term gains in economic growth that result in no long-term increase in growth but in much higher inflation.[5] The central dynamic of these analyses—and the occasion for theorizing about policy credibility—is the process by which private economic actors formulate their expectations about future inflation. To avoid needless inflation, policymakers need to claim credibly that they do not intend to push unemployment below the "natural rate" (the lowest rate of unemployment that can

2. This is a reasonable interpretation of Downs's argument about party reliability. Anthony Downs, *An Economic Theory of Democracy* (Harper and Row, 1957), for example, pp. 104–05. For a review of some of the relevant theoretical work, see John Ferejohn, "Do Candidates Tell the Truth?" presented at the Downs Conference, University of California, Irvine, October 1988. A characteristic of much of the Downsian literature is an assumption that parties can make binding precommitments. See, for example, Randall L. Calvert, "Robustness of the Multidimensional Voting Model: Candidate Motivations, Uncertainty, and Convergence," *American Journal of Political Science*, vol. 29 (February 1985), pp. 69–95.

3. See, among other things, Alberto Alesina, "Credibility and Policy Convergence in a Two-Party System with Rational Voters," *American Economic Review*, vol. 78 (September 1988), pp. 796–805. In general, time inconsistency, or incentives to pursue different policies in the short run and long run, disappears if actors sufficiently value future outcomes. See Robert J. Barro and David B. Gordon, "Rules, Discretion, and Reputation in a Model of Monetary Policy," *Journal of Monetary Economics*, vol. 12 (July 1983), p. 113.

4. John Ferejohn, "Incumbent Performance and Electoral Control," *Public Choice*, vol. 50 (1986), pp. 5–25.

5. This is not the place for an extensive review and critique. A useful introduction is found in Keith Blackburn and Michael Christensen, "Monetary Policy and Policy Credibility: Theories and Evidence," *Journal of Economic Literature*, vol. 27 (March 1989), pp. 1–45. See also Finn E. Kydland and Edward C. Prescott, "Rules Rather Than Discretion: The Inconsistency of Optimal Plans," *Journal of Political Economy*, vol. 85 (June 1977), pp. 473–

be sustained without increasing the rate of inflation). Some circumstances may lead politicians to cheat (that is, ignore the long run) precisely because observers cannot clearly tell what they are doing or recently did. In such a case, policymakers would knowingly generate inflation precisely because they could reap the benefits of higher growth in the short run while dodging the blame for inflation in the long run.

This literature arouses concern for the conditions or institutions that could guarantee that policymakers not be drawn into this inflation trap. The essential element in these solutions is that they provide a way of committing policy in advance to a particular substantive direction. This commitment must be made in a fashion credible to other economic participants. The electoral mechanisms just mentioned, which punish politicians who abandon their commitments, could be part of such a process. Any mechanism that reliably imposes significant costs on politicians for "cheating" can contribute to credible commitments. One such mechanism could be, for example, a highly organized labor force that would adjust wage demands swiftly in response to inflation to nullify any gains in economic growth from inflating.[6] More typically, the ways suggested to create credible commitments include making sure that policymakers have an overwhelmingly obvious ideological aversion to inflation;[7] entrusting monetary

---

91; Kenneth Rogoff, "The Optimal Degree of Commitment to an Intermediate Monetary Target," *Quarterly Journal of Economics*, vol. 100 (November 1985), pp. 1169–89; and Barro and Gordon, "Rules, Discretion, and Reputation."

6. The more fragmented and uncoordinated the labor movement, it has been suggested, the more likely labor will be at an informational disadvantage compared with the public sector. This makes the private sector less capable of deterring public sector "cheating." As Blackburn and Christensen put it, the private sector in such systems is not in a position to take the necessary collective action "to maintain and improve its reputation" for punishing public sector "cheating." "Monetary Policy and Policy Credibility," p. 23, n. 29. Cameron's data on unionization and labor organization centralization show that only two EMS countries had both above average levels of centralization and more than 40 percent unionization of the labor force—Denmark and Belgium. The countries with the greatest unionization and most centralized union structures have been outside the EMS (although some have engaged in deutsche mark targeting): Austria, Norway, and Sweden. This state of affairs may confirm the suggestion of Blackburn and Christensen that an additional external source of discipline is useful for EC countries. David R. Cameron, "Social Democracy, Corporatism, Labor Quiescence, and the Representation of Economic Interest in Advanced Capitalist Society," in John H. Goldthorpe, ed., *Order and Conflict in Contemporary Capitalism* (Oxford University Press, 1984), pp. 143–78. See also A. Newell and J. S. V. Symons, "Corporatism, Laissez-Faire, and the Rise in Unemployment," *European Economic Review*, vol. 31 (June 1987), pp. 567–614.

7. Blackburn and Christensen, "Monetary Policy and Policy Credibility," p. 21. Rogoff proposes similarly that the central banker should be a conservative who places a greater

policy to an independent central bank; and specifying by law policy rules that preclude inflating.[8]

This theoretical concern for credibility of the inflation commitment is precisely the concern that preoccupied the authors of the Delors Report. The fear that future policymakers will not resist the temptation of seeking short-run economic growth despite the cost of long-run inflation pervades and dominates the discussions about economic and monetary union. In a typical observation, Samuel Brittan has written that the great benefits of monetary union would arise if such a union were "run with a commitment to price stability approaching that of the Bundesbank." This "credible commitment" cannot be achieved, Brittan claims, unless other policy commitments are checked and institutional structures are appropriate.[9]

The European Monetary System and Credibility

To understand how the search for credibility figures in the events unfolding in Europe and how the theoretical literature on credibility helps one to understand these events, I first consider the European Monetary System.[10] Experience with the EMS has contributed significantly to the enthusiasm for 1992. The EMS policy rules may contribute to policy credibility; the Bundesbank, which is at the center of the EMS, is an independent central bank whose credibility may be valued by other EMS participants.

---

weight on fighting inflation than "society" does. Rogoff also points out that in the event of an unanticipated shock, the conservative's response is "distorted." "Optimal Degree of Commitment," p. 1179.

8. Blackburn and Christensen observe laconically that "the fact that such legislation is not observed in actual economies seems to be an unequivocal indictment of its undesirability or impracticality." "Monetary Policy and Policy Credibility," p. 15. As Barro has pointed out, an optimal policy rule would require some advance specification of the conditions that would justify a deviation from that rule, and even such "contingent rules" require additional institutional mechanisms to guarantee that there is no cheating. Robert J. Barro, "Rules versus Discretion," in Colin D. Campbell and William R. Dougan, eds., *Alternative Monetary Regimes* (Johns Hopkins University Press, 1986), pp. 21–23.

9. Samuel Brittan, "Why ERM Needs Monetary Union," *Financial Times*, October 25, 1990, p. 20. Brittan writes, "The Bank will certainly not have this credibility if Neil Kinnock has his way and it is committed to regional policies and so-called 'growth,' while being completely subordinate to governments."

10. In this chapter I adopt the conventional and technically incorrect practice of failing to distinguish between the European Monetary System and the exchange rate mechanism of the EMS. Countries may be signatories of the EMS treaty without participating in the ERM. The analysis here, and in the literature referred to, addresses participation in the ERM.

The Theory of Policy Credibility and the EMS

How might a credible anti-inflation policy be facilitated by participation in an international regime such as the EMS? Is a promise to try to protect a multilateral exchange rate more credible or effective than a promise unilaterally to defend a bilateral exchange rate (as with Austria and Switzerland) or a promise to hit a growth rate for a monetary aggregate, prices, or nominal gross domestic product?

Fixed exchange rates can contribute to policy credibility because of the variability in the *real* exchange rate *between* realignments of the nominal rates. This variability results from inflation differentials with the rest of the world and, it has been argued, has the effect of making domestic inflation more costly from the perspective of policymakers.[11] Jeroen J. M. Kremers claims that EMS participants gain credibility because of the additional costs placed on inflation in such a system. Before realignments of exchange rates, inflation results in loss of international competitiveness. Moreover, EMS practice is to limit the eventual amount of devaluation to an amount less than inflation; consequently, an added discipline occurs because the inflation losses are never fully accommodated in the subsequent revaluation.[12]

In an analysis of hypothetical EMS relationships between Germany and France, Jacques Melitz postulates two costs that can affect the behavior of policymakers in a quasi-fixed exchange rate system.[13] One is the cost of preventing capital outflows in the country with higher inflation rates between exchange rate realignments (the other, discussed below, is political.) Capital outflows are prevented either by imposing direct regulatory controls on capital flows or by keeping interest rates high. Like the costs identified by Kremers, these are real costs, but policymakers could assume identical costs simply by announcing their intent to peg their exchange rate to another country's rate with the possibility of periodic realignments.

11. Francesco Giavazzi and Alberto Giovannini, *Limiting Exchange Rate Flexibility: The European Monetary System* (MIT Press, 1989), pp. 104–10. This account presents results similar to those in Francesco Giavazzi and Marco Pagano, "The Advantages of Tying One's Hands: EMS Discipline and Central Bank Credibility," *European Economic Review*, vol. 32 (June 1988), pp. 1055–82.

12. Jeroen J. M. Kremers, "Gaining Policy Credibility in the EMS: The Case of Ireland," WP-89-36 (Washington: International Monetary Fund, April 1989), pp. 116–45.

13. Jacques Melitz, "Monetary Discipline and Cooperation in the European Monetary System: A Synthesis," in Francesco Giavazzi, Stefano Micossi, and Marcus Miller, eds., *The European Monetary System* (Cambridge University Press, 1988), pp. 54–57.

It is by no means clear that the credibility gains, if any, of EMS-type (multilateral) exchange rate arrangements arise from the details of the rules for adjusting or defending central rates.

Francesco Giavazzi and Alberto Giovannini identify two costs of participating in a multilateral exchange rate system that increase the credibility of the system. The first is the cost associated with persuading partners of the need for realignments in exchange rates. The second cost arises because too frequent adjustments of parities imply a de facto abandoning of the system.[14] I argue below that the first cost is not inherent in the EMS. Moreover, what can make credible a commitment to bear this cost if the cost of negotiation really is much greater than the total cost of acting unilaterally? The second cost is characteristic of any commitment to any rule and thus is of no special standing in considering a rule for exchange rates. Indeed, these economic analyses generally do not help much in understanding how the EMS has contributed to the making of substantive policy commitments in Europe.

The second cost Melitz identified is political. "In case of a political agreement about the exchange rate, they [voters] hold their political leaders responsible for devaluations. Devaluations cost votes."[15] As before, it is not clear why devaluations are more costly for politicians in the context of a formal exchange rate system than in an announced unilateral commitment to maintain the value of the exchange rate. This seems to be, in effect, an assertion that voters are more likely to hold their leaders to account for policy pledges made to other national leaders than for pledges made only to the voters. The problems of making credible policy pledges are not considered at all. In short, something like national pride must be involved in Melitz's argument, which, if correct, is an interesting invocation of apparently irrational factors in a model of rational choice. Melitz notes that "devaluations of the franc and the lira since 1979 have generally been a political embarrassment [in domestic politics]."[16] It is by no means clear why devaluation should have been more of an embarrassment to an incumbent (and thus a more effective constraint) than inflation, unemployment, worsening trade deficits, or the failure to meet an exchange rate commitment assumed unilaterally.

One obvious answer for the greater credibility of an EMS-type commitment may be found in the logic of repeated games and the complex nature

14. Giavazzi and Giovannini, *Limiting Exchange Rate Flexibility*, p. 104.
15. Melitz, "Monetary Discipline and Cooperation," p. 58.
16. Melitz, "Monetary Discipline and Cooperation," p. 68.

of the interactions in the EC. The EMS is just one of many "games" that EC countries play.[17] In the overall EC structure there are many opportunities for punishing noncooperation across games, and there may be a parallel value across games of establishing a reputation for cooperativeness. However, this possibility does not figure prominently in the literature explicitly dealing with credibility and the EMS. Although this chapter is too brief to explore these multiple games in any detail, such games are a key element of the institutional context in which the EMS must be understood.

Capital Markets and Commitment

The independent actions of international financial markets, can, as Melitz mentioned, make cheating costly. This has typically not been the focus of reputational analyses, but it is worth discussing for several reasons. In a system of *flexible* exchange rates, the attempts by a domestic policymaker to generate surprise inflation in order to increase employment would show up, perhaps very rapidly, in currency depreciation. Depreciation would bring in train an increase of the price of imports and a relative shift in consumption to domestic goods. This would improve the trade balance, but it would also produce a fall in the domestic standard of living. Sluggishness in adjusting to higher import prices may mean that over some period both inflation and the trade balance may deteriorate. Indeed, this discipline is precisely the kind of discipline lauded by the former British prime minister Margaret Thatcher.

In a system of fixed exchange rates (or adjustable peg system like the EMS), the costs of inflation for domestic policymakers involve the costs (owing to variation in interest rates) of defending the exchange rate. Movement of the exchange rate around the central rate signals the possible existence of underlying problems. Precisely because there is a target exchange rate, something missing from a system of fully flexible exchange rates, international capital can be a more powerful constraint on domestic policymakers. A target rate becomes more costly to defend as it becomes

17. The Common Agricultural Policy is, of course, directly related to the logic of the European Monetary System. On a larger scale, Hanrieder argues that the Germans have "preferred a European institutional context for implementing their national policies, shying away from purely national justifications and trying to avoid the perception that they were striving for national independence of action or heavy-handed political influence." Wolfram F. Hanrieder, *Germany, America, Europe: Forty Years of German Foreign Policy* (Yale University Press, 1989), p. 305.

more likely that it will be changed—and credibility undermined. In a system of flexible exchange rates, policy credibility can be vigorously and rapidly tested. This possibility suggests a question to bear in mind for later in the discussion: what happens to this source of policy commitment in a program of economic and monetary union?

Generating EMS Credibility: A Brief Historical Look

According to conventional wisdom, the dominant place in the EMS of the Bundesbank and its highly credible attachment to the inflation objective have been central to EMS successes in reducing the variability of exchange rates and in generating a convergence in inflation rates.[18] Lucas Papademos, an economist and adviser to the Governor of the Bank of Greece, observed that a view "shared by most European central bank officials [is] that the EMS has not only imposed greater discipline on the policies of inflation-prone countries, but that it has indeed facilitated the disinflation process by allowing these countries to use the system to influence expectations and enhance the credibility of domestic policies." Giavazzi and Giovannini assert that "most observers" agree with this view. They agree that the EMS is "an arrangement for France and Italy to purchase a commitment to low inflation by accepting German monetary policy."[19]

In fact, the conventional wisdom overstates what the EMS institutions achieved. As noted, the conventional wisdom focuses on the exchange rate constraint and the rules for realigning parities. At the outset of the EMS, however, these EMS institutions were not a particularly effective source of credibility for domestic policy (see the appendix for a brief description of these institutions). The EMS treaty, one between central banks, says nothing about the adjustment of central rates. In a related resolution of the European Council, it was agreed that central rate adjustments would be "subject to mutual agreement by a common procedure," a vague formula consistent with essentially unilateral action in the first few realignments.[20] The EMS by itself was a very limited surrender of

18. See, for example, the account of David Folkerts-Landau and Donald J. Mathieson, "The European Monetary System in the Context of the Integration of European Financial Markets," Occasional Paper 66 (Washington: International Monetary Fund, October 1989).

19. Lucas Papademos, "Discussion," in Giavazzi, Micossi, and Miller, eds., *European Monetary System*, p. 359; and Giavazzi and Giovannini, *Limiting Exchange Rate Flexibility*, p. 85.

20. Jacques van Ypersele, with Jean-Claude Koeune, *The European Monetary System: Origins, Operation, and Outlook* (Brussels: Commission of the European Communities,

sovereignty, and it certainly did not subordinate other countries to the Bundesbank—as initial Bundesbank misgivings about the EMS amply demonstrated.

In the early years of the EMS a series of changes occurred in the internal politics of several EMS countries that solidified their commitment to a policy orientation consistent with the then-current conventional wisdom. Such policy adjustments were observed in the early 1980s in Belgium, Denmark, Ireland, Italy, and France; many observers put special emphasis on the changes in France. Massimo Russo and Giuseppe Tullio identify a sharp distinction between EMS performance before and after March 1983.[21] In short, domestic political commitments made the EMS credible in the early 1980s, not the other way around. The EMS may now have an excellent reputation, but the effect of having a reputation is very different from the problem of acquiring one. EMS institutions did not possess any inherent credibility; they acquired credibility because of the demonstrated willingness of participating governments to bear political costs.

An extensive discussion of these "new" policy commitments in member countries is not possible here, but a summary of two cases is in order. The argument is that policy commitments necessary for the perpetuation of the EMS preceded any EMS capability to provide a binding constraint on domestic policymakers. These commitments, of course, were made in a context that included the existence of EMS institutions. In at least one case, the choice was explicitly conceptualized as a choice between the costs of being in EMS institutions and the costs of withdrawing. Nonetheless, the contribution of the EMS was subtle and quite different from the economists' models emphasizing the imposition of new costs.

1985); the treaty is reproduced on pp. 129–33; the European Council resolution is on pp. 122–25; the quotation is on p. 123. On the history, see Tommaso Padoa-Schioppa, "Policy Cooperation and the EMS Experience," in Willem H. Buiter and Richard C. Marston, eds., *International Economic Policy Coordination* (Cambridge University Press, 1985), pp. 350–51.

21. Jean-Jacques Rey, "Discussion," in Giavazzi, Micossi, and Miller, eds., *European Monetary System*, pp. 136–39; Tommaso Padoa-Schioppa, "The European Monetary System: A Long-Term View," in ibid., pp. 369–84; Massimo Russo and Giuseppe Tullio, "Monetary Policy Coordination within the European Monetary System: Is There a Rule?" in ibid., pp. 292–356; and Kremers, "Gaining Policy Credibility in the EMS," pp. 133–38. Giavazzi and Giovannini themselves present evidence showing that the credibility effects of the EMS emerged only in the period 1982–84. *Limiting Exchange Rate Flexibility*, pp. 124–25.

FRANCE. Politically, developments in France have appeared especially significant in that a Socialist government substantially surrendered control of its monetary policy to the Bundesbank. There is no doubt that President François Mitterrand could have abandoned the EMS commitment if he had chosen to do so—probably shattering the EMS. Arguably, the costs to the Mitterrand government of pursuing an aggressively expansionist economic policy would not have been very different even in the absence of the EMS—that is, that the EMS itself added little to the constraint. In the early years of the Mitterrand government, there was a sharp debate framed as a choice between domestic objectives and external constraints.[22] In 1983 France's leadership chose to bow before external constraints, fearing a precipitous drop in the franc, the swift depletion of foreign exchange reserves, budgetary laxity, and resurgent inflation.[23] France's future economic prosperity depended on economic stability and trade, and in the existing international environment the room for maneuver was limited, EMS or not.

However, even in this case the EMS commitment did constrain French policymakers in a special way. The very existence of an EMS commitment, dating from before the Mitterrand government's election, guaranteed that the president's economic decisions would be framed in a particular way. The EMS commitment forced Mitterrand to confront decisions about the exchange rate (and, by implication, the stance of macroeconomic policy) and the nature of French participation in the European Community that could otherwise have been avoided. Without the EMS commitment, the devaluation of the franc would not have required explicit government decisions. If the EMS had not been a *treaty* commitment, the Mitterrand government might have more easily abandoned a policy of pegging the franc to the deutsche mark, since it would have been a commitment of

22. David R. Cameron, "The Colors of a Rose: On the Ambiguous Record of French Socialism," paper presented at the 1987 meeting of the American Political Science Association; and Peter A. Hall, *Governing the Economy: The Politics of State Intervention in Britain and France* (Oxford University Press, 1986), chap. 8. The nature of the financial reforms in France is detailed in Didier Bruneel, "Recent Evolution of Financial Structures and Monetary Policy in France," in Donald R. Hodgman and Geoffrey E. Wood, eds., *Macroeconomic Policy and Economic Interdependence* (St. Martin's Press, 1989), pp. 3–61. See also Jeffrey Sachs and Charles Wyplosz, "The Economic Consequences of President Mitterrand," *Economic Policy*, vol. 2 (April 1986), pp. 261–321; and Philip G. Cerny, "The 'Little Big Bang' in Paris: Financial Market Deregulation in a *Dirigiste* System," *European Journal of Political Research*, vol. 17 (March 1989), pp. 169–92.

23. Cameron, "Colors of a Rose," p. 80.

the prior, now defeated, government. Because the EMS had already become a visible symbol of Europe, debate about leaving the EMS was "synonymous with the debate over abandoning other spheres of cooperation in Europe."[24] That is, the choice was not simply about whether to stand up to international capital markets, to create socialism in one country; it was a choice whether to abandon a whole array of European commitments and opportunities for leadership.

Jacques Delors, a leading figure in the 1983 debate, had argued for more economic cooperation among the industrialized countries. His conception clearly focused on the imperative to succeed in international competition.[25] Historically, in understanding where the credibility of the EMS commitment comes from, one needs to see that France's policy decisions of 1982–83 were critical and that they involved much more than simply declining to leave the EMS.

ITALY. At the outset of the EMS, officials at the Bank of Italy doubted that Italy could make a credible commitment to a system of quasi-fixed exchange rates.[26] Since the early 1980s a series of actions in Italy have established the commitment of the authorities—the Treasury as well as the Bank of Italy—to abandon quantitative controls and move toward market-allocative mechanisms. These steps have indicated a commitment to try to confront problems of large budget deficits and a willingness by monetary authorities, as Giorgio Basevi puts it, "to tie their own hands."[27]

24. Sachs and Wyplosz, "Economic Consequences of Mitterrand," pp. 294–95. See also Peter Ludlow, "Beyond 1992: Europe and Its Western Partners," CEPS Paper 38 (Brussels: Centre for European Policy Studies, 1989), p. 23; and Giavazzi and Giovannini, *Limiting Exchange Rate Flexibility*, chap. 8.

25. This theme continued to dominate Delors through the 1980s. In early 1990 Delors created a stir in France by publicly repudiating central elements of Mitterrand's economic doctrine as contrary to the actions that were "necessary for economic survival." "Le communiqué du Conseil des Ministres," *Le Monde*, January 26, 1990, p. 8; and E. S. Browning, "Capital-Needy French Industry Achieves Some Easing of Anti-Privatization Policy," *Wall Street Journal* (European edition), January 26, 1990, p. A5A.

26. Luigi Spaventa, "Italy Joins the EMS—A Political History," *Occasional Paper* 32 (Johns Hopkins University Bologna Center, June 1980), pp. 67–93. Thanks to John Goodman for making this source available.

27. Giorgio Basevi, "Liberalization of Capital Movements in the European Community: A Proposal, with Special Reference to the Case of Italy," in Commission of the European Communities, *European Economy*, no. 36: *Creation of a European Financial Area: Liberalization of Capital Movements and Financial Integration in the Community* (May 1988), p. 74. See also the analysis in John Benjamin Goodman, "The Politics of Monetary Policy in France, Italy, and Germany, 1973–85," Ph.D. dissertation, Harvard University, 1987.

The first of these was the divorce between the Bank of Italy and the Treasury in 1981, relieving the bank of the unlimited obligation to purchase any Treasury bills unsold at monthly auctions.[28] In 1983 administrative credit controls were abandoned and there followed a public announcement of a determination to accept the domestic implications of membership in the EMS.[29] Significant labor reforms occurred in the early 1980s, culminating in very important reforms in 1985 in the system of wage indexation (Scala Mobile) that many observers had argued was inflationary.[30] These latter reforms, "painful to introduce," consolidated a certain amount of credibility for Italian monetary policy but were almost certainly possible only because of prior efforts to create policy credibility. In these efforts, some observers credit the EMS with making an independent contribution to that policy credibility.[31]

Italian officials have discussed EMS membership in terms of consolidating the conditions for economic growth and integrating their economy more with others in Europe. The developments of the 1980s, especially the increasing openness of the Italian financial sector, have been explicitly linked to the need to build international credibility.[32] In 1987 the Italian government expressed a desire to make the liberalization of capital flows irreversible so as to tie the hands of any future parliaments.[33]

28. The Bank of Italy was, however, still obliged to extend credit to the Treasury through an overdraft facility up to 14 percent of public expenditure. Marco Pagano, "The Management of Public Debt and Financial Markets," in Francesco Giavazzi and Luigi Spaventa, eds., *High Public Debt: The Italian Experience* (Cambridge University Press, 1988), p. 137. See also Gerald A. Epstein and Juliet B. Schor, "The Divorce of the Banca d'Italia and the Italian Treasury: A Case Study of Central Bank Independence," in Peter Lange and Marino Regini, eds., *State, Market, and Social Regulation: New Perspectives on Italy* (Cambridge University Press, 1989), pp. 147–64.

29. For a penetrating examination of monetary policy in the early 1980s, see Guido Tabellini, "Monetary and Fiscal Policy Coordination with a High Public Debt," in Giavazzi and Spaventa, eds., *High Public Debt*, especially pp. 96–99.

30. For an overview of these developments, see Gianprimo Cella, "Criteria of Regulation in Italian Industrial Relations: A Case of Weak Institutions," in Lange and Regini, eds., *State, Market, and Social Regulation*, pp. 167–85.

31. Ray Barrell, "Has the EMS Changed Wage and Price Behaviour in Europe?" *National Institute Economic Review*, vol. 134 (November 1990), pp. 64–72.

32. Mario Sarcinelli, "Towards Financial Integration in a European and International Context: Exchange Liberalization in Italy," *Review of Economic Conditions in Italy*, May–August 1987, pp. 125–46. Credibility is discussed on p. 141. Sarcinelli was minister of foreign trade at the time. Formerly he had been a deputy director-general at the Banca d'Italia. See also Basevi, "Liberalization of Capital Movements," p. 75.

33. Sarcinelli, "Towards Financial Integration," p. 144.

Summary

In reviewing the early development of the EMS, a Belgian central banker noted that by about 1982, "The costs of economic divergence within the ERM [exchange rate mechanism of the EMS] had become obvious, and *they were unlikely to disappear simply by opting out of the system.* Several factors account for this, such as the degree of openness of the countries concerned, the various facets of their linkages within the EEC, or the previous experience of opting out of the exchange arrangement."[34] The search for growth with low inflation led naturally to a search for a formula to guarantee stable economic relations with major trading partners. The rapid growth of international capital flows in liberalized markets with more rapid telecommunications made it attractive for countries to enter formal cooperative agreements to manage exchange rates rather than to rely on bilateral arrangements.[35]

The specific economic and political conditions of the time are undoubtedly of great importance in understanding how the EMS could take shape and succeed: there was a strong consensus on policy objectives, policy theories, and policy challenges (inflation, monetarism and rational expectations, and deregulation); the system was able to function for many years without the need of adjusting to serious economic shocks; there was a substantial continuity of supportive top leadership in many of the key countries.

The EMS has come to represent a commitment by governments to reassure markets, to remove uncertainty about exchange rates as an impediment to commerce, and to reduce imported inflation. Recent studies suggest that during the EMS period several desirable developments in economic performance have occurred in the participating countries. Inflation rates have declined and converged; money growth rates have declined and converged; intra-EMS exchange rate stability has increased; and, in at least some cases, the volatility of real exchange rates has decreased.[36]

34. Rey, "Discussion," p. 138 (emphasis added).

35. Data on the magnitudes of international capital flows are impressive. The stock of international financial assets is estimated to have doubled in the period 1984–88 (that is, a compound annual growth rate of nearly 20 percent). This growth accompanied rapid innovation in financial markets and faster international transmission of financial impulses via improved telecommunications technology. For a useful account see John B. Goodman and Louis W. Pauly, "The New Politics of International Capital Mobility," paper prepared for the 1990 annual meeting of the American Political Science Association.

36. See, for example, Frank McDonald and George Zis, "The European Monetary System: Towards 1992 and Beyond," *Journal of Common Market Studies*, vol. 27 (March

However, the means by which the EMS creates credible policy commitments is almost certainly not to be found in the institutions of the EMS for adjusting exchange rates. Rather, the EMS has become credible because national political leaders made policy commitments that were mutually reinforcing with those of the EMS. The EMS did contribute to making those commitments, but in ways very different from the ways anticipated in the mainstream economic literature on policy credibility.[37]

According to the academic literature on policy credibility, an institution for enforcing commitments is supposed to work by imposing additional costs on policymakers for taking a short-run view of policy. It may be more accurate to think of the EMS as functioning as an effective policy constraint by providing new benefits and by framing policy choice in an effective way.

Rather than impose new costs, the EMS reduces political and economic costs for domestic policymakers. Economically, the EMS provides facilities to finance interventions for stabilizing the exchange rate. Thus the exchange rate can be defended without the degree of adjustment of domestic interest rates that would otherwise be required.[38] Politically, the EMS reduces costs for policymakers by plausibly assigning controversial decisions to a presumably fair, multilateral setting. Although in fact the government has exactly the same kinds of short-run discretionary options as before (that is, one can always leave the EMS or one can peg unilaterally to the deutsche mark), it is politically useful to have a policy one prefers "imposed" from somewhere else when it involves short-run costs.[39]

Rather than impose new costs, the EMS frames issues in economic policy debates more effectively or more acceptably than can be done otherwise. For example, using a multilateral system of parities may be

1989), pp. 183–202; Giavazzi and Giovannini, *Limiting Exchange Rate Flexibility*, esp. chaps. 2, 5; M. J. Artis, "The European Monetary System: An Evaluation," *Journal of Policy Modeling*, vol. 9 (Spring 1987), pp. 175–98; and Michael J. Artis and Mark P. Taylor, "Exchange Rates, Interest Rates, Capital Controls, and the European Monetary System: Assessing the Track Record," in Giavazzi, Micossi, and Miller, eds., *European Monetary System*, pp. 185–206.

37. Indeed, if the EMS created credibility for governments rather than the other way around, then late-joining members like Spain and the United Kingdom would have experienced distinctive and dramatic benefits following entry in the exchange rate mechanism. While this hypothesis cannot be examined here in detail, there is ample room for doubt on the matter.

38. The sources of financing for these purposes were increased and made more useful to governments after 1987. See the appendix.

39. In the U.S. literature on the Federal Reserve, this is, of course, the "scapegoat" hypothesis; see Edward J. Kane, "External Pressures and the Operations of the Fed," in Raymond E. Lombra and Willard E. Witte, eds., *Political Economy of International and*

less symbolically objectionable than simply pegging to a single currency. By focusing discussion on currency movements relative to a parity grid or in terms of a divergence indicator, the EMS can highlight preexisting costs of inflation and price-setting processes without imposing new costs. This mechanism should enhance policy commitments whenever there is inconsistency in benefit streams between the long run and the short run.

Because the exchange rate mechanism sets limits on exchange rate fluctuations, it provides a structure indicating when member state governments are expected to act or not act. In this way, the EMS forces issues onto the agenda that might otherwise be bypassed. Moreover, these issues have a powerful symbolic quality because the EMS has come to be one of the most visible, positively valued elements of European cooperation. Though the EMS commitment could be renounced, renunciation would have to be public. It would draw strong reactions from capital markets as well as from other governments in other negotiating contexts. Thus the renunciation of the EMS commitment would be costly in most cases, but *these* costs have not been the focus of most prior analysis.

Rather than impose new costs, a system like the EMS gives policymakers some possibilities for gaining policy effectiveness through collective action when little or no opportunity exists for individual action. The EMS involves a joint obligation to intervene to protect the parity grid, and it provides financing arrangements to help weak currencies defend their exchange rates. As the system has developed, it has also provided some possibility for nations to exercise a voice in critical policy decisions, whereas there might otherwise have been none.

Credibility of Economic and Monetary Union

The European single market program (1992) raises many of the issues discussed in the literature on policy credibility. Not only is the credibility of the program in question, but 1992 is seriously concerned with eliminating or minimizing a broad range of policy-based distortions of the sort postulated to raise the natural rate of unemployment. Market liberalization—"free movement of goods, persons, services, and capital"—has been touted as a way to increase output at a stroke. This freedom would, by

Domestic Monetary Relations (Iowa State University Press, 1982), pp. 211–32; and John T. Woolley, *Monetary Politics: The Federal Reserve and the Politics of Monetary Policy* (Cambridge University Press, 1984), chap. 9.

definition, reduce the "temptation to cheat" that figures so prominently in the literature on policy credibility. The importance of controlling inflation as an overarching policy goal was noted at the outset of this chapter and bears repeating here.

At the Maastricht summit of 1991, agreement was reached on a future economic and monetary union (EMU) with a European central bank, the irrevocable fixing of exchange rates, and, eventually, the substitution of a single currency for separate national currencies. Each of these moves brings new political challenges to be overcome. Interestingly, while each step forward eliminates some problems of credibility by making it more and more difficult for individual nations to contemplate leaving the system, the problem of credibly committing a new supranational central bank to a future policy course looms very large.

The Single Market in Financial Services as a Test of Policy Credibility

Perhaps no element of the single European market is as important to European leaders as is the single market in financial services. The Single European Act called for the creation of a financial services market with free movement of capital and freedom of competition in financial services throughout the full range of those services. Progress in this direction was evident even before the Single European Act was ratified in 1987, and action in the member states toward implementation of the single market has been substantial. As of mid-1990, barriers to capital mobility had been almost completely removed in the most important financial markets. Action to implement the Second Banking Directive, governing the single market in banking services, was already at an advanced stage.[40] By early 1991 there were signs of significant progress in opening markets in securities and in insurance.

This act by governments to completely expose their policies to the harsh evaluation of international financial markets is an act of great confidence and a profound test for the credibility of exchange rate policy and, by implication, of inflation policy. Free capital movements in a system of quasi-fixed exchange rates in the European Monetary System bring in

40. George Zavvos, "Banking Integration in the European Community," *Northwestern Journal of International Business and Law*, vol. 9 (Winter 1989), pp. 572–87; and George Zavvos, "Towards a European Banking Act," *Common Market Law Review*, vol. 25 (Summer 1988), pp. 263–89.

their train powerful pressures for coordination and harmonization in several other policy areas: monetary and economic policy, tax policy, regional policy, and social policy. With quasi-fixed exchange rates, individual national authorities no longer control their domestic money supply, and interest rate policy must be oriented toward protecting the exchange rate.

Thus national policymakers have strong incentives to pursue consistent and mutually reinforcing policies. Because action in the other policy areas affects the ability of national-level policymakers to follow a noninflationary monetary policy, international capital markets will search for policy inconsistencies and bring powerful pressures to bear on the exchange rates of countries that have defined inconsistent objectives. Since tax policy directly affects the returns that investors receive, differences in the tax treatment of capital will produce differential capital flows that could have long-run implications for economic growth. Observers argue that these pressures can be contained only through further political integration, which must eventually take an institutional form, or through abrupt fragmentation.

With free capital flows, divergent inflation rates will result in substantial differences in interest rates and potentially in pressure to adjust exchange rates or reimpose controls on capital flows. But the logic of 1992 and the EMS preclude such adjustments. With fixed exchange rates and free capital movements, it is not possible to have an independent (national-level) monetary policy. In such a system, greater policy coordination is essential, and greater convergence among economic structures is desirable. This point has been made with great force in a stream of commentaries and reports. [41]

Through the current period one sees gradual moves toward a greater coordination of policy and the reiteration of a determination to carry through on the process of economic and monetary union. The cumulative effect of this momentum is to make it more costly for any particular nation to reverse its prior commitment. Because this governmental process is accompanied by new ventures in the private sector—cross-border mergers

41. The conclusion is by no means new among economists. For the recent statements see Commission of the European Communities, *European Economy*, no. 36, esp. Charles Wyplosz, "Capital Flow Liberalization and the EMS: A French Perspective," pp. 85–103; and Folkerts-Landau and Mathieson, "European Monetary System." Padoa-Schioppa in "European Monetary System" discusses a similar notion, which he calls "the inconsistent quartet."

and investment flows—and by increasing horizontal collaboration and cooperation between mid-level public policymakers, additional layers and forms of commitment are created. Thus while the speed of motion toward, and the precise institutional shape of, EMU remains in question, public sector commitments to the essential ingredients are increasingly difficult to reverse. The commitments to EMU gain credibility by virtue of the increasing costs of reversal.

However, even though the basic commitment to create a system requiring a common monetary policy—and eventually a common money—is becoming less reversible, the important issue remains whether policymakers can create a monetary policy regime credibly committed to anti-inflation policy. Thus much of the debate about the terms of monetary union has concerned the way to define institutions that would preserve and reinforce the current level of anti-inflation commitment. Indeed, the debate between the Thatcher government and others about the future course of economic and monetary union can be easily interpreted as a debate about whether a new institution and fixed exchange rates will, in fact, be as strongly anti-inflation as a system of adjustable rates.

The EuroFed as a Solution to Credibility Questions

According to Karl-Otto Pöhl, former head of the Bundesbank, "If we are to have a European monetary regime, then it has to be as good as, for example, the Bundesbank's. And a European central bank can only achieve price stability if it is independent in its monetary policies of the EC institutions and governments."[42] European leaders are putting great stake in the design of the central bank—the EuroFed. Undoubtedly their concern is correct. The issue for both the academic audience and the policymaker is the same: can policy commitments be embodied more credibly in institutional rules than in simple statements of policy?

In late 1991 plans for the a new European central bank were finalized at the European summit at Maastricht. The overall design of the proposed institution remained remarkably consistent from the Delors Report, through the draft of the Committee of Central Bank Governors, to the final treaty.[43] As I shall shortly show, relative to other independent central

42. Quoted in Wolfgang Münchau, "Hard Ecu, Harder Problems Says Pöhl," *The Times*, June 26, 1990, p. 23.
43. Compare Delors Report, paragraphs 31 through 34; Committee of Governors of the Central Banks of the Member States of the European Economic Community, "Draft Statute

banks, in its institutional details the "EuroFed" is much less like the U.S. Federal Reserve System (the Fed) than like the Bundesbank.[44]

The proposed EuroFed would be created with an explicit mandate to maintain price stability, like the Bundesbank and unlike the Federal Reserve. Since central bankers everywhere are believed to care more about price stability than anything else, this aim would presumably have little effect on their preferences. The bank's bargaining position with respect to other institutions might well be stronger if it could point to such an injunction.

The proposed EuroFed Council would be composed of the governors of the twelve-member central banks and a six-member executive board. This is like the Bundesbank Council, which includes the eleven presidents of the land central banks and the seven members of the Bundesbank directorate.[45] As a constitutional structure, it is a representative design. It is unlike the Federal Open Market Committee, which includes seven members of the Board of Governors of the Fed and five voting members from the twelve district banks (one of whom is always from New York). Some evidence from the United States suggests that the more distant central bankers are from elected officials, the more likely they are to favor a more stringent anti-inflation policy.[46] This means that recruitment patterns, processes for appointment and dismissal, and voting rules are especially important. Length of term has not been shown to be systematically linked to policy behavior.

The governors serving on the EuroFed Council would be appointed by member state governments for terms of not less than five years. Member governments would not consult with the EuroFed Council before selecting

---

of the European System of Central Banks and of the European Central Bank," November 27, 1990; and "Mapping the Road to Monetary Union, *Financial Times*, December 12, 1991, p. 5. Other proposals were developed by the Commission, by the Monetary Committee, and by various member states.

44. In the early stages, it seemed likely that the term EuroFed would acquire official status. I continue to use the term here for simplicity.

45. Following German economic and monetary union, proposals were advanced in late 1990 to redefine the territories covered by the regional banks so that they no longer coincide precisely with the Länder. Otherwise, the size of the council would grow to twenty-three voting members with the addition of representatives of five land central banks from the former East German territory. Terence Roth, "German Reunification Creates Problems for Poehl in Bid to Realign Bundesbank," *Wall Street Journal*, October 12, 1990, p. B4F.

46. Federal Reserve district bank presidents are overwhelmingly likely to dissent in favor of more restrictive monetary policy, whereas Board members have been more likely to dissent in favor of ease. Woolley, *Monetary Politics*, p. 64. In the United States the district

the governors—unlike the Bundesbank system.[47] Federal Reserve district
bank presidents also serve five-year terms but are nominated by district
bank boards of directors, subject to approval by the board of governors.
Elected officials at all levels have little or no say in the selection of district
bank presidents. Top Bundesbank officials are appointed to eight-year
terms, and Federal Reserve board governors are appointed to fourteen-
year terms.

The members of the proposed EuroFed executive board would be
appointed to eight-year terms by the European Council, following consultation with the Central Bank Council and the European Parliament. In
the German procedure, the government nominates and the president
appoints, and there is no official requirement for parliamentary consultation. In the U.S. procedure, the U.S. Senate has the opportunity to veto
presidential appointments to the Federal Reserve Board.

The partisan affiliation of the appointing president has been important
in predicting the policy stance of Federal Reserve Board members. Thus
the procedures by which the EuroFed Council would approve appointments ("common accord") are as important as is the possibility for the
emergence of enduring ideological divisions within the council. Although
the initial appointees might be carefully selected for their acceptability to
financial interests, the almost certain development of enduring policy or
partisan divisions within the European Council means that these divisions
may be eventually reflected in the preferences of the members of the
executive board of the EuroFed. The possibility of reappointment has
been very important in the United States. At least two cases have been
documented of Federal Reserve chairmen altering their behavior to satisfy
incumbent presidents near the time of their possible reappointment—
they have "run for reelection."[48] The final statutes of the EuroFed exclude
any reappointment. Unlike the situation currently in some member states
(for instance, Italy and France), no members of the EuroFed Council,
including the governors of state member central banks, could be dismissed

---

bank presidents are neither nominated nor confirmed by elected officials. The opposite is
true in Germany, where anecdotal evidence suggests that the most liberal votes in the
Central Bank Council come from Land Central Bank presidents.

47. Such consultation in Germany's case seems not to have been a reliable means for the
Bundesbank Council to shape the decisions of Land Governments. Personal communication
from John Goodman.

48. The case of William McChesney Martin is discussed in Woolley, *Monetary Politics*;
the case of Arthur Burns is discussed in William Grieder, *Secrets of the Temple: How the
Federal Reserve Runs the Country* (Simon and Shuster, 1987).

except for personal misconduct. "Compulsory retirement" of members of the executive board would be only by the European Court of Justice, and a member state's action could be appealed to the Court.[49]

As for voting rules, all members of the EuroFed Council would have equal votes except on issues having to do with the creation of the bank's capital and its foreign reserve assets. This issue has been, appropriately, the object of considerable discussion.[50] Voting rules determine which preferences count and when. Under the Maastricht treaty, the EuroFed board, which would inevitably have an advantageous strategic position by virtue of its access to superior information, would need only three additional votes to carry any issue.[51] In both the Bundesbank Council and the Federal Open Market Committee, each member has an equal vote.

As in the Bundesbank, the president of the European Council and an unspecified "member of the Commission" could attend meetings of the EuroFed Council and participate in debate. The president of the EuroFed would be entitled to attend meetings of the European Council when matters relating to monetary policy were discussed. No such reciprocal privileges link the Fed and the executive branch in the United States, although there is no scarcity of opportunities for informal consultation. Indeed, one of the most important institutional reforms of the Fed in the 1930s involved removing the secretary of the treasury as a voting member of the Federal Open Market Committee. The EuroFed would report annually to the European Council and Parliament, a requirement that has an analog in the Federal Reserve but not in the Bundesbank.[52] This

49. These provisions apparently reflect preexisting precedents in the EC and thus demonstrate the emergence of a distinctive European constitutional order.

50. Compare an earlier proposal for weighted voting described in David Buchan, "Brussels Struggles to Balance Power at Top of Planned Eurofed," *Financial Times*, May 17, 1990, p. 3. Members of the Committee of Governors apparently believe that equal voting weights will contribute to creating a sense of a collegial unity and that unequally weighted votes would emphasize national differences.

51. A detailed discussion of this and related points is in C. A. E. Goodhart, "The Draft Statute of the European System of Central Banks: A Commentary," LSE Financial Markets Group, Special Paper Series 37 (1991). See also C. A. E. Goodhart, "An Assessment of EMU," *Royal Bank of Scotland Review*, no. 170 (June 1991), pp. 3–25.

52. The proposed dual reporting of the EuroFed is notable precisely because most European central banks, which are accountable to the government, have little or no direct contacts with parliaments. Lance T. LeLoup and John T. Woolley, "Legislative Oversight of Monetary Policy in France, Germany, Great Britain, and the United States," in David M. Olson and Michael L. Mezey, eds., *Legislatures and the Policy Process: The Dilemmas of Economic Policy* (Cambridge University Press, 1990), pp. 25–28; and John T. Woolley and

reporting would probably provide an occasion for public questioning of EuroFed officials, at least in the case of the Parliament. However, as long as the European Parliament is without clear authority to change the EuroFed statutes (an authority enjoyed by the U.S. Congress), this possibility would have little practical effect.

In summary, the internal institutional structure of the proposed EuroFed gives great power to the directorate and makes the entire institution independent of instructions from other European institutions. Its federal structure much more closely resembles the Federal Reserve of the period 1914–30 than it does the modern day Federal Reserve System in the United States. The EuroFed design allows none of the potential for decentralized policy action of the early Federal Reserve. Nor is it conceivable that there could be a system of independent policy determination and implementation by the member state representatives on the EuroFed Council as was true in the United States with the Open Market Policy Committee of the 1920s.

Among students of central bank independence, these kinds of factors are considered equaled, if not exceeded, in importance by legal requirements whose aim is to prohibit the monetizing of public debt. For example, in many cases statutes prohibit the fiscal authority from automatically financing budgetary expenditures at the central bank. This prohibition would also characterize the EuroFed. However, only in Greece, Spain, and Italy is there now an automatic credit line for governments, and legal prohibitions on automatic financing have not prevented central banks from accommodating government deficits.[53]

Lance T. LeLoup, "The Adequacy of the Electoral Motive in Explaining Legislative Attention to Monetary Policy," *Comparative Politics*, vol. 22 (October 1989), pp. 63–82. See also the proposal in Jean-Victor Louis, *Vers un système européen de banques centrales: projet de dispositions organiques* (Brussels: Institut d'Etudes européennes, Université de Bruxelles, 1989), pp. 28–30, which anticipates a much closer relationship between the European Central Bank and the Commission than with either of the other main institutions.

53. As of the end of January 1991, a fixed ceiling on absolute amounts that could be borrowed in Belgium was limited to Fr. 15 billion (equal to less than 5 percent of 1987 government budget deficits) solely for facilitating the Treasury's day-to-day cash management. Limits are defined in percentages of current public expenditures in the other three countries. Commission of the European Communities, *European Economy*, no. 42: *Facing the Challenges of the Early 1990s* (November 1989), esp. "The Community Economy at the Turn of the Decade," p. 70. As noted (note 28), the Bank of Italy's divorce from the Treasury was not absolute. George D. Demopoulos, George M. Katsimbris, and Stephen M. Miller, "Monetary Policy and Central-Bank Financing of Government Budget Deficits: A Cross-Country Comparison," *European Economic Review*, vol. 31 (July 1987), pp. 1023–50.

In short, the EuroFed will be fully equipped with all the institutional paraphernalia of central bank independence. The only possible problem is if it turns out that central bank independence does not reliably (that is, credibly) produce low inflation. The critical issue can be put as a nonobservable counterfactual question: would German inflation policy be substantially different with a nonindependent central bank than it is with one? To what degree does the anti-inflation commitment arise from preexisting, historically derived policy preferences and policy coalitions, and to what degree is it created by the structure of the institution? It is certainly a plausible supposition that the attitudes that make Germany a low-inflation country are the same attitudes that tolerate an independent institution like the Bundesbank.

The argument for the institutional view is theoretical and empirical. The theoretical part is essentially the observation that when legitimate authority for a set of decisions is granted to an agent that is not subject to any requirements for concurrent majorities or outside approval, then outsiders must always entertain some doubt about how the agency will perform. In particular, outsiders must have doubts about whether the agency will attend to (or accommodate) preferences other than those of the members of the agency.

The empirical part is the finding of some researchers that more formally independent central banks have tended to have lower inflation rates on average than less independent central banks.[54] The empirical evidence is certainly not without ambiguity, however. A telling argument against this claim is the research by students of inflation and inflation expectations, which discusses at length how to create a credible anti-inflation program in the United States—where there is an independent central bank.[55]

54. Michael Parkin and Robin Bade, "Central Bank Laws and Monetary Policy," University of Western Ontario, 1985, as cited in Blackburn and Christensen, "Monetary Policy and Policy Credibility," no. 33, p. 27; and Richard C. K. Brudekin and Thomas D. Willett, "Central Bank Reform: The Federal Reserve in International Perspective," Claremont McKenna College, Claremont, California. There is no systematic historical research that might demonstrate whether change in behavior has been reliably linked to change in legal status.

55. Thomas J. Sargent, *Rational Expectations and Inflation* (Harper and Row, 1986); Leland B. Yeager, *Experiences with Stopping Inflation* (Washington: American Enterprise Institute for Public Policy Research, 1982); Herbert Stein, "Achieving Credibility," in William Fellner, ed., *Contemporary Economic Problems, 1980* (Washington: American Enterprise Institute for Public Policy Research, 1980), pp. 39–75; and John B. Taylor, "Establishing Credibility: A Rational Expectations Viewpoint," *American Economic Review*, vol. 72 (May 1982), pp. 81–85.

Perhaps the strongest claim to credibility on behalf of the proposed EuroFed is this one: the EuroFed design has been agreed on, and a prototype, the European Monetary Institute, will be in operation long before there exists an equally coherent and capable European institution exercising sovereign power in any other important realm of policy.[56] This development will be unprecedented in the modern history of central banking. Never before has a powerful, autonomous central bank been established to govern a monetary union that was not itself the creation of preexisting political institutions unambiguously in a position to express the national sovereign will.[57]

Political institutions are in the first instance attempts by policymakers to commit to particular divisions of labor in the political economy. One may well have doubts about the importance of institutions independent of the distribution of policy preferences in the polity. However, the rules and regulations that govern the ongoing behavior of institutions may become very important, particularly if they are credited by observers, rightly or wrongly, as embodying particular substantive policy commitments. These attributions are in part what gives institutional structures their special political meaning.

By joining political institutions that signal the commitment of policymakers to inflation fighting (independent central banks) with economic institutions that permit high levels of capital mobility, policymakers structure a particularly important set of reinforcing relationships. Any proposal to alter the political institutions would call into question the credibility of the substantive policy commitment, producing an automatic, market-based penalty for higher expected inflation rates. In this case, to policymakers, the response of market expectations would be harmful, since it

56. Already in stage one of EMU the Committee of Central Bank Governors has taken on additional responsibilities for surveillance and commentary on national policies (publicly if it chooses) and has a small, independent staff.

57. The most plausible analogue is, again, in the Länder bank predecessors to the Bundesbank during Allied occupation. For some of the relevant histories, see Gianni Toniolo, ed., *Central Banks' Independence in Historical Perspective* (Berlin: Walter de Gruyter, 1988); and Marcello de Cecco and Alberto Giovannini, eds., *A European Central Bank: Perspectives on Monetary Unification after Ten Years of the EMS* (Cambridge University Press, 1989). This is not to say that the issue of democratic control of the EuroFed has gone unexamined even by the most ardent supporters of a Bundesbank-type structure. See Karl-Otto Pöhl, "Plaidoyer pour une Politique Monetaire Independante," *Le Monde*, January 18, 1990, p. 1; and Peter Norman, "Pöhl Presents Powerful Case for a 'Euro-Bundesbank,'"

would tend to lower employment below the natural rate, presumably a bad thing for incumbents. Therein lies the peculiar significance of the combination of the EuroFed structural details and the freeing of European capital markets.

Policy Interdependencies and Credibility

By the same token, however, policy interdependencies may continue to challenge the credibility of the anti-inflation commitment by calling into question the viability of the proposal for monetary union. This discussion must necessarily be brief, but it is important to touch on two areas: taxes and budget deficits.

TAXES. The single market program has yet to deal successfully with national differences in the tax treatment of capital gains, interest, and dividends. The withholding tax on interest payments to nonresidents ranges widely in the EC, depending on the countries involved. For example, a German resident may be subject to no withholding on interest income from Denmark, France, Ireland, Luxembourg, the Netherlands, and the United Kingdom, but may be subject to tax rates from 10–25 percent on interest income earned in Belgium, Greece, Italy, Portugal, and Spain.[58] Similar ranges apply for withholding on dividends. In some jurisdictions, there are additional capital gains taxes for certain investments.

Considerable energy and effort has already been devoted to advising foreign investors about the most profitable locations for investment based on the consideration of taxes. There is convincing evidence that investors are very sensitive to differences in tax rates. In this respect, one may anticipate considerable market pressure to equalize tax rates. At the margin, such equalization may be important for securing necessary investment capital. Failure to equalize may lead to persistent differences in economic performance and, in turn, strains inconsistent with economic and monetary union.

BUDGETARY BALANCES. As it develops, the countries that have levied the highest taxes on capital are also the countries with the most persistent problems of budget deficits (Italy, Greece, Portugal, and Spain). The

Financial Times, January 17, 1990, pp. 2, 20. From a democratic point of view, says Pöhl, a central bank will be legitimate if it is created by a treaty among democratic governments and ratified by democratically elected parliaments.

58. Alberto Giovannini, "National Tax Systems versus the European Capital Market," *Economic Policy*, no. 9 (October 1989), p. 354. See also the figures in Vittorio Grilli, "Financial Markets and 1992," *Brookings Papers on Economic Activity*, 2:1989, pp. 301–24.

amount of government debt outstanding is already an important determinant of interest rates in Europe. After monetary union, will it be conceivable that a country might default on its debt? This event is generally regarded as not possible. Given the basic rule of public finance that all debt must be repaid eventually, the obvious difficulty in some countries of reducing the deficit suggests an eventual threat to the credibility of the anti-inflation commitment in economic and monetary union. Many European policymakers fear that if budget deficits in weak countries are not controlled, then there is nothing inherent in the system to guarantee virtuous stability. Indeed, they argue, a potential instability arises from the fact that fixed exchange rates remove from lenders any exchange risk, while deepening political linkages remove any default risk.

The Delors Report recognized this problem and proposed that at some point "it would seem necessary to develop both binding rules and procedures for budgetary policy."[59] The Maastricht treaty did, indeed, include provisions for monitoring the overall budget position of member states and for punishing states that persist in running "excessive deficits." Even so, the proponents of economic and monetary union will surely face many challenges that arise from the relatively weak collective capacity in economic policy compared with that created in monetary policy.

Conclusion

Nowhere has the interdependence of political and economic institutions been more clear than in the opening of European capital markets and the creation of the single European market in financial services. In the eyes of virtually all analysts, these developments, coupled with a commitment to near-fixed exchange rates in the European Monetary System, create a logical necessity for the further development of institutions of monetary cooperation, and, eventually, monetary union. Though an apparent logical necessity, it is by no means practically ensured. Nonetheless, the choices European governments have made about the scope to allow market institutions have further constrained, perhaps irreversibly, the choices of these

59. Delors Report, paragraph 33 (emphasis deleted). Compare, however, the September 1, 1989, speech of the Bank of England governor, Robin Leigh-Pemberton, in which he states that "neither I—nor, I think, my colleagues on the Committee—saw a need for specific and detailed budgetary rules." Robin Leigh-Pemberton, "Europe 1992: Some Monetary Policy Issues," *Economic Review of the Federal Reserve Bank of Kansas City*, vol. 74 (September–October 1989), p. 7.

same governments in economic policy. Certainly by late 1991 the determination of EC governments to proceed with economic and monetary union seemed very firm.[60]

The concerns of academic analysis for devising institutional structures that permit—or compel—policymakers to bind themselves to a long-run policy perspective have echoed throughout the European debate. That academic work considers especially the consequences of not being able to make credible policy commitments. Unfortunately, the literature is better at showing that the inability to make binding commitments may cause problems than at revealing how such commitments may be made.

The EMS experience is supposed to have demonstrated how an external commitment can effectively tie the hands of domestic policymakers. However, I have argued that it is more accurate to think of the EMS as gaining credibility because of domestic policy commitments made by national-level politicians. In my view, therein lies the most sobering challenge for the proponents of EMU. Fighting and winning domestic political battles were required to make the EMS effective. That experience and the generally positive experience of the EMS have been essential in paving the way for serious discussion of EMU. As the process of monetary coordination continues in the context of an increasingly open single market, the commitments to EMU will become irreversible. However, that will not eliminate concerns about the policy pursued in a unified monetary regime. In the future, there will be more domestic political fights to be won before EMU can become a reality with high credibility pertaining to inflation policy.

The policy environment prior to full monetary union will provide a test of credibility which can substantially guarantee that entry to monetary union is accompanied by a commitment to fight inflation. That test is provided during stages one and two by the exchange rate pressures that will follow from inconsistent or unsustainable national-level policies.

The EMS experience shows that effective policy commitments need not be based simply on institutions that punish politicians for weakness. Undoubtedly, by making cheating costly, policy commitments can be made highly credible. However, credible commitments may also flow from institutional arrangements that allow policymakers to deflect short-term political costs onto a scapegoat institution so they can pursue longer-term goals. Obviously, the EuroFed is intended to perform this function,

60. At Maastricht it was agreed that the second stage would begin January 1, 1994. Entry to the third stage could come at any time after that (following favorable reports and decisions) but would be no later than January 1, 1999.

whatever the true preferences of policymakers may be. Institutions that create new means to assist policymakers in reaching their goals—for example, the intermediate financing mechanisms of the EMS—actually lower some of the costs of persisting in a policy commitment, making other costs easier to bear and credibility easier to build.

Credible policy commitments may be reinforced by framing effects. Policy can be framed to emphasize the long run rather than the short run and to demonstrate the interconnectedness of policy. The EMS apparatus of parity grids and divergence indicators may have helped in this regard. So may the fact that special, highly visible acts would be required for any member to abandon the commitment to the EMS. Certainly the simple fact of more frequent positive references to the system in economic discourse have had a framing effect. It is by no means clear what rhetorical device is available to fill this gap in EMU.

Several favorable conditions have promoted progress toward monetary union. Conditions in the external economy have facilitated steps by major governments to make firm and credible commitments to a system of near-fixed exchange rates. This process has gained legitimacy through apparent success. Economies have prospered; inflation has fallen; exchange rates have been stabilized. In short, the sunk costs in the current arrangements are great, and their efficacy has been accepted by both policymakers and expert observers.

The efforts to create a zone of monetary stability have been reinforced by increased trade and by efforts to solidify military and political alliances. Overarching this structure has been a belief in the plain necessity to prepare to thrive in an emerging highly competitive global economy. Time will tell if these conditions have been special, and if progress was contingent on their continuing, or if by institutional design and credible commitments this progress can be sustained even in a less hospitable economic and political environment.

Appendix: The Institutions of the European Monetary System

The EMS is a system of semifixed exchange rates that links the currencies of most of the EC member states in what is known as the exchange rate mechanism. The EMS began as an almost purely cooperative structure—that is, there was no autonomous capacity to regulate or constrain the behavior of the participants. However, as it evolved in the 1980s, the

EMS came to function as a binding constraint for several governments. Although there is no central, supranational decisionmaking authority, the institutions of cooperation have assumed an increasingly important role in policy coordination and mutual surveillance. These are, as Robert O. Keohane points out, essential elements of institutions.[61]

Structure of the EMS

The structure of the EMS is somewhat arcane in its precise details, but the general logic is simple enough.[62] All EC countries are members of the EMS (which is technically an agreement between central banks), and all but two (Greece, Portugal) participate in the exchange rate mechanism (ERM). At the center of the EMS is an accounting currency, the European currency unit (ECU), which is a basket of all the EMS currencies.[63] The weights of each currency in the currency basket are arrived at by negotiation but are intended to reflect the relative economic sizes of the various countries.

The countries in the ERM are linked with one another through a series of official fixed rates. Although the rates are, technically, defined in terms of the ECU, they comprise a grid of bilateral exchange rate relationships in which the ECU plays no special role. One of the fundamental institutional rules of the EMS is that (with the exception of the Spanish peseta as of January 1990 and the British pound sterling as of October 1990) market exchange rates may not vary more than plus or minus 2.25 percent around the official exchange rate. At the fluctuation limit, central banks must intervene; the central bank of the weaker currency sells the stronger currency, and the central bank of the stronger currency buys the weaker currency.[64] As Giavazzi and Giovannini show for 1983–86, a substantial share of intervention has occurred before the margins were reached.[65]

A significant institutional reform of the EMS occurred in the September 1987 Nyborg agreements. These facilitated the borrowing of reserves for intramarginal interventions from the "very short-term financing facility" (which had previously been restricted only to supporting compulsory

61. Robert O. Keohane, "International Institutions: Two Approaches," *International Studies Quarterly*, vol. 32 (December 1988), p. 386.

62. See Giavazzi and Giovannini, *Limiting Exchange Rate Flexibility*, esp. chaps. 1, 2; and van Ypersele with Koeune, *European Monetary System*.

63. Data on currency weights in the ECU and central rates are published in Eurostat, "ECU-EMS Information," Theme 2, Economy and Finance, Series B, Short-term trends.

64. Giavazzi and Giovannini, *Limiting Exchange Rate Flexibility*, p. 34.

65. Giavazzi and Giovannini, *Limiting Exchange Rate Flexibility*, p. 65.

interventions at the margins) and lengthened the time in which such short-term loans must be repaid. These agreements also increased the responsibilities of the Committee of Governors for policy surveillance and short-term policy coordination.[66]

The EMS structure also includes something called the "divergence indicator," which is intended to show how a particular currency is performing relative to all the other EMS currencies simultaneously. If, for example, because of some localized economic shock, the exchange rates of a particular currency were depreciating simultaneously against all other EMS currencies, the divergence indicator would make this situation clear. In this case the presumption (but not the obligation) is that the country with the divergent currency would bear a special (asymmetrical) obligation to take action. The divergence indicator has been strongly criticized on technical grounds,[67] and it has not been accorded any special significance either in assessing member state performance or in motivating action.[68]

Many observers argue that since 1983 the EMS has in fact become a system for joint decisions in setting exchange rate parities.[69] Padoa-Schioppa, a key participant-observer, reports that the setting of central rates has become the result of "truly collective decisions." He also argues that countries with weak currencies have never been allowed to devalue without also implementing economic adjustment packages. Thus the setting of exchange rates—one of the hallmarks of sovereignty—has already become, in part, a European Community decision.[70] Community influence extends to defining the conditions under which states prepared to revalue may do so. These institutions do not yet have the capacity to require revaluations, nor is there consensus on the conditions that would require

66. Jacques Delors, "Economic and Monetary Union and Relaunching the Construction of Europe," in *Collection of Papers Submitted to the Committee for the Study of Economic and Monetary Union* (Luxembourg, 1989), p. 66; Lamberto Dini, "A New Phase in the European Monetary System—Exchange-Rate Constraint, Capital Liberalisation, and Policy Coordination: A Report of the Conference Panel Discussion," in Giavazzi, Micossi, and Miller, eds., *European Monetary System*, pp. 385–88; and *European Economy*, no. 38: *The European Financial Area: Situation and Outlook* (November 1988), pp. 133–44. These new facilities were used immediately thereafter in November in a coordinated interest-rate action by the Bundesbank and the Banque de France.

67. Giavazzi and Giovannini, *Limiting Exchange Rate Flexibility*, p. 35-37.

68. For example, "General Discussion," in Giavazzi, Micossi, and Miller, eds., *European Monetary System*, pp. 415–17.

69. For example, Artis, "European Monetary System."

70. Tommaso Padoa-Schioppa, *Efficiency, Stability, and Equity: A Strategy for the Evolution of the Economic System of the European Community: A Report* (Oxford University Press, 1987), p. 371.

revaluations. In early 1990, for example, the Germans were unable to win agreement to an exchange rate realignment that they sought.[71] Another report notes progress in cooperative target setting for monetary policy in the framework of EMS discussions.[72] Overall, it seems that a basic economic policy consensus has been built up through these consultations, that common understandings about policy have been achieved, and that some genuinely collective actions have been observed.

Decisionmaking Institutions of the EMS

European monetary institutions circa 1989 also included three formal consultative bodies (of which the first two are most important): the Monetary Committee, the Committee of Central Bank Governors, and the Banking Advisory Committee.

THE MONETARY COMMITTEE. There are two main organizational structures that integrate and serve to maintain the EMS. One of these is the Monetary Committee, and the other is the Committee of Central Bank Governors. The Monetary Committee, dating from 1958, includes high officials of finance ministries and central banks. It was initially conceived as an advisory body to the European Council and the Commission of the European Communities, which could provide advice either on request or at its own initiative.[73]

Since 1964 the Monetary Committee has been officially designated as the place for consultation between member states in the field of international monetary relations.[74] The committee is central to the preparation of monetary decisions within the European Community, of which parity changes are the most visible and perhaps the most important. Parity

71. There was a kind of catch-22 in this case. Refusing to revalue was apparently regarded by some governments as a measure of their capacity and determination to defend fixed parities; revaluation would have been interpreted in Germany as evidence that conditions were not yet right for further steps toward monetary union. Tim Carrington, "European Monetary System Is Facing Increasing Strain amid East Bloc Shifts," *Wall Street Journal,* January 22, 1990, p. A9A; and George Melloan, "Thatcher Has Won the Monetary Unity Battle," *Wall Street Journal,* January 15, 1990, p. A13.

72. Padoa-Schioppa, *Efficiency, Stability, and Equity,* pp. 77–78. Others are not quite so enthusiastically positive. See the cautious evaluation in Sarcinelli, "Towards Financial Integration in a European and International Context," p. 129.

73. Andreas Kees, "The Monetary Committee of the European Community," *Kredit und Kapital,* vol. 20, no. 2 (1987), p. 258.

74. Hans O. Schmitt, "Capital Markets and the Unification of Europe," *World Politics,* vol. 20 (January 1968), pp. 228–44, esp. p. 241.

decisions are not made in the European Council but in the Council of Economics and Finance Ministers. According to Andreas Kees, the Monetary Committee has been the locus of decision concerning parities in some cases.[75] The Monetary Committee monitors economic and policy developments in the member states, and "on this road good progress has been made in recent years."[76]

THE COMMITTEE OF GOVERNORS. The Committee of Governors was created in 1964 as a consultative body, and it works closely with the Monetary Committee, with which its membership overlaps. The committee was initiated in a context of concern about limiting German hegemony in financial matters. The Commission expressed hope at the time that the committee would serve as the nucleus for a "federal-type banking system" and that by 1970 it would be making "centralized decisions."[77] The secretary of each committee is present at the other committee's meetings.[78] The committee is, by statute, free of instructions from both national and Community authorities.[79] Although there were proposals from the Werner Report to increase the powers of the committee, until 1987, it was formally nothing more than a forum for the exchange of views.[80] The Nyborg agreements increased the responsibilities of the committee for the surveillance of policy.[81]

THE BANKING ADVISORY COMMITTEE. The Banking Advisory Committee was established in 1977 (as part of the First Banking Directive) and brings together the top banking supervisors from each member state. Up until the Second Banking Directive, the committee was both consultative and advisory to the Commission on certain regulatory matters. Although this committee is of little direct importance to the conduct of monetary policy,

75. Kees, "Monetary Committee," p. 264.
76. Kees, "Monetary Committee," p. 261.
77. Schmitt, "Capital Markets and the Unification of Europe," p. 241.
78. Kees, "Monetary Committee," p. 259.
79. Karl-Otto Pöhl, "The Further Development of the European Monetary System," in Collection of Papers Submitted to the Committee for the Study of Economic and Monetary Union, p. 145.
80. Gunter D. Baer and Tommaso Padoa-Schioppa, 1989. "The Werner Report Revisited," in Collection of Papers Submitted to the Committee for the Study of Economic and Monetary Union, pp. 53–56.
81. Jacques Delors, "Economic and Monetary Union and Relaunching the Construction of Europe," in Collection of Papers Submitted to the Committee for the Study of Economic and Monetary Union, p. 66.

it is important in promoting and enforcing the movement toward greater competition in financial services. In the opinion of Commission observers, the Banking Advisory Committee has been marked by an increasing sense of independent "European" identity and a commitment to completing the single market.

In the emerging structure of financial regulation, the Banking Advisory Committee assumes additional responsibilities in the Second Banking Directive (and in a related directive dealing with capital ratios). In making "technical adaptations" to implement the directive, the Commission proposes draft language to the committee, which, using the weighted voting procedures followed in the European Council, then votes whether to approve the Commission's proposal. The measures are adopted if the committee approves. Otherwise, the proposal is submitted to the council, which has three months in which to veto the Commission's proposal.[82]

82. This is an instance of *comitology*, the assigning of quasi-legislative powers to committees that nominally advise the Commission. In a wry commentary, Blumann has suggested that better terms might be *comitomanie* or *comitolatrie*. Claude Blumann, "La Commission, Agent d'Execution du Droit Communautaire: La Comitologie," in Jean-Victor Louis and Denis Waelbroeck, eds., *La Commission au coeur du système institutionnel des Communautés européennes* (Brussels: Institut d'Etudes européennes, Université de Bruxelles, 1989), pp. 49–70.

Chapter 6

Structural Policy in the European Community

GARY MARKS

O NE OF the central elements of 1992 is a structural policy to increase "economic and social cohesion" in the European Community by "reducing disparities between the various regions and the backwardness of the least-favored regions."[1] The call for greater regional equality within the Community is not in itself new, but, for the first time, it has been accompanied by a serious financial commitment. In recent years a significant shift of resources to the three Funds responsible for regional integration has taken place (the European Regional Development Fund, the European Social Fund, and the Guidance Section of the Agricultural Guidance and Guarantee Fund). Following the general admonition of the Single European Act, in February 1988 the European Council agreed to double, in real terms, the resources available to the Funds between 1987 and 1993. By 1993 the budget appropriations for the Funds will increase to ECU 14 billion (European currency units), or about 25 percent of the total Community budget. At Maastricht a separate, legally binding protocol provides for additional regional aid and budgetary reform, and the treaty itself includes a new cohesion fund to help the poorest member states—Spain, Portugal, Greece, and Ireland – shoulder the cost of environmental and infrastructural projects.

I would like to thank my fellow contributors to the Brookings project on 1992 and my collaborators on the Consortium for 1992 for their numerous suggestions and crticisms. I am especially indebted to several administrators in the Commission of the European Communities for their aid and to Jeffrey Anderson, Michael Shackleton, and Helen Wallace for comments on this chapter. The remaining faults are my own.
1. Single European Act, 1986, article 130a.

Alongside this impressive budgeting expansion there have been fundamental innovations in the administration of the structural Funds. The
Fund administrations are coming to play a pivotal role in allocating resources and in developing and monitoring programs. For the first time the
administrations are creating policy networks that encompass subnational
governments and private interests in individual regions.[2]

The reforms of the structural Funds raise basic questions about the
distribution of authority and decisionmaking power across the Community, member states, and regional governments. To what extent are the
Community institutions responsible for structural policy developing independence from member states? Do these institutional innovations indicate
a fundamental shift in European political integration? Is it possible to
discern the outline of a new political order, a Europe of the regions, in
which states are outflanked by subnational governments dealing directly
with Community-wide bodies? Or is a new political disorder emerging
that escapes previous conceptualizations of the European polity?

To explain the growth of funding for structural policy I adopt a state-
centric perspective, focusing on member states conceived as unitary
actors. But in coming to grips with the changing relations of power and
authority involved in the reforms of the structural Funds, I adopt a more
open-textured, multilevel perspective in which EC institutions are seen
as independent political actors, and member states appear as complex
political institutions in contested national and regional political arenas.

This contrast is not the result of ambiguity about what the European
Community or the state really is but instead reflects different explanatory
strategies for contrasting political phenomena. Member states dominate
the allocation of resources within the EC, and if one wishes to explain the
growth of the budget for structural policy, a state-centric model is a useful
theoretical starting point.[3] The allocation of scarce resources within the

2. These innovations are only beginning to receive systematic attention either in the
scholarly literature (of which there is very little) or in the news sources. Apart from writings
cited elsewhere in this chapter, the major expression of intellectual interest in the structural
reforms is the current project on the European Community and the regions conducted by
Giuliano Bianchi, Rolf Jurgen Grote, Robert Leonardi, and Raffaella Y. Nanetti and others
at the European University Institute, Florence.

3. See Helen Wallace, "Negotiations and Coalition Formation in the European Community," *Government and Opposition*, vol. 20 (Autumn 1985), pp. 453–72, for a discussion of
theoretical approaches to different bargaining contexts. Wallace points out that a game theory
approach based on unitary and rational actors is appropriate in a few situations, including
the EC budget.

EC usually has a transparent zero-sum character, and this leads to intense bargaining among member states. If this interaction were the sum total of the European Community, then one might describe the Community merely as a set of rules within which member states make decisions. But there are also several policy sectors, including the internal market, the environment, the legal system, and structural policy, in which EC institutions can be autonomous and powerful. In these sectors member state governments must vie with supranational and, in some cases, subnational governments. Thus instead of assuming that member states have political control of the decisionmaking process, one must examine whether such control exists, and to the extent it does, one must ask how that is changing.

The Growth of the Structural Funds

The demand for a reduction of regional inequalities was present at the origin of the European Community. The preamble to the Treaty of Rome stated that member states are "anxious to strengthen the unity of their economies and to ensure their harmonious development by reducing the differences existing between the various regions and the backwardness of the less favored regions."[4] But while the legal framework for subsequent development existed, no plans were put forward for achieving this goal. The founders of the Community believed that greater regional equality could be achieved as a by-product of economic integration and growth and so did not feel the need to target individual regions directly. It was also stressed that poorer regions would benefit disproportionately from two Community-wide programs: the European Social Fund, which assists worker retraining in high-unemployment sectors, and the European Investment Bank, which provides low-interest loans.[5] In addition, the political impetus for a regional fund was limited among the original six member

4. Preamble, Treaty of Rome, 1957.
5. See John Mawson, Mario Ruis Martins, and John T. Gibney, "The Development of the European Community Regional Policy," in Michael Keating and Barry Jones, eds., *Regions in the European Community* (Oxford: Clarendon Press, 1985), pp. 20–59; Willem Molle and Jean Paelinck, "Regional Policy," in Peter Coffey, ed., *Economic Policies of the Common Market* (St. Martin's Press, 1979), pp. 146–71; and Marja-Liisa Kiljunen, "Regional Disparities and Policy in the EEC," in Dudley Seers and Constantine Vaitsos, eds., *Integration and Unequal Development: The Experience of the EEC* (St. Martin's Press, 1980), pp. 119–222. In addition, the European Coal and Steel Community provided aid for regions that had difficulties in reconverting to other activities, and the European Agricultural Fund provided funds for modernization in agricultural areas. However, the overall effects of the European Agricultural Fund are not progressive among member states according to Jan de

states. Only Italy contained a sizable region, the Mezzogiorno, which was far less developed than the rest, and the problems of this region could be dealt with in an ad hoc manner. It was not until the early 1970s, when Britain and Ireland—both with severe regional problem areas—were negotiating to join the EC, that Italy's long-standing call for a regional policy was galvanized into a new European Regional Development Fund.[6] The budget of the ERDF grew steadily, if unspectacularly, from its establishment in 1975 until the decision to double the proportion of the budget devoted to the lagging regions.[7]

Can Side Payments Explain the Doubling of Structural Funds?

The most straightforward explanation for the growth of the structural Funds is that they are a side payment or bribe paid by the wealthier members to the poorer peripheral members of the EC in return for their assent to the 1992 package of economic liberalization. Although the structural Funds aid some industrially declining regions in the wealthier countries, including parts of the Saarland in western Germany, the overall effect of the policy is to transfer resources from Belgium, Denmark, Germany, France, and the Netherlands to Greece, Spain, Ireland, Italy, and Portugal, with the United Kingdom remaining more or less neutral.

Table 6-1 sets out hypothetical payoffs for one rich and one peripheral country, say Germany and Portugal, respectively. Given that the cooperation of both countries is necessary to create a unified competitive market and that the combined welfare of these countries is increased by doing so, then the key to economic liberalization is finding some way of distributing the benefits so that both countries will be impelled toward a combined optimal solution. If one assumes that the benefits of 1992 are highly skewed and that some countries stand to lose (B), they will demand some kind of

---

Veer, "National Effects of CAP Trade Liberalization," in Second Tarditi and others, eds., *Agricultural Trade Liberalization and the European Community* (Oxford: Clarendon Press, 1989), pp. 99–109; and Kenneth J. Thomson, "Budgetary and Economic Effects of CAP Trade Liberalization," in ibid, pp. 110–19.

6. Claude André, Jean-François Drevet, and Eneko Landaburu, "Regional Consequences of the Internal Market," in *Contemporary European Affairs: 1992 and After*, vol. 1 (1989), pp. 205–14.

7. In 1975 the ERDF was allocated ECU 257.6 million, 4.8 percent of total EC spending. In 1987 its allocation was ECU 3,311 million, 9.1 percent of total EC spending. Commission of the European Communities, *The Regions of the Enlarged Community: Third Periodic Report on the Social and Economic Situation and Development of the Regions of the Community, Summary and Conclusions* (Luxembourg, 1987).

Table 6-1. *Hypothetical Payoffs Resulting from Economic Liberalization and Structural Policy*[a]

Country	Status quo pre-1992 (A)	1992 (B)	1992 + structural policy (C)
Germany	x	x + 10	x + 6
Portugal	y	y − 2	y + 2

a. x and y are constants.

side payment in return for their agreement to go along. Hence one should expect to see some policy mix along the lines of C, combining economic liberalization with a side payment (that is, structural policy) paid to potential losers.

The economic basis for the model sketched above is the hypothesis that the weaker economies on the periphery of the EC—Northern Ireland, Ireland, Portugal, Spain, southern Italy, and Greece—are vulnerable to liberalized competition with the far stronger economies of the core. Though it is generally agreed that the aggregate effects of 1992 are beneficial for the EC as a whole—most estimates of the positive net impact on the gross domestic product of the EC are in the range of 4 to 6 percent—the distributional effects of 1992 are uncertain and contested.[8]

According to neoclassical economic theory, an increase in the geographic scope of competition will tend to equalize factor prices in the affected regions.[9] Poorer countries and regions will benefit as labor moves to higher-wage areas and firms relocate in low-wage areas. However, several arguments have been put forward in the scholarly literature and in EC reports that suggest this scenario is overoptimistic.[10] Although

8. For estimates of the total net impact of 1992, see Paolo Cecchini, with Michael Catinat and Alexis Jacquemin, *The European Challenge: 1992, The Benefits of the Single European Market*, tr. John Robinson (Aldershot: Wildwood House, 1988).

9. Richard A. Bilas, *Microeconomic Theory*, 2d ed. (McGraw-Hill, 1971), chap. 11; and Bo Södersten, *International Economics* (Harper and Row, 1970), chap. 5.

10. The chief arguments are as follows. First mobility of labor within the EC after 1992 will be constrained by continuing linguistic and cultural diversity. The opening up of a European economic market is not expected to replicate the development of national markets based on more homogenous populations, which precipitated large migrations of labor to high-wage and high-employment areas. In any case, large migration flows in response to job opportunities are likely to have significant social and political costs for regions that lose skilled labor and for those that must accommodate the incoming population. Depopulated regions face economic and communal obsolescence; magnet regions face overcrowding and tension between local and immigrant populations. See Iain Begg, "European Integration and Re-

the Fund administrations avoid making precise predictions about the distributional consequences of 1992 across regions and member states, their reports stress the potential downside for the weaker regions and economies:

Peripheral areas . . . are, in many cases, quite remote from the major demand and supply centers and are much less densely populated than the Community as a whole. . . . The special problems they face stem in part from their location, with which are associated higher transport costs, longer transport and travel times, longer delivery periods, higher storage costs, fewer opportunities to achieve size-related cost savings, and more difficult access to information. These factors hamper exploitation of the development opportunities and incentives arising from the internal market.[11]

---

gional Policy," *Oxford Review of Economic Policy*, vol. 5 (Summer 1989), pp. 90–104; and Allan M. Williams, *The Western European Economy: A Geography of Post-War Development* (London: Hutchinson, 1987), p. 259.

Second, the assumption about capital mobility in response to cheap labor is vitiated in key sectors, including most technologically innovative industries that rely on a sophisticated communication infrastructure and a pool of highly skilled labor. Recent studies have emphasized the difficulties of attracting private capital to declining industrial areas and less-developed regions. Evidence also shows that capital mobility within the Organization for Economic Cooperation and Development during the postwar period has been relatively limited. For a discussion of the difficulties faced in structural policy designed to attract high-technology industry, see Nils Diederich and Ulrich Hilpert, "Statliche Politik and Nicht-Intendierte Konsequenzen," unpublished proposal, Free University of Berlin, July 1989; and Ulrich Hilpert, ed., *State Policies and Techno-Industrial Innovation* (London: Routledge, 1990). See also Andrea Boltho, "European and United States Regional Differentials: A Note," *Oxford Review of Economic Policy*, vol. 5 (Summer 1989), pp. 105–15.

Creation of a competitive market within the EC will take place in the virtual absence of fiscal and welfare policies that have countered regional disparities in European societies that previously developed national markets. The present conception of 1992 includes a common market in the absence of equalizing fiscal and social instruments (including progressive direct taxes, welfare transfers, and public expenditure) that have accompanied such markets in the past. The potential for regional disparities will be exacerbated if, as planned, member states integrate their monetary policies, thus denying less developed countries strategic devaluation as a means of promoting exports. See Dudley Seers, "Theoretical Aspects of Unequal Development at Different Spacial Levels," in Seers and Vaitsos, eds., *Integration and Unequal Development*. In addition, harmonization of labor regulations to avoid "social dumping" would deprive backward areas and countries of differential advantages in the final cost of labor. See, for example, Herbert Giersch, "EC 1992: Competition Is the Clue," *European Affairs*, vol. 3 (Autumn 1989), pp. 10–17.

11. Commission of the European Communities, *Regions of the Enlarged Community*, p. ix.

However, to know that the policy is grounded in an evaluation of potential economic costs and benefits across regions does not reveal why it was enacted. Fairness is only one consideration, and by no means the most important one, in determining which policies are enacted and which are not. Moreover, in this case potential losers are in the minority. The major recipients of structural aid, regions on the southern and western peripheries of Europe, encompass only about one-fifth of the EC's population. Except for the Italian Mezzogiorno, the poorest regions are in countries that are recent members of the EC; as a result, they have had less opportunity to shape the Community's institutions in their favor. To explain the shift in resources to the poorer regions, one must analyze the economic implications of 1992 in the context of the decisionmaking process in the European Community.

Economic concerns about the distribution of the costs and benefits of 1992 were particularly forceful because it has rarely been possible for a majority of member states to enforce policy changes on a minority. The effective mode of decisionmaking in the EC from the Luxembourg Compromise of 1966 until modified by the Single European Act has been unanimity voting. The challenge for innovators has thus been to find ways of paying off recalcitrant member states by combining issues in such a way that every member state benefits.[12] In contrast to the familiar politics of majority voting, which is driven by the need to create majority coalitions, the politics of unanimity voting is one of creating bundles of issues to distribute potential gains so that no voter wishes to block the legislation.[13]

---

12. The Single European Act has introduced modified majority voting, except when member states' essential national interests are affected. However, the conditions under which this concern is true are determined by member states themselves. The logic of the analysis runs along similar, though weaker, lines when applied to modified majority voting. On the institutional evolution of decision rules in the EC, see Helen Wallace, "The Best Is the Enemy of the 'Could': Bargaining in the European Community," in Tarditi and others, eds., Agricultural Trade Liberalization, pp. 193–206; and the chapter by Guy Peters in this volume. Discussions of the consequences of unanimity voting are found in James M. Buchanan and Gordon Tullock, The Calculus of Consent: Logical Foundations of Constitutional Democracy (University of Michigan Press, 1962); and Dennis C. Mueller, Public Choice II (Cambridge: Cambridge University Press, 1989). My approach contrasts with the analysis of unanimity voting in H. Wayne Moyer, "The CAP in a Single Market: Magnitude, Significance and Obstacles," paper presented at the annual meeting of the American Political Science Association, 1989.

13. The logic of the situation is essentially the same if a temporal dimension is added to the model. Under iterated unanimity voting, a voter wishing to veto will have to take into account the negative effects of this vote on future relations with other voters, as well as the present costs and benefits of the legislation.

Politically, the growth of the structural Funds is explained by this model as a side payment to potential loser member states that could otherwise have blocked economic liberalization and the overall gains it was expected to bring. The countries that will gain significantly from the growth of the structural Funds—Greece, Spain, Ireland, Italy, and Portugal—encompass a minority of the total population of the EC, yet because their assent to the package of economic reforms was necessary for its passage, they were powerfully positioned to demand a side payment.[14] According to the model sketched above, this side payment reflects the expected costs of 1992 for the peripheral economies of the EC. Economic liberalization generated both the prospect of losing ground by weaker economies and an overall economic gain that could finance side payments without any real sacrifice by the rich.

This simple model of decisionmaking helps explain the rachetlike character of institutional change in the EC, in which sustained blockage is punctuated by complex and far-reaching reform. On the one hand, unanimity rules lead to extended stalemate, where every conceivable innovation is blocked by recalcitrant voters. On the other hand, when change comes, it is in the shape of complex agreements that shift the status quo on several fronts simultaneously. Thus economic liberalization is decisive not only on its own account but also because it involves expected benefits large enough to finance side payments to those who believe they will not benefit. The shift in Community resources to the structural Funds can be seen as a *forced spillover*, in which the prospect of a breakthrough in one arena created intense pressure for innovation in others.

A model focusing on side payments as a forced spillover is useful for understanding previous key episodes of policy innovation in structural policy in the EC. The debate about the creation of some institutional mechanism for regional subvention in the early 1970s, culminating in the establishment of a Regional Fund in 1975, took place in the wake of the first enlargement of the Community with the addition of the United Kingdom and Ireland. Both countries had endemic regional problems that led them to side with Italy in its long-standing demand for a Community regional policy. At the same time the budgetary process in the EC virtually ground to a halt as Britain demanded special treatment because of its position as a large net contributor to the budget. Although the creation of

14. The United Kingdom does not stand to be a net gainer from the growth of the structural Funds. Its share of ERDF funding from 1986 to 1988 was 16.42 percent, compared with its population share in the EC-12 of 17.6 percent.

a Regional Fund was rooted in a diffuse and long-standing commitment to economic cohesion, the timing of the innovation was driven by the need to consolidate a newly enlarged Community in a period of particularly hard national bargaining about relative contributions to the budget.[15]

The expansion of structural policy with the introduction of Integrated Mediterranean Programs (IMPs) in 1984 for Greece, southern Italy, and parts of southern France can also be seen as a forced spillover. These states demanded a side payment to offset the increased agricultural competition that was bound to result from the inclusion of Spain and Portugal in the Community. The outcome was a new form of integrated structural policy targeted at the regions that had the most to lose.[16]

The side-payment model sketched out above provides an elegant explanation of the growth of structural policy in the EC. But it is problematic in one important respect. Though the logic of the model is powerful, the effects of 1992 for the poorer peripheral countries in the EC are ambiguous. The view that economic liberalization will hurt the weaker economies in the EC is contested. A recently published study of the distributional benefits of economic liberalization published in *Economic Policy* finds that Portugal, Greece, Spain, and, to a lesser extent, the United Kingdom stand to gain the most. With the removal of nontariff barriers, Portugal, Greece, and Spain will be able to further specialize in labor-intensive commodities, such as shoes and textiles, for which there are still untapped economies of scale. In contrast, available economies of scale have for the most part already been realized in the northern countries. The study concludes that "the main beneficiaries of the 1992 programme are . . . likely to be the Southern European countries, both in terms of exploiting comparative advantage and in terms of exhausting scale economies."[17]

Economic data on the past performance of individual countries and regions in the EC do not confirm the picture of a widening gap between rich and poor (table 6-2). During the past two decades the four states that have the weakest economies, with a per capita gross national product of

15. See Helen Wallace, "Distributional Politics: Dividing Up the Community Cake," in Helen Wallace, William Wallace, and Carole Webb, eds., *Policy-Making in the European Community*, 2d ed. (Chichester: John Wiley and Sons, 1983), pp. 81–113.

16. Commission of the European Communities, *Les Programmes Intégrés Méditerranéens* (Luxembourg: Office for Official Publications of the European Communities, May 1989).

17. Damien J. Neven, "EEC Integration towards 1992: Some Distributional Aspects," *Economic Policy*, no. 10 (April 1990), pp. 14–62; quotation on p. 46.

Table 6-2. *Real GDP per Capita in EC Member States, 1960–88*

Country	1960–88	1960–68	1968–73	1973–79	1979–88
Belgium	3.0	3.9	5.3	2.1	1.7
Denmark	2.5	3.8	3.3	1.6	1.7
France	3.0	4.2	4.6	2.3	1.4
Germany	2.7	3.1	4.0	2.5	1.7
Greece	4.1	6.7	7.8	2.6	0.9
Ireland	3.1	3.8	3.5	3.3	2.0
Italy	3.5	5.0	3.9	3.2	2.2
Luxembourg	2.4	2.1	4.9	0.7	2.5
Netherlands	2.3	3.5	3.7	1.9	0.7
Portugal	4.0	5.7	8.9	1.3	1.8
Spain	3.7	6.4	5.7	1.1	1.9
United Kingdom	2.2	2.3	3.0	1.5	2.0
Average for Greece, Ireland, Portugal, Spain	3.7	5.7	6.5	2.1	1.7
Total EC	2.8	3.8	4.2	2.1	1.7

Source: Organization for Economic Cooperation and Development Economic Outlook, *Historical Statistics 1960–1988* (Paris, 1990), table 3.2.

less than 75 percent of the EC average—Portugal, Greece, Spain, and Ireland—have grown at an annual per capita rate of 3.7 percent, compared with a 2.8 percent rate for the EC as a whole, even though the population increased more rapidly in the poorer societies. The relative gains of the four peripheral countries were concentrated in the 1960s and early 1970s. Their combined economic growth from the early 1970s is neither better nor worse than the average of EC member states. Although the aggregate evidence does not suggest that absolute differences between rich and poor countries have narrowed significantly, it is important to note that absolute levels of economic welfare before the 1992 reforms (the constants x and y in table 6-1) are irrelevant for the side-payment theory just discussed.

This picture is consistent with the available regional data, summarized in table 6-3. Between 1973 and 1982 the poorest regions of the EC experienced greater economic growth, absolutely and per capita, than the richest regions. Both population and employment increased faster in the poorest regions than in the richest. The differences are not large, particularly when Spain and Portugal are included, and it is clear that even if these trends continued, it would take decades for the gap to disappear. However, once again, there are few signs that the economic position of

Table 6-3. *Regional Growth in Real GDP, Population,
and Employment in the Twenty-five Strongest and Weakest
EC Regions, 1973–82*
Average annual percent change

Area of growth and years	Average of regions[a]					
	EC-10[b]			EC-12		
	25 weakest	25 strongest	All	25 weakest	25 strongest	All
Real GDP per capita						
1973–79	2.4	2.2	2.1	. . .	. . .	. . .
1977–82	2.0	1.3	1.3	1.4	1.3	1.2
1973–82	1.8	1.7	1.5	. . .	. . .	. . .
Real GDP						
1973–79	3.0	2.3	2.4	. . .	. . .	. . .
1977–82	2.5	1.6	1.6	2.1	1.6	1.6
1973–82	2.4	1.8	1.7	. . .	. . .	. . .
Population						
1973–79	0.6	0.1	0.3	. . .	. . .	. . .
1977–82	0.4	0.2	0.3	0.7	0.2	0.3
1973–82	0.5	0.1	0.3	. . .	. . .	. . .
Real GDP/employment						
1973–79	2.2	2.5	2.2	. . .	. . .	. . .
1977–82	1.9	1.6	1.6	2.5	1.6	1.8
1973–82	1.7	2.1	1.8	. . .	. . .	. . .
Employment						
1973–79	0.8	−0.2	0.2	. . .	. . .	. . .
1977–82	0.6	−0.03	−0.02	−0.4	−0.03	−0.3
1973–82	0.6	−0.3	−0.1	. . .	. . .	. . .

Source: Commission of the European Communities, *The Regions of the Enlarged Community: Third Periodic Report on the Social and Economic Situation and Development of the Regions of the Community, Summary and Conclusions* (Luxembourg, 1987), p. 131.
a. Level 2 regions ranked by real level of GDP per capita at beginning of each period.
b. All EC members except Spain and Portugal.

the weaker economies is deteriorating either in absolute terms or relative to the EC as a whole.

A detailed report written for the Commission of the Economic Communities in 1988, based on data for 1977–83, finds that although peripheral regions have one-third of the EC's population and only one quarter of its gross domestic product, along with 39 percent of its unemployment, they have also had higher rates of per capita economic growth and employment growth in recent years. Absolute income levels are lower than the average for central regions in 98 percent of the peripheral regions, but 83 percent of the peripheral regions have had growth rates higher than the average for central regions.[18]

These data do not settle the issue, but they do raise serious doubts about the view that the structural Funds are a side payment to losers. To attempt to predict the distributional consequences of economic liberalization would reach far beyond the present chapter. However, an essential point has already been made, namely, that the distributional consequences of economic liberalization are contested and, above all, uncertain. Economic theory speaks on the regional distribution of economic growth with more than one voice; we do not know if we can extrapolate past trends into the future; and the international economic context within which 1992 will be played out is unpredictable.[19] To accept the explanation of side payments as just discussed and as assumed in the literature on structural policy, one must be prepared to make the highly dubious assumption that winners and losers can be distinguished in advance of the process of economic liberalization.

Rethinking Side Payments

There seem to be two ways to develop a more convincing explanation. First, one can try to formulate the side-payment explanation on a more subtle and convincing basis by building uncertainty about outcomes into the model itself and arguing that the poorer societies were paid because of their greater vulnerability to any given economic loss should it occur. Second, one can argue that the structural Funds were a response to new conceptions of fairness and equality that intensified demands for redistribution on behalf of the poorer societies and created a greater willingness to concede such demands on the part of the richer societies.

There are plausible grounds for believing that the risk of economic recession is harder for a less affluent society to bear. In the first place

18. David Keeble, John Offord, and Sheila Walker, *Peripheral Regions in a Community of Twelve Member States* (Luxembourg: Commission of the European Communities, 1988), pp. 104, 111.

19. There are many other sources of uncertainty. For example, the levels of external tariffs for the EC as a whole are unknown, and this information is likely to be critical for the distribution of gains and losses across regions according to Cambridge Economic Consultants, "The Regional Impact of Policies Implemented in the Context of Completing the Community's Internal Market by 1992," Final Report to the Commission of the European Communities (n.d.).

poorer societies lack a cushion of affluence against economic downturns. A large proportion of the wages of many workers in those societies is spent on meeting basic needs for food, clothing, and shelter, and a loss of real income, or at worst unemployment, must hit them especially hard. Generally speaking, the less affluent a society is, the more its citizens will be sensitive to a given percentage change in their consumption. This response is reinforced because poorer societies are less able to fund welfare systems to counter the effects of economic adversity. For the poorest countries in the EC the 1992 project is part of an acute struggle to develop a decent standard of economic well-being.

The hypothesis that the least affluent member states face disproportionate costs as a result of the uncertainties of economic liberalization also has a political basis. The countries with the most severe regional problems— Portugal, Spain, Greece, and Ireland—are recent members of the Community and as a result are particularly prone to a negative political fallout if their hopes for economic growth as a result of economic liberalization are shattered. Although support for the Community has developed within the core EC-6 members over three decades, mass publics in the new member countries are just now becoming accustomed to the idea.[20] Because citizens in the poorer member countries have expanding opportunities to compare their life chances with citizens elsewhere in the Community, their expectations may rise faster than their governments can fulfill them. Despite the fears voiced by many economists that the weaker regions may suffer as a result of 1992, mass publics in the least affluent countries tend to be more, not less, optimistic about the effects of the economic liberalization.[21] For governments in these societies, the economic risk associated with 1992 seems particularly threatening. If these countries suffer as a result of 1992, the fundamental political issue of the benefits of EC membership will be raised in a particularly direct and transparent fashion. Without the political capital of support for the EC built up over decades, 1992 may turn out to be a harsh test for the most recent members of the Community.

20. According to Eurobarometer polls, overall support for membership of the EC remains on average lower among publics in the newer members than in the EC-6, although the gap has been narrowing in recent years. This is true even if one excludes the two more affluent newer members, the United Kingdom and Denmark, where levels of support for membership have been particularly low.

21. Commission of the European Communities, "Awareness of '1992': The Single Market," *Eurobarometer: Public Opinion in the European Community*, no. 30 (December 1988), table 3, p. 20.

Finally, three southern members—Portugal, Spain, and Greece—are facing the uncertainty of economic liberalization while undergoing the fundamental political transition to liberal democracy. On the one hand, this transition provides a source of legitimacy for membership in the European Community. Membership is viewed as a confirmation of new-found democratic status.[22] But on the other hand, governments in these societies are particularly vulnerable to economic dislocation, especially when it can be blamed on prior political choices. The possibility of economic dislocation arising from fundamental changes in the competitive environment is a challenge for even the most stable democracy; for a newly established democratic regime it can be daunting.[23]

An explanation for the growth of the structural Funds focusing on the differential costs of economic risk adds complexity to the side-payment model. But the model has one major advantage: it does not rest on the questionable assumption that winners and losers can be distinguished in advance of the implementation of 1992. Instead of sweeping the unpredictability of the process aside, it builds unpredictability into the explanation and poses the question whether the risks of the policy fall more on some societies than on others.

Demands for Redistribution

A second approach, which is by no means mutually exclusive with the focus on risk, is to explain the growth of the structural Funds as a result of changing conceptions of fairness leading to new demands and a new willingness to meet those demands. For several centuries conceptions of justice, freedom, and equality have been monopolized by the modern state as the only practicable arena for achieving the good society. But there are signs that this mind-set is changing. Many educated younger people, particularly those active in the EC, regard the state as just one of several legitimate arenas for achieving the public good.[24]

---

22. Edward P. Moxon-Browne, "Spain and the European Community in the 1990s," paper presented at the 1989 Conference of the European Community Studies Association, George Mason University, May 1989.

23. See, for example, Wolfgang Merkel, "Vom Ende der Diktaturen zum Binnenmarkt 1993: Griechenland, Portugal und Spanien auf dem Weg zurück nach Europe," *Aus Politik und Zeitgeschichte*, no. 51 (December 14, 1990), pp. 3–14.

24. Ronald Inglehart, *Culture Shift in Advanced Industrial Society* (Princeton University Press, 1990), pp. 417–21.

Demands for a regionally redistributive policy are reinforced by the severity of regional disparities in the enlarged Community. While economic inequalities among the original EC-6 were fairly narrow, those among the newly enlarged EC-12 are extremely wide. These contrasts are reflected at the regional level. Of the thirty-two regions with the greatest economic problems (as identified by the EC's synthetic index) all but eight are found in Portugal (counted as one region), Spain, or Greece.[25] Regional disparities within the EC are far greater than among states in the United States.[26] At the extremes, the per capita gross domestic product of the poorest regions, including Thrakis in Greece, and southern Portugal, is just one-sixth that of Groningen or Hamburg.

The sheer existence of such disparities does not, of course, mean that they will mobilize demands for redistribution. Most injustices are politically dormant. It seems likely, though, that the thrust of the 1992 package, its focus on liberal economic reforms in an attempt to increase productivity and growth, helped mobilize demands for a more egalitarian distribution not simply of the immediate benefits that 1992 was expected to bring but of the European economic pie as a whole. Given that the poorer societies were essential partners in the creation of the integrated market, why, one might ask, should they not derive a fairer share of the benefits of the international division of labor? At the same time, the deepening of the institutions of the EC made the stark inequalities that exist seem less inevitable and therefore more pressing. Little time is spent worrying about inequalities that are acts of nature, but those that seem to be under human control can provoke intense conflict. In this case, the creation of more powerful European political institutions has extended the sphere of the political (and thus of potential disagreement and conflict) to encompass issues that were formerly believed, quite accurately, to be beyond human manipulation.

While state-based realpolitik dominates the Council of Ministers, many proponents of regional policy in Brussels and Strasbourg are motivated by ethical concerns about regional disparities that have long been influential within individual states. A frequently voiced argument is that regional

25. Commission of the European Communities, *Regions of the Enlarged Community*, pp. 169–75.

26. The Gini coefficient for the EC-12 divided into fifty-nine regions is 0.13, while that for the forty-eight contiguous United States is 0.072. Boltho, "European and United States Regional Differentials."

disparities should be tackled because they are a barrier to further integration.[27] Underlying this practical concern is the realization that if the Community is to gain the loyalty of individual citizens, it must provide for the expression of basic moral concerns for justice and equality that have formerly been confined to nation states. These arguments have frequently been expressed in the European Parliament, which has become closely identified with the cause of structural spending in the poorer regions. Regional and social items fall under the quarter of the budget that is deemed "noncompulsory expenditure," and as a result the European Parliament has been able to increase spending in this area.[28]

Reform of the Structural Funds

The growth of funding for the weaker regions has been accompanied by some fundamental reforms of the decisionmaking procedures of the structural Funds. The Funds are in the process of being transformed by several open-ended, more or less contested innovations, whose consequences are likely to be only partly those intended by the makers.

The main institutional and procedural reforms are as follows:[29]

Elaboration of explicit priorities for the overall distribution of the structural budget. These priorities are justified as a necessary step in transforming structural policy into an instrument with real economic impact by focusing spending in those regions with the worst problems. The

27. David Coombes, "The Politics of Scale: European Economic Integration, Spatial Disparity, and Local Development," paper presented at the May 1989 Conference of the European Community Studies Association, Fairfax, Va.; and Harvey Armstrong, "Community Regional Policy," in Juliet Lodge, ed., *The European Community and the Challenge of the Future* (St. Martin's Press, 1989), pp. 167–85. For a general statement along these lines, see Lynn Krieger Mytelka, "The Salience of Gains in Third-World Integrative Systems," *World Politics*, vol. 25 (January 1973), pp. 236–50.

28. See Michael Shackleton, "The Budget of the European Community," in Lodge, ed., *European Community*, pp. 129–47; and chapter 3 in this volume.

29. Bruce Millan, "Regional Policy in Europe of the 1990s," opening address to the International Congress on Regional Policy held in Madrid May 30-31, 1989; and Armstrong, "Community Regional Policy." The 1988 reforms are detailed in Council Regulation (EEC) No. 2052/88 of 24 June 1988, *Official Journal of the European Communities*, no. L 185 (July 15, 1988), p. 9; Council Regulation (EEC) No. 4253/88 of 19 December 1988, *Official Journal of the European Communities*, no. L 374 (December 31, 1988), p. 1; and Council Regulation (EEC) No. 4254/88 of 19 December 1988, *Official Journal of the European Communities*, no. L 374 (December 31, 1988), p. 15. The reforms are summarized in Commission of the European Communities, *Guide to the Reform of the Community's Structural Funds* (Luxembourg: Office for Official Publications of the European Community, 1989).

Figure 6-1. *Regions of the European Community Eligible under Objective 1 of the Structural Funds*[a]

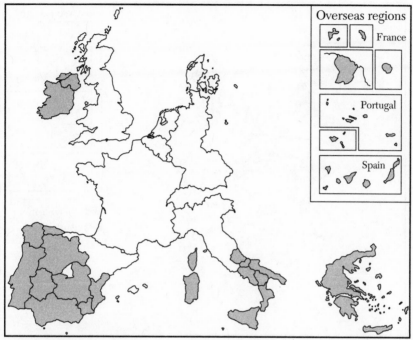

Source: Commission of the European Communities, *The New Structural Policies of the European Community*, European File (June–July 1990), p. 10.
a. Regions lagging behind in development.

following five priorities for structural spending were put forward by the Commission and approved by the Council of Ministers at the Brussels summit of February 1988.[30]

Objective 1 is to promote economic development in regions with a per capita gross domestic product of less than 75 percent of the EC average. The areas covered are Northern Ireland, Ireland, Portugal, large parts of Spain, Corsica and the French overseas departments, southern Italy, and Greece, which together encompass 21.5 percent of the population of the EC (see figure 6-1). Beginning in 1989 these regions were to receive

30. The objectives are drawn from Commission of the European Communities, *Annual Report on the Implementation of the Reform of the Structural Funds, 1989* (Brussels, 1990), pp. 1–4. See also Commission of the European Communities, "Good News for the Regions," *Information*, March 8, 1989.

Figure 6-2. *Regions of the European Community Eligible under Objective 2 of the Structural Funds*[a]

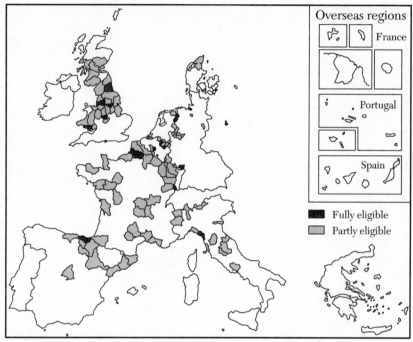

Source: EC Commission, *New Structural Policies*, p. 11.
a. Industrial areas in decline.

about 80 percent of the resources available to the European Regional Development Fund and the bulk of structural funding as a whole, ECU 38.3 billion of the total multiannual structural budget of ECU 60.3 billion for 1989–93, or 63.5 percent of total appropriations. The Funds are now able to meet up to three-quarters (from one-half before 1989) of the cost of approved measures in objective 1 regions, thereby reducing the burden on indigenous funding.

Objective 2 is to convert regions seriously affected by industrial decline. A total of sixty regions in the United Kingdom, France, Italy, Spain, Germany, Denmark, Belgium, and Luxembourg, encompassing between 16 and 17 percent of the population of the EC, are slated to receive structural aid under this criterion (see figure 6-2). The appropriation for 1989–93 is ECU 7.2 billion.

Objective 3 is to combat long-term unemployment, and objective 4 is to facilitate the occupational integration of young people. These objectives, which are combined for budgetary purposes, apply to the EC as a whole. Their appropriation for 1989–93 is ECU 7.45 billion.

Objective 5a is to speed up adjustment in agricultural structures, particularly marketing and processing, across the EC, and objective 5b is rural development in selected regions, particularly those regions covered under objective 1. Objective 5b is directed to fifty-six regions encompassing 5 percent of the EC's population. Appropriations for objective 5a and 5b for 1989–93 are ECU 3.415 billion and ECU 2.795 billion, respectively.

Change in emphasis from projects to programs. Rather than support individual projects proposed by member states, the structural Funds will increasingly combine their interventions in larger financial commitments running over longer periods of time (three to five years) for multifaceted programs called Community Support Frameworks (CSFs). This shift in emphasis was initiated by the Commission in 1984 with the development of Integrated Mediterranean Programs and was extended and refined in the 1988 reforms, particularly affecting the role of regional authorities. Whereas project funding is usually directed to roads, building, and other infrastructural investment, program funding includes diverse forms of aid for local industry and services (for example, direct productive investments in private industry, provision of consulting services, research and development, and technical and vocational training) designed to stimulate indigenous development. In contrast to project grants, which are straightforward financial transfers to member states for schemes that they would probably undertake in any case, programs allow the Funds themselves to shape policy. There are three categories of programs: national programs of Community interest drawn up as part of member-state regional aid schemes in the form of Community Support Frameworks (these include the IMPs); specific Community measures taken on the Commission's initiative outside of the regular budget; and Community initiatives conceived by the Commission: STAR (grants for advanced telecommunication services), VALOREN (grants for exploiting indigenous energy sources), RENAVEL (conversion of shipbuilding areas), RESIDER (conversion of steel areas), and, since 1989, RECHAR (to diversify the economic base of coal-mining areas), ENVIREG (to help lagging regions with their environmental problems), STRIDE (to increase regional capacities for research, technology, and innovation), INTERREG (to encourage cooperation between border regions), REGIS (to integrate peripheral island regions into the Community), REGEN (to integrate gas and electric transmission networks), EUROFORM, NOW, HORIZON (initiatives concerned with vocational training in the Community as a whole), PRISMA (to help lagging regions meet Community-wide quality standards), LEADER (to promote rural development), and TELEMATIQUE (to develop advanced telecommunications services in objective 1 regions).

Increased role for the Funds in allocating expenditures across and within member states. Fifteen percent of the ERDF budget (ECU 3.8 billion for 1989 to 1993) is at the discretion of the Commission for the Community initiatives just listed. The allocations for objectives 3 and 4 are determined by the ratio of the long-term unemployed and the number of unemployed under twenty-five years old in each member state to the number in the EC as a whole. The remainder of the structural budget is allocated among member states on the basis of broad ranges rather than fixed quotas. The ranges are wide: the difference between the lower and upper limit is roughly one-third the value of the lower limit.[31] A member state is entitled to the lower limit, but any transfers above this line are at the discretion of the Commission. In deciding where to target expenditures above the minimum margins, the Commission is directed to favor projects and programs that are deemed of value to the Community as a whole. Under new regulations agreed at the Brussels summit, the role of the Commission in policy formulation is formalized and enhanced. Member states submit detailed plans that become the basis for negotiations between the Commission, the member state, and the regional authorities concerned. As a result of these negotiations, CSFs are established for each region, and these are used by the Commission to make final decisions about levels of funding.

Coordination among the Funds. The notion of a structural policy encompassing the Regional Fund, Social Fund, and Guidance Section of the Agricultural Fund, as elaborated in the 1988 reforms, demands increased institutional coordination. The priorities for spending that came into force in 1989 apply to the entire budgets of these Funds, and in many cases the Funds must cooperate on individual programs. A new Directorate-General, DG XXII (Coordination of Structural Instruments), has been set up to coordinate the three structural Funds and link their interventions

31. Commission of the European Communities, *European Regional Development Fund: Thirteenth Annual Report*, pp. 74–75.

to those of other EC agencies, particularly the European Investment Bank, which makes extensive loans (ECU 7 billion in 1989) for income-generating projects.

Increased role for regional authorities. In the project approach the Funds were conceived of as financial controllers, at arm's length from regional governments. But the 1988 regulations envisage a three-sided partnership of the Commission, member states, and regional authorities in drawing up, financing, and monitoring Community Support Frameworks. Under the reforms, representatives from regional governments are included in numerous and lengthy meetings, a legally mandated "direct dialogue," in which the Commission explores funding priorities, alternative means of financing CSFs, and effective means of implementing them.[32] For some CSFs, especially those detailing conversion policies in agricultural areas, the partnership has extended beyond the regional level to include affected local authorities. Besides its attempt to include subnational governments in the planning process, the Commission has also sought to increase the share of funding that is allocated directly to regional authorities by shifting emphasis away from large-scale infrastructural spending in favor of local development-oriented operations such as training, technical assistance, and direct investment in local business.

These reforms have been justified in terms of administrative efficiency and economic rationality, and to enforce the principle of additionality, in which programs receiving a grant from the Funds are supported by member states in addition to, and not as a substitute for, existing planned public expenditure. But they also share an interesting and consequential set of political bottom lines. First, they increase the autonomy of the Commission and the respective Directorates-General in allocating resources among individual programs and even among member states. Patterns of spending for the European Regional Development Fund from 1985 to 1987 reveal wide differences in the ability of member states to compete for funds in excess of their lower limits. Italy was allocated 30.9 percent of the margin resources, compared with its lower limit of 21.62 percent, while several other member states received shares of the margin at roughly the same rate as their lower limit. For example, the United Kingdom received 15.91 percent of the margin resources, compared with its lower limit of 14.6 percent.[33]

32. Commission of the European Communities, *Annual Report on the Implementation of the Reform of the Structural Funds, 1989*, p. 8.

33. Commission of the European Communities, *European Regional Development Fund: Thirteenth Annual Report*, pp. 73–74.

Second, the reforms of the structural Funds extend the EC's administrative reach into the regions and into individual programs in the regions. Although in the past the Funds were a straightforward device for financial transfers to member states, under the 1988 reforms Fund administrators are called on to actively formulate Community Support Frameworks with subnational government administrators. The program approach emphasizes what are called "immaterial" investments, investments that enhance indigenous entrepreneurial and management skills, especially of small- and medium-sized firms, as distinct from large-scale infrastructural investments. For the first time systematic efforts will be made to evaluate the ongoing performance of individual programs. Since 1989 the Funds have had a larger stake in the programs they help pay for. The cap on the EC's share of funding for particular programs will increase from 50 percent to 75 percent, and these funds will be made available as "global grants," managed by public or semipublic bodies in the regions. Together, these changes give the Funds substantial functions and power resources in the regions.

In short, the reforms have set in motion a process of institution building that strengthens the Commission; that attempts to technocratize—and in a narrow sense depoliticize—a key and growing policy area; and that, by creating direct links between the Funds and regional political institutions, challenges centralized decisionmaking within member states.

Outflanking the State?

Reforms in structural policy have created new possibilities for EC decisionmakers to deal directly with political actors in individual regions in creating, sustaining, and monitoring comprehensive development programs over several years or even decades. For the first time it seems possible to conceive of a practical basis for visions of a new European political order in which increasing centralization of decisionmaking in the EC is counterbalanced by the emergence of powerful regional institutions linked directly to the center. Are states now being outflanked on the one side by the transfer of authority to the EC and on the other by incentives for newly assertive and politically meaningful regional bodies? To put the issue in its sharpest form, is this the beginning of the end of the state in Western Europe?

This is the ideal of proponents of a "Europe of the regions," who have long argued that European states reflect neither the diverse cultures, languages, and identities of Europeans nor the most practical geographical units of economic life in conurbations and regions that, like the Lille-Roubaix-Tourcoing region in France and Belgium, often span state boundaries. While the vision of a federal European Community has never really threatened the legitimacy of the state, a Europe of the regions accords with basic aspirations for enhanced participation in smaller political units that have been expressed by many young educated people across Western Europe. Such a conception has also been pressed by various geographically based cultural minorities. Welsh, Bretons, Basques, and Catalans have joined the Bureau of Unrepresented Nations set up in Brussels in 1977. A charter expressing the demand for a Europe of the regions has been signed by several cultural and ethnic parties, including Plaid Cymru, the Flemish Volksunie, and the Friesland party.[34] Germany's regional governments, the Länder, have demanded, and have been granted, observer status on several EC bodies.

Over the last two decades governments across Western Europe have experimented with ways to deconcentrate and decentralize decisionmaking to mollify ethno-linguistic minorities, bring policy provision nearer policy receivers, cushion demands on the state, and reduce the central tax burden.[35] Belgium has been transformed from a unitary into a federal polity; Italy, France, and Spain, previously highly centralized political systems, have created a comprehensive layer of regional government; and Greece, and to a lesser extent Portugal, has moved more tentatively in the same direction, mainly in response to the financial advantages of subnational participation in the EC's structural policy. Only Germany, which is a federal polity in a culturally homogenous society, has moved steadily in the opposite direction. Ireland remains highly centralized, though there are pressures for the creation of regional government, and in the United Kingdom recent conservative governments have restricted the autonomy of subnational governments and resisted demands for devolution.

Recent developments in the regions in response to the structural re-

34. Anne Daltrop, *Politics and the European Community*, 2d ed. (London: Longman, 1986), p. 119.

35. See Michael Keating, *State and Regional Nationalism: Territorial Politics and the European State* (London: Harvester-Wheatsheaf, 1988), chap. 8; Robert J. Bennett, ed., *Decentralization, Local Governments, and Markets: Towards a Post-Welfare Agenda* (Oxford: Clarendon Press, 1990); Mark Kesselman, "The End of Jacobinism? The Socialist Regime and Decentralization," *Contemporary French Civilization*, vol. 8 (Fall–Winter 1983–84), pp. 84–103; and L. J. Sharpe, "The Growth and Decentralization of the Modern Democratic State," *European Journal of Political Research*, vol. 16 (July 1988), pp. 365–80.

GARY MARKS

214

forms indicate the potential for the mobilization of regional governments and regionally based interest groups intent on gaining direct access to EC decisionmaking. Virtually every regional government receiving significant structural funds is now directly represented in Brussels (and in many cases Strasbourg), where they shepherd their proposals through the Community political process, monitor EC regulations, and lobby the Commission and Parliament. Pan-European associations of regional and local governments, including the Association des Régions d'Europe and the Union Nationale des Villes et Pouvoirs Locaux, are now consulted by the Commission on matters of structural policy. For its part, the Commission has opened offices in several regions. The structural reforms have enabled local and regional governments to serve as the new interlocutors of the Commission, a role that challenges the traditional monopoly of national governments to mediate between domestic and international affairs.

It is perhaps tempting to extrapolate an emerging new order in these developments in which regional units come to displace national state structures. But one vital factor cannot be ignored: the responses of states themselves.[36] National governments have been adept at outflanking the reforms by channeling contacts through central ministries, constraining the autonomy of subnational governments, and challenging the legitimacy of EC intervention at the regional level.[37] Instead of offering a new institutional equilibrium to replace the system of state domination, 1992 and the reforms of the structural Funds are creating a dynamic and indeterminate situation characterized by conflicting conceptions of the scope and especially the locus of decisionmaking.[38] The reforms have created new and untried issues of governance and jurisdiction; they have spawned new

36. Steven D. Krasner, "Sovereignty: An Institutional Perspective," in James A. Caporaso, ed., *The Elusive State: International and Comparative Perspectives* (Sage Publications, 1989), pp. 69–96.

37. See Barry Jones, "Conclusion," in Keating and Jones, eds., *Regions in the European Community*, pp. 234–45.

38. Occasionally this slips out in the usually dry and unedifying official EC publications, as in the Commission's most recent *Annual Report on the Implementation of the Reform of the Structural Funds, 1989*: "This major operation brought together authorities which did not necessarily share the same views at the outset. It assembled, around the table of partnership, three different administrative levels (regional, national and Community). . . . Negotiation of the CSFs also provided the first real opportunity for exchanges between the Commission departments and regional administrations. The discussions were enriching for all and led to greater mutual understanding. An assessment of the partnership has to take account of the particular institutional structure of each Member State, which meant that in some cases it was more limited than one would have wished" (p. 5).

arenas in which decisionmaking will take place; and they have multiplied the number and type of groups that contend for influence over substantive outcomes and, more important, for control over the decisionmaking process.

Given the role of individual states in contesting outcomes, one should not expect convergence within the Community as a whole. Structural intervention in the regions seems to be leading to continued, and perhaps even enhanced, national differentiation that reflects varying strengths and types of regional government and varying state strategies and capacities.[39]

Member states are powerfully positioned in the constitution and decisionmaking process of the Community. Constitutionally, the European Community is a club of monolithic states.[40] To the extent that subnational units of governance exist in the Community, they do so at the behest of the member states. They have no legal standing independent of the states of which they are a part. This constitutional focus on the state and the central position of the Council of Ministers, composed solely of representatives of national governments, has led many observers to the conclusion that far from weakening the state, the creation of the EC has strengthened states, particularly in subgovernmental relations.[41]

In Ireland and Portugal, where central governments have pursued national rather than regional development programs, the EC's structural Funds are essentially engaged in regional policy without regions. These countries qualify in their entirety for objective 1 funding, and they have so far been successful in their refusal to countenance any regional focus for EC funding. In Ireland receipts from the European Regional Development Fund go directly into the Public Capital Program, a centralized fund that does not discriminate among regions. However, the Funds have been able to indirectly pressure member states through their discretionary control of a sizable share of the structural budget. Ireland has recently created subregions based on its counties so as to better compete for structural funds.[42]

39. See Thomas O. Hueglin, "Regionalism in Western Europe: Conceptual Problems of a New Political Perspective," *Comparative Politics*, vol. 18 (July 1986), pp. 439–58. Krasner, "Sovereignty," presents some general arguments to this effect (pp. 69–96).

40. Jones, "Conclusion," pp. 243–44.

41. L. J. Sharpe, "Fragmentation and Territoriality in the European State System," *International Political Science Review*, vol. 10 (July 1989), pp. 223–38.

42. Joseph E. Thompson, "The European Community and Northern Ireland," paper presented at the 1989 Conference of the European Community Studies Association, George Mason University, May 1989.

The double-edged politics involved in the creation of policy networks linking the regions and the EC are especially sharp in Britain. Since the mid-1980s competition for structural funding has intensified. With the adoption of discretionary allocations, the British government accepted the need for increased regional and local participation in framing budget requests. Community departments have been set up in local authorities in regions meeting objectives 1 and 2 criteria. Regional civil servants have begun to lobby directly in the EC through members of the European Parliament and by setting up their own offices in Brussels. The Northern Development Company, which was established in the northeast of England in 1986 to coordinate interests in the region, now provides information about funding opportunities in the Community and serves as a conduit for direct contacts between EC and local officials.[43]

But the national government has been determined to maintain a strong grip over the process as a whole. Local and regional authorities must work through the Department of Trade and Industry at Whitehall whether they wish to apply for a single project or for a comprehensive program. In fact, the British government refuses to recognize the difference between these types of funding: both are simply factored into the budget as a whole and effectively replace existing spending. The government views the structural Funds as a budgetary mechanism offsetting a portion of British payments to the EC. The perception is that the government, not the EC, should decide how this money should be spent. The justification for involving subnational governments in regional planning is simply to maximize the transfer of resources from Brussels to London. While it struggles to adapt to changing criteria of selection of programs by mobilizing local authorities in planning agencies, Whitehall finds itself opposing the basic thrust of the reforms, resisting "an additional layer of bureaucratic planning which in our view would result in the Commission imposing its own preferences on Member States' planning priorities." If the Department of Trade and Industry were to have its way, "There will never be a common Community regional policy in the sense that we already have a Common Agricultural Policy and a common commercial policy."[44]

43. Jeffrey J. Anderson, "When Market and Territory Collide: Thatcherism and the Politics of Regional Decline," *West European Politics*, vol. 13 (April 1990), pp. 234–57.

44. House of Lords Select Committee on the European Communities, European Regional Development Fund, *23rd Report* (1983-84) (London: Her Majesty's Stationery Office, 1984), p. 115.

Predictably, the government has resisted the Commission's most recent attempts to decentralize structural planning. In November 1989 the secretary for trade and industry, Nicholas Ridley, refused to accede to the Commission's demand that local authorities play an independent role in creating development plans.[45] Community Support Frameworks forwarded to the Commission by the United Kingdom have emphasized centralized infrastructural spending—for example, to modernize the water industry—instead of creating local enterprise agencies and other ongoing concerns that would involve local government participation.

But once policy networks linking subnational governments to the EC have been created, there is no certainty that they can be dominated by national government. Local authorities are well aware that their interests diverge from those of the government. In the words of a leader of the Scottish local authority association, "The objectives and interests of local authorities individually—or perhaps in a local grouping—are not necessarily the same as those of government. Local authorities at present and no doubt under the amended regulations seek to attract maximum European funding into their areas. It is not necessarily an objective that, taken globally across the country, will commend itself to the Government."[46]

Until now, national governments have been fairly successful in protecting their prerogatives over regional policy. They exercise a constitutional monopoly mandated in the Treaty of Rome and in subsequent legal cases in the process of intermediating interests between subnational governments and the EC. The extension of the functions of the Community may even give some national governments an expanding role as the interlocutor between domestic and European interests. Moreover, national governments have important advantages in any direct conflict with subnational governments, deriving from their financial powers, legitimacy, and high levels of prior institutionalization.[47] The weight of these advantages varies from state to state and from region to region, but even in Germany, where subnational governments are strongest relative to the federal state, most observers argue that the EC has

45. Hazel Duffy and Anthony Moreton, "Challenge to EC Commission Plan for Regional Funds," *Financial Times*, November 20, 1989, p. 7.
46. House of Lords Select Committee, *23rd Report*, pp. 93–94.
47. Sharpe, "Fragmentation and Territoriality in the European State System."

consolidated the power of the central government at the expense of the Länder.[48]

Despite the entrenched position of national governments in the EC, the development of structural policy at the Community level has given subnational governments a new arena for pressing their demands. It is not at all surprising that regional governments and Community institutions should regard each other as useful potential allies in bargaining with member states.[49] Though member states retain considerable resources for regional policymaking, the growth of informal networks linking regions and the EC is a resource for subnational governments in mobilizing support behind regional claims and for the Commission in framing a European structural policy.

Sources of Uncertainty

This chapter has attempted to describe and analyze developments in structural policy that are in process and contested rather than fully realized. No one has yet seen the intended and unintended consequences of the reforms or their durability. Three sources of indeterminacy appear crucial: the geographical boundaries of the Community are unsettled, particularly for east central Europe; political relations between the major institutional actors in the Community are still in flux, with the possibility that member states will attempt to reassert their "sovereignty"; and, finally, implementation cannot be taken for granted. Implementing the structural reforms provides significant scope for administrative overextension and bureaucratic infighting among the Funds.

The inclusion of East Germany in the Community by virtue of unification with West Germany and the possible further enlargement of the Community to include east-central European states (Hungary and Czechoslovakia are the most likely candidates) make predictions of the future of structural policy, or of the EC in general, highly problematic. In the first place, it seems clear that policy coordination based on minimal reciprocity,

48. Gerhard Bahrenberg, "West Germany: From Decentralization in Theory to Centralization in Practice," in Robert Bennett, ed., *Territory and Administration in Europe* (London: Pinter, 1989), pp. 255–70; and Hans-Georg Gerstenlauer, "German *Länder* in the European Community," in Keating and Jones, eds., *Regions in the European Community*, pp. 173–90.

49. Fritz W. Scharpf, "Interorganizational Policy Studies: Issues, Concepts and Perspectives," in Kenneth Hanf and Fritz W. Scharpf, eds., *Interorganizational Policy Making: Limits to Coordination and Central Control* (London: Sage Publications, 1978), pp. 345–70.

let alone harmonization, would be much more difficult in an EC that encompasses parts of east central Europe. It seems reasonable to expect that the more *extensive* the EC becomes, the more difficult the task of institutionalizing *intensive* decisionmaking powers or political authority will be.

An opening to the East would greatly magnify the demands on structural policy. To some extent this challenge is already occurring with the integration of former East Germany into the EC. The Kohl government renounced any claim against current structural spending but agreed to a total of ECU 3 billion in additional structural spending for the period 1991–93. The cost would be much greater if other east-central European countries joined. Czechoslovakia and Hungary have a combined population of 26 million, and their inclusion in the EC along with eastern Germany would add another two-thirds to the population living in objective 1 regions. If the next likeliest eastern contender for membership, Poland, is included, the population of the less-developed regions doubles. An opening to the East would therefore internalize enormous regional problems that the present structural policy is not equipped to handle.

The consequences of developments in east central Europe for the EC are already being felt, particularly by the peripheral regions. The revolutions of 1989 and subsequent calls for large-scale aid and investment raise the specter of a zero-sum game between the southern and eastern peripheries of Europe for scarce international finance. If expected private German (and French) investment in Portugal, Spain, and Greece does not materialize, these countries may try to secure more investment through the channel of the Funds. Public figures in these countries have already voiced concern about the potential diversion of investment away from their economies to east central Europe. Bargaining among member states about the future size and distribution of the structural Funds may become more conflictual even if the EC does not open further to the East.

Despite the recent growth of the Commission's influence in allocating the structural budget across priorities and among member states, the member states dominate the budgetary process as a whole and may claim back the powers they have ceded to the structural Funds. The Funds have gained influence in the allocation process because they dispense the budget, but their role is still in flux. Member states tend to be jealous of whatever political benefits accrue from regional dispensations and are sometimes unwilling to advertise Community involvement in popular projects. To the extent that member states view the benefits of regional policy in zero-sum terms, the role of the structural Funds as an active participant rather than as a mechanism for bargains worked out among the member states is likely to be contested. In addition, member-state administrators complain about the complexity of the funding process for Community programs and argue that the structural Funds are merely another layer of bureaucracy.[50] If calculations of national outcomes continue to dominate budgetary politics, the leeway given the structural Funds may erode under the pressure of bargaining among member states.

In the absence of a deeply rooted and generally held sense of Europeanness among mass publics, it is very difficult for the structural Funds to legitimate an extension of their powers of redistribution among member states. Ultimately, the role of the structural Funds, alongside other EC institutions, will be constrained by cultural identifications, and these are likely to change only slowly. In the absence of strong external legitimation, the appearance of an autonomous role for the structural Funds governed by technocratic standards and an overarching European interest may really be a dressing up of conventional national bargaining. In some cases it is evident that technocratic standards are elaborated post hoc to justify bargains hammered out in the Council of Ministers.[51]

Finally, the reforms present administrative tasks that the Funds are ill-equipped to handle. The structural reforms place a heavy reliance on policy coordination and DG XXII has been established with this purpose in mind. Effective coordination demands power, and it is still unclear whether this new, very small Directorate-General will have the authority to fulfill its responsibilities. Some insiders have suggested that DG XXII should be elevated above the three structural Funds by being made responsible to the president of the Commission. At present, DG XXII is dependent on the intangible resource of "moral leadership." There is significant potential for institutional conflict between DG XXII and the larger, more established Directorate-Generals.

The expansion of the responsibilities of the structural Funds has not been matched by an increase in the numbers of administrators or by the

50. House of Lords Select Committee, *23rd Report*, p. 13.

51. For example, one middle-level bureaucrat I spoke to was told to manufacture a technocratic justification for Britain's 38 percent share of ERDF assistance under objective 2.

hiring of people with regional expertise. The problem is particularly severe in the Regional Fund (DG XVI). In the past the administrators of DG XVI acted as financial controllers for projects that were designed and carried out by member states or regional bodies. With the shift to a program approach, the need is to find people who are competent to go to the regions, explore potential sites and programs, and monitor their subsequent performance. The Funds are chronically understaffed, and the staff they have are poorly equipped to carry out their new functions.[52]

Conceptualizing the European Community

One of the clearest things to emerge from an overview of structural policy in the EC is that it is in flux: new conceptions of the role of the Commission are being pressed into institutional form; subnational governments are being mobilized in unconventional ways; and states are responding to financial incentives offered by the Funds and to various internal demands, including the desire for control over relations between subnational governments and the Community. Some very basic, and perhaps surprising, features of the emerging political landscape are visible now, and it would be well to make them explicit in concluding this chapter. Instead of the advent of some new political order, however distant, one finds an emerging political disorder; instead of a neat, two-sided process involving member states and Community institutions, one finds a complex, multilayered, decisionmaking process stretching beneath the state as well as above it; instead of a consistent pattern of policymaking across policy areas, one finds extremely wide and persistent variations. In short, the European Community seems to be part of a new political (dis)order that is multilayered, constitutionally open-ended, and programmatically diverse.

A distinctive characteristic of the process of structural reform is its open-endedness. Instead of posing a new federal political order as the eventual outcome of the process, the reforms increase uncertainty and conflict by creating new functions, challenging central state bureaucracies, and mobilizing regional interests. The structural reforms challenge both state control of regional policy and state monopoly of intergovernmental relations. Unprecedented policy networks are being created that link

---

52. This point was raised by several fund administrators in interviews. See also House of Lords Select Committee, *23rd Report*, p. 13.

the EC directly to regional governments and interests. It would not be surprising to see regional governments and regionally based private groups across different member states forming coalitions to press their common interests in the EC. But, at the same time, it seems unlikely that a tidy polity will emerge at either the supranational, the national, or the subnational level.[53]

The structural reforms are the outcome of conscious institutional creativity, yet they are not modeled on a prior plan for creating a new political system. The reforms are inductively problem driven, not deductively constitution based. As a result, there is no sense of finality about them. This is not to deny that regional policy, and European integration in general, has taken place within an ongoing debate between alternative conceptions of a European polity, encompassing, for example, a Europe of the regions in which states would wither away, a federated Europe tying together existing member states, a free-trade Europe dominated politically by autonomous member states, and so forth. But these models of the good polity have not determined the reform process. They are attempts to abstract general principles or tendencies from the process of European integration, rather than architectural master plans. In practice, structural policy, and arguably many other policy areas, have been open-ended in a way that has escaped those who have thought of grand architectural plans or final destinations.

Structural policy, unlike policy areas that have dominated thinking about European integration in the past, cannot usefully be conceptualized as a two-sided process between member states and the European Community. The outcome cannot be understood as some point along a continuum ranging from a loose confederation of strong member states on the one side to a federal Euro-state on the other. Formulations constrained to member states and Community institutions miss a critical element of the whole picture: the role of subnational governments. Instead of a two-sided process, a far more complex, open-textured, and fluid situation is emerging in which subnational governments interact with the EC and cross-nationally. Policymakers are confronted not simply with the issue of how much decisionmaking to centralize in Brussels but with how disparate levels of government both within and beyond the national state fit together.

---

53. The result may be the kind of bargaining described by Leonardo Parri, "Territorial Political Exchange in Federal and Unitary Countries," *West European Politics*, vol. 12 (July 1989), pp. 197–219.

The polar conceptions of a Europe of the regions versus a state-dominated Europe are unsatisfactory not because something in-between is emerging but because elements of both may coexist in a conceptually untidy, multilayered polity. The Weberian conception of the state, rooted in the monopolistic control of the legitimate means of coercion within some given territory, reveals less and less about the realities of political power and decisionmaking in Western Europe. Visions of a Europe of the regions have an air of unreality about them because they do not explain how existing states will wither away.

There is little reason to believe that the experience of structural policy will be replicated in other policy areas in the EC. On the contrary, there are enormous contrasts across policy areas within the EC. If the experience of policymaking within member states is any guide, there is no reason to assume that such contrasts are just a transitional phase. Throughout its existence the EC has been oriented as a means to discrete, diverse, contested, and contingent goals that have been specific to particular policy areas.[54] The result is an immensely complex and variegated structure, or, more accurately, a set of structures, that reflects the logic of numerous individual policy areas and the consequences of their intricate connections. If one tries to discern a pattern of governance, one finds variations ranging from a virtual unitary suprastate in the sphere of trade barrier regulation to loose coordination of virtually autonomous member states in most fields of education policy to multilayered intergovernmental relations in structural policy. The institutional structure of provision in each policy area reflects the logic of individual programs and the distribution of power among their providers and recipients more than constitutional structure.[55] Policy diversity is a fundamental and enduring characteristic of the EC. The overall shape of the Community is the result of the accretion of numerous bargains about specific policies and their institutional frameworks.[56]

54. In this context Haas speaks of the "autonomy of functional contexts." Ernst B. Haas, "International Integration: The European and the Universal Process," *International Organization*, vol. 15 (Summer 1961), p. 376; see also Haas, "The Study of Regional Integration: Reflections on the Joy and Anguish of Pretheorizing," in Leon N. Lindberg and Stuart A. Sheingold, eds., *Regional Integration: Theory and Research* (Harvard University Press, 1971), pp. 3–42.

55. John B. Goodman, "Do All Roads Lead to Brussels? Economic Policymaking in the European Community," paper prepared for the American Enterprise Institute's conference on the United States and Europe in the 1990s, Washington, March 1990.

56. Helen Wallace, "National Bulls in the Community China Shop: The Role of National

With some exaggeration, one can say that the European Community, like the modern state, has been created self-consciously with respect to its parts but not to its whole.[57]

Government in Community Policy-Making," in Wallace, Wallace, and Webb, eds., *Policy-Making in the European Communities*, pp. 33–68.

57. I explore the comparison between European integration and state-building at more length in "Structural Policy, European Integration, and the State," paper presented at the meeting of the Consortium for 1992 at the University of North Carolina, March 1991.

Chapter 7

The Politics of the Social Dimension

PETER LANGE

MUCH OF THE attention given the 1992 process of European economic integration has focused on the aggregate benefits of a fully developed internal market. This positive attention marks a shift away from Europe's preoccupation with "eurosclerosis" and "europessimism" in the mid-1980s, toward a renewed faith in Europe's future. The Cecchini report of 1988 with its predictions of substantial European benefits in growth and employment from integration is the fullest expression of this new "euro-optimism." Yet it is also clear that a fully integrated and barrier-free internal market, and the attached commitment to reduce and eventually to eliminate barriers to external trade, is likely to have significant *distributional consequences*.

From a political standpoint, these effects should be understood in sectoral, territorial, and class terms. Some sectors, or some firms within them, will reap substantial and relatively immediate benefits from less costly access to other European markets and are likely to respond well to exposure to international competition. Others can be expected to suffer, at least in the short run. There is also good reason to believe that these sectoral and firm effects will, at least in the beginning, benefit some regions of the European Community much more than others.[1] Thus, even

I have greatly benefited from the comments of Helen Wallace and Wolfgang Wessels of the Brookings Project on 1992 and from the always detailed and insightful commentary of Geoffrey Garrett. I also wish to thank my colleagues in the Consortium on 1992 for their comments on an earlier version of the chapter. Brian Loynd provided invaluable assistance in the preparation of this study; Cynthia Irvin, Sig Vitols, and John Constantelos helped with specific research tasks.

1. Tommaso Padoa-Schioppa and others, *Efficiency, Stability, and Equity: A Strategy for the Evolution of the Economic System of the European Community* (Oxford University Press, 1987).

if one assumes that the opening of trade both internally and externally will raise the aggregate return to the EC, there are likely to be substantial differences in the distribution of gains across regions. There is, therefore, a potential that in an EC in which states still hold the ultimate power of decision, economic losers, either individual or group, could withdraw political support from the specific measures needed to implement full integration of the market, thereby depriving the Community of a major source of additional economic welfare.[2]

In addition to the sectoral and territorial effects, market integration may have substantial distributional consequences between social classes and the fragments within them.[3] The Single European Act (SEA) and the 1992 project are often interpreted as the instruments of large European businesses and financial firms—that is, as the tools of "capital."[4] The measures, therefore, have raised fears among European unions and the European Left that integration will promote an erosion of workers' existing social benefits (or, at the least, slow the extension of such benefits) and that it will weaken labor's position in industrial-relations institutions.[5] Thus the single market would be associated with a decline in the *social* wages of workers and would increase the risks they face from "social dumping" and "social competition."[6] It would also potentially aggravate

2. Padoa-Schioppa and others, *Efficiency, Stability, and Equity*, pp. 89–102.

3. The term *social classes* is used broadly and fairly loosely here. It is intended to differentiate those whose interests in the production and distribution process are usually represented by trade unions from those whose interests are represented by employers, business, or commercial associations. In general, this usage differentiates those who make their living primarily from the ownership or management of financial, manufacturing, or service firms from those who make their living primarily from working for those firms or for the government.

For a discussion of how the distributional effects of market integration are perceived, see Paul Teague, "Constitution or Regime? The Social Dimension to the 1992 Project," *British Journal of Industrial Relations*, vol. 27 (November 1989), pp. 310–29.

4. Andrew Moravcsik, "Negotiating the Single Act: National Interests and Conventional Statecraft in the European Community," Harvard University, Center for International Affairs, 1989. Wayne Sandholtz and John Zysman, "1992: Recasting the European Bargain," *World Politics*, vol. 42 (October 1989), pp. 95–128.

5. *The Social Dimension of the Internal Market* (Brussels: European Trade Union Institute, 1988).

6. *Social wages* are composed of the benefits paid to workers at the expense of employers or the government. They include health benefits, unemployment insurance, disability benefits, and the like. There are substantial cross-national differences in the coverage and systems for payment of social wages across the EC member states. These benefits are referred to as the social wage because they are paid to workers above their "market" wage and represent a significant portion both of their total compensation and of the costs to employers of hiring

already existing cross-national disparities in social protection. In contrast to labor, capitalists would gain bargaining power, flexibility, and direct economic advantage through lower social costs and weaker union influence in collective bargaining.

Interest groups, political parties, governments, and Community officials have responded in both principled and pragmatic ways to the distributional consequences—or more often the expectation of them—of the 1992 process. As in earlier periods of market extension and deepening, those committed to restraining market forces in the name of communal, religious, or egalitarian values[7] have sought to counteract the deregulatory thrust of the 1992 process at the national level with "reregulation" at the Community level. In addition, others, fearful that the distributional conflicts within the Community could stall creation of the single goods-and-services market, have sought to devise policies that could sufficiently allay the concerns of potential losers in order to gain their consent to market integration (see chapter 6). Still others have argued that free markets should be accompanied by social policies that improve the quality of the work force and facilitate rapid adjustment to changes in Community and international demand. This approach would secure European firms market niches in a dynamically evolving international marketplace by promoting the spread throughout the Community of a "European model of production."[8]

---

them. *Social dumping* is the pejorative term applied to the idea that production will shift to employers using substandard employment practices. It could occur through production shifting to employers in countries where the social costs of production, including both the social wage and regulatory control, are lower; through the threat that firms will shift their investment to low social-cost countries, thereby providing them with a lever to win social-cost concessions in the sites where they are already located. See Hugh G. Mosley, "The Social Dimension of European Integration," *International Labour Review*, vol. 129 (March–April 1990), pp. 147–64. *Social competition* is also a pejorative term applied to the idea that national governments and unions in collective bargaining, faced with the prospect of social dumping, will lower standards to meet the cross-national competition and thereby maintain production and employment. See Teague, "Constitution or Regime?"; and Stephen J. Silvia, "The Social Charter of the European Community: A Defeat for European Labor," *Industrial and Labor Relations Review*, vol. 44 (July 1991), pp. 626–43.

7. Karl Polanyi, *The Great Transformation* (New York: Farrar and Rinehart, 1944).

8. The "European model of production" refers to a mode of producing goods and services which relies on comparatively well paid, highly skilled, trained, and organized workers that receive extensive social benefits, in combination with relatively high levels of production technology. The skills of the workers and the cooperation of management and unions in the workplace allow for the use of more complex, flexible, and productive technology than elsewhere. The high wages, social benefits—including a well-developed educational and training system—and union leadership ensure a more reliable, low-error, low-turnover work force. The result is that the average per unit production costs are not significantly higher

The politics of the social dimension—the interests and institutions involved in developing social policy—is directed toward protecting and improving the rights and the quality of life of workers throughout the Community as the integration process moves ahead. Social policy also works to
ensure the widespread availability of the skilled and flexible work force
necessary for the European model of production. The Commission of the
European Communities and the Council of Ministers have committed
themselves to the implementation of the single goods-and-services market
by 1992. Many officials have also recognized that, at least in principle,
market integration should "extend beyond the single market to solidarity
through economic and social cohesion, to the social dimension." Thus,
alongside "market Europe," there should be a "social Europe" with a "human face."[9]

This chapter concerns the politics of the social dimension. I examine
the dynamics among interest groups, member states, and Community
institutions in the context of EC rulemaking procedures, or "decision
rules."[10] This combination of factors will determine the character of social
policy that is likely to develop out of the pressures generated by the creation
of the single market. Although the social dimension encompasses both
social and industrial-relations policies, I focus here on the former.[11]

Two arguments predominate in the chapter. First, I maintain that while
it may seem that the political alignments which have historically shaped
conflict over social policy in Europe will dominate the debate in the EC

---

than in lower-wage, lower-skill, lower-benefit settings and that the goods are of comparatively
high quality. Competitiveness results from a favorable mix of cost and quality. The "European
model of development" (discussed later) would seek to make the European model of production increasingly characteristic of goods and services produced throughout Europe rather
than in just the more developed countries and regions, as is now the case. See Commission
of the European Communities, Directorate-General for Employment, Industrial Relations
and Social Affairs, *Employment in Europe* (Luxembourg, 1990); and David Soskice, "The
Institutional Infrastructure for International Competitiveness: A Comparative Analysis of
the UK and Germany," in A. B. Atkinson and R. Brunetta, eds., *The Economics of the New
Europe* (London: Macmillan, forthcoming).

9. Juliet Lodge, "Social Europe," *Journal of European Integration*, vol. 13 (Winter–
Spring 1990), p. 2.

10. "Decision rules" refers here to the operative ways decisions are made in the EC. I
argue that understanding the decision rules in the EC is necessary in order to understand
how actors within the EC pursue their interests through strategic behavior and how these
strategies interact to produce the policies that have (and have not) been undertaken.

11. For a general review of the history of the social dimension, see Lodge, "Social
Europe."

over social issues, this is unlikely to be true.[12] Insofar as such alignments have appeared, they have been the product of a particular combination of EC decision rules and the preferences of specific governments which have allowed symbolic politics to prevail over interest politics. Second, I argue that in the face of recent changes—a movement in government positions on European issues, a shift away from the formulation of policies toward their passage, and the possibility of changes in decision rules—interest politics is likely to come to the fore. To the extent that it does, the social policies of the EC are likely to be fragmented, partial, and piecemeal, responding more to complex configurations of special interests than to any broad principle developed by stable political and social coalitions.

In developing these arguments, I should like to emphasize that a study of the politics of the social dimension is, like much of the rest of the analysis of the 1992 process, an effort to hit a moving target. As will become evident, the social dimension is primarily a set of symbolic gestures, general policy commitments, and a few hotly debated, specific EC proposals. The key political dynamics of the social dimension are only just now emerging, as the effort is made to adopt and implement particular policy directives embodying the general principles. As a result, I stress here the logic of the policy process rather than the content of specific policy initiatives. Such an approach is not only prudent but unavoidable, given the current state of policy implementation in the social dimension.

The Social Dimension

Definitions of the social dimension of the Community abound. Here I use a simple, and expansive, one: the social dimension of the 1992 process comprises all those policies, or proposed policies, for the EC and its mem-

---

12. The rise of the welfare state and protective policies for workers generally took place with employers, their associations, and political parties on one side and the workers, their unions, and political parties on the other. There were, of course, exceptions, including both state interventionist policies by governments of the Right (for example, Bismarckian Germany) and Catholic and Christian parties with strong ties to the workers' movement and to social Catholic doctrines. Nonetheless, it has been expected that the class alignments and conflicts that earlier played such an important role in welfare-state development would also assume such a role in the struggle over European social policies in the 1992 process and beyond. For historical discussions, see Gaston V. Rimlinger, *Welfare Policy and Industrialization in Europe, America, and Russia* (Wiley, 1971); and Peter Flora and Arnold J. Heidenheimer, eds., *The Development of Welfare States in Europe and America* (New Burnswick, N.J.: Transaction Books, 1981).

ber states that provide or would provide rights, opportunities, benefits, or protections to actual, potential, or former participants in the labor market.[13] In empirical terms, the social dimension has, most recently, been clearly formulated in three documents: the Charter of Fundamental Social Rights (also called the Social Charter or simply the Charter), which represents a covenant among the member states to a set of social rights and which all EC members agreed to with the exception of Great Britain;[14] the associated Action Program,[15] which stipulates forty-seven specific proposals intended to implement the principles agreed to in the charter; and the proposed Community legislation governing industrial relations in European firms.[16] This chapter examines those aspects of the social dimension covered by the first two documents, which most closely parallel what is generally considered worker protection, worker rights, and labor-related welfare-state policy.

Within this framework, two polar positions on the appropriate regulatory role for the Community can be identified. First, there are those who favor an essentially decentralized, or hands-off, approach and would limit Community legislation to a fairly narrow set of questions, including minimum health and safety standards, the rights of women, children, and the handicapped with respect to employment, and issues on which the policies of member states have significant effects on other countries. Member governments and collective bargaining units within countries would be given ample room to determine the appropriate level of worker rights in the competitive economic environment created by the 1992 process. In

13. The rights and entitlements of women in the labor market have been given special attention, as have those of migrant workers.

14. The charter would confer rights in most of the major areas covered by labor laws in the member states. It includes rights pertinent to matters such as work time, vacation time, the rights of part-time workers, minimum pay and other standards, child labor, sex discrimination, social security, and organizing and bargaining rights. See Commission of the European Communities, "Community Charter of Fundamental Social Rights: Draft," COM (89)471 (Brussels, October 1989). Special attention has been given to issues concerning equal employment opportunities for women and protection for pregnant women and women who have recently given birth. See Commission of the European Communities, Information Services of the European Community, "Progress Report on the Social Charter" (newsletter), London, May 28, 1991.

15. Commission of the European Communities, "Communication from the Commission Concerning Its Action Programme Relating to the Implementation of the Community Charter of Basic Social Rights for Workers," COM (89)568 (Brussels, November 1989).

16. See "Draft Directive on European Works Councils," *European Industrial Relations Review* (London), no. 206 (March 1991), pp. 12–14. Overall, the social dimension can be argued to consist of four important areas of policy: working conditions, freedom of movement of workers, employee participation, and structural funds for particular problems created by the implementation of the single market or European economic development more generally.

this decentralized system, "subsidiarity," a principle articulated by Jacques Delors, would be given maximum scope. Under subsidiarity, policy decisions would be made on a level as close as possible to the one on which they are implemented while remaining consonant with the basic principles of social justice.[17] This can be called the neoliberal, or minimalist, approach to the social dimension.[18]

A second approach—which one can call social protectionist—would give much greater scope to Community responsibilities for guaranteeing the living and working conditions of workers throughout the EC. It would strive toward a "harmonization" of national standards without an accompanying devaluation of the achievements of workers in any national context. Thus, it would effectively raise the standards in countries where they had been low and maintain them where they had been high. This approach has been linked more recently to a "developmentalist" strategy articulated by some both inside and outside the European Commission. It would rationalize EC-level social policy not so much in terms of rights or the need to satisfy particular constituencies but as essential to promoting development in the less-developed regions of the Community in ways that encourage the spread of the European model of production. By fostering a trained, protected, and therefore flexible work force, while at the same time gradually raising labor costs for firms, EC-level social policy would provide both carrots and sticks for firms to upgrade their technology and to compete in markets in which European firms have the most favorable prospects in the coming decade. Over time, such policies and their firm-level consequences would erode regional disparities within the Community. A social-protectionist approach requires the EC to take an interventionist role in setting social benefits, doing so on the basis of normative principles established at the Community level.[19]

Europeans are divided over which approach is best. Until the end of 1990, debate over the social dimension generally followed predictable

17. Karlheinz Neunreither, "Euphoria about Subsidiarity? The Constitutional Debate in the European Community," *Political Science and European Unification* (London School of Economics), no. 2 (Spring 1991), pp. 1–3.

18. Commission of the European Communities, Directorate-General for Employment, Social Affairs, and Education, *The Social Dimension of the Internal Market: Special Report of the Interdepartmental Working Party,* Social Europe spec. ed. (Brussels, 1988), p. 63; and Teague, "Constitution or Regime?"

19. Commission of the European Communities, *Social Dimension of the Internal Market,* pp. 62–63; Teague, "Constitution or Regime?"; and interviews conducted by author, November 1990.

political and interest-group alignments, based on traditional cleavage lines and preferences already expressed in national struggles over welfare-state policies. Political parties and governments on the Left, as well as Christian Democrats with their traditions of social responsibility and close links to Catholic labor movements, national trade unions, and the European Trade Union Confederation (ETUC), have favored the social-protectionist vision. Political parties and governments with a distinct neoliberal profile, national employers' associations, and UNICE, the European employers' association, have favored the minimalist approach.

Within EC institutions, the European Parliament has aggressively pressed the interventionist approach, even going so far as to threaten to hold up single-market measures through the cooperation procedure if more rapid progress was not made in the Commission and the Council of Ministers to pass substantive measures called for in the Action Program.[20] In the Council of Ministers and European Council, states have been divided, primarily in accordance with the ideological hue of their government.[21] The Commission under Delors, especially the Directorate-General V (DG V), the body charged with primary responsibility for the social dimension, has appeared to favor the more social-protectionist vision and has increasingly voiced its developmentalist perspective.[22] The Commission and the Directorate have, however, usually accommodated the realities of the balance of power in the Council of Ministers.

Indeed, because of the dynamics of the Council, it is the neoliberals who have thus far largely triumphed. As the debate over the Charter

20. The cooperation procedure was established as part of the Single European Act. It increases the role of the European Parliament in the formulation and amendment of legislation proposed by the Commission to the Council of Ministers. It applies only to legislative matters subject to qualified majority decisions. For a more detailed discussion, see Neill Nugent, *The Government and Politics of the European Community* (Duke University Press, 1989).

21. One possible exception has been the "social democratic" stance taken by the German government. This has been attributed to the social Catholicism of the Christian Democratic Union–Christian Social Union (CDU-CSU) coalition. It is also possible to explain this position, however, in terms of the economic self-interest of many German employers (and unions) who might benefit from having their competitors in lower social-cost countries pay higher, EC-imposed social benefits. Insofar as this is true, it becomes impossible to disentangle the ideological and material explanations of the government's position.

22. Commission of the European Communities, Directorate-General for Employment, Industrial Relations, and Social Affairs, *Health and Safety at Work in the European Communities,* Social Europe (Luxembourg, 1990); and interviews conducted by the author, November 1990.

moved through various stages, culminating (for the moment) in the decisions taken in December 1989 at the European Council meeting in Strasbourg, it increasingly became a statement of principles or, at times, an affirmation of regulations embodied in already existing national and international standards, regulations, and laws. The role for Community intervention narrowed, and with subsidiarity assuming greater importance as a policy criterion, the role assigned to national governments, especially to the "social partners" through collective bargaining, expanded. The British government, as the preeminent neoliberal state, used the Community institutions, particularly the unanimity rule governing most of the issues in the Charter, to impose a minimalist vision.[23] In this effort, Britain was seconded by UNICE.[24] A more social-protectionist vision has been promoted by ETUC and by several member states, including, prominently, Spain, France, and Germany.[25] A similar history could be traced for the Action Program, although the dynamic governing the politics of passage of its specific measures is becoming increasingly unsettled.[26]

It might be thought that the history of the Social Charter and the social dimension provides the best source of insight into the likely institutional, political, and policy outcomes in post-1992 Europe. If so, patterns of political cleavage around the social issues should largely repeat those that marked the development of welfare states at the national level: one should expect relatively unified action by the organizations representing European labor and capital around their alternative visions of the social dimension; one should also expect that governments of the member states would align themselves with the alternative positions depending on their partisan composition; and finally, the European Left and socially progressive Christian Democrats should tend to push the issues in the social dimension "up" the European decisionmaking structure to the Community level,

23. Silvia, "Social Charter of the European Community."
24. Secretary General Z. J. A. Tyskiewicz, "European Social Policy: Striking the Right Balance" (text of speech), Union of Industrial and Employers' Confederations of Europe, Brussels, 1989.
25. Silvia, "Social Charter of the European Community."
26. There are some exceptions to this pattern. Significant provisions have been enacted at the European level regarding equal opportunity in the workplace and employment for women, migrants, and the handicapped. In addition, there has been progress on minimum health and safety standards at the workplace for all workers, with specific protections for women, children, and the handicapped. These measures implement article 119 of the Treaty of Rome, which requires "equal pay for equal work" for men and women. For an excellent, concise discussion, see Mosley, "Social Dimension of European Integration."

while the conservatives and employers should seek to push them "down" to the member states and, where possible, to decentralized collective bargaining. Paul Teague summarizes such expectations:

> Overall, it is hard to avoid the conclusion that the extent to which the Community adopts a *dirigiste* or deregulated social dimension to the 1992 SEA will depend on the outcome of some hard political bargaining, if not total political confrontation, between the 'maximalists', led by the Commission and perhaps Mitterrand, and the 'minimalists', led by the British government and the European employers' organizations.[27]

If recent history is used as the guide, the outcome of this struggle should be determined above all by political developments in the member states. To the extent that unions recover strength in the market and those parties committed to a social-protectionist approach gain governmental power, a more Community-level interventionist approach should be expected. The balance of power in the Council should change, and pressure should be brought to bear on employers, thereby unleashing the maximalist tendencies of the Commission. Changes in Community decision rules, making more social issues subject to qualified majority voting, would also facilitate this shift. Such a rule change was made at the Maastricht summit in December 1991, although, surprisingly, outside the framework of treaty revisions agreed to in the intergovernmental conference on political change in the EC.[28] Under these conditions, some have argued that corporatist-like institutions at the Community level, perhaps including Europeanwide sectoral collective bargaining, would develop.[29]

---

27. Teague, "Constitution or Regime?" p. 326.

28. In December 1990 the European Council inaugurated two intergovernmental conferences. One of these is expected to establish the process for the implementation of European monetary union. The other is dedicated to reviewing and seeking reform of the political structures and decisionmaking rules of the Community.

29. Michael Baun, "Europe 1992 and Trade Union Politics: Towards a European 'Industrial Relations Space'?" paper prepared for the Seventh International Conference of Europeanists, Washington, March 23–25, 1990; and Daniel K. Tarullo, "Can the European 'Social Market' Survive 1992?" *The American Prospect* (Spring 1991), pp. 61–72. The argument here is based on an analogy between the development of corporatist practices at the national level and what would happen at the Community level. Faced with strong unions and a politically powerful Left, employers would see in corporatist bargaining practices a way of ensuring the stable political-economic environment necessary for them to exploit the opportunities of market integration and economic openness.

By contrast, history would also teach that, insofar as conservative, and especially neoliberal, parties continue to dominate one or more of the major member-state governments, and labor continues to be relatively weak, European-level social policy should remain largely symbolic, with standards being set through more decentralized procedures. In such a scenario, the combination of social dumping and social competition might lead to a progressive erosion of workers' living and working conditions and of the power of the national labor movements, thereby creating what, for labor and the Left, would be a vicious circle.

I would argue, however, that extrapolating the future politics of the social dimension from its recent history, or from the history of welfare-state development at the nation-state level, is likely to produce fundamentally flawed predictions. Such a historical approach is based on an incorrect understanding both of the alignments of interests on social issues and of how the conflicts and coalitions among those interests intersect with Community rules. With regard to the first point, the structure of institutional rules and government alignments in the years since the Community embarked on the single-market program has prompted a misleading perception of the positions of governments and interest groups (a false "revelation of preferences") on the social dimension. As to the second point, recent changes in government positions and changes in Community decisionmaking rules are likely to produce a pattern very different from what recent experience would lead one to expect. In the rest of the chapter, I enlarge on these two points and their significance for the future politics of the social dimension. The twelve numbered paragraphs indicate the steps of the argument, which are then elaborated on in ensuing paragraphs.

Interests, Rules, Governments, and the Social Dimension, 1985–90

"Things will move towards the lowest common denominator," [says] one British official, perhaps a touch too smugly. "And that's us." [30]

1. The structure of interests with respect to the social dimension is extremely complex, and no Europeanwide position by labor or capital is

30. "The Spoilers," *The Economist*, March 9, 1991, p. 44.

to be expected. Interests of workers and employers vary with specific issues in the social dimension by country, sector, and firm. Thus the likely stances of their representative organizations will also differ. The social dimension is, therefore, not, as is often argued, one in which cross-national coalitions of workers and employers, unions and employer associations can be expected to confront each other at the European level around alternative, internally consistent visions of "Social Europe."

The complexity of interests on the social dimension arises from the direct and indirect social costs that firms incur in order to employ workers, as well as from the rules and regulations that constrain employers' prerogatives in making decisions about how goods are to be produced most profitably. These social costs and rules vary across European countries, most immediately because national policies and collective bargaining vary.[31] In the European and international marketplaces, it is likely that firms in different countries and regions, operating under different social-cost regimes and institutionalized constraints (as well as diverse infrastructural and other conditions outside their control), have developed unique internal equilibria with regard to how they employ workers and capital in order to remain competitive.[32]

Under these conditions, changes in the direct and indirect social costs to firms and the rules governing how they can deal with their work force are likely to have an effect on competitiveness. For example, EC-imposed standards above current EC minima would represent increased costs for firms operating below the new standards, thereby potentially reducing their competitiveness. For firms operating above the standard, however, they would represent advantages as high standards become entry barriers to low-cost competitors. Potential conflicts of interest therefore arise

31. Mosley, "Social Dimension of European Integration."
32. Commission of the European Communities, *Employment in Europe*; and Mosley, "Social Dimension of European Integration." In a number of sectors cross-national differences in social costs (and in the costs of environmental and other regulations) are apparently compensated for by differences in the systems by which these costs are paid (the burden falling on employers varies significantly across countries) and by differences in the productivity arising from differences in workers' skill levels, the quality of technology, and other factors. The result is that the *per unit cost* of production does not reflect the differences in social costs and is often fairly similar across nations. It might furthermore be argued that the differences in the kinds of technology and work organization that employers can develop across countries are themselves partly the result of the different quality of welfare-state provision. See also Mosley, "Social Dimension of European Integration"; and Soskice, "Institutional Infrastructure for International Competitiveness."

among firms that operate in the same sector but have different social costs, technologies, and production techniques.[33]

Such differences may well influence the positions of both employers and workers. To think of just one possible example, they could encourage workers in the low-cost firms—who fear that an increase in social costs will endanger their employment—to side with their employers against higher EC standards and to pressure their sectoral union to urge such a stance on the national government, the political party with which the union may have close affiliations, and the ETUC. The universalistic principle used to justify what can be interpreted as a self-interested stance would be the priority of employment.

Workers in the higher-cost firms might also side with their employers, but with the countervailing goal of encouraging the adoption of higher standards. The rationale here might be that market liberalization should not impede the development of decent working and living conditions in the less-developed areas of Europe, and such a stance might be linked to arguments about the need to encourage the "European model of development." In this case, then, implicit, if not explicit, cross-class alliances from a different set of workers, unions, and employers (some of them from the same sectors or countries, or both) would be evident.

Clearly, responses to Community actions will vary with the firm, sector, and specific social issue, and they can be expected to produce different intra- and international coalitions and positions among national unions and employers' associations depending on the specific policy proposal. It may

33. This is true whether cross-national differences in social costs are associated with advantages for firms in the low-cost countries or are associated with different types of production that lead to similar per unit costs for firms in the same sector across countries. In the former case, European harmonization will either confirm existing advantages for low social-cost producers (harmonization at the "bottom") and thereby reinforce the fears of social dumping and social competition, or reduce such advantages (harmonization "up"), thereby depriving firms in the poorer countries of competitive advantages. In the latter case, harmonization will, respectively, either permit competition among firms across countries to continue as it has been or impose costs on firms that have, so far, prospered because of their ability to use less productive technologies with cheaper (but also less skilled and less reliable) labor. In either case, firms and their workers across countries do not necessarily have the same interests in social policies. Eliminating internal frontiers in the EC market is, however, more likely to have significant short-run effects—and thus to generate sharp political responses to the extent that cross-national differences in social costs provide real competitive advantage. But the evidence increasingly appears to be that such advantages are not nearly as great as once assumed. See Commission of the European Communities, *Employment in Europe*; and Mosley, "Social Dimension of European Integration."

seem overly cynical to stress the role of self-interest, but the logic of representation in a highly competitive environment certainly encourages attention to it. I do not mean to suggest that ideology and solidarity will play
no role, but it seems both naive and ahistorical to ignore the substantial
dissonance of interest within classes, and the possible confluence of interest
across classes, that occurs within and across nations in an environment of
intense economic competitiveness and rapid economic change.

2. The positions taken by national governments in the Council of Ministers and the European Council on the social dimension are particularly
prone to pressures from domestic interest associations.

One way to explicate this point is by drawing a contrast with the
domestic politics of EC regional policy. Regional policy is likely to cause
far fewer conflictual pressures on national governments than social policy.
First, those who *directly* bear the costs of regional policy are the governments of the member states. These governments are keenly aware of the
utility of regional redistribution to sustain support for market integration
and thus are likely to be committed to it (see chapter 6). Second, the costs
to citizens of regional policy are highly diffuse and hidden; they are
incorporated into the general systems of national taxation (essentially the
value-added tax [VAT], an indirect tax) and further obscured by the complex payments schemes through which national governments support
Community activities. It is therefore unlikely that domestic pressures will
build for net-contributor governments to resist regional policy, although
the governments may have their own reasons for wanting to keep down
their contributions. As appears to have been the case for Great Britain
under Prime Minister Margaret Thatcher, governments may also try to
mobilize their citizenry on the contributions issue in order to generate
domestic political support (using the EC as the external "threat") or to
increase their bargaining leverage in Brussels on other issues. In effect,
governments can support regional redistribution as a means to legitimate
full market integration relatively free of domestic pressures from those
paying the costs. And obviously the governments in countries that are net
beneficiaries are likely to see regional policy as a useful mechanism for
legitimating the 1992 process.

Not so for social policy. The short-run costs and benefits associated with
the implementation of numerous social policies would be immediately
apparent to workers, firm owners, or both. The consequences of the
policies are often borne directly by the firm, as increases in the costs of
production or increases in the barriers to entry, and also borne by workers,

as threats to their employment prospects and to their social and economic rights and benefits. These expectations might not be accurate, but both workers and firms are likely to base their opinions on them. Furthermore, the organizations representing workers and firms are likely to perceive these potential costs (or benefits) and seek to promote their constituents' interests in the appropriate political arenas.[34] Thus domestic politics is far more likely to affect government stances on policies in the social dimension than on regional policy.

3. The preceding arguments mean that national governments will be faced with conflicting pressures from different class and sectoral forces as they are required to act at the European level.

Because the domestic politics of the social dimension can be highly divisive, national governments may well have to choose between which domestic interests to accommodate and which to resist. How they make this decision is likely to depend on how they balance electoral self-interest, especially regarding economic performance, with loyalty to traditional core constituencies and with the power of more ideological party activists. The balance struck can be expected to vary significantly across governments and the parties within them. What seems certain is that national governments will have to take positions that satisfy some interests while alienating others. Governments of neither the Left nor the Right will easily fit the complex configuration of national interests into the framework of their ideologies or their traditional policy stances on social questions. Coalition governments may face even greater difficulties. Delicate compromises designed to maximize partisan political and national economic interests are likely. Over time, governments may begin to appear inconsistent and even incoherent.

The extent to which any specific national government faces such dilemmas will depend on how potential policies in the social dimension affect groups to which the party needs to pay attention. Where there is congruence between party ideology and the preferences of groups to which the party is responsive for partisan reasons, positions may be coherent, broad,

---

34. It is also true that the interests of the constituents of specific national unions may themselves be divided. This could happen if the union incorporates workers from different sectors, or if firms within the sector covered by the union vary considerably in their interna tional competitiveness (particularly if there has been much subsidization or protection). Fragmentation becomes increasingly likely as the scope of the union expands. When unions are faced with internal conflicts, the likelihood that they can effectively represent their constituents declines, and that leads to greater possibilities for fragmented interest representation. A similar case can be made for employers' associations.

and stable. Similarly, the less the government is concerned about its reelection prospects, the less it will need to adhere closely to the positions of voters and the more it can pursue its ideological inclinations.

At the moment, however, this complexity is not revealed in Community decisionmaking on the social dimension. Instead, there has been the *appearance* of Europeanwide confrontation around the issues of the Social Charter and the Action Program (as well as the European Company Law) between the neoliberal and the social-protectionist coalitions, and the latter has seemingly failed to carry the day in any but symbolic terms. Perhaps the preceding arguments are inaccurate, reflecting an unduly political and national perspective and an excessive emphasis on narrow self-interest. Perhaps they underestimate the role of functionalist logic and spillovers from the single market to social protection, of broader-scale commitments to Europe, and of ideology as a counterbalance to narrowly defined self-interest. But I do not think so.

I would argue that the current debates do not accurately reflect the interests and preferences of the relevant economic and political actors, nor do they capture the likely future political dynamics and policy outcomes in the social dimension. To understand why this is true, one needs to understand the intersection among the rules governing Community-level decisionmaking on social issues, the positions assumed by particular governments, and the strategies that other governments and interest groups have pursued in response.

4. The current rules of the EC require unanimity on almost all social issues. Only those issues that are directly concerned with the health and safety of workers or that have direct and immediate implications for the development of the single market fall under qualified majority decisionmaking.[35] Under the unanimity rule,

—if a government declares a position at the outset and convinces the other governments that it will not change its position,

35. Both these criteria for determining whether an issue is subject to qualified majority voting are themselves disputed in their application. Whether an issue really is a matter of health and safety at the workplace or involves interference with the single market is subject to conflict between those who want extended EC activity in the social dimension and those who want to keep such activity at a minimum. The debate over which voting rule should apply to a proposed directive becomes a surrogate dispute over the substance of the directive itself. This emerged clearly in interviews with business and labor representatives working in Brussels (interviews conducted by the author, November 1990). See also Philippe Meyer, "Key Year for 'Social Europe,'" *Industrial Relations Europe: 1992 Supplement* (newsletter), vol. 19 (February 1991), p. 3S.

—if all other governments would prefer the intransigent government's position to the status quo, and

—if all governments have a relatively accurate knowledge of the positions of the other governments,

then the intransigent government's position will become the winning position, thereby determining the level of social-policy intervention undertaken by the Community. The other Community governments and socioeconomic actors expect and understand this process.

The Thatcher government assumed such an intransigent stance on social issues for much of the period from 1985 to the prime minister's departure at the end of 1990.[36] Thatcher was thereby able to impose a largely "minimalist" position on the role played by the Community in social policy.[37] Illustrative of the firmness of her stance is the fact that she failed to sign the Social Charter, even in its watered-down and largely symbolic form, and despite the fact that all other members of the Community were agreed on its acceptance.

In addition, it might be thought that Thatcher's intransigence could come only at considerable cost, because other governments could threaten to punish Britain on other issues about which it wanted to see Community progress. Thatcher, however, could not have been persuaded to change her minimalist stance under threat of linkage, because outside of decisions creating the single market, to which all members were committed and which required only qualified majorities, Thatcher's positions were usually as close or closer to the status quo than those of the other governments. As a result, since unanimity was the decision rule governing those areas, there was no real room for effective linkage: little real pressure could be applied because Britain held effective "veto" power over much Community policymaking.

Finally, Thatcher's intransigence on the social dimension and her ability to convince others that she was committed to resistance may not have depended solely on her perseverance in the face of opposition. It may also be that many of the economic interests to which she owed allegiance and on which she relied for political support were also committed to a minimalist

36. Teague, "Constitution or Regime?"; and Silvia, "Social Charter of the European Community."

37. It should be noted that the position of the intransigent need only be preferred by all others to the status quo. In the case under consideration, however, it is also true that Britain's position is closer to the status quo than the position of any other government.

stance. Furthermore, she clearly would have gained little electorally or politically from assuming a position closer to that of the Labour party and the Trades Union Congress, especially when her reelection prospects remained quite strong.[38]

5. As a result, there was little incentive for governments to support positions on the social dimension that might have been costly to them in partisan terms, even if the result of such positions would, if implemented, harm the competitiveness of important domestic interests as well as national economic performance. As a corollary, governments have been inclined to take the politically and ideologically convenient position on social issues, taking little heed of the expressed positions of domestic parties to whom they owe little or no political loyalty. Because the governments could largely predict what the actual EC outcome would be on the social dimension, they have not needed to worry about the actual economic impact of their platforms. Their partisan political preferences or their commitment to party activists has been able to take precedence. In other words, parties have been able to engage in what is best understood as "cheap talk."

6. Similarly, national associations representing workers or employers have had little incentive to take any position other than the one most politically and ideologically convenient. The leaders have known that their positions were likely to be of little consequence economically, and so have those particular groups within their constituency who might suffer economically were the position implemented but who otherwise would be in ideological sympathy with the stance of the leadership.

7. This environment of cheap talk suggests that current stances on social policy by governments and national interest groups do not accurately reflect the structure of interests and possible future positions of these actors. These stances also do not reflect with any accuracy the potential distributional consequences and conflicts over issues in the social dimension that might be expected to result from the implementation of the Single European Act. To the extent that the Community-level associations representing business (UNICE) and labor (ETUC) aggregate the preferences of their member associations, their current positions also cannot be assumed to reflect capital's and labor's positions at the EC level.

38. Support for Thatcher's EC positions within her own party and among traditionally conservative interest groups that might have favored a somewhat more flexible stance toward aspects of European integration, such as monetary union, only began to decay publicly when the Conservative party's reelection prospects began to dim in the fall of 1990.

The gulf between policy positions and seeming interests can explain a seemingly paradoxical alignment of national governments on the social dimension. During the run-up to the passage of the Social Charter and Action Program, Germany, France, Belgium, and Spain were the most fervent supporters of a social-protectionist interpretation, while Britain was an extremely intransigent advocate of the minimalist position. This configuration presents two possible dilemmas. On the one hand, the coalition for a more social-protectionist approach was ideologically heterogeneous, with leftist governments in France and Spain but a conservative (sometimes neoliberal) one in Germany. On the other hand, Britain's isolation would seem surprising, since other countries in the Community, including possibly Spain, had large economic interests that would be damaged by higher Community standards. These interests include not only profit-seeking employers but also employment-oriented workers and unions.

Drawing on the argument developed here, however, one can identify a resolution of these dilemmas. For Germany, an ideologically based explanation would root that nation's position in the social conservatism of German Catholicism and in the traditions of state paternalism. It should also be recognized, however, that the German government's position on the social dimension is pragmatic too: it may agree with (or at least not damage) the interests of many major German employers,[39] workers, and unions and may also take into consideration the political interest of the CDU-CSU government, which can use the position to appeal to voters on the Left margin of their constituency. At the same time, since talk is cheap, those German interests that might be threatened by the government's position need not be very concerned.[40] Moreover, they may believe their long-term interests lie with the current government's remaining in office. Ideology may be the explanation, but upon close examination, political self-interest is more compelling.

This logic can also explain the position of the Spanish government. Although support for a more aggressive approach to the social dimension might not be economically attractive to many Spanish employers and workers if they were actually forced to live with its full consequences, they have not had much motivation to mobilize against it because the

39. Andrei S. Markovits and Alexander Otto, "The West German Trade Unions and the Challenge of 1992," paper prepared for the Seventh Conference of Europeanists, Washington, March 23–25, 1990.

40. Markovits and Otto, "West German Trade Unions and the Challenge of 1992."

government's position represents cheap talk. At the same time, for the Spanish Socialist government, support for a more socially progressive vision of EC-level policy is consistent with traditional party ideology and is likely to create less internal opposition among party activists and union ideologues. Gaining the support of those groups is particularly important and difficult for the government in light of the generally moderate and often technocratic policies that it has pursued for several years. Again, cheap talk allows the government to adopt a politically rewarding position without having to confront the economically—and eventually politically— damaging effects if such a position were adopted at the Community level.

By now it should be clear that the patterns of policy development over the first five years of the single-market program may not serve as accurate guides to future policy development. The intersection of government preferences and the decision rules governing most issues within the social dimension (unanimity) have afforded governments, and relevant social interests, the luxury of not having to come to terms with the complex, underlying structure of interests that implementation of specific social policies would entail. However, it may be that the pattern of explicit policy alignments will be transformed into a much different one, given changes in the political and economic environment. I now turn to these issues.

The Evolving Politics of the Social Dimension

With No Thatcher to Assail, Europe's Unity Stalls.[41]

Chief among these was the growing pressure to use the intergovernmental conference on political reform of the Community to change the decision rules to make implementation of the principles of the Social Charter more possible. This was combined with a change in British leadership and a greater flexibility of the new government toward a growth in Community power as long as Britain retained its policy autonomy. These developments combined at the Maastricht summit in December 1991 to create a new, if highly unconventional, institutional setting for the making of policy in the social dimension. In this section, I examine the dynamic set in motion by the fall of Prime Minister

41. *New York Times*, March 17, 1991, p. 10.

Thatcher and the intergovernmental conferences, using the analysis I developed earlier to draw conclusions about likely post-Maastricht developments.

8. The preceding discussion indicated that if one or both of the following were to occur,

—the British government adopted a more flexible posture on social issues, and

—the operative rules governing EC social policymaking were changed such that a large proportion of them would be considered under a qualified-majority decision rule,

then both interest groups and national governments would be confronted with far more difficult and complex choices on EC social issues, and policy coherence would become less likely. The reason for this is that they would no longer be able to engage in cheap talk while hiding behind Britain's intransigence. As a result, they would have to aggregate among a highly heterogeneous and fragmented set of economic interests created by the distributional consequences of the completion of the internal market.

Thatcher's fall in November 1990 by a coup from within her own party had many causes, not the least of which was fear that she would lead the party to defeat in the next election. Another contributing factor may have been the disagreement within her cabinet and party over Britain's role in the evolving EC.[42] These disputes were over substance and tactics. A number of Thatcher's colleagues, including her former foreign secretary, Sir Geoffrey Howe, argued that Britain had much to gain from membership in the Community and from monetary union, which was the most pressing issue at the time of her defeat. Thatcher's resistance to the latter threatened the future of European monetary union (EMU) negotiations as well as Britain's ability to participate effectively in Community negotiations on other issues—including the specifics of single-market implementation.[43]

42. David Buchan and John Wyles, "EC Moves toward Fuller Union without UK Support," *Financial Times*, October 29, 1990, p. 1.

43. See Philip Stephens, "Howe Blasts Thatcher on EC," *Financial Times*, November 14, 1990, p. 1. As an example, even after Thatcher departed, Mrs. Vasso Papandreou, the commissioner for social affairs (DG V), warned that the completion of the European internal market by the end of 1992 is in jeopardy because of Britain's refusal to agree to elements of the European Commission's social action programme. Diane Summers, "Brussels Says Single Market Threatened by U.K. Attitude," *Financial Times*, January 15, 1991, p. 9.

Similar arguments were made about the further development of the political rules of the Community, especially in the context of the proposed intergovernmental conference.[44]

Britain was seen as isolated. The British public, Conservative backbenchers, and cabinet members increasingly saw Thatcher's position less as an appropriate defense of British sovereignty and more as stubborn posturing. Thatcher's stance came to be perceived in Britain for what it had already become to the rest of the EC: a screen behind which the other member states could avoid responsibility for not doing what they did not want to do, while ignoring Britain's opposition to the things they did want to do.[45]

This history is important for it indicates the forces working on Prime Minister John Major's stance toward Europe and EC reform in the first year of his tenure. First, the new prime minister had strong incentives to be less publicly belligerent, whatever the final position Britain might pursue. This he has clearly done.[46] Second, Britain's position on monetary union has changed as a result of its entry into the exchange rate mechanism of the European Monetary System (EMS).[47] Third, Britain under Major has inevitably had to become a full participant in the negotiations surrounding the intergovernmental conferences on monetary union and political reform. Thus the political costs of uniformly pursuing Thatcherite positions on the EC have risen substantially since he took office.

The consequences for the politics of the social dimension flowing from these changes were unclear until the Maastricht summit. On the one hand, Britain could gain in *international* political bargaining with its EC partners by appearing more flexible on social dimension issues. This was all the more true because Major, unlike Thatcher, was susceptible to

44. Philip Stephens, "Thatcher to Defend Opposition to Emu," *Financial Times*, October 30, 1990, p. 1.

45. In an interview with a high-level official at the Council of Ministers, I was told that no one any longer paid attention to British positions, for they understood that on the important questions Thatcher would eventually either concede or let the others decide, while vainly proclaiming her opposition in principle.

46. Alan Riding, "With No Thatcher to Assail, Europe's Unity Stalls," *New York Times*, March 17, 1991, p. 10.

47. Great Britain entered the EMS on October 8, 1990. The reasons cited for Thatcher's acquiescence include pressure from pro-EC members of her party, posturing for the next national election, and an attempt to gain enough influence in EMU negotiations to scuttle or, at least, weaken it or to maintain Britain's autonomy. See "Going for It," *The Economist*, October 13, 1990, pp. 14–15.

linkage politics, in which other governments might make Britain pay a political cost in terms of its interests in the EMU or political reform negotiations if it remained inflexible on social issues. On the other hand, politics inside the Conservative party, especially pressure from the Thatcherite wing, could make it very costly in terms of British *domestic* politics for Major to make concessions in the social area that would appear to threaten the Thatcher "social revolution" in Britain. With a political election looming, such costs became all the more palpable.

The potential for changes in Britain's posture on social issues was not in itself sufficient to place the social dimension on the active agenda of the EC. Two developments at the EC level, however, made the avoidance of social issues more difficult. First, passage of the Action Program in December 1989 created a mandate for social-policy implementation which the commissioner for social affairs and the eurocrats of DG V readily took up. In 1990 they placed five proposed directives on the table, several of which quickly proved controversial.[48] Furthermore, the Commission's commitment to social policy was buttressed by action in the European Parliament which criticized the Commission, and even more the Council of Ministers, for proceeding too slowly and timidly with its efforts to provide a social dimension to the single-market program.[49] The Parliament threatened to use the cooperation procedure to slow progress on the single-market directives if the social dimension did not receive greater priority.

Second, the intergovernmental conference devoted to political governance of the Community provided an inescapable arena for debate over how social issues should be treated. The Commission, some of the member states (Belgium, Holland, Germany, and Italy), and at times Delors have been arguing that most social legislation should be governed by qualified majority voting in the Council and that the European Parliament should have greater power.[50] There was considerable controversy over such a

---

48. "EC Involvement Scheme Adds to Business Disquiet on 92," and "Controversy Grows over EC 'Atypical Work' Drafts," *Industrial Relations Europe*, vol. 18 (December 1990), pp. 1, 2.

49. "Controversy Surrounds Draft Atypical Work Directives," *European Industrial Relations Review*, no. 203 (December 1990), p. 11. On October 24, 1990, the European Parliament voted down one of three proposed directives on atypical work because of its legal basis under article 100 instead of article 100a; most parliamentarians felt that directives on working conditions should be subject to qualified majority voting.

50. "Who Wants to Live in the Brave New Europe?" *The Economist*, December 1, 1990, pp. 46–47.

proposal. Nonetheless, its inclusion among the items of the conference necessarily meant that the social dimension and the decision rules governing the passage of directives would be on the Community's agenda.

In light of these conditions and the earlier analysis, one can form several hypotheses about how the politics of the social dimension was likely to proceed before Maastricht, and after.

9. The partial change in Britain's posture, the seeming aggressiveness of the Commission with regard to the Action Program, the pressures from the European Parliament, and the intergovernmental conferences and the increased possibilities for linkage politics all made it likely that EC intervention in the social dimension would grow. This becomes increasingly probable once the social effects of the single-market program are felt. The intersection of rules and member-state positions, which had damned European-level interventionism, came under increasing pressure before Maastricht. The decisions taken there fundamentally alter the strategic context in which social dimension policy will be made in the coming years. It is worthwhile to look both at what happened before the summit and at the situation that the decisions of the summit have created.

During the year leading up to Maastricht, the Commission undertook significant efforts to produce directives covering five issues raised in the Action Program. The issues concerned "atypical" (or part-time) work, organization of work time, contents of employment contracts and proof of their existence, information and consultation with workers within EC-scale companies, and protection for pregnant women and new mothers. In each of these areas, the Commission put directives on the table that would greatly increase EC-level intervention—generally through the establishment of standards that would be binding on all member states.[51]

An example illustrating both the type of proposed intervention and the aggressiveness of the Commission was its proposal to set a minimum standard of social benefits to which "atypical" employees (those not working a "normal" or full-time workweek) would be entitled. The proposal clearly would represent a substantial intervention into matters that to date have been subject only to national laws and collective bargaining agreements.

What is particularly striking about the proposal, however, is that the Commission maintained that the directive falls under article 100a of the Treaty of Rome (distortions of competition) and can therefore be passed by a qualified majority vote. This is consistent with the opinion of the

---

51. Meyer, "Key Year for Social Europe," p. 3S.

European Parliament as well as that of the ETUC but is strongly opposed by UNICE. On the basis of past experience, however, the benefits issues covered by the draft directive would not qualify as distortions of competition and would, therefore, fall instead under article 100, requiring a unanimous vote in the Council of Ministers.

Before Maastricht it appeared that despite the Commission's activism and the willingness of some member states to support it, these and all similar proposals would fail to be transformed into directives in the near future.[52] As the summit approached, British resistance to EC-level interventionism in social dimension issues increased. This was true both for specific Commission policy proposals and for use of the intergovernmental conference on political reform to alter the decision rules governing the social dimension. Britain made clear its firm opposition to any rules changes that would subject more social policy directives to passage by qualified majority. To maintain Conservative party unity—and perhaps also by conviction—Major declared his unwillingness to give up British policy autonomy in social policy areas that had been at the heart of the Thatcher "revolution." It appeared that Britain might be willing to scuttle political treaty revision through use of its veto rather than permit EC use of qualified majority voting to make decisions in social policy areas.

Such an outcome was avoided through the most unusual and unpredictable of compromises. In the face of a likely British veto, the other eleven member states signed a separate protocol on social policy that allows them to use EC "institutions, procedures and mechanisms" to formulate and implement social policies on which they agree. The protocol expands both the issues in the social dimension that are subject to EC intervention and, among those, the ones that can be decided by qualified majority. There remain, however, many qualifiers that could, in the future, lead to substantial disputes even among the Eleven.

The protocol is, however, outside the Treaty of Rome, and therefore

52. Meyer, "Key Year for Social Europe," p. 3S. This proposed directive, and the rules extension that it would entail, was one of the issues on which Z. J. A. Tyskiewicz, secretary-general of UNICE, expressed the greatest dismay with the social dimension, the Action Program, and the Commission's stance. Interview with Z. J. A. Tyskiewicz, November 1990. In addition, as little as one week before the Maastricht summit, the Commission's proposal on working time—a Europeanwide 48-hour maximum work week and specific weekly day-off provisions—was shelved by the social affairs ministers primarily because of continued British resistance. The proposal could have been passed over British objections by qualified majority because the Commission had tabled the proposed directive as a health and safety measure, but the ministers chose, instead, to postpone further consideration indefinitely. Andrew Hill, "EC Working Time Directive Shelved," *Financial Times*, December 4, 1991, p. 2.

decisions taken under it will not have the status of EC law but will come into effect only through their translation into national laws. The agreement to go outside the treaty means that no provisions passed using the protocol will require enactment by Britain or be grounds for claims by British citizens against British employers or the government. Effectively, Britain retains its policy autonomy on those issues that it considers outside the current treaty provisions regarding the social dimension. The other eleven members can pursue a more EC-level interventionist social agenda, and on an expanded set of questions can do so by qualified majority.[53]

In sum, after Maastricht, there is considerably more *potential* for EC interventionism than before, for no longer can Britain veto most initiatives. Of course, under the decision rules of the protocol, there is also distinctly less opportunity for cheap talk. The question, therefore, becomes what kind of policy in the social dimension is to be expected.

10. Under the new conditions, there is no reason to still expect similar associations in different countries, or associations representing different groups of workers or employers in the same country, to adopt similar stances. There is also no reason to expect that national governments composed of parties from either the Left or the Right will necessarily take the same positions on social issues. There is also no reason to expect that the European associations representing workers (ETUC) and employers (UNICE) will be forceful representatives of coherent positions on social issues.

Some empirical evidence shows that these kinds of divisions were emerging even before Maastricht. First, in the early months of 1991, in conjunction with the intergovernmental conference concerned with the political arrangements of the EC, several countries that traditionally favored strong EC-level intervention in the social dimension pressed for changes in the Community rules that would bring most social issues under qualified majority voting. Belgium led the way in this regard.[54] The Socialist government of Spain led by Felipe Gonzales, however, acted as a spoiler in these negotiations. Spain called for the creation of special budgetary funds for the poorer countries of the Community as a precondition for the enactment of the rule changes. Spain's expressed fear was that

53. "Separate Protocol on the Quality of Life," *Financial Times*, December 12, 1991, p. 6. See also David Gardner, "Astonishing Compromise Threatens to Create a Brussels Benefit for the Legal Fraternity," ibid., p. 2.

54. "Pressures Mount to Extend Majority Voting on Council," *European Industrial Relations Review* (London School of Economics), no. 203 (December 1990), p. 2.

the decision-rule changes would lead to the passage of directives that would be costly for the poor countries to implement. The costs would be both direct and indirect through lost competitiveness. As a result, Socialist-governed Spain tied its possible support for decision-rule changes to enhanced economic support from the wealthier member states. Its position won support from the other poorer countries of the Community.[55]

A second example of growing division involves Britain, which expressed opposition to the proposed directive regarding the payment on a pro-rata basis of social benefits to atypical workers and to the Commission's proposal that it be subject to qualified majority voting. To the surprise of many, in the early months of 1991 the British opposition was echoed by Denmark, Ireland, Luxembourg, Spain, and Germany.[56] Opposition by Spain and Germany was particularly surprising in light of their generally supportive positions in the past regarding the social dimension.

Third, UNICE, the representative association for employers at the European level, is composed of representatives from the national confederations of employers in the member states. As a result, it offers no real opportunities for sectoral business interests to be directly represented in its negotiations and consultations with the Commission and Council. Increasingly, however, trans-European associations supporting the interests of sectoral employers are being developed at the EC level and are setting up offices in Brussels. In addition, DG V of the Commission has begun to foster sectoral discussions over specific directives or other initiatives of the Commission. As a result, UNICE appears in danger of losing its privileged position in bargaining with the Commission, and increased opportunities are appearing for specific sectoral initiatives that may not coincide with the aggregated positions favored by UNICE.[57]

These examples suggest the fragmentation developing out of the effort to push ahead with aspects of the social dimension. With the disappearance of the opportunities for cheap talk, the growing pressures on the commission for progress on social policy, and the Maastricht social policy protocol, more intervention at the European level seems likely.

---

55. "The Spoilers," p. 44. At Maastricht, an alliance of the poorer countries won an agreement for an increase in structural funds. "Spain Welcomes Cohesion," *Financial Times*, December 12, 1991, p. 4. It should be noted that Spain also had more specific budgetary concerns.

56. Lucy Kellaway, "EC Ministers Balk at Commission's Social Measures," *Financial Times*, November 27, 1990, p. 2.

57. Interviews with administrators of DG V and representatives of relevant business associations, Brussels, November 1991.

11. Such intervention will probably be quite uneven in its application across policy areas.

The likelihood of EC intervention in any one of the forty-seven specific areas indicated in the Action Program or in any new areas identified by the Commission or the member states will usually result from one of two processes: alliances of convenience among a subset of countries with common economic or political interests, with the remaining countries either having no significant interest or making concessions because of linkage or (more bluntly) logrolling; or generalized agreements among all the member states when there are no significant distributional consequences from the proposed measure. As a result, the development of broad-based European-level intervention in social and industrial-relations policy, replicating the welfare-state patterns that evolved in response to the spread of markets within states, seems improbable.

The Maastricht protocol has created the opportunity for greater EC social policy intervention. In doing so, however, it is also likely to bring to the surface differences in interests that will prompt a patchwork of policies, some at the EC level, others at the national level, and still others at the regional level or decided through collective bargaining. This pattern of policies will be the product of temporary coalitions of governments using the decision rules at the EC level to respond to domestic interest pressures and political calculations rather than of consistent alliances based on shared ideological principles or coherent policy principles.

The Social Dimension and the Evolution of European Institutions

What place should these conclusions claim in the study of the political economy of European integration? What factors might lead to a different outcome from the one this analysis suggests? In the social-science literature concerned with international integration, a contrast is often drawn between "neorealist" theory, which tends toward skepticism about the likelihood of integration among states, and "neofunctionalism," which often leads to more optimistic expectations.[58] Where does this study fall?

Insofar as I have focused on the likely interactions between states and the interests of national governments in the context of the decision rules

58. Stanley Hoffman and Robert O. Keohane, "European Integration and Neofunctional Theory: Community Politics and Institutional Change," paper prepared for the workshop Dynamics of European Integration, Florence, September 10–12, 1989. See also chapter 2.

of the Community, this analysis has had a neorealist cast, and so too have its conclusions. The question that arises, however, is whether neofunctionalist pressures might promote outcomes more consistent with a fully integrationist view of the shape of the social dimension. Neofunctionalist analysis would lead one to expect two kinds of related processes to promote integration: spillover from one policy area in which integration is going forward into another, and pressures from transnational actors with an interest in promoting a fully integrated outcome.

The spillover hypothesis would argue that the attainment of a single goods-and-services market or full market integration would create problems and inconsistencies in social policy that could only be resolved by more consistent European-level social policy. In particular, differences in social costs across European states would constitute barriers to trade and competitive advantages (or disadvantages) that could only be resolved by "harmonization" at the European level. Concerns about social dumping and social competition, and the need to counteract these through Community legislation, are proof of the need for EC regulation to those who fear that without such intervention harmonization would be achieved through market mechanisms at the lowest common denominator.

Upon reflection, however, it is not clear that pressures for harmonization are as strong as initially believed. Most important in this regard is the discovery that, despite differences in the social costs for producers across member states, the competitiveness of similar products produced in different countries in the Community often does not greatly vary.[59] The reason seems to be that firms in these countries establish different mixes among infrastructure, skills, training, and technology that allow them to remain competitive. No clear cross-national disadvantages for the higher labor- and social-cost countries are evident.

This finding has two implications for the likely pattern of social policy. First, because the higher social-cost countries are typically the more powerful in the Community (for example, Germany), the impetus for harmonization at the EC level is less than a simple neofunctional perspective would suggest. More generally, the absence of consequential cost differentials lessens the functionalist pressures for harmonization overall. There is no compelling "need" to harmonize social policies in order for the single market to operate effectively. Under these conditions, national,

59. Commission of the European Communities, *Employment in Europe*; and Mosley, "Social Dimension of European Integration."

sectoral, and more specific, if fragmentary, interests are more likely to govern social policy.

Of course, it may be that transnational actors with interests in a fully integrated, European-level, social dimension could seize control of these issues and impose their own agenda. It is not clear, however, who these transnational actors would be. One possibility is ETUC. There is some evidence that unions have tended to work together at the European level to promote implementation of social policies, using the fear of social dumping and social competition as a source of unity. Union cohesion, however, has not yet been thoroughly tested, for little of the Action Program has been implemented. Furthermore, ETUC has, to date, been relatively ineffective in EC negotiations. The employers' association, UNICE, has been considerably more effective; its policy has been to stress subsidiarity, decentralized collective bargaining, and national legislation. Its support for European intervention is largely confined to health and safety measures and standard setting. On decision rules, it consistently favors the maintenance of unanimity rules where they exist.[60]

A second possible transnational actor promoting the social dimension would be the commission—specifically DG V and President Delors. In most neofunctional accounts, Community officials take on a particularly important role in promoting integration. They have a stake in the integration process, as well as an ideology committed to greater cooperation. Moreover, as regards the social dimension, there is a widespread impression that the Directorate officials charged with implementing the Action Program have been intent on fulfilling their mandate. The commissioner took a highly active role in 1989 by ensuring that the Social Charter was translated into an action program, and the officials of the Directorate were referred to as "closet social democrats" by a business representative interviewed in November 1990. Finally, it was Delors who initially gave new impetus to the social dimension in 1987 when he argued that the single market had to have a "human face."

There is, nonetheless, good reason to believe that the Commission and its president will not be the impetus for a more aggressive pursuit of broad, social democratic or maximalist aspects of the social dimension. I learned from interviews with officials in DG V that their intention is to further those aspects of the Action Program that seem most likely to

60. Interviews with EC, ETUC, and UNICE officials, November 1990.

promote economic development in the less-developed regions, such as gradual implementation of social-welfare provisions that would maintain pressure on employers to move to higher levels of technology and more efficient forms of work organization. The officials also intend to use the program to make a positive contribution to the creation of fully free markets in labor supply through increased labor mobility (for example, through common programs of vocational training that would be available throughout the Community).[61]

I found little enthusiasm for generalized movement toward a European "welfare state," in part, perhaps, because the officials were keenly aware they could not attain such a goal. One official noted that Delors was more committed to other aspects of integration (in particular, monetary union) and would certainly sacrifice the social dimension to attain it.[62] Another indicated that the enthusiasm of the European Parliament for the social dimension, and thus the extent of pressure it was placing on the Commission, was directly related to its efforts to augment its power among Community institutions in light of the forthcoming intergovernmental conference. For this official, the Parliament, too, was only instrumentally committed to the social dimension.[63]

The full accuracy of these views is not at issue, although considerable evidence has been presented that they are well founded in experience. What counts is that, on the basis of these expectations, even those Community officials with seemingly the greatest stake in promoting widespread implementation of the social dimension are inclined to pursue directives in areas where consensus among interests and member states is more likely or areas they think essential to achieving the single goods-and-services market. Combined with the lack of strong generalized pressure for spillover into the social dimension, the absence of actors with a commitment to the broad facets of the Action Program argues for the weakness of neofunctionalist processes in this area. Instead, the underlying pattern of conflicting and fragmentary interests, and of decision rules that encourage governance of EC policymaking by governments responsive to these interests, seems likely to prevail for the foreseeable future.

What, then, will be the policy pattern in the social dimension?

61. Interviews with officials of DG V, November 1990.
62. Interview with official of European Community staff of the Council of Ministers, November 1990.
63. Interview with official of the European Commission, November 1990.

12. There is at present no reason to expect the development of broad-based, European-level intervention in social (and industrial-relations) policy. The combination of fragmented interests, a continued critical role for governments, and a particular set of decision rules governing Community social policy implies that no general European social "model" is likely to develop. A social democratic or neocorporatist Europe, redistributing to the "losers" as markets become freer, is improbable. More likely is a neopluralist social Europe in which temporary coalitions of interests and governments form around proposals for specific European interventions in the social area, while other social issues are left to national or subnational governments or to the results of collective bargaining.

Chapter 8

Thinking about the European Future: The Uses of Comparison

ALBERTA M. SBRAGIA

A S THIS book shows, the European Community is not a political entity that is easily understood. Unique in its institutional structure, it is neither a state nor an international organization. The lack of the normal political lubricants, such as transnational political parties, renders the Community, to use Helen Wallace's words, "a part-formed political system."[1] The Community is, therefore, particularly dependent on the attributes of formal institutions. It is not accidental that the question of institutional reform has been perennially debated within the Community and that the Single European Act linked the creation of a single market to new pathways of governance. The evolution of institutions, the allocation of power among institutions, and the questions of legitimacy linked to such allocation are critical to the governance of the Community and its policy capacity.

Given the current institutional structure, the issue of how much national governments should shape Community policymaking rests at the heart of debates about the long-term future of the Community. As the Community institutions (propelled by the decisions taken at Maastricht in December 1991) take on responsibility for an increasing number of policy competences, as the European Parliament presses for an ever-stronger role in the structure of governance, as the European Court of Justice continues to exercise judicial review, and as the institutional challenges posed by future enlargement become clearer, so the role of national

1. Helen Wallace, "The Best Is the Enemy of the 'Could': Bargaining in the European Community," in Secondo Tarditi and others, eds., *Agricultural Trade Liberalization and the European Community* (Oxford: Clarendon Press, 1989), p. 205.

governments in Community decisionmaking will be constantly debated. As the "nation-state" truly becomes the "member state" in the post-Maastricht Community, it is the fate of national governments that will shape the Community's political future.

The thrust of future debate was indicated by the Commission's position during the negotiations leading to the Maastricht Summit that it favored "keeping to the course charted by the Treaty of Rome, leading eventually to a federal-type organization."[2] The Commission's aspiration will face two contradictory impulses. The Community's institutional structure reflects the fact that the Community is based on treaties rather than a constitution. Further, the territorial dimension within the Community is, even by comparative standards, very powerful. The future institutional design of the Community, therefore, is unlikely to submerge national governments into some kind of federation, as conventionally defined. On the other hand, as enlargement becomes a more urgent issue over the next decade, and as the Community takes on more duties, the pressure for increasing the federal characteristics of the Community will increase.

Is it possible to "federalize" the Community significantly while retaining a key policymaking role for national governments? This chapter considers some relevant ideas about comparative federalism, which may help in thinking about some of the critical issues in future institution building.[3]

2. Commission of the European Communities, "Commission Opinion of 21 October 1990 on the Proposal for Amendment of the Treaty Establishing the European Economic Community with a View to Political Union," Com (900) 600 final (Brussels, October 23, 1990). The idea of a federal Europe subsequently became the object of vehement British criticism. Britain argued that it could not accept language in a draft treaty that described the Community as "a union with a federal goal." David Buchan, "Britain Rejects EC Treaty 'with a Federal Goal,'" *Financial Times*, June 18, 1991, p. 1. Denmark also objected, and the opposition party called the idea of a federal state unacceptable. David Buchan, "Defining 'Federalism' Fans Confusion," *Financial Times*, June 19, 1991, p. 16. In France, the government supported the movement toward a federal structure, but strong antifederalist sentiments were voiced by the Gaullists. Ian Davidson, "Braced for Turbulence," *Financial Times*, June 17, 1991, sec. 3, p. 3. The Maastricht agreement dropped the word "federal."

3. This chapter is written very much in the spirit expressed by Krislov, Ehlermann, and Weiler: "The decline of confident assertions about the proper model for integration has . . . some curiously liberating consequences, not all of them discouraging. The absence of a clear model, for one thing, makes ad hoc analogies more appropriate and justifiable. If one may not specify what are clear analogies, less clear ones may be appropriate." Samuel Krislov, Claus-Dieter Ehlermann, and Joseph Weiler, "The Political Organs and the Decision-Making Process in the United States and the European Community," in Mauro Cappelletti, Monica Seccombe, and Joseph Weiler, eds., *Integration through Law: Europe and the American Federal Experience*, vol. 1: *Methods, Tools and Institutions*, bk. 2: *Political Organs, Integration Techniques and Judicial Process* (Berlin: Walter de Gruyter, 1986), p. 10.

Since territory is central to federal arrangements, the chapter focuses on the implications for Community governance of the Community's strong territorial dimension. In particular, it outlines the conflict between the representation of territory and the representation of voters as a crucial element in the debate over the appropriate decisionmaking role of national governments.

Federalism in Comparative Context

The role of national governments remains a real problem for those who see the construction of Europe as somehow transcending the nation-state and, in particular, overriding the role of national governments in Community decisionmaking. The notion of a federal Europe is used by both opponents and supporters of a more tightly integrated Europe to symbolize a decline in the influence of national governments.

The debate over an appropriate role for national governments in decisionmaking is linked to the issue of making the Community somehow accountable to the electorate so that it is rendered more democratic. A federal structure, based on a "citizens' Europe," stands as the alternative to a Europe of nation-states. The question of how to balance the weight of the national governments and that of the "European electorate" is central to the debate about institutional power. In addressing this balance, the future institutional architecture of the Community will be making a statement about how democracy is defined within the Community.

The striking feature of the debate about the future institutional shape of the Community is the way in which the participants use the terms "federalism" or "federal." Although scholars of federalism find it impossible to agree on a common definition,[4] both advocates and opponents of a more federalist Community tend to assume that such a definition, clear and incontrovertible, does exist. Although federalists tend to think of a federation as protecting cultural heterogeneity and guaranteeing the rights of

4. See, for example, William H. Stewart, "Metaphors, Models, and the Development of Federal Theory," *Publius*, vol. 12 (Spring 1982), pp. 5–24. Furthermore, there have been sharp differences within the federalist movement, broadly defined, as to the appropriate vision for a federal Europe. The so-called integral federalists, who emphasize integrating economic activity and who are inspired by the writings of Pierre-Joseph Proudhon, differed from the Hamilton federalists, who emphasized institutional and constitutional integration. See Lutz Roemheld, *Integral Federalism: Model for Europe—A Way Towards a Personal Group Society: Historical Development, Philosophy, State, Economy, Society*, trans. Hazel Bongert (Frankfurt am Main: Peter Lang, 1990), pp. 147–71.

constituent units, antifederalists tend to downplay the role that subsidiarity assumes in federalist thinking and emphasize the loss of freedom that a once-sovereign state suffers upon joining a federal union that by definition circumscribes its powers.[5]

The term "United States of Europe" sums up the most common expression of a federal Europe.[6] For many analysts the late twentieth-century American model of federalism, with its strong sovereign federal government insulated in many ways from state governments, represents the prototype of a federated Europe.[7] Other federal systems are often referred to only in passing.[8] Perhaps most important, the possibility of exercising originality in designing future Community institutions is not fully acknowledged.[9] Ironically, the debate over future institutional development does

5. For a good description of the way federalists view federalism as protecting heterogeneity and diversity as well as of the variety of institutional forms with which they feel comfortable, see Ernest Wistrich, *After 1992: The United States of Europe* (London: Routledge, 1989), pp. 94–106. By contrast, Dominic Lawson argues, "Advocates of monetary union have a blind spot on economic sovereignty and, by extension, democracy. Perhaps they think . . . that to have a slight democratic control over a European finance minister running a pan European money supply would be no different from having complete democratic control of a British Chancellor with complete responsibility for the supply of banknotes in Britain." Dominic Lawson, "Dreams of the Europhiles," *Financial Times*, June 8–June 9, 1991, p. xxii. For a discussion of "subsidiarity," see Marc Wilke and Helen Wallace, *Subsidiarity: Approaches to Power-Sharing in the European Community*, Royal Institute of International Affairs, Discussion Paper 27 (London, 1990).

6. Robert O. Keohane and Stanley Hoffmann, "Conclusions: Community Politics and Institutional Change," in William Wallace, ed., *The Dynamics of European Integration* (London: Pinter, 1990), p. 278; Roemheld, *Integral Federalism*, p. 151; and Wistrich, *After 1992*. Chancellor Kohl, in an address to the German Parliament, stated, "We want to develop [the EC] in the direction of European union and thereby lay the foundation stone of the United States of Europe." David Buchan, "Italy's EC Proposals Run into Trouble," *Financial Times*, November 23, 1990, p. 3. For the principal study comparing the United States and the Community, see Cappelletti, Seccombe, and Weiler, eds., *Integration through Law*.

7. It is usually forgotten that until after the Civil War popular usage referred to the United States in the plural. "The United States are" rather than "The United States is" was the common formulation.

8. Many analysts of American federalism also assume that the American model is the prototype of the federal model. Samuel Beer, for example, writes, "At Philadelphia in 1787, it is generally recognized, the Americans invented federalism as it has come to be understood since that time." Samuel H. Beer, "Federalism, Nationalism, and Democracy in America," *American Political Science Review*, vol. 72 (March 1978), p. 13.

9. Vincent Ostrom shows a judicious balance in using the American experience to think about the European Community. He argues, "To find a theory useful for thinking about problems does *not* mean that Europe should copy the American model. . . . The task, rather, is to use conceptions and the associated theoretical apparatus as intellectual tools to think through problems and make an independent assessment of appropriate ways for addressing the problems of contemporary Europe." Vincent Ostrom, *The Political Theory of a Com-*

not live up to the originality of institutional design manifested at the time of the Community's founding.

Federalism is arguably an exercise in institutional creativity—it is not necessarily a replication of existing institutional designs. The political debate about federalism does not reflect the elasticity of federalism as an organizing concept, an elasticity that many scholars argue makes the concept too imprecise for rigorous theorizing. What is bad for theory, of course, can be fertile for institution building. Daniel Elazar, widely recognized as a leading student of federalism, has thought more about the manifestations of federalism than most. Federalism, in his view, is not to be equated with a federal state (the most common equation found in political debate). He concludes that

> using the federal principle does not necessarily mean establishing a federal system in the conventional sense of a modern federal state. The essence of federalism is not to be found in a particular set of institutions but in the institutionalization of particular relationships among the participants in political life. Consequently, federalism is a phenomenon that provides many options for the organization of political authority and power; as long as the proper relations are created, a wide variety of political structures can be developed that are consistent with federal principles.[10]

Although the academic literature on the subject often argues that federalism as such has common constitutional characteristics, actual federations vary significantly in how they organize the power of constituent units

---

pound Republic: Designing the American Experiment, 2d ed. (University of Nebraska Press, 1987), p. 9.

10. Daniel J. Elazar, *Exploring Federalism* (University of Alabama Press, 1987), pp. 11–12. By contrast, Keohane and Hoffman do not view federalism in the way Elazar does. They seem to equate federalism with a federal state. They argue, "The inappropriateness of statist, strictly inter-governmental or even confederal models of how European politics operates stems from the inconsistency of these images with the network metaphor or the semi-lattice model, which serve as the best approximation to the evolving reality. 'Supranationality,' despite the unfortunate connotations of federalism encrusted onto the term, is compatible with these notions. The Community political system can best be visualized as an elaborate set of networks, closely linked in some ways, partially decomposed in others, whose results depend on the political style in the ascendant at the moment." Keohane and Hoffmann, "Conclusions," p. 282.

within the overall framework of power in the system.[11] Further, the widespread federalization of once unitary systems introduces still more variation in any possible definition of federalism. Using the United States as the referent for debates about federalism, therefore, obscures the dynamism, the complexities, and the strikingly wide range of potentially federalist institutional arrangements.

It also does not encourage asking the question, as Elazar does, whether one can potentially design federalism, that is, conceptualize federal arrangements outside a constitutionally based federation.[12] Since the Community is clearly not a federation, and since the question whether it will ever become a federation is still open, many analysts do not feel that using concepts drawn from federalism is appropriate in analyzing Community activities. They ignore the possibility that one can have what might be called segmented federalism, that is, treaty-based federal arrangements in certain policy arenas, without having a formal, constitutionally based federation.

In a similar vein, insisting on the need to have a federation before

11. Arend Lijphart argues that at least a rough consensus exists in the literature on the constitutional characteristics of federalism. The primary characteristic is "a guaranteed division of power between central and regional governments." He goes on to conclude that "five secondary characteristics of federalism can be identified: a written constitution, bicameralism, equal or disproportionately strong representation of the smaller component units in the federal chamber, decentralized government, and the right of the component units to be involved in the process of amending the federal constitution but to change their own constitutions unilaterally." Arend Lijphart, "Consociation and Federation: Conceptual and Empirical Links," *Canadian Journal of Political Science*, vol. 12 (September 1979), p. 502. Murray Forsyth, however, indicates how difficult it is to cleanly distinguish between a so-called confederation or federal union, on the one hand, and a federal state on the other. Forsyth distinguishes between a political union having a federal government and a "federal state." For example, Forsyth argues that the United States from 1789 until the Civil War was not unequivocally a federal state. Murray Forsyth, *Unions of States: The Theory and Practice of Confederation* (Leicester University Press, 1981), p. 4. By contrast, William Riker disagrees with Forsyth's interpretation of the pre–Civil War American federation. Riker argues that "the change from the Articles to the Constitution was the main step in centralization, and a more or less steady state has continued since then." William H. Riker, "Introduction," in *The Development of American Federalism* (Boston: Kluwer Academic Publishers, 1987), p. xi. See also Daniel J. Elazar, "Confederation and Federal Liberty," *Publius*, vol. 12 (Fall 1982), pp. 1–14.

12. For a discussion of how federation and federalism are or are not related to each other, see Michael Burgess, "Federalism and Federation in Western Europe," in Burgess, ed., *Federalism and Federation in Western Europe* (London: Croom Helm, 1986), pp. 15–33; and Preston King, *Federalism and Federation* (London: Croom Helm, 1982). The existence of a constitution, of a constitutional structure, has traditionally been central for most federalists. See Daniel J. Elazar, "The Role of Federalism in Political Integration," in Elazar, ed., *Federalism and Political Integration* (Ramat Gan, Israel: Turtledove, 1979), pp. 42–44.

discussing federalism ignores the fact that federalism has a political as well as a constitutional meaning. Although thus far, existing federations have combined constitutional and political characteristics, one option available to the Community is to implement the political dimension of federalism without its constitutional dimension. Thus a federal-type organization could evolve without becoming a constitutionally based federation in the traditional sense.

Missing from the current political and scholarly debate is an appreciation of the various institutional arrangements possible under federalism.[13] Further, there is a lack of acknowledgment of the "silent dialogue" that has gone on among the founders of federations and that accounts for the uniqueness of each system in the way it deals with the claims of territory. That self-consciousness about designing institutions in response to the problem of territory makes the study of federations useful in thinking about the Community's future.

For example, the American, Canadian, and Australian founders of their respective federations deliberately designed institutions in reaction to models of which they disapproved.[14] Negative models (often imperfectly

13. See, for example, Pinder's discussion of the shortcomings of federalist analysis in this regard. John Pinder, "European Community and Nation-State: A Case for a Neo-Federalism?" *International Affairs*, vol. 62 (Winter 1985–1986), pp. 50–51.

14. The Austrians rejected their own previous federal arrangement. The postwar Austrian model of federalism, which gives relatively little power to the provinces, was a modification of their previous, more strongly federal system. Peter Katzenstein points out, "For a variety of reasons the Austrians adopted at the end of World War II a constitution that was based not on the constitution of 1920 (in which federal principles had been relatively strong) but on the constitutional amendments of 1929 (which had centralized political power in the national center and, in particular, in the hands of the president)." Peter J. Katzenstein, "Center-Periphery Relations in a Consociational Democracy: Austria and Kleinwalsertal," in Sidney Tarrow, Peter J. Katzenstein, and Luigi Graziano, eds., *Territorial Politics in Industrial Nations* (Praeger, 1978), pp. 127–28.

For its part, the German system has not faced the problems that have confronted the American one in deciding which powers belong to the federation. One reason has to do with the existence of the American model. Gunter Kisker argues that "another reason for the rather strict construction of the constitutional distribution of powers between the federation and the *Länder* is that the provisions were drafted as precisely as possible, just because the fathers of the West German constitution wanted to prevent what the U.S. Supreme Court did, and had to do, to the corresponding provisions of the U.S. Constitution." Gunter Kisker, "The West German Federal Constitutional Court as Guardian of the Federal System," *Publius*, vol. 19 (Fall 1989), p. 46.

For a discussion of the debates on the question of whether to choose a Bundesrat or an American-style senate, see Peter H. Merkl, *The Origin of the West German Republic* (New York: Oxford University Press, 1963), pp. 66–73; and John Ford Golay, *The Founding of the Federal Republic of Germany* (University of Chicago Press, 1958), pp. 44–59.

understood) were important in these attempts at institutional design. J. W. Schulte Nordholt concludes that, in the American case, "the Founding Fathers, especially James Madison, studied the Dutch past and used it, or better, rejected it, for their own purposes."[15] In a more positive vein, Samuel Beer argues that the founders' "inventiveness consisted precisely in combining elements taken from two incompatible constructions of, respectively, Montesquieu and Hume."[16]

The Canadian Fathers of Confederation, for their part, rejected what they understood as the American model of federalism.[17] The Australians in turn rejected Canada's model.[18] In Canada and Australia, however, the wishes of the founders were contradicted by the evolution of the respective systems. Canada, designed to have a strong national government, is now "one of the most decentralized operative federations in the world," while Australia, which "knowingly emphasized states rights," is now comparatively centralized.[19] Self-consciousness about designing institutions does not ensure they will evolve as planned.

Analytic Costs and Benefits of Comparison

The study of the Community can benefit from the scholarly literature on comparative federalism because the influence of territorial boundaries finds strong echoes in such writing. Considering the impact of what Ivo

15. J. W. Schulte Nordholt, "The Example of the Dutch Republic for American Federalism," in J. C. Boogman and G. N. Van der Plaat, eds., *Federalism: History and Current Significance of a Form of Government* (The Hague: Martinus Nijhoff, 1980), p. 67. Riker, however, argues that the framers used an "inaccurate description and poorly written history not as foreign experience from which they could learn, but as a metaphor for domestic experience from which they had *already* learned very much. Thus, Dutch federalism is twice and distantly removed from American." William H. Riker, "Dutch and American Federalism," in Riker, ed., *Development of American Federalism*, p. 64.

16. Beer, "Federalism, Nationalism, and Democracy in America," p. 13.

17. In challenging some aspects of the conventional wisdom concerning the birth of the Canadian Confederation, Robert C. Vipond summarizes such wisdom well: "If the Canadian Fathers of Confederation held any truth to be self-evident, it was that the Americans had made a fundamental constitutional mistake in 1787. . . . And it is usually said that the Canadians, in designing a federal system, explicitly rejected the American model and the 'federal principle' on which it is based." Robert C. Vipond, "1787 and 1867: The Federal Principle and Canadian Confederation Reconsidered," *Canadian Journal of Political Science*, vol. 22 (March 1989), pp. 3–4.

18. Bruce W. Hodgins, "The Plans of Mice and Men," in Bruce W. Hodgins, Don Wright, and W. H. Heick, eds., *Federalism in Canada and Australia: The Early Years* (Waterloo, Ontario: Wilfrid Laurier University Press, 1978), p. 14.

19. Hodgins, "Plans of Mice and Men," p. 4.

D. Duchacek calls "territorial communities" on politics within federations can help one to understand politics within the Community.[20] That said, however, it is also true that the integrative processes of the Community are in some sense anachronistic when viewed through the lens of federalism. Contemporary examples of federalization within the industrialized world represent "the deintegration of formerly unitary states . . . a process quite unlike the federalization as integration that marks the origin of most of the older federations."[21] The process of federalization in Belgium in the 1980s, for example, was profoundly different from what it had been in the United States, Canada, or Australia.

In turn, comparing the Community with the older federations also has serious problems. For example, the current version of the American federation is far different from its early version; comparing the Community to the mature American federation will lead to very different lines of inquiry than will comparing it to the early federation. The same is true of the Australian federation. Yet comparing the Community to the early years of either the American or Australian federation is problematic, for the intervening centuries have seen the development of the mixed economy, a democratic culture, and strong administrative apparatuses in all advanced societies.[22] The economic, social, and political context within which federalization is currently taking place is so different from the context in which the older federations emerged that comparison is difficult.

The comparative literature on federalism and federalization is nonetheless intriguing. Certainly, it points out how striking is the emergence of a federal-type organization through integration rather than disintegration. Federalization through integrative rather than deintegrative processes is so rare in the late twentieth century that scholars of contemporary federalism do not pay it much heed.

Second, the literature cautions against trying to overgeneralize about the processes of integration. Samuel Beer has argued that modernization in the technological and economic arena is the key to understanding a

20. Ivo D. Duchacek, *Comparative Federalism: The Territorial Dimension of Politics* (Holt, Rinehart and Winston, 1970), p. 20.

21. Maureen Covell, "Federalization and Federalism: Belgium and Canada," in Herman Bakvis and William M. Chandler, eds., *Federalism and the Role of the State* (University of Toronto Press, 1987), p. 58.

22. I acknowledge Joseph Weiler's suggestion of this line of thought.

general thrust toward centralization.[23] However, the deintegrative experience of once-unitary states as well as Canada argues that such an argument, even if true for the United States, cannot be easily generalized.[24] The relationship between territorial politics and economic interdependence seems to be more complex than that posited by Beer.

Though it may be true, as many theorists of international relations would argue, that economic interdependence and international cooperation accompany each other,[25] it is also true that such interdependence does not necessarily seem to create pressures for increased intrastate integration. Within the European Community, subnational governments in Belgium, Spain, Portugal, Italy, and France have become more important at the same time as their national governments have participated in integrative processes at the Community level.[26] If nothing else, the literature on federalism should sensitize one to the possibility that the Community's institutions may give national governments an opportunity to compartmentalize decisionmaking about (interstate) integration and thus separate it from decisionmaking about (intrastate) deintegration.

I do not wish to be misunderstood. The literature on federalism and

23. Samuel H. Beer, "The Modernization of American Federalism," *Publius*, vol. 3 (Fall 1973), pp. 49–95.

24. For a discussion of Beer's argument within the Canadian context, see Richard Simeon and Ian Robinson, *State, Society, and the Development of Canadian Federalism* (University of Toronto Press, 1990), pp. 121–28.

25. See Richard N. Cooper, *The Economics of Interdependence: Economic Policy in the Atlantic Community* (McGraw Hill, 1968); Robert O. Keohane, "Multilateralism: An Agenda for Research," *International Journal*, vol. 45 (Autumn 1990), pp. 731–64; and Miles Kahler, "The Survival of the State in European International Relations," in Charles S. Maier, ed., *Changing Boundaries of the Political: Essays on the Evolving Balance between the State and Society, Public and Private in Europe* (Cambridge: Cambridge University Press, 1987), pp. 287–319.

26. See, for example, Robert J. Bennett, "Decentralization, Intergovernmental Relations and Markets: Towards a Post-Welfare Agenda?" in Robert J. Bennett, ed., *Decentralization, Local Governments, and Markets: Towards a Post-Welfare Agenda* (Oxford: Clarendon Press, 1990), pp. 1–26; Douglas E. Ashford, "Decentralizing France: Spatial and Functional Tensions," in Bennett, ed., *Decentralization, Local Governments, and Markets*, pp. 354–68; and Robert Leonardi, Raffaella Y. Nanetti, and Robert D. Putnam, "Italy: Territorial Politics in the Post-War Years: The Case of Regional Reform," *West European Politics*, vol. 10 (October 1987), pp. 88–107. For a discussion of regional governments' new role in the economy, see *Regionalisation in France, Italy and Spain*, Papers Presented at a Seminar on National-Regional Conflicts in Economic Policy-Making in France, Italy, and Spain, June 9–10, 1983, at the International Center for Economics and Related Disciplines (London School of Economics, 1984). See also Gary Marks's chapter in this volume.

federalization does not offer a map of where the Community is going. It does, however, offer guideposts to the tensions the Community is most likely to experience even if it does not actually develop into a "federal-type organization." A more systematic exploration of the institutional range of democratic federal systems can help broaden the scope of analysis when one is thinking, either in scholarly or in political terms, about the future long-term shape of government within the Community.

This chapter addresses the scholarly dimension,[27] but it may be that in this case scholarship has something to say, however partial, about the world of political choice. Ideally, both opponents and proponents of a more federal Europe would find an analytic, as opposed to a political, treatment of federalism useful in thinking about the future. Such a treatment can sketch the repertoire of existing institutional responses to the dilemmas of size and diversity. The designers of Community institutions can perhaps use such a sketch in shaping their own, inevitably original as well as hybrid, institutional answer to that same dilemma.

For scholars, the application of comparative frameworks in analyzing the Community can illuminate processes outside the Community as well as inside.[28] Perhaps the study of the Community will stimulate scholars of politics within unitary states and federations to rethink what they have so far taken as givens. Hence the study of the Community could both be incorporated into and contribute to the study of comparative politics rather than be isolated from the general conceptual and theoretical concerns of

27. The concept of federalism as applied to the Community carries emotional political connotations and is embedded in an ongoing, politically charged debate about the future of the Community. Discussions of federalism are inevitably viewed as possessing intrinsically political dimensions. By contrast, in the United States, federalism has an important analytic scholarly dimension that dominates its usage. The political dimension is decidedly minor. In this chapter, I am analyzing federalism from an analytic perspective and am thus drawing on the American tradition of analyzing federalism from a scholarly perspective.

28. John Pinder argues that "although it may well be legitimate to see the development of the Community up to now as a process of incremental federalism, little attention has been paid to this possibility." "European Community and Nation-State," p. 50. In a similar vein, Nathan and Balmaceda are attempting to establish a framework by which to study comparative federalism. They do not include the European Community in their sample of countries, but they do note that "a number of reviewers have also suggested that the EEC be included." Richard P. Nathan and Margarita M. Balmaceda, "Comparing Federal Systems of Government," in Bennett, ed., Decentralization, Local Governments, and Markets, p. 63, note 1. I argue that the study of the Community and the study of comparative federalism can be mutually beneficial even though I am well aware of Nathan and Balmaceda's point that "a consensus appears to have emerged that modern federalism is a political form that defies close specification" (p. 60).

political scientists interested in comparing political systems. Although the Community is unique, analysis is more likely to suffer from studying it in isolation from other systems than from using the comparative method in less than ideal circumstances.

The Problem of National Governments

The dichotomy pervading much European debate on the future of the Community is evident in Christopher Tugendhat's discussion of the tensions within the Community: "Federalism and intergovernmentalism, supranationalism and cooperation between different nationalities: two different concepts of Europe . . . have been vying with each other since the earliest days of the Community."[29] Typically, federal arrangements have been viewed as being in opposition to "intergovernmentalism"—the two are seen as mutually exclusive. In that vein, integration within the Community is assumed to be correlated with the weakening of the role of national governments.

In both neofunctionalist and federalist analysis, a strengthening of a center or of the general power has become linked to the subordination, the weakening, of the current member states' powers, a ceding of sovereignty by the states.[30] In both models, the Community's institutions would be strong to the extent they were insulated from the reach of national governments.[31] Neofunctionalist theory, for example, gradually came to

29. Christopher Tugendhat, *Making Sense of Europe* (Viking, 1986), p. 71.

30. The view of theorists is shared by many who see the Community as transcending the nation-state. Helen Wallace describes the initial hopes for the Community as being a new polity: "The touchstone of progress towards that grand design would be the transfer of power away from the worn out governments of the member states to a new and dynamic European level of government. . . . Some looked towards a European federation in which the old nation states would be transformed into residual authorities with continued though reduced political scope. Others saw the Community as becoming responsible for all the most vital areas of policy-making, leaving the member governments to act as its agents." "Institutions in a Decentralised Community: Ambitious Dreams and Painful Reality," in Bernard Burrows, Geoffrey Denton, and Geoffrey Edwards, eds., *Federal Solutions to European Issues* (St. Martin's Press, 1978), p. 26. See also William Wallace, *The Transformation of Western Europe* (New York: Council on Foreign Relations Press, 1990), pp. 60–64.

31. For federalists, such independence is analogous to the independence of the American federal government from the state governments. Scharpf describes the American system of federalism by concluding that "the exercise of federal government functions is formally independent of the governments of the American states, and those functions that have been taken over by the federal government are effectively nationalized." Fritz W. Scharpf, "The Joint-Decision Trap: Lessons from German Federalism and European Integration," *Public Administration*, vol. 66 (Autumn 1988), p. 242.

be understood as positing that a supranational government would gradually take over many of the powers of the national government.[32] In federal models, a center, acting independently of its constituent units, takes over certain functions even if those units retain significant powers. The federal government is sovereign in its domain as specified by a constitution establishing the federation.

Under both models, sovereign institutions in the new entity will be sovereign precisely because they are independent of the control of the constituent units' governments. They are responsible to voters rather than to governments. An entity in which sovereign "general" institutions do not exist is assumed to be simply a confederal body.

The building of European institutions, therefore, has been conceptualized as an enterprise in which national governments had to be circumvented, weakened, or otherwise displaced from their preeminent place. Both pro- and anti-integrationists have identified the representation of the Community interest with the Commission and, more recently, with the European Parliament, not with those institutions representing national

32. Neofunctionalist theory has several strands, and therefore the treatment given by neofunctionalist theory to the concept of supranationality is a matter of spirited debate. Keohane and Hoffmann put forth the view that "the conception of supranationality . . . has suffered grievous misinterpretation and stereotyping over the years. For Haas, supranationality did not mean that Community institutions exercise authority over national governments. . . . That is, supranationality is not at the end of a continuum, whose other end is occupied by strict intergovernmentalism. Instead supranationality refers to a process or style of decision-making, 'a cumulative pattern of accommodation in which the participants . . . seek to attain agreements by means of compromises upgrading common interests.' Haas saw this process as implying structurally 'the existence of governmental authorities closer to the archetype of federation that any past international organization, but not yet identical with it.' " Keohane and Hoffmann, "Conclusions," p. 280.

For their part, Lindberg and Scheingold, in their now-classic (neofunctional) work argued that "observers have usually described the Community institutional system in terms of conflicts between supranational power and national sovereignty. To do so is to assume that each gain in capability at the European level necessarily implies a loss of capability at the national level. We reject this 'zero sum' interpretation. . . . The relationship . . . between the European Community and the national political systems is more nearly a symbiotic relationship than a competitive one." Leon N. Lindberg and Stuart A. Scheingold, *Europe's Would-Be Polity: Patterns of Change in the European Community* (Prentice-Hall, 1970), pp. 94–95. For a particularly sophisticated view of neofunctionalism, see Leon N. Lindberg, "Political Integration as a Multidimensional Phenomenon Requiring Multivariate Measurements," in Lindberg and Stuart A. Scheingold, eds., *Regional Integration: Theory and Research* (Harvard University Press, 1971), pp. 45–127. Scholars who drew on neofunctionalist theory in the 1970s and 1980s, however, tended to disregard Lindberg and Scheingold's formulation. Their use of the theory's concept was not as nuanced as the theory's originators might have wished.

interests such as the Council of Ministers and the European Council. The Community is thought to be strong to the extent that its policies transcend the collectivity of national interests, and the strength of the Commission has been seen as a rough approximation of the likelihood of such transcendence occurring.

A strong Community has not been envisaged as involving the assertive representation of the institutional self-interests of each member government. Similarly, a situation like the present one in which each national government shares power *with other national governments* rather than have power exercised over them by a political center does not constitute integration as originally imagined. Founders of the Community such as Jean Monnet wanted far more than the "joint exercise of pooled sovereignty."[33]

The Commission acts as a truly pivotal institution, as chapters 2, 3, and 6 make clear. The Commission does have some powers normally attributed to a center. Yet the national governments have, through the use of qualified majority voting, accepted the sharing of power with one another rather than with the Commission.[34] Integration has thus proceeded through the willingness of national governments to submit to one another—not to the Commission. The supposed motor of European integration has not been allowed to displace national prerogatives.

The successful protection by national governments of their collective role has led those committed to further integration to regard national governments as necessarily part of the problem and not part of the solution.[35] Governments are especially problematic because the electorate is conspicuous by its absence. The European Parliament is the ultimate check on executive power only insofar as that power is manifested in the

33. That is the description of the current decisionmaking framework given by the Commission in its report on political union. "Commission Opinion of 21 October 1990," p. 3.

34. It can be argued that the single market program shows the willingness of national governments to share power with market forces. How much "sharing" is occurring is unclear, however. Technical standards, critical for the shaping of markets, are being formulated through an evolving institutional structure in which representatives of national governments seem to play a central role. See Michelle Egan, "Associative Regulation in the European Community: The Case of Technical Standards," paper delivered at the European Community Studies Association Biennial Conference, George Mason University, May 1991. I thank Michelle Egan for having brought the politics of standard setting to my attention.

35. Paul Taylor, for example, argued that the level of integration "refers to the manner in which the [functional] areas are organized—in particular, the extent to which they are ruled from new centers which can act independently of governments." Paul Taylor, "The Politics of the European Communities: The Confederal Phase," *World Politics*, vol. 27 (April 1975), p. 343.

Commission. The member states, acting in the Council of Ministers, are consequently the ultimate decisionmakers. Introducing qualified majority voting under the Single European Act has not changed, constitutionally, the *collective* weight of the nation-state.[36] Even after Maastricht the Parliament will depend on the Commission and the Council of Ministers for much of its policy impact.

Why did many scholars interested in the phenomenon of integration misjudge the power of national governments? I would argue that they underestimated the importance of both the fact that the Community was a creature of a treaty rather than a constitution and the strength of the territorial dimension within the Community. The latter was exceptionally strong on its own as well as being mobilized and represented by national governments. These two factors, which at times reinforce each other, made the likelihood of minimizing the importance of national governments very unlikely indeed.

The Significance of a Treaty instead of a Constitution

The six founding members of the Community signed the Treaty of Rome rather than attend a constitutional convention. That fact has meant that the evolution of the Community is intrinsically tied to how national governments view their role in the Community.[37] Traditionally, students

36. In brief, the votes of each member country are not equal—it is not a system of "one country, one vote." France, Germany, the United Kingdom, and Italy each have ten votes; the other member countries each have fewer, with Luxembourg having only two votes. For a proposal to be approved under the rules of qualified majority voting, fifty-four (out of a total of seventy-six) votes need to be cast in favor. Twenty-three negative votes are sufficient to kill the proposal. The introduction of qualified majority voting does not alter the constitutional position of the Commission in comparison with the Council of Ministers. However, it does increase the Commission's tactical position compared with the Council's because the Commission has a wider range of negotiating tactics it can use to advance its positions. It can threaten to discount the votes of a particularly obstructionist member government and can anticipate coalition behavior in its formulation of proposals presented to the Council.

37. For a discussion of the differences between the Treaty of Rome and the U.S. Constitution, see Samuel Krislov, Claus-Dieter Ehlermann, and Joseph Weiler, "The Political Organs and the Decision-Making Process in the United States and the European Community," in Cappelletti, Seccombe, and Weiler, eds., *Integration through Law*, vol. 1, bk. 2, pp. 13–16. Further, it is useful to remember that within the United States, one population is governed exclusively by the Constitution, while another population is governed by a complex mix of treaties and constitutional provisions. Native Americans living on Indian reservations have a very different relationship with the national government than anyone else does, and the impact of international law as expressed in treaties is largely responsible for their special status. Although their legal status is complex, recognized tribes living on

of international relations, used to studying the role of states in international negotiations and international organizations, assume that states will be preeminent. Neofunctionalist scholars, however, were struck by the potential of the Commission· to transcend the conventional categories of interstate relations. Yet the very framework within which the Commission was established, that is, the Treaty of Rome, was destined to undergird the power of national governments as decisionmakers.

In federal systems, subnational governments are critical to amending the constitution. Yet even in countries like Canada, where all provinces must agree to amendment, the federal government must be negotiated with by the federation's constituent units.[38] The result of the negotiations may not be completely to the federal government's liking, but it is certainly one of the central negotiating parties and its approval is necessary.

When institutions are constructed by treaty, however, the signatories-to-be negotiate with one another, and those signatories are only national governments. The Commission could become a signatory only if the member states changed the treaties to this effect (an unlikely step, to say the least). While it participates in the negotiations, its position can be ignored by the negotiating governments. The use of a treaty institutionalizes the importance of national governments, especially since by definition a treaty is only binding on those countries that sign it.

Second, a treaty allows national governments to segment the process of institution building. Although some legal scholars argue that the Treaty

---

reservations have a higher status in the federal system than do the states themselves. Indian reservations, therefore, are often not subject to state laws, have their own judicial system, and recognize tribal law. Their special status is particularly important in the environmental policy arena. The possibility of living under treaty arrangements within a federation is suggestive of the institutional creativity and flexibility possible under federalism. For an introduction to the status of Native Americans in the American federal system, see Les Houston, "The States and Indian Jurisdiction," *State Government*, vol. 51 (Winter 1978), pp. 20–27; Vine Deloria, Jr., ed., *American Indian Policy in the Twentieth Century* (University of Oklahoma Press, 1985); and Sharon O'Brien, ed., *American Indian Tribal Governments* (University of Oklahoma Press, 1989), pp. 255–88. In Canada, aboriginal people also have special treaty rights under the Constitution Act of 1867. See J. Anthony Long and Menno Boldt, eds., *Governments in Conflict? Provinces and Indian Nations in Canada* (University of Toronto Press, 1988).

38. Donald V. Smiley, *Canada in Question: Federalism in the Seventies* (Toronto: McGraw-Hill Ryerson, 1972), pp. 42–43; and Douglas V. Verney, *Three Civilizations, Two Cultures, One State: Canada's Political Traditions* (Duke University Press, 1986), pp. 359, 398. For a discussion of the German amendment process, see also Sharpf, "Joint-Decision Trap," pp. 245–47.

of Rome has been "constitutionalized" in the legal arena,[39] it is important to note that the use of the treaty mechanism allows such constitutionalization to be limited, very explicitly, by the member states. For example, the Single European Act clearly delineates which actions of the member states will not be subject to the European Court of Justice. Thus the practice of judicial review can be segmented by treaty in a way that is extremely difficult by constitutional means.[40] In a similar vein, it is only because the national governments decided that Jacques Delors should chair the committee which wrote the Delors Report on Economic and Monetary Union that the Commission was involved at all. If the national governments had decided to exclude the Commission from the discussions on economic and monetary union, they could have done so.

Finally, national governments can disregard developments in one area of policy when they negotiate treaties in other areas. A treaty on political union can be signed quite apart from the Treaty of Rome. Whereas amendments to a constitution resemble a continuing dialogue with previous political and constitutional developments, the formulation of new treaties can differentiate among whatever institutional innovations were made in previous treaties.[41] Treaties allow for much greater discontinuity in institutional development, a disjuncture that permits national governments to control the timing and shape of institution building relatively closely.[42]

Third, the process of creating institutions by treaty maximizes the power of the executive within all the national governments concerned. Treaties are negotiated by executives, even though they are ratified by

39. See Joseph Weiler, "The Community System: The Dual Character of Supra-nationalism," in *Yearbook of European Law, 1981*, vol. 1 (Oxford University Press, 1982), pp. 267–306.

40. In the United States, Congress throughout the nineteenth century exercised the right to impose differential, and often burdensome, conditions on territories wishing to become a state. Yet in the twentieth century, the Supreme Court "challenged Congress' right to set invidious admission conditions and asserted its own jurisdiction over the state-making process." Peter S. Onuf, "New State Equality: The Ambiguous History of a Constitutional Principle," *Publius*, vol. 18 (Fall 1988), p. 53. In the Community, it is unlikely that the European Court would be able to mount such a challenge.

41. Accession treaties, signed by new members as they join the Community, are an exception. New members must accept the existing body of EC law and institutional arrangements.

42. That is not to say that the Commission in particular does not have an impact on such institutional development. In the bargaining process between states, which underlies institutional change, the Community institutions can offer helpful suggestions or generate favorable conditions.

legislatures. Because the Community was created through treaties, then, not only are national governments entrenched but the executive branch is strengthened in comparison with their respective national legislatures. This dynamic within the relationship between national executives and national legislatures needs to be recognized as particularly important in designing future Community institutions.

The Territorial Dimension

The national governments that sign treaties are governments of a specific territorial unit. Governments, institutionally, represent the territorial cleavages in the Community that have received international recognition. Yet even if national governments as such did not exercise institutionalized strength in the Community, politics would still have a powerful territorial dimension. The legacy of the European sovereign state is that national boundaries are extraordinarily important shapers of most aspects of life. The territorial claims that national governments represent, therefore, are exceedingly strong.

It is nearly impossible to overestimate the importance of national boundaries as key organizers of political power and economic wealth within the Community. National identity, political party organizations, party systems, partisan identity, interest groups, taxing and spending arrangements, educational systems, electoral constituencies, the internal organization of the state, executive-legislative relations, the appointment of commissioners and European Court justices, the role of the judiciary, legal systems, and administrative apparatuses are all defined by national territory.

The ties across territory are relatively weak in critical areas. Most individuals in the Community, for example, speak only their national language and thus cannot communicate across territory. Feelings of social solidarity are also constrained by national boundaries in the central area of taxation. As Richard Rose has pointed out, "The fraternal feelings of socialists are dissipated if anyone suggests that in a federal Europe, northern European workers would pay higher taxes to provide social benefits for less well-off workers in southern Europe."[43]

Even "peripheral" regions within the nation-state suffer that status due to the definition of national territory. As Sharpe argues, "peripheral

43. Richard Rose, "Is Europe a Community?" *Public Opinion*, vol. 12 (May–June 1989), p. 43.

regions are peripheral because the boundary of the state has made them so. . . . The Midi is peripheral to Paris, but not to Spain's twin economic heartlands, the Basque country and Catalonia; nor is it peripheral to the Italian economic centre—the Turin-Genoa-Milan triangle. With the exception of those regions on the very limits of human habitation . . . the boundaries of the West European national state alone determine peripherality."[44]

The territorial dimension is so strong, therefore, that based on the experience of other federal systems characterized by territorial diversity, it would be felt even if sovereign Community institutions were agreed to. That is, even if national governments as such did not participate in the Community's policymaking process, Community politics would certainly be shaped, and probably dominated, by territorial considerations.[45] National boundaries would continue to matter enormously if a federal Europe were constructed.

The Impact of Treaty and Territory on Institutions

The evolution of institutions in the Community illustrates the impact of treaties and national governments. The chapters in this book give a good sense of how this development has occurred. The role of the European Council is an often-discussed manifestation of intergovernmentalism, and its importance is presented in David Cameron's chapter. Gary Marks has outlined how Regional Funds have been established and funded as a result of national government claims and bargaining strategies. Guy Peters, for his part, has discussed the interdependence between the Commission and the Council of Ministers.

It is useful here simply to point out that the intersection between the use of treaty negotiations and the role of national governments is nowhere more present than in the agreements made at Maastricht about the EuroFed. As John Woolley points out, the proposed central bank is far more federal than the Federal Reserve System in the United

44. L. J. Sharpe, "Fragmentation and Territoriality in the European State System," *International Political Science Review*, vol. 10 (July 1989), p. 236.

45. Although it is important to remember that in the United Kingdom the centralized unitary state has indeed been able to minimize the political role of strong territorial differences, it is unlikely that the Community could develop that degree of "central" authority. For a seminal history of the territorial dimension in the United Kingdom, see Hugh F. Kearney, *The British Isles: A History of Four Nations* (Cambridge: Cambridge University Press, 1989). See also Richard Rose, *The Territorial Dimension in Government: Understanding the United Kingdom* (Chatham, N.J.: Chatham House, 1982).

States. Whereas national central banks will be represented in the EuroFed's governing structure, neither American governors, state banking commissioners, nor state legislatures are represented on the governing councils of the Federal Reserve. The proposed bank resembles the constitution of the Bundesbank, which is governed in such a way that all the territorial units of the German federation are formally represented. (If proposed changes in its structure are implemented, the Bundesbank will still be far more federal than the Federal Reserve.) The central bank agreed to at Maastricht thus will not be a sovereign institution (that is, insulated from its constituent units) in the way the American Federal Reserve is. Rather, the member governments' central banks will pool sovereignty—they will all participate in its governance. They will not cede sovereignty to a European institution that excludes their direct participation.

The effect of the territorial dimension on the European Court of Justice, the most sovereign of the Community's policymaking institutions, perhaps best illustrates the power of territorial claims even when not mobilized by national governments. As Martin Shapiro points out, the Court was created by the Treaty of Rome and has come to exercise significant powers of judicial review over the laws of the member states. Yet the Court has done so by using the highest (as well as lower) national courts as its partners.

Through a procedure in which the national courts ask the European Court of Justice for preliminary references and preliminary rulings, which they then render as their own verdict, the Court has been able to impose the supremacy of Community law. Such a procedure, however, distinguishes the Court from, for example, the Supreme Court in the United States. In the Community's legal system, national judiciaries play a pivotal role in contrast to, for example, the subordinate role played by American state judiciaries.

In the United States, the Supreme Court delivers its own verdict, which is then binding on both federal and state courts. In the Community, the European Court uses the national judiciary to render its verdicts, thus harnessing the national judicial and legal order to the Court's interpretation of whether national and Community law are compatible. Weiler argues, "What is important, indeed crucial, is the fact that it *is* the national court acting in tandem with the European Court which gives the formal final decision on the compatibility of the national measure with Community law. . . . [T]he supranational system—in a synthesis of international law and constitutional law—puts the inherently stronger *national* system in the service of the transnational order."[46]

The Court, then, incorporates territorially based judicial systems into its decisionmaking structure in a way alien to, for example, the American system of judicial review.[47] The Community's legal order has been constructed with the active cooperation and partnership of the national courts as opposed to their subordination.

Territory versus Electorate

As Guy Peters points out in chapter 3, the "democratic deficit" is causing widespread concern among scholars and policymakers. The deficit, in the eyes of many, is due to the lack of power exercised by the European Parliament. In this view, the institution representing the individual citizens of the member-state countries does not have enough of a say in the workings of the Community. The weaknesses of the European Parliament are somewhat less than they were before the Single European Act and the decisions taken at Maastricht, but nonetheless the Parliament is too weak to provide the kind of democratic accountability conventionally implied by the term *democracy*.[48] Further, the creation of a EuroFed, as John Woolley points out, will make such a deficit even more striking.

46. Weiler, "Community System," p. 301 (emphasis in the original). See also Renaud Dehousse and Joseph H. H. Weiler, "The Legal Dimension," in Wallace, ed., *Dynamics of European Integration*, pp. 254–55.

47. Such an organizational structure tends to act as a guarantor of the claims of territoriality. Jacqué and Weiler argue that the advent of qualified majority voting has made the delineation of competences between the Community and the member states necessary in order to forestall a rebellion by the national courts. Jean Paul Jacqué and Joseph H. H. Weiler, *On the Road to European Union—A New Judicial Architecture* (Florence: European University Institute, 1990). By contrast, Robert F. Nagel argues that, in the American case, "jurists and scholars tend to . . . undervalue judicial protection of principles that allocate decision-making responsibilities among governmental units." *Constitutional Cultures: The Mentality and Consequences of Judicial Review* (University of California Press, 1989), p. 64. The relationship between the European Court and national courts resembles in some ways the relationship among courts within the Federal Republic of Germany. In the Federal Republic, "there are no federal courts at the *Land* or regional level. Except for the Federal Constitutional Court, original jurisdiction is vested almost completely in *Land* courts, even in cases concerning the application of federal statutes." Kisker, "West German Federal Constitutional Court," p. 37. Furthermore, the Constitutional Court is linked to the Bundesrat in that the latter selects one-half of the Constitutional Court's judges. Philip M. Blair, *Federalism and Judicial Review in West Germany* (Oxford: Clarendon Press, 1981), p. 13.

48. For a discussion of the pressures leading to passage of the Single European Act, including the role of the federalists, see Andrew Moravcsik, "Negotiating the Single Euro-

Although it could be argued that the Community is indeed democratic since the member governments are democratically elected, the indirect link between the individual citizen and the directives approved by the Council of Ministers troubles those who believe that the link between voter and policymaker should be more direct, more robust. From the perspective of committed federalists, the representation of governments in the Council of Ministers and the European Council is less legitimate than the representation of individual voters. Representation as used in political discourse refers to voters rather than to governments, for the representation of the individual voter has come to dominate notions about democracy and therefore has a much greater legitimacy than does the representation of territorial government as an institution.[49]

Analysts who give overriding importance to the representation of individuals regard the representation of the "institutional self-interests of governments"[50] as belonging to a confederation rather than to a federation. In a federal system, according to this view, a sovereign Community must by definition represent individual voters as opposed to the governments of member states. In brief, national governments are associated with confederation, while electoral representation is linked to the development of Community institutions independent of national governments.

It is ironic that many federalists in Europe have been so unwilling to consider the possibility that the development of the corporate personality of the Community will inevitably be institutionally linked to the politics of territory. Federalists have been so critical of the role of national governments in the current institutional structure that they have downplayed the fact that federations are created, above all, because of concerns with

pean Act: National Interests and Conventional Statecraft in the European Community," *International Organization*, vol. 45 (Winter 1991), pp. 19–56; and Wayne Sandholtz and John Zysman, "1992: Recasting the European Bargain," *World Politics* vol. 42 (October 1989), pp. 95–128. For a discussion of the larger context within which the Single European Act was approved, see Alberta Sbragia, "Asymmetrical Integration: Institutional Development and the Single European Act," in Dale L. Smith and James Lee Ray, eds., *The 1992 Project and the Future of Integration in Europe* (Sharpe, forthcoming).

49. Theorists of representation have typically focused on representation as linked to voters and elections. Those who have not focused on the representation of persons have focused on the representation of groups or classes. The representation of territorial governments, as opposed to constituents bounded by a territorial boundary, is conspicuously absent. See Hanna Pitkin, *The Concept of Representation* (University of California Press, 1967).

50. The term is used by Fritz W. Scharpf in a seminal article on the Community, one from which I have drawn liberally. Scharpf, "Joint-Decision Trap," p. 254.

territorial or ethnic politics. Cleavages, whether cultural or territorial, are the sine qua non of federal arrangements.[51]

The focus on electoral representation as the pivot around which the hoped-for federal constitutional order would revolve has its roots in the desire for a political center that would anchor the corporate development of the Community. That center is not rooted in territorial cleavage and the representation of that cleavage but, in this view, is meant to transcend such divisions, to represent the European interest.

Writing about Altiero Spinelli, perhaps the best-known European federalist, Michael Burgess concluded that "the mistake which Spinelli attributed to Monnet was inherent in the functional approach which neglected to deal with the organisation of political power at the European level. The political centre thus remained weak and impotent, lacking the capacity to go much beyond what existed and unable to adapt to new forces and problems encountered at the European level. . . . The missing element from Monnet's Europe is the King: the crucial political element without which Europe is in chaos."[52]

Yet most federal systems are established as federations precisely to avoid or replace a king. In their wish to see a "United States of Europe," European federalists railed against a confederation of sovereign states to such an extent that they tended to conceptualize a federal Europe without the institutionalization of territorial politics. In their view, a body representing a European electorate would constitute a strong political center— and the representation of the member states' governments as governments would become tangential at best.

From a comparative point of view, such an analysis is problematic. Territorial politics is so important in polities characterized by territorial cleavages that the representation of territorial claims is bound to be a likely feature of politics in similar contexts. Because of the role of territorial boundaries as the central organizing units of Community political and economic life, it is extremely difficult to imagine a federated Community,

51. For an interesting discussion of how territorial cleavages may intersect other types of cleavages (such as linguistic or ethnic ones), see Lijphart, "Consociation and Federation," pp. 499–515.

52. Michael Burgess, "Federalism and European Union: Past, Present and Future," paper delivered at the meeting of the European Community Studies Association, George Mason University, May 24–25, 1989, p. 8. For a discussion of differences among European federalists, see Ilam Greilsammer, "Some Observations on European Federalism," in Elazar, ed., *Federalism and Political Integration*, pp. 107–32.

much less a federal-type organization, in which territorial politics would not play a central, and most probably a dominant, role.

The Institutional Representation of Territorial Government

But how are territorial politics to be defined? And how can the participation of constituent units in central decisionmaking be organized? Sidney Tarrow has argued that "in mobilized political systems . . . there are two basic principles of representation: territorial representation based on the choice of officials through geographic areas, and functional representation based on professional, class, and interest organization."[53] Generally, the literature on territorial politics within the nation-state assumes that territoriality will lose ground to the imperatives of functional representation, this being inevitable (it is claimed) because of the complexities of modernization and the extension of the welfare state. Territorial politics is equated with decentralization, typically in the governmental administration of services, with the establishment of new regional governments, or with the exercise of influence by territorially based officials such as mayors in shaping the policies of the center.[54]

53. Sidney Tarrow, "Introduction," in Tarrow, Katzenstein, and Graziano, eds., *Territorial Politics in Industrial Nations*, p. 4.

54. The literature on the various aspects of territorial politics as outlined here is very large. Of particular importance are Bennett, ed., *Decentralization, Local Governments, and Markets*; Douglas E. Ashford, *British Dogmatism and French Pragmatism: Central-Local Policymaking in the Welfare State* (London: Allen and Unwin, 1982); Tarrow, Katzenstein, and Graziano, eds., *Territorial Politics in Industrial Nations*; L. J. Sharpe, ed., *Decentralist Trends in Western Democracies* (London: Sage, 1979); Yves Meny and Vincent Wright, eds., *Centre-Periphery Relations in Western Europe* (London: Allen and Unwin, 1985); Sidney Tarrow, *Between Center and Periphery: Grassroots Politicians in Italy and France* (Yale University Press, 1977); Michael Keating, *State and Regional Nationalism: Territorial Politics and the European State* (Harvester-Wheatsheaf, 1988); R. A. W. Rhodes, *Control and Power in Central-Local Government Relations* (Westmead, U.K.: Gower, 1981); Beer, "Modernization of American Federalism," pp. 49–95; Suzanne Farkas, *Urban Lobbying: Mayors in the Federal Arena* (New York University Press, 1971); Donald H. Haider, *When Governments Come to Washington: Governors, Mayors and Intergovernmental Lobbying* (Free Press, 1974); Jim Bulpitt, *Territory and Power in the United Kingdom: An Interpretation* (Manchester University Press, 1983); Rose, *The Territorial Dimension in Government*; Patrick Le Gales, "New Issues around Decentralisation and Urban Policy in France: A Reform of the State Administration to Match Local Dynamism?" paper delivered at the World Congress of Sociology, July 1990; R. A. W. Rhodes and Vincent Wright, eds., special issue on "Tensions in the Territorial Politics of Western Europe," *West European Politics*, vol. 10 (October 1987); and Jeffrey Joseph Anderson, *Territory, Economy, and the State: Politics against Markets in Declining Industrial Regions* (Cambridge University Press, forthcoming).

Such a notion of territorial politics is a far cry from the role played by national governments in the European Community. The dimension of territoriality is so strong within the Community and the role played by national governments is so decisive that one needs to look elsewhere for possible guides to thinking about the role of territorial politics in the Community.

It is perhaps instructive that the president of the American Political Science Association, in his presidential address of 1978, dealt with American federalism by focusing on the concept of representation. By contrast, the president of the Canadian Political Science Association, in his 1977 address, stressed the importance, in the Canadian context, of governments as institutions. The latter both manipulate the federal system and structure state-society relations. This difference reflects the very different ways in which federalism in the two countries has evolved, and it cautions against assuming that the American variant of federalism is the only relevant one to discussions of the Community.

The American model of federalism can be thought of as constituting a model of territorial politics in which territory plays the role of defining the geographic locus of representation. States are "aggregates of electors."[55] Members of the House of Representatives represent territorially defined districts, and senators represent the electorate in their respective states. However, no one in Congress represents the institutional interests of state governments.[56] Territory simply "packages" the representation of individuals; the corporate interests of the governments of that territory are not constitutionally represented.

Even when senators were elected by state legislatures (pre-1913), the role of the Senate as a legislative body was not defined as one that represented the interests of state legislatures. Elmer Schattschneider points out that "in a series of decisions, the Senate first established the principle that individual senators are not bound by the instructions of state legislatures."[57] Certainly, since 1913, senators represent the electorate, not the state legislature or the governor's office. Americans, whether policymakers or

55. Campbell Sharman, "Second Chambers," in Bakvis and Chandler, eds., *Federalism and the Role of the State*, p. 84.

56. The same is true of the Australian legislative system. In practice, Australian "senators have become primarily representatives of their parties rather than of their states." Donald V. Smiley and Ronald L. Watts, *Intrastate Federalism in Canada* (University of Toronto Press, 1985), p. 57.

57. Elmer Eric Schattschneider, *Semisovereign People: A Realist's View of Democracy in America* (Holt, Rinehart, and Winston, 1960), p. 14.

scholars, acknowledge the institutional self-interests of government fairly infrequently (although such interest is expressed, for example, when one government sues another in the courts). Other than through the require-ment that the approval of three-fourths of state legislatures is needed to amend the Constitution, the interests of state governments as institutions (as opposed to the interests of constituencies defined by state boundaries) do not play an important role in the American political system.[58]

Canadians, owing to their very different history of federalism, have begun to view the role of government rather differently. Alan Cairns, for example, argued that analysts of Canadian federalism, with their expecta-tions that modernization would lead to greater centralization, had failed to "treat government with appropriate seriousness."[59] He went on to argue that the provincial governments had an ability to protect their interests that had been overlooked: "Possessed of tenacious instincts for their own preservation and growth, the governments of Canadian federalism have endowed the cleavages between provinces, and between provinces and nation which attended their birth, with an ever more comprehensive political meaning."[60]

The assertion of provincial self-interest has occurred in Canada despite institutional obstacles. Canada, as a parliamentary federation in which the Westminister model of responsible party government is operative, does not have an elected second chamber in which provincial interests are

58. Interestingly, the governor's office has not been viewed as playing an important role in linking national and state government. In the period before 1913, the state legislatures, not the governor, selected U.S. senators. During the Constitutional Convention, the idea of the governor choosing the senators was not even discussed as an option. The framers of the Constitution viewed state legislatures as the repository of legitimacy. As Haynes points out, "It had been by their legislatures that the thirteen Colonies made protest against British oppression, and later prepared for common resistance. Throughout the war it had been the state legislatures which elected the governors and most of the other officers, both civil and military." George H. Haynes, *The Elections of Senators* (Henry Holt, 1906), p. 17. In a similar vein, advocates of strengthening the states' influence on national policymaking argue for repealing the Seventeenth Amendment, thereby returning to the pre-1913 system of choosing senators, rather than giving the governor a role in the process of choice. See, for example, Ronald M. Peters, Jr., "Repeal the Seventeenth? A Reform Proposal for the Political Crisis of Our Time," *Extensions*, Spring 1990, p. 2.

59. Alan C. Cairns, "The Governments and Societies of Canadian Federalism," *Canadian Journal of Political Science*, vol. 10 (December 1977), p. 698. By contrast, Samuel Beer argued that in the United States modernization has led to the strengthening of the federal government. State governments have not been able to stem the effects of economic and technological change. See Beer, "Modernization of American Federalism."

60. Cairns, "Governments and Societies of Canadian Federalism," p. 700.

represented.[61] Nor is the representation that does exist in the Senate disproportionate to population.[62] Finally, for many reasons, Canadian members of Parliament exhibit high degrees of party discipline (higher than British members of Parliament). Such party cohesion minimizes the representation of constituencies territorially defined or of the interests of provincial governments as such.[63]

Nonetheless, finding a constitutional ally in the (British) Judicial Committee of the Privy Council during the nineteenth century, the provinces have been able to increase their powers in the Canadian system.[64] The requirement that provincial governments must unanimously approve amendments to the Constitution (contrasted with the three-fourths majority required in the United States) has given the provinces a strong position in the federal system.

Still a different model of federalism is presented by Germany's federal system.[65] In fact, German federalism illustrates the elasticity of federal arrangements in two important ways. First, it shows how unique institutions can be created at the national level. In Winfried Steffani's words, "Unlike the British Constitution, the German Constitution established not a pure parliamentary system but a federative one manifested by the existence of two legislative organs at the national level, the Bundestag and the Bundesrat."[66]

Second, the German federation differs from other federal systems in how power is divided among governments. Reissert and Schaefer conclude,

61. Smiley and Watts argue that nonlegislative mechanisms (such as provincial representation in the Cabinet) allow regional interests to be represented. Smiley and Watts, *Intrastate Federalism in Canada*, pp. 64–90.

62. Campbell Sharman points out, "In Canada . . . the terms of political debate at the time of Confederation were not ones that put provincial equality of representation in the national legislature as high on the agenda, and the composition of the Canadian Senate, while based on regional representation, largely mirrored the dominance that the two largest provinces, Ontario and Quebec, had in the lower house by virtue of their population." "Second Chambers," p. 83.

63. For a discussion of the impact of party cohesion on territorially based representation in Canada, see Smiley and Watts, *Intrastate Federalism in Canada*, pp. 91–115.

64. See, for example, Verney, *Three Civilizations, Two Cultures, One State*, pp. 136–37.

65. See the special issue on "Federalism and Intergovernmental Relations in West Germany: A Fortieth Year Appraisal," ed. Arthur B. Gunlicks, *Publius*, vol. 19 (Fall 1989).

66. Winfried Steffani, "The Bundestag at the Intersection of Four Systems," in Norman J. Ornstein, ed., *The Role of the Legislature in Western Democracies* (Washington: American Enterprise Institute for Public Policy Research, 1981), p. 57. The Australian system is similar in that it has imposed an upper chamber representing interests territorially defined onto a parliamentary system.

"The division of responsibilities between the federation and the states in the Federal Republic differs significantly from that in other federal systems: responsibilities are not divided by policy areas, but by functions in the policy-making process. Each level of government is primarily responsible for either legislative or administrative and financial functions in the policy process, and it performs these functions within almost all policy areas."[67] In the policymaking process, the federal government legislates, and the state governments implement policy. The federal level does not administer its own policies, for administration falls under the states' jurisdiction.

The power of the states in the system comes from their near monopoly in administration and, more interestingly for current purposes, from their direct participation in the decisionmaking process at the federal level. Such participation is linked to the unique system of representation that underlies the German federation. The German federal system recognizes the representation of two distinct entities—voters and governments. Voters are represented in the Bundestag, to which the executive is accountable. The state governments themselves are represented in the Bundesrat, the second chamber, which exercises an absolute veto over legislation affecting the Länder. Arend Lijphart describes the Bundesrat as "a unique federal chamber, composed of representatives of the executives of the member states of the federation—usually ministers in the member state cabinets."[68]

The system of representation within the German system, therefore, differs significantly from that found in other federal systems. The German second chamber represents what Fritz Scharpf terms the "institutional self-interests"[69] of the executive branch of the Länder governments, the Länder's dominant political authority. Rather than having the members of the upper house selected either by the state legislature or by voters, the German system puts the selection process in the hands of the German states' executive. The Länder cabinets select and instruct the members of the Bundesrat.

67. Bernd Reissert and Gunther F. Schaefer, "Centre-Periphery Relations in the Federal Republic of Germany," in Meny and Wright, eds., *Centre-Periphery Relations in Western Europe*, pp. 105–06. See also Nevil Johnson, *State and Government in the Federal Republic of Germany: The Executive at Work*, 2d ed. (Oxford: Pergamon Press, 1983), pp. 120, 117–68.

68. Arend Lijphart, "Bicameralism: Canadian Senate Reform in Comparative Perspective," in Bakvis and Chandler, eds., *Federalism and the Role of the State*, p. 103.

69. Scharpf, "Joint-Decision Trap," p. 254.

By contrast, even when nineteenth-century American senators were chosen by state government, they were chosen by the state legislature and not by the governor. Further, the degree of instruction received from the legislature was neither high nor well enforced.[70] Gunter Kisker concludes that "the Bundesrat speaks for the 'States as States' even more than the U.S. Senate did before 1913, when its members were elected by the state legislatures."[71]

The German model, therefore, represents an important institutional innovation in federalism and helps us to grasp how the constituent units of a system may, as institutions, participate in central decisionmaking. The German system treats state governments as institutions seriously, to paraphrase Alan Cairns. The relevance of the German model for the role of national governments in the Community has been pointed out in a seminal article by Fritz Scharpf. He argues that advocates of a " 'United Europe' had in mind . . . a federal system fashioned after the American model. What was created, however, were institutional arrangements corresponding more closely to the tradition of German federalism. . . . More specifically . . . Länder governments have a significant share in the exercise of many of the important functions of the federal government. It is in this regard that German federalism is most comparable to the European Community."[72]

70. William H. Riker, "The Senate and American Federalism," in Riker, ed., *Development of American Federalism*, pp. 135–56.

71. Kisker, "West German Federal Constitutional Court," p. 37. In a similar vein, Hans-Georg Wehling states, "One could speak of the *Bundesrat* as an assembly of *Land* ambassadors, but the *Land* governments cannot entrust just anyone with this task: the members of the *Bundesrat* as well as their representatives have to be members of their *Land* cabinet. . . . Because the members are subject to instructions by their *Land* government, the votes of one *Land* can only be cast as a bloc. . . . The right to vote, then, is not given to the individual members of the *Bundesrat* but to the *Länder* represented by the *Land* governments." Hans-Georg Wehling, "The Bundesrat," *Publius*, vol. 19 (Fall 1989), p. 54.

72. Scharpf, "Joint-Decision Trap," pp. 242–43. The similarities between the Community's institutional arrangements and those of the German system have been noted within the Community. For example, Jacobs and others point out that the conciliation procedure in Parliament "is almost identical to that of the "Conciliation Committee" (*Vermittlungsausschuss*) in the Federal Republic of Germany, where one Minister for each *Land* from the *Bundesrat* meets with an equivalent sized delegation from the *Bundestag* to thrash out compromises where the positions of the two chambers diverge. The difference is that in the Community, at the end of the negotiations, whatever the result, it is up to one side, namely the Council, to adopt the act in question." Francis Jacobs and Richard Corbett, with Michael Shackleton, *The European Parliament* (Boulder, Colo.: Westview Press, 1990), p. 8.

The Länder are not represented in the sense that constituents are; rather, "they are direct participants in central decision processes."[73] The German system, therefore, allows direct participation by constituent governments in the policymaking carried on at the "center." Such a system does not fit the standard Anglo-Saxon notions of federalism, based as they are on independent spheres of power. German federalism incorporates a great deal of intergovernmentalism, therefore, and provides a springboard for thinking about possible governmental arrangements in which the governments of constituent units retain significant power.

Although the details of how the Bundesrat functions in the German federation (such as the impact of political parties) are not our concern, it is important to note that the second chamber has become more rather than less powerful over time. The Federal Constitutional Court has expanded "the number of matters that are within the jurisdiction of the federation but which cannot be handled by the *Bundestag* without the consent of the *Bundesrat*." Because of the court's decisions, "almost two-thirds of all federal legislation [is subject] to the approval of the *Bundesrat*."[74]

The extent of the Länder's power has recently been demonstrated as the intragovernmental debate has raged in Germany about how to pay for unification as well as how to restructure the Bundesbank, given the need to incorporate the new Länder into the central bank's federal organization and system of representation.[75] In both instances, the Länder were a formidable force, which the federal executive and the Bundesbank had to take very seriously. Although party politics certainly affects how the interests of the Länder are looked after in the Bundesrat, the representation of Länder interests as such also takes place. The institutional as well as

73. Scharpf, "Joint-Decision Trap," p. 254.

74. Kisker, "West German Federal Constitutional Court," pp. 50–51. This is a higher figure than Nevil Johnson's. Johnson, writing earlier, had concluded that roughly 55 percent of all legislation had to be approved by the Bundesrat. *State and Government in the Federal Republic of Germany*, pp. 127–28.

Although the Bundesrat is increasing its influence within the German policymaking system, it is still not, as an institution, coequal with the Bundestag. Lijphart's comparative classification of bicameral systems, for example, classified the German one as a "moderately asymmetrical" bicameral legislature whereas the American bicameral legislative system is classified as fully "symmetrical." The American Senate has formally equal powers with the House of Representatives and is thus able to cast an absolute veto on every piece of legislation, whereas the Bundesrat's powers are more circumscribed. Lijphart, "Bicameralism," p. 111.

75. See, for example, David Marsh, "Bundesbank Dispute Ends in Byzantine Deal," *Financial Times*, June 14, 1991, p. 2; and Peter Norman, "Upper House Rejects Bundesbank Restructuring," *Financial Times*, November 30–December 1, 1991, p. 2.

the partisan self-interest of the Länder is represented.[76] The Bundesrat is interesting because it allows the governments of the federation's constituent units to participate in the making of federal legislation. The institutionalization of the territorial dimension in the Bundesrat represents an alternative to, for example, the way the American system represents territorial claims. The Bundesrat institutionalizes a conception of representation different from that operative in the American system.

The Question of Representation

The representative scheme underlying the Bundesrat is fundamentally different from that involved in other federal systems. Whereas in nineteenth-century America indirect election by state legislatures selected the members of the federal upper house, the German system allows the executives of the German state governments to participate directly in the national policymaking process. The German system, in a sense, incorporates direct democracy—of governments rather than individuals. In a strict sense, then, the state governments are not "represented" but are participants and decisionmakers in national policymaking.

From a historical and comparative point of view, such an innovation in representation is striking. Samuel Beer argues that an emphasis on representation, on self-government rather than on the classic attributes of American federalism, was at the core of the design of the American federal system. For Beer, the existence of independent spheres of jurisdiction for the national and state governments, so-called dual federalism, was "only one and a secondary feature" of the new polity designed in Philadelphia. Beer argues that "dual federalism was a means to representational federalism."[77] In a similar vein, Heinz Eulau concludes that "the great innovation in political theory implicit in the American Constitution consisted in the theoretical fusion of two basic principles of governmental engineering— the principle of federation and the principle of representation."[78]

The American model of federalism introduced the idea of equal representation of states in the Senate, indirect election by state legislatures of

76. Carl Cavanagh Hodge, "The Supremacy of Politics: Federalism and Parties in Western Europe," *West European Politics*, vol. 10 (April 1987), p. 262.

77. Beer, "Federalism, Nationalism, and Democracy in America," pp. 9–10.

78. Heinz Eulau, "Polarity in Representational Federalism: A Neglected Theme of Political Theory," in Heinz Eulau and John C. Wahlke, eds., *The Politics of Representation: Continuities in Theory and Research* (Beverly Hills, Sage Publications, 1978), p. 91.

senators, and direct election of the House of Representatives. The idea of representation in the upper house disproportionate to population was adopted by the Australians, and of course all democracies, whether federations or unitary states, gradually accepted the notion of the lower house being directly elected. Further, the Americans switched to direct elections for their Senate in the twentieth century, paralleling Australia's decision.[79]

The German system, therefore, represents the first major challenge to the assumptions about representation made by the framers of the American Constitution. Indirect election by various types of legislatures to upper houses still exists (the French Senate and the Dutch Senate are indirectly elected), but no other democratic system institutionalizes the direct participation of the executives of the constituent units of the federation.

The German model of federalism raises an alternative to the way representation and territory are traditionally linked. Rather than considering territory as a "package" in which individual voters exercise their choice in choosing the members of sovereign institutions, the Bundesrat offers an example of an institution wielding general power in which the interests of territorial governments (defined as executives rather than legislatures) are protected by those very governments. The "general" power does not need to be thought of as separate from the power of the constituent units—the latter is integral to the construction of the former.

The representation of governments rather than individuals is so unusual that it does not fit conventional notions of democracy. Even though those governments are responsible to directly elected legislatures, indirect representation is viewed with deep suspicion by current theorists of democracy. In a similar vein, the participation of constituent units in the exercise of the general or federal power is so atypical that scholars of federalism have felt impelled to categorize it as a deviation from normal federalism.

Yet the representation of territorially based governments does provide a method of facilitating integration, of achieving federalism, without submerging the interests of the constituent units. It does offer the possibility of federalization through indirect rather than direct representation—or of combining direct and indirect representation in a way that gives the collectivity of national governments (but not individual governments) the

79. Australia's Senate exemplifies the problems of imposing a powerful territorially based second house onto a British-derived system of parliamentary government (as opposed to the German system of parliamentary government or the American system of executive-legislative relations based on the separation of powers). See Sharman, "Second Chambers," pp. 85–96.

right of absolute veto. It thus presents an alternative to models that assume that federalization must necessarily be characterized by either a supranational executive or by parliamentary sovereignty. It essentially allows one to think about the exercise of public authority without imposing a center-periphery model on such an exercise.

Although the Bundesrat is universally referred to as unique, its significance for possibilities in designing federal institutional structures has probably been underestimated. The German system offers an alternative way of conceptualizing federalism, for the Bundesrat offers an alternative way of thinking about how constituent units of a federation can participate in the work of the "center."[80] The German system raises the possibility that, at the Community-level, a federal-type organization could operate without a center as traditionally conceptualized, so long as the national governments are willing to abide by qualified majority voting, abide by judicial review in case of disputes, allow the Commission to exercise policy leadership, and permit the Parliament to exercise some (even coequal) power. In that sense, a center could conceivably be constructed by member governments without its being detached from the collectivity of constituent units, in this case national governments.

Conclusion

The decisionmaking process evolving in the Community gives a key role to governments—national government at the moment, and according to Gary Marks, subnational government increasingly in selected arenas. The role of interest groups and political parties needs to be investigated further, as do "policy communities." Nonetheless, governments will continue to be central actors. The interaction between governments and the Commission on the one hand and the European Parliament on the other will shape policymaking within the Community. Territorial politics rather than the interest politics frequently thought of as corporatist in national

80. It is perhaps striking to some that this discussion has focused on representation rather than on efficient policymaking or an optimal policy process. Fritz Scharpf argues that the role of the Bundesrat often leads to suboptimal policy outcomes in the Federal Republic. Yet any variant of federalism is likely to be more concerned with balancing claims of representation than with issues of efficiency or rationality in policymaking. Managing diversity typically requires "side payments" in order to reach consensus, and such payments may run counter to the rational allocation of resources. The European Community is not likely to engage in rational policymaking, if rational is defined as economists and cost-benefit analysts might.

contexts are likely to be highlighted in a Community evolving along federalist lines.

The Council of Ministers, in which national governments act, is the critical institutional forum in which territorial politics play themselves out. As Wolfgang Streeck and Philippe C. Schmitter point out, the Council "halted any attempt by supranational bodies, especially the Commission and the Parliament, to cultivate a strong constituency of organized interests that would in turn have enhanced the status of supranational Community institutions as an incipient sovereign government."[81] Organized, functional interests are not insignificant in the Community and their importance is increasing.[82] Nonetheless, they typically must use, and will need to keep using, channels provided by national governments in order to maximize their influence.

For that reason, the authors in this volume have given significantly more weight to national governments than to interest groups or political parties. That is also why the federalist theme underlies, either explicitly or implicitly, much of their analysis of the Community's system of policymaking. In studies of national politics, it is often possible to ignore territorial politics but impossible to overlook political parties and organized interests (business and labor especially). Peter Lange's chapter makes that clear. By contrast, territorial politics play a central, though not an exclusive, role in the Community.

Politics and policymaking in the European Community force one to rethink the role of government. At the Community level, governments bargain with other governments—and, significantly, with the Commission—rather than with business and labor. The role of political parties is problematic at best. Organized interest groups and political parties will undoubtedly become more significant in the years ahead. Policy communities are likely to be influential under selected conditions. Yet it is unlikely that national governments will be displaced from playing a significant role.

The member states of Europe are unlikely to become the equivalent of the American states. National governments will be forced to share power

81. Wolfgang Streeck and Philippe C. Schmitter, "From National Corporatism to Transnational Pluralism: Organized Interests in the Single European Market," *Politics and Society*, vol. 19 (June 1991), p. 142.

82. Svein S. Andersen and Kjell A. Eliassen, "European Community Lobbying," *European Journal of Political Research*, vol. 20 (September 1991), pp. 173–87; and Bruno Julien, "Euro-Lobbying Invades Berlaymont," *European Affairs*, vol. 4 (Autumn 1990), pp. 28–33.

with the European Parliament and the Commission, but they will continue to participate in the making of Community-wide decisions. National prime ministers will not become the functional equivalents of American governors. The political system they are gradually constructing, therefore, will be an original one. The insistence on the representation of territorially defined governments, in fact, will lead to a reconceptualization of federalism, representation, and the functions of government.

Appendix

A Thumbnail Sketch of the Principal Institutions of the European Community

Commission: Consists of seventeen members, including a president and six vice presidents, appointed by the governments of the twelve member states for renewable terms of four years; the president and vice presidents have renewable terms of two years. (The number of members may be reduced after the Maastricht treaty comes into effect.) No member state can have more than two members on the Commission. The Commission's main functions are to ensure the application of the provisions of the Treaty of Rome and the other relevant treaties; to serve as the executive arm of the EC, issuing decisions and regulations to implement treaty provisions; to initiate Community policy; and to defend the Community interest in the Council of Ministers. The Commission provides much of the leadership and momentum in the Community's policymaking process.

Council of Ministers: Consists of representatives of the governments of the member states, each government normally sending one of its ministers, according to the subject discussed. The foreign minister is each country's "main" representative, but other ministers often meet for specialized Council meetings. The Council ensures the coordination of the general economic policies of the Community and takes decisions necessary for carrying out the treaties. It makes the final decisions on all important issues. Qualified majority voting is permitted in certain policy areas, while unanimity is required in others. A Committee of Permanent Representatives (COREPER) prepares and coordinates the Council's work.

European Council: Consists of the Heads of State (the French president) or Government (prime ministers) of the twelve member countries, who meet twice a year in a "summit" with their foreign ministers, the president of the Commission, and one of the Commission's vice presidents. Outside of the "Community framework"—the European Council's decisions do not fall within the jurisdiction of the European Court of Justice—the European Council makes the strategic decisions about the Community's development.

European Parliament: Consists of 518 members who are directly elected by the citizens of the member states. The members of Parliament, however, sit in political, not national, groups. The Parliament meets about twelve times a year, usually for one week at a time. It advises on legislation, scrutinizes the Community budget, and exercises some democratic control over the Commission and the Council of Ministers. But the often-used term *democratic deficit* refers to the European Parliament's relative lack of power within the Community's institutional structure.

Court of Justice: Consists of thirteen judges and six advocates-general, all appointed for renewable six-year terms by the governments of the member states. The Court ensures the observance of law in the interpretation and application of the treaties and in the implementation of regulations issued by the Council of Ministers or the Commission.

Index

Action Program, 230, 232, 254
  EC intervention in, 252
  Implementation of, 253
  Social dimension and, 240
Adenauer, Konrad, 59
Ad Hoc Committee on Institutional
  Affairs, 55, 61
Agricultural Guidance and Guarantee
  Fund, 191, 210
Agricultural programs, 61–62
Allison, Graham, 115
American federal system, 5, 12–13, 260–
  61n, 263–64, 265, 271–72n, 281–82,
  287–88
American Political Science Association,
  278
American politics, state vs. federal, 3–4
Andorra, 16
Association des Régions d'Europe, 214
Australia, federal system, 263–64, 265,
  281n, 288
Austria, EC membership, 16, 29

Balance of trade, 68–70, 164
Banking Advisory Committee, 188,
  189–90
Bank of Italy, 168–69
Basevi, Giorgio, 168
Beer, Samuel, 264, 265–66, 287
Belgium
  Shift to conservatism, 57
  Social dimension and, 250
Berlin Wall, 67
Bill of Rights, United States, 150,
  153
Bretton Woods system of fixed exchange
  rates, 47

Britain
  Atypical work proposal and, 251
  Budget rebate dispute with EC, 33,
    55n, 59–63, 198–99
  EC membership, 14
  EMS and, 246
  Fall of Thatcher government and, 244–46
  Opposition to monetary union, 84
  Privy Council Judicial Committee, 283
  Relations with EC, 59–63, 198–99
  Shift to conservatism, 57
  Social Charter and, 241
  Social dimension and, 11, 13, 233, 241–
    50
  Structural Funds and, 216–17
  Trade and Industry Department, 216
  Voting in European Council and, 84
  See also Maastricht summit; Major,
    John; Thatcher, Margaret
Brittan, Samuel, 161
Buchan, David, 52–53, 167
Budget contributions, EC-member nations
  and, 61–62
Budget deficits, 182–83
Budget process in European Community
  Assessment, 97–98
  Expenditures, 96–97
  Revenue, 94–96
Budget rebates
  Britain's dispute with EC, 33, 55n,
    59–63, 198–99
  EC-member nations and, 61–62
Bundesbank, 67
  Compared with EuroFed, 176–79
  EMS and, 165–66, 167
  Federal structure of, 276
  Relationship to Länder, 286

Bundesbank Council, 176, 178
Bundesrat, 283–89
Bundestag, 283–86
Bureaucratic policymaking, 76–77, 115–21
Bureaucratic politics, 6–7, 115–21
Bureau of Unrepresented Nations, 213
Burgess, Michael, 279

Cairns, Alan, 282, 285
Canada
  Federal system, 263–64, 282–83
Canadian Political Science Association, 281
Capital markets, 164–65
  Mobility of, 196n
Cassis de Dijon, 52–53, 64, 129–34,
  154–55
Cecchini report, 225
Charter of Fundamental Social Rights,
  151, 230, 233, 240, 241, 254
Christian Democrats, social dimension
  and, 233–34
Cockfield, Lord, 35, 51
Colchester, Nicholas, 52–53, 67
Colombo, Emilio, 54–56
Commission v. French Republic, 139n,
  142–43
Commission v. Italian Republic, 139n,
  142–43
Committee of Central Bank Governors,
  188, 189
Committee of Permanent Representatives
  (COREPER), 80–82
Community Support Frameworks, 209–11,
  214n
Confederation of European Industries of
  the European Community, 49
Conference on Security and Cooperation
  in Europe, European Community
  security and, 19
Consumer prices, EC-member nations
  and, 47–48
Cooperation procedure, 101
COREPER. See Committee of Permanent
  Representatives
Costa v. ENEL, 52, 126–27n
Council of Europe, 3
Council of Ministers, 3
  Administrative judicial review and,
    141–42
  Adoption of 1992 program, 23–24
  Agriculture Council, 80
  As protector of territorial politics, 290
  Bureaucratic politics, 116, 119
  Economics and Finance Ministers Coun-
    cil, 80
  European Parliament and, 54–55, 90–92

Functions, 78–85
General Affairs Council, 80
Harmonization, 129
History of 1992 program and, 23–24, 32
Legal basis for action, 146–47
National governments and, 4–5
Organization of, 78–85
Parochialism and, 81–82
Policymaking and, 101–02
Powers, 12
Relationship with European Commis-
  sion, 81–82, 88–89
Secretariat of the Council, 82, 89
Structural spending priorities, 206–08
See also Qualified majority voting
Court cases
  Cassis de Dijon, 52–53, 64, 129–34,
    154–55
  Commission v. French Republic, 139n,
    142–43
  Commission v. Italian Republic, 139n,
    142–43
  Costa v. ENEL, 52, 126–27n
  Jean Reyners v. Belgian state, 124n
  Van Gend en Loos v. Nederlandse
    Administratie der Belastingen, 52,
    126–27n
Court of Human Rights, 149
Craxi, Bettino, 84
Crocodile Club, 101
Currency realignments, 46–47
Current account balances of EC-member
  nations, 39–40, 43
Czechoslovakia, membership in European
  Community, 14, 16

Davignon, Etienne, 49–50, 52
de Gaulle, Charles, 29, 59
Delors Committee, 71–73, 157
Delors, Jacques, 31, 34, 51, 76, 86, 103,
  273
  Advocacy of SEA, 106
  Bureaucratic politics and, 116–17
  EMU and, 27
  French debate over EMS and, 168
  Social dimension and, 254
  Subsidiarity, 110–11, 231
  Views on federalism, 110–11
Delors Report, 157–58, 273
  Budgetary policy, 183
  EuroFed and, 175
  Inflation and, 161
Denmark
  EC membership, 14
  Shift to conservatism, 57
Deregulation, 134–41

Dillon's rule, 111
Directives, 102, 138–39, 141
  83/189, 139–40
  First Banking Directive, 189
  Human rights, 152–53
  Second Banking Directive, 173, 189–90
Directorates-General, 87–88
  Bureaucratic politics and, 117, 119
  Competition with each other, 107
  DG III, 52
  DG V, 232, 247, 251, 254
  DG XVI, 221
  DG XV, 87
  DG XXII, 210–11, 220
  Structural Funds and, 210–11
Domestic policy, relationship to foreign
  policy, 65–67
Dooge Committee, 23, 51, 100
Dooge, James, 55
Downs, Anthony, 115
Duchacek, Ivo D., 264–65

Eastern European countries
  Changes in affecting EC, 29
  EC membership, 16
  Structural policy and, 218–19
Economic and monetary union (EMU), 9,
  34, 184–85
  Policy credibility and, 172–85
  Pursuit of, 26–27
  Steps toward in 1989–90, 71–72
  Thatcher and, 245–46
  See also Maastricht summit
Economic data
  EC-member nations, 36–45, 199–200
  EC regions, 94–95, 200–01
Economistic view of 1992 program, 1
EFTA. See European Free Trade Associ-
  ation
Elazar, Daniel, 261
Employment growth by EC regions,
  200–01
EMS. See European Monetary System
EMU. See Economic and monetary union
Enlargement of European Community,
  13–18
  Differentiating among new entrants,
  17–18
Environmental issues, 21
Environmental policy, 107n
Environmental regulations, 135–38
EPC. See European political cooperation
ERDF. See European Regional Develop-
  ment Fund
ESPRIT. See European Strategic Program
  for Information Technology

ETUC. See European Trade Union Con-
  federation
Eulau, Heinz, 287
Eurobarometer polls, 203n
EuroFed (European central bank), 8, 14,
  27, 72, 184
  Bundesbank compared with, 176–79
  Delors Report and, 157, 175
  European Council and, 177–78
  European Court of Justice and, 178
  European Parliament and, 178–79
  Federal structure of, 275–76
  Inflation and, 9, 180–82
  Policy credibility and, 175–83
  U.S. Federal Reserve System and,
  176–79
  See also Maastricht summit
EuroFed Council, 176–78, 179
European Agricultural Fund, 193n
European business, internal market initia-
  tive and, 48–50
European central bank. See EuroFed
European Coal and Steel Community,
  26n, 59, 193n
European Commission
  Administrative judicial review and,
  141–43
  Bureaucratic politics, 116–20
  Communications with EC-member
  states, 3
  European Parliament and, 90–92
  Executive accountability and, 98–100
  Federalism and, 269–71
  Functions of, 85–89
  History of 1992 program and, 32–35
  Internal market initiative and, 51–52
  Legal basis for action, 146–47
  Maastricht and, 85, 86
  National governments and, 4–5, 289–91
  Organization, 85–89
  Policymaking and, 7, 101–03
  President's powers, 99–100
  Relationship with Council of Ministers,
  81–82, 88–89
  Social dimension and, 232, 249–50
  Structural Funds and, 10, 211
  Structural spending, 210
  Subnational bodies and, 10, 289
European Company Law, 240
European Convention on Human Rights,
  149, 151, 153
European Council, 3
  Ad Hoc Committee on Institutional
  Affairs, 55, 61
  Composition, 78
  EuroFed and, 177–78

European Parliament and, 54–56
History of *1992* program and, 23–24,
    31–35
Internal market initiative and, 63–64
National governments and, 4–5
Selection of European Commission pres-
    ident and, 86
Social dimension and, 232–34
Yugoslav conflict and, 20
European Court of Justice, 13, 15
Administrative judicial review, 141–45
As policymaker, 7–8
Composition, 124
Direct effect doctrine, 126–27
EuroFed and, 178
Federal structure of, 276–77
Free movement of goods and, 128–34
Human rights, 148–52
Internal market initiative and, 52–53
Jurisdiction, 124–28
Legal basis for EC actions, 145–48
National governments and, 4–5
SEA and, 126–27, 154–56
European Free Trade Association (EFTA),
    29–30
European Investment Bank, 193, 211
European model of production, 227–28
European Monetary Institute, 181
European Monetary System (EMS), 8, 45–
    48, 80, 183–85
Banking Advisory Committee, 188,
    189–90
Britain and, 246
Bundesbank and, 165–66, 167
Committee of Central Bank Governors,
    188, 189
France and, 167–68
Historical development, 165–72
Institutions of, 185–90
Italy and, 168–69
Monetary Committee, 188–89
Policy credibility and, 161–72
Structure of, 185–90
European Parliament, 5, 14, 51, 289
Bureaucratic politics, 116, 118
Committees, 90–91
Council of Ministers and, 54–55, 90–92
EuroFed and, 178–79
European Commission and, 90–91
European Council and, 54–56
Executive accountability and, 98–100
Expenditures of EC and, 96–97
Federalism and, 269–71
Functions, 90–92
Internal market initiative and, 53–56
National governments and, 289–91

Organization, 90–92
Policymaking fragmentation and, 118
Policymaking under SEA, 100–01
Powers, 12, 13, 90, 92
Role under *1992* program, 24
Social dimension and, 232, 247–48,
    255
Structural spending and, 206
See also Maastricht summit
European political cooperation (EPC), 105
European Polity model, 113–15
European Regional Development Fund,
    13, 191, 194, 208, 210–11
Britain's share, 198n
Ireland, 215
European reserve fund, 157–58
European Social Fund, 191, 193, 210
European Strategic Program for
    Information Technology (ESPRIT), 50,
    52
European Trade Union Confederation
    (ETUC), 232, 233, 237, 242, 248–49,
    250, 254
European Union Treaty, 101
Eurosclerosis, 225
Exchange rates, 47, 173–74
Decisions concerning changes, 162–72
Policy credibility and, 162–72
Undervaluation strategy, 44–45
Expenditures of European Community,
    96–97

Federalism, 109–12
American model, 13, 260–61n, 263–64,
    265, 271n, 281–82, 287–88
Analytic costs, 264–68
As model for EC, 257–91
Australian model, 263–64, 265, 281n,
    287–88
Canadian model, 263–64, 282–83
Comparison of, 13, 259–68
Contrasted with confederation, 278
EC national governments and, 268–77
European Commission and, 269–71
European Parliament and, 269–71
German model, 13, 283–89
Integrative vs. deintegrative processes,
    265
Territorial dimension and, 274–75
Treaty vs. constitution, 271–74
Federal Open Market Committee, 176,
    178, 179
Federal Reserve System, contrasted with
    proposed EuroFed, 176–79
Federal systems. *See* Federalism

Financial services
  Policy credibility and, 173–75
  Single market development, 173–75
Flemish Volksunie, 213
Foreign policy, 18–22
  Relationship to domestic policy, 65–67
  SEA and, 104–05
France
  EMS and, 167–68
  Relations with Germany, 59–60
  Shift to conservatism, 58
  Social dimension and, 243–44
Free movement of goods, 128–34
French Declaration of the Rights of Man, 150
Friesland party, 213
Functionalist theorists of supernational integration, 110
Fundamental rights, 148–54

General Agreement on Tariffs and Trade (GATT), 22
Genscher, Hans-Dietrich, 54–56
German Customs Union, 48n
Germany
  EC dominance in 1990s, 67–71
  Federal system, 13, 283–89
  Inflation, 47
  Länder, 213, 218, 284–87
  Relations with France, 59–60
  Saarland, 194
  Shift to conservatism, 58
  Social dimension and, 243–44
  Yugoslav crisis, 20
Giavazzi, Francesco, 163, 165, 186
Giovannini, Alberto, 163, 165, 186
Giscard d'Estaing, Valéry, 45–48
Gonzales, Felipe, 250
Greece, membership in European Community, 14

Hamilton federalists, 259n
Harmonization, 120, 140
  Directives and, 138–39
  Free movement of goods and, 128–29
  National regulations and, 132–35
  Social costs and, 237n
  Social dimension and, 252–54
  Value-added tax and, 94n
Health regulations, 135–38
Heisler, Martino, 113
Howe, Sir Geoffrey, 245
Human rights, 148–52
  Future of, 152–54
Hungary, membership in European Community, 14, 16

Ideological preferences of EC-member nations, 56–59
IMPs. See Integrated Mediterranean Programs
Inflation, 157–58, 159–61
  Delors Report and, 161
  EC-member nations and, 47–48
  EuroFed and, 180–82
  Labor and, 160
Information Technologies Commission, 52
Institutional analysis of European Community, 105–21
  As nation state, 107–09
  Bureaucratic politics, 115–21
  European Polity model, 113–15
  Federalism, 109–12
  Overview, 105–07
Institutionalized intergovernmentalism in European Community, 63, 65–67
Integrated Mediterranean Programs (IMPs), 199, 209
Interest groups
  Influences on social dimension, 238–40
  Social dimension and, 11
Internal Market Council, 33, 52
Internal market initiative
  Economic factors leading to, 35–50
  History, 31–35
  Institutional factors leading to, 50–56
  Political factors leading to, 56–64
Ireland
  EC membership, 14
  Public Capital Program, 215
  Structural Funds and, 215
Italy
  EMS and, 168–69
  Mezzogiorno region, 194, 197

Japan
  EC trade restrictions against, 43–44
  Trade, 36–37
Jean Reyners v. Belgian State, 124n
Jenkins, Roy, 86, 106
Joint-decision trap, 120–21

Kangaroo Group, 39n
Kees, Andreas, 189
Keohane, Robert O., 186
Kisker, Gunter, 285
Kohl, Helmut, 58, 59, 71–72
Koopmans, T., 154
Kremers, Jeroen J. M., 162
Kvavik, Robert B., 113

Labor
  Inflation and, 160

Mobility of, 195n
Social dimension of, 233n, 235–38
Unions, 160n
See also European Trade Union Confederation; Union of Industrial and Employers' Confederations of Europe
Länder. *See* Germany, Länder
Lijphart, Arend, 284
Lubbers, Ruud, 57
Luxembourg Compromise of *1966*, 14, 29, 54n, 84, 122, 197

Maastricht summit, 2, 3, 5, 6, 9, 12, 15, 24, 75, 79, 121, 257, 258
Britain and, 11, 14, 244–45, 249–50
EMU and, 25–26, 27, 61, 73–74, 173, 183
Enlargement of Community and, 16–17
European central bank and, 8, 13–14, 27, 72, 73–74, 157, 173, 175–76, 178, 275
European Commission and, 85, 86
European Parliament and, 5, 13–14, 86, 91, 92, 118, 271, 277
Foreign and security policy, 15, 19–20, 104
Qualified majority voting, 16
Regional aid, 13, 191
Single currency and, 8, 13–14, 27, 72
Social dimension and, 11, 13, 234, 244–45, 246, 248, 249–50, 251, 252
Subsidiarity and, 110
Madison, James, 264
Major, John, 246–47, 249
Martens, Wilfried, 57
Megaproject, 49–50, 52
Melitz, Jacques, 162
Mitterrand, François, 24, 31, 55, 59, 71–72, 167
Monnet, Jean, 26, 270, 279
Morgenthau, Hans, 27
Mutual recognition doctrine, 53, 120, 129, 134–35

Narjes, Karl-Heinz, 31
National governments
European Commission and, 289–91
European Parliament and, 289–91
Federalism and, 268–77
Role in EC, 4–5
National veto, 54–56
Neoclassical economic theory, 195
Neofunctionalist theories, 268–69
Regional integration, 25–27
Social dimension and, 252–55
Supernational integration, 110

Neorealist theories
International relations, 27–30
Social dimension and, 252–55
Netherlands, shift to conservatism, 57
1992 initiative. See Internal market initiative
Nordholt, J. W. Schulte, 264
North Atlantic Treaty Organization, European Community security policy and, 18
Northern Development Company, 216
Nyborg agreements, 186–87, 189

Open Market Policy Committee, 179
Organization for Economic Cooperation and Development, 196n

Padoa-Schioppa, Tommaso, 26, 187
Papademos, Lucas, 165
Philips Petroleum, 49, 50
Picket-fence federalism, 112
Plaid Cymru, 213
Pöhl, Karl-Otto, 175
Poland, membership in European Community, 14, 16
Policy credibility
EMS and, 161–72
EMU and, 172–85
Establishment of, 158–61
EuroFed and, 175–83
Exchange rates and, 162–72
Policymaking, 100–05
Bureaucratic, 76–77, 115–21
Council of Ministers, 101–02
Fragmentation of, 118
Political preferences of EC-member nations, 56–59
Political processes in European Community, 93–105
Budget process, 93–98
Executive accountability, 98–100
Policymaking, 100–05
Population growth by European Community regions, 200–01
Portugal
EC membership, 14, 15
Qualified majority voting and, 16
Structural Funds and, 215
President of European Commission, bureaucratic politics and, 116–17, 121
Prussian Customs Union, 48n
Putnam, Robert, 66

Qualified majority voting, 16, 54–56, 82–85, 120–21, 134–35, 240n, 271
Application uncertainty, 146–48

Atypical work proposal and, 248
Effect of, 122
Harmonization and, 140
Internal market and, 24
New membership and, 16
Social dimension and, 234, 247, 248–50
States' interest and, 197n
Trade regulation harmonization and, 132
Use of, 16–17
See also Maastricht summit

Rasmussen, Hjalte, 154
Recessions, impact of, 202–03
Regional development policy. *See* Structural policy
Regional Fund, 220
Creation of, 198–99
See also European Regional Development Fund
Regulations, 102, 141–43
Reissert, Bernd, 283–84
Revenue sources, 94–96
Rewe Zentral AG, 53
Ridley, Nicholas, 85, 217
Rights. *See* Human rights
Rose, Richard, 274
Roundtable of European Industrialists, 49
Rulemaking in European Community, 102, 136
Implementation of rules, 103–04
Russo, Massimo, 166

Safety regulations, 135–38
Schaefer, Gunther F., 283–84
Scharpf, Fritz, 113, 120, 285–86, 289n
Schattschneider, Elmer, 281
Schlüter, Poul, 57
Schmidt, Helmut, 45–48, 58, 59
Schmitter, Philippe C., 290
SEA. *See* Single European Act
Security policy, 18–22, 104–05
Sharpe, L. J., 274–75
Siemens, 49, 50
Single European Act, 14, 71, 73
Adoption of, 24
Amendments to Treaty of Rome article *100*, 146–47
Article *13*, 131, 136
Article *14*, 131, 136
Article *15*, 136
Article *16*, 136
Article *18*, 131, 137
Article *19*, 131, 137
Article *130*, 137
EC institutions' powers and, 101

European Court of Justice and, 126–27, 154–56
European Parliament as enhanced by, 91–92
Financial services, 173
Foreign policy and, 104–05
Institutional consequences of, 3
Modified majority voting and, 197n
Monetary union and, 84
Product standards, 143–45
"Race to the bottom" risk and, 132–33
Significance regarding governments' powers, 2
Structural Funds and, 191
Structural policy and, 9
Social dimension
Belgium and, 250
Britain and, 11, 13, 233, 241–50
Christian Democrats and, 233–34
Definition, 229–30
Delors and, 254
European Commission and, 232, 249–50
European Council and, 232–34
European Parliament and, 232, 247–48, 255
Europeanwide capital position and, 235–38
Europeanwide labor position and, 235–38
France and, 243–44
Germany and, 243–44
Interest groups and, 11, 238–40
Minimalist approach, 230–35
Neofunctionalism and, 252–55
Neorealist theory and, 252–55
Qualified majority voting and, 234, 247, 248–50
Social protectionist approach, 231–35
Spain and, 243–44, 250–51
Thatcher and, 241–42, 244–46
Unanimity rule, 240–44
See also Maastricht summit
Social policy. *See* Social dimension
Social wages, 226–27n
Solemn Declaration on European Union, 105
Soviet Union
Changes in affecting EC, 29
Disintegration of, 19
Spain
EC membership, 14–15
Qualified majority voting and, 16
Social dimension and, 243–44, 250–51
Spinelli, Altiero, 54–56, 279
Steffani, Winfried, 283
Streeck, Wolfgang, 290

Structural Funds, 96, 191–224
  Britain, 216–17
  Coordination among, 210–11
  Growth of, 194–206
  Ireland, 215
  Portugal, 215
  Programs vs. projects, 209–10
  Reform of, 206–12
  Regional authorities and, 210–12,
    221–24
  Viewed as equitable redistributions,
    204–06
  Viewed as "side payments," 194–204
Structural policy, 10, 191–224
  EC-member nations and, 212–18,
    219–20, 221–24
  Effect of Eastern European countries
    on, 218–19
  Effect on state authority, 212–18,
    219–20, 221–24
  Implementation, 220
  Spending priorities, 206–08
  Subnational governments and, 210–12,
    221–24
Stuttgart declaration, 54–56
Subnational governments, structural policy
  and, 210–12, 221–24
Subsidiarity, 110–11, 231
Supreme Court, U.S., contrasted with
  European Court of Justice, 276–77
Sweden, membership in European Com-
  munity, 16, 29

Tarrow, Sidney, 280
Teague, Paul, 234
Territorial dimension
  Effect on Institutions, 275–77
  Federalism and, 274–75
  Institutional representation and, 280–87
Territorial politics, 289–91
Territorial representation, 277–91
Thatcher, Margaret, 29–30, 61–63, 84, 164
  Effect of fall on British policy toward
    EC, 244–46
  Effect of fall on social dimension,
    244–46
  EMU and, 245–46
  Government programs, 57
  Modification of stance toward EC, 114
  Social dimension and, 11, 241–42,
    244–46
  See also Britain
Theoretical perspectives on 1992
  Neofunctionalist theories of regional
    integration, 25–27

Neorealist theories of international rela-
    tions, 27–30
Thorn, Gaston, 31–32, 51–52
Tindemans, Leo, 31, 54
Trade
  Balance of trade among EC-member
    nations, 68–70, 164
  Canada, 36–37
  EC-member nations, 36–40
  Exports of EC-member nations to each
    other, 68
  Japan, 36–37
  Restrictions, 43–44
  United States, 36–37
  See also European Trade Union
    Confederation; Union of Industrial
    and Employers' Confederations of
    Europe
Treaties
  Constitution vs. treaty, 271–74
  Impact on institutions, 275–77
  Territories and, 274–75
Treaty of Friendship, 1963, 59
Treaty of Rome, 8, 217, 249
  Article 8, 131, 136
  Article 36, 129, 133, 137–40, 143, 152
  Article 57, 136
  Article 99, 146
  Article 100, 131–32, 135, 137–38, 140,
    142, 146–47, 152, 248
  Article 169, 125, 142
  Article 170, 125
  Article 171, 125
  Article 173, 149
  Article 177, 126–27, 139, 143
  Article 189, 139
  Article 235, 145–48
  Federalism and, 271–73
  Structural policy and, 193
Tugendhat, Christopher, 268
Tullio, Giuseppe, 166

Unanimity rule, social dimension and,
    240–44
Union of Industrial and Employers' Con-
  federations of Europe (UNICE), 232,
    233, 242, 249, 250, 251, 252, 254
United Kingdom. See Britain
United Nations, 94
United States
  Articles of Confederation, 94
  Bill of Rights, 150, 153
  Comparison with EC, 2–4
  European defense role, 19
  Federal Reserve System, 176–79
  Supreme Court, 276–77

Structural Funds, 96, 191–224
  Britain, 216–17
  Coordination among, 210–11
  Growth of, 194–206
  Ireland, 215
  Portugal, 215
  Programs vs. projects, 209–10
  Reform of, 206–12
  Regional authorities and, 210–12, 221–24
  Viewed as equitable redistributions, 204–06
  Viewed as "side payments," 194–204
Structural policy, 10, 191–224
  EC-member nations and, 212–18, 219–20, 221–24
  Effect of Eastern European countries on, 218–19
  Effect on state authority, 212–18, 219–20, 221–24
  Implementation, 220
  Spending priorities, 206–08
  Subnational governments and, 210–12, 221–24
Stuttgart declaration, 54–56
Subnational governments, structural policy and, 210–12, 221–24
Subsidiarity, 110–11, 231
Supreme Court, U.S., contrasted with European Court of Justice, 276–77
Sweden, membership in European Community, 16, 29

Tarrow, Sidney, 280
Teague, Paul, 234
Territorial dimension
  Effect on Institutions, 275–77
  Federalism and, 274–75
  Institutional representation and, 280–87
Territorial politics, 289–91
Territorial representation, 277–91
Thatcher, Margaret, 29–30, 61–63, 84, 164
  Effect of fall on British policy toward EC, 244–46
  Effect of fall on social dimension, 244–46
  EMU and, 245–46
  Government programs, 57
  Modification of stance toward EC, 114
  Social dimension and, 11, 241–42, 244–46
  See also Britain
Theoretical perspectives on 1992
  Neofunctionalist theories of regional integration, 25–27

Neorealist theories of international relations, 27–30
Thorn, Gaston, 31–32, 51–52
Tindemans, Leo, 31, 54
Trade
  Balance of trade among EC-member nations, 68–70, 164
  Canada, 36–37
  EC-member nations, 36–40
  Exports of EC-member nations to each other, 68
  Japan, 36–37
  Restrictions, 43–44
  United States, 36–37
  See also European Trade Union Confederation; Union of Industrial and Employers' Confederations of Europe
Treaties
  Constitution vs. treaty, 271–74
  Impact on institutions, 275–77
  Territories and, 274–75
Treaty of Friendship, 1963, 59
Treaty of Rome, 8, 217, 249
  Article 8, 131, 136
  Article 36, 129, 133, 137–40, 143, 152
  Article 57, 136
  Article 99, 146
  Article 100, 131–32, 135, 137–38, 140, 142, 146–47, 152, 248
  Article 169, 125, 142
  Article 170, 125
  Article 171, 125
  Article 173, 149
  Article 177, 126–27, 139, 143
  Article 189, 139
  Article 235, 145–48
  Federalism and, 271–73
  Structural policy and, 193
Tugendhat, Christopher, 268
Tullio, Giuseppe, 166

Unanimity rule, social dimension and, 240–44
Union of Industrial and Employers' Confederations of Europe (UNICE), 232, 233, 242, 249, 250, 251, 252, 254
United Kingdom. See Britain
United Nations, 94
United States
  Articles of Confederation, 94
  Bill of Rights, 150, 153
  Comparison with EC, 2–4
  European defense role, 19
  Federal Reserve System, 176–79
  Supreme Court, 276–77

Atypical work proposal and, 248
Effect of, 122
Harmonization and, 140
Internal market and, 24
New membership and, 16
Social dimension and, 234, 247, 248–50
States' interest and, 197n
Trade regulation harmonization and, 132
Use of, 16–17
See also Maastricht summit

Rasmussen, Hjalte, 154
Recessions, impact of, 202–03
Regional development policy. *See* Structural policy
Regional Fund, 220
Creation of, 198–99
See also European Regional Development Fund
Regulations, 102, 141–43
Reissert, Bernd, 283–84
Revenue sources, 94–96
Rewe Zentral AG, 53
Ridley, Nicholas, 85, 217
Rights. *See* Human rights
Rose, Richard, 274
Roundtable of European Industrialists, 49
Rulemaking in European Community, 102, 136
Implementation of rules, 103–04
Russo, Massimo, 166

Safety regulations, 135–38
Schaefer, Gunther F., 283–84
Scharpf, Fritz, 113, 120, 285–86, 289n
Schattschneider, Elmer, 281
Schlüter, Poul, 57
Schmidt, Helmut, 45–48, 58, 59
Schmitter, Philippe C., 290
SEA. *See* Single European Act
Security policy, 18–22, 104–05
Sharpe, L. J., 274–75
Siemens, 49, 50
Single European Act, 14, 71, 73
Adoption of, 24
Amendments to Treaty of Rome article *100*, 146–47
Article *13*, 131, 136
Article *14*, 131, 136
Article *15*, 136
Article *16*, 136
Article *18*, 131, 137
Article *19*, 131, 137
Article *130*, 137
EC institutions' powers and, 101

European Court of Justice and, 126–27, 154–56
European Parliament as enhanced by, 91–92
Financial services, 173
Foreign policy and, 104–05
Institutional consequences of, 3
Modified majority voting and, 197n
Monetary union and, 84
Product standards, 143–45
"Race to the bottom" risk and, 132–33
Significance regarding governments' powers, 2
Structural Funds and, 191
Structural policy and, 9
Social dimension
Belgium and, 250
Britain and, 11, 13, 233, 241–50
Christian Democrats and, 233–34
Definition, 229–30
Delors and, 254
European Commission and, 232, 249–50
European Council and, 232–34
European Parliament and, 232, 247–48, 255
Europeanwide capital position and, 235–38
Europeanwide labor position and, 235–38
France and, 243–44
Germany and, 243–44
Interest groups and, 11, 238–40
Minimalist approach, 230–35
Neofunctionalism and, 252–55
Neorealist theory and, 252–55
Qualified majority voting and, 234, 247, 248–50
Social protectionist approach, 231–35
Spain and, 243–44, 250–51
Thatcher and, 241–42, 244–46
Unanimity rule, 240–44
See also Maastricht summit
Social policy. *See* Social dimension
Social wages, 226–27n
Solemn Declaration on European Union, 105
Soviet Union
Changes in affecting EC, 29
Disintegration of, 19
Spain
EC membership, 14–15
Qualified majority voting and, 16
Social dimension and, 243–44, 250–51
Spinelli, Altiero, 54–56, 279
Steffani, Winfried, 283
Streeck, Wolfgang, 290

Trade, 36–37
See also American federal
system

Value-added tax, 94–95, 154–55, 238
Van Gend en Loos v. *Nederlandse
Administratie der Belastingen*, 52,
126–27n

Wallace, Helen, 257
Waltz, Kenneth, 28

Weiler, Joseph, 276–77
Werner Report, 31, 189
Western European Union, European
Community security policy and, 19
Westminister model of party government,
282–83
WEU. *See* Western European Union

Yom Kippur War, 31
Yugoslav crisis, 20–21

DATE DUE

HIGHSMITH 45-220